St. Louis Community College

Forest Park
Florissant Valley
Meramec

Instructional Resources
St. Louis, Missouri

GAYLORD

Working with Carter G. Woodson, the Father of Black History

Working with Carter G. Woodson, the Father of Black History

A Diary, 1928–1930

Lorenzo J. Greene

Edited, with an Introduction, by
Arvarh E. Strickland

Louisiana State University Press
Baton Rouge and London

Copyright © 1989 by Louisiana State University Press
All rights reserved
Manufactured in the United States of America
First printing
98 97 96 95 94 93 92 91 90 89   5 4 3 2 1

Designer: Patricia D. Crowder
Typeface: Linotron 202 Bembo
Typesetter: The Composing Room of Michigan, Inc.
Printer: Thomson Shore, Inc.
Binder: John H. Dekker & Sons, Inc.

This publication has been supported by the National Endowment for the Humanities,
a federal agency which supports the study of such fields as history, philosophy,
literature, and languages.

LIBRARY OF CONGRESS CATALOGING-IN-PUBLICATION DATA

Greene, Lorenzo Johnston, 1899–
   Working with Carter G. Woodson, the father of Black
history.
   Bibliography: p.
   Includes index.
   1. Woodson, Carter Godwin, 1875–1950. 2. Greene,
Lorenzo Johnston, 1899–   Diaries. 3. Afro-American
historians—Biography. 4. Historians—United States—
Biography. I. Strickland, Arvarh E. 5. Afro-Americans—
Historiography. II. Title.
E185.97.W77G74 1989   973'.0496073   88-32588
ISBN 0-8071-1473-1 (alk. paper)

The paper in this book meets the guidelines for permanence and durability of the
Committee on Production Guidelines for Book Longevity of the Council on Library
Resources. ∞

To the memory of

Dr. Charles Harris Wesley

Teacher, historian, author, administrator, churchman, collaborator, mentor, and friend, whose interest and advice made this work possible

Contents

Illustrations

Foreword

Charles Harris Wesley

Dr. Carter G. Woodson, founder of the Association for the Study of Negro Life and History, has always been regarded by the membership of that organization as the Father of Negro History. In 1946 in the *Negro History Bulletin,* he described a group of the association's black historians in these words: "The later historians are just as much interested as their predecessors to see their social, economic and political problems solved, but they have tended to leave agitation and propaganda to specialists who have shown capacity along this line, while the historians by publishing the truth in scientific form may accomplish as much in their own way."

This statement is true of all black historians who have worked in the fields of both history and political activism. Dr. Woodson chose to work as a historian, but Dr. Lorenzo J. Greene worked in both fields. This dual role seemed to come naturally to him, as it did to some others in the association. In this book Dr. Greene tells an interesting, even gripping, story about his study, work, travel, research, and writing for the ASNLH and its Associated Publishers.

It was in Ansonia, Connecticut, on November 16, 1899, that Lorenzo Johnston Greene was born, the sixth of nine children of Willis Hamilton Greene and Harriett Coleman Greene. After attending elementary and high school in his native city, he entered Howard University with the intention of studying medicine. He shaped his purpose toward this goal but, after completing his pre-medical work, decided to earn a baccalaureate degree before entering medical school. In his senior year he enrolled in history courses and in 1924 graduated with a B.A. degree (*cum laude*). His studies in history brought him in contact with Professors Walter Dyson and Leo Hansberry, as well as myself, and together we influenced him to make history his life's work.

Greene went on to Columbia University in New York City, where he was awarded an M.A. in history in 1926 and the Ph.D. in 1942. His dissertation was published by Columbia University Press that same year under the title *The Negro in Colonial New England, 1620–1776*. In 1966 it was reprinted by the Kennikat Press, and in 1968 it was reprinted again, in paperback by the Atheneum Press, with a new preface by Dr. Benjamin Quarles, as a volume in the Studies in American Negro Life series edited by Dr. August Meier.

While Greene was engaged in graduate study at Columbia University, I gave him a letter of introduction to Dr. Woodson. In it I expressed the hope that Woodson might be able to assist Greene in financing his studies at Columbia. But it was not until several years later, in March, 1928, that Greene was actually employed as a research associate and field investigator for the ASNLH. His early writings came from his experiences in this position. Greene and Woodson were coauthors of *The Negro Wage Earner* (1930), and Greene and Myra Colson Callis collaborated on *Negro Employment in the District of Columbia* (1932). A third publication in this period was *Negro Housing* (1933), which Greene wrote with Charles S. Johnson of Fisk University.

Among the writings of his later years, "Massacre at Fort Pillow" in *Battles of the Civil War*, edited by C. A. Harper (1962), was a contribution of notable value. With Antonio F. Holland and Gary R. Kremer he wrote "The Role of the Negro in Missouri History, 1719–1970," in the *Official Manual of Missouri* for 1973–1974. He also edited the *Midwest Journal* at Lincoln University in Missouri from 1949 to 1955. Greene collaborated again with Holland and Kremer on *Missouri's Black Heritage*, which was published by the Forum Press in 1980. Thus, Greene wrote of the sections of the nation in which he lived and worked—New England, Washington, D.C., and Missouri.

Greene was extremely active in the movement for civil rights and for the general advancement of the cause of black people. As a result, in 1957 he was appointed to the Missouri Advisory Committee to the United States Commission on Civil Rights and in 1959 he wrote a report entitled *The Desegregation of Public Schools in Missouri* for the commission. He followed it up with another report on the same subject in 1962. Greene was unanimously elected president of the ASNLH for the term 1963–1964, during which I served with him as executive director.

The author of the diary that follows was personally known to me through the years as student, teacher, professor, researcher, investigator, colleague, and friend. I served with him in most of these capacities and endeavors, which would have tried the souls of many men. But for both of us, these were satisfying and enjoyable years, for in spite of the numerous diff culties, we were working for a cause that we loved. I watched as Greene became a scholar of renown, the author of numerous books and articles in history and social science, and an able lecturer and worthy historian.

Other early members of the ASNLH should record their life stories, especially their experiences relating to the organization and Dr. Woodson. As we all know, Woodson never had the opportunity to write his autobiography and so we have only what has been and will be written by others. However, persons such as Dr. Greene can fill in many of the gaps that now exist in the story of Dr. Woodson's endeavors. In his diary Greene supplies the facts to show us that Dr. Woodson was a fascinating man, a hard worker who achieved much despite the obstacles and often the antipathy that he faced.

Greene's diary gives a significant picture of the early years of the discipline of Negro history, when its founder, Dr. Woodson, carried on the work of the ASNLH with only two investigators to assist him. During the years 1928–1930, Greene was a field investigator, and the story of his life during this period, especially his efforts on behalf of the ANSLH, should inspire black historians and other people to carry on the struggle to make men and women of darker hue the equals of others in all areas of life. For it is not only those who struggle and fight for freedom in activist organizations who are of value to the movement, but also those who quietly, as individuals and in small groups, work, write, and talk for the cause. Woodson and Greene spent their lives spreading knowledge of black history, and some of their efforts are depicted in this book.

In 1980, when he was honored by the Lincoln University alumni, Greene explained the motivation behind his endeavors in black history. "I had a feeling it was necessary to give those students pride in themselves," he said. He also stated: "I felt it my duty because of what Woodson and Historian Charles H. Wesley instilled in me. They gave me an inspiration to do something for my race, instilled in me the knowledge and pride that I belonged to a group that had achieved."

Dr. Greene's wife, Dr. Thomasina Talley Greene, a daughter of Thomas W. Talley, longtime professor of chemistry at Fisk University, and their son, Lorenzo Thomas Greene, are a great family. A concert pianist and a teacher of music, she has devoted herself to white and black students through the years, giving of herself freely to the community and its children. Dr. Greene stood with them over the rough places and the smooth ones, and all moved forward with him.

Small of stature but big of heart, Greene was much more than a history teacher. He was an active scholar who also lived outside the classroom and in the community. He knew that our people would be moved forward by his efforts, and he wanted to move forward with them. He lived and believed with the historians on the mountaintop, but he also lived and believed with the people in the valley and moved with them out of the lowlands into the hills. This was the historian, the leader, the man whom I knew.

Editor's Acknowledgments

Editing this book has been a labor of love. Working with Lorenzo J. Greene in the final preparation of his diary for publication further cemented an already close friendship. I am deeply grateful for the many hours Lorenzo spent with me, helping me to know and understand the people and events he recorded and the milieu in which it all happened.

Nevertheless, we did not do it alone. In his preface, Lorenzo thanks those who provided assistance to him at earlier stages; some of these people, along with others, helped me in this final stage.

Dottie and J. Leonard Bates opened their home to me on several occasions and facilitated my use of materials in the University of Illinois Library. Ruth Jones of Old Dominion University permitted herself to be imposed upon in the name of friendship and did research for me in the Virginia State Library in Richmond.

This project placed me deeply in debt to librarians. I am especially grateful to Anne Edwards of Ellis Library, University of Missouri—Columbia, for her valuable assistance. Felix Unaeze and Willie Green of Page Library, Lincoln University, also provided help in locating and copying materials.

Patty Eggleston and Susan Patrick began the word-processing task of converting the edited manuscript to finished copy, and Janet Winn's dedicated and efficient work brought the project to completion.

It is not possible to name all of the people who deserve to be listed as contributors to this project, but I owe special thanks to Ida Mae Wolff, Nancy Taube, Carolyn Dorsey, and Antonio Holland. Marie Sloan assisted me in more ways than I can list here.

My son Bruce was pressed into service as a temporary research assistant, and the work he started was continued by Denyse Sturges. William Wood picked up where they stopped, and his careful work and good judgment were of great help to me.

The task was easier because of the cooperation of several University of Missouri administrators, including Gerard Clarfield, Milton Glick, and Jay Barton. Word processing was funded by a grant from the Research Council of the Graduate School, University of Missouri—Columbia.

Editor's Introduction

In the 1980s, August Meier and Elliott Rudwick, two prolific chroniclers of the black American experience, turned their attention to the development of Afro-American history as a field for scholarly research. The book that resulted from their investigation has as its principal theme the "analysis of the process by which black history, originally a Jim Crow specialty ignored by nearly the entire profession, became legitimated into one of the liveliest and most active fields of study in American history."[1] Even though it is a faithful reflection of the state of things in the history profession between 1915 and 1980, there is still a certain arrogance in dating the legitimacy of the field from the decade of the 1960s, when white scholars began working in the field without apology and black scholars entered it without believing they were jeopardizing their careers by doing so.[2]

The legitimacy of Afro-American history, if it needed legitimatizing, resulted from the work and dedication of Carter Godwin Woodson, who "with his drive and vision was virtually single-handedly responsible for establishing Afro-American history as a historical specialty."[3] Not only did he found the Association for the Study of Negro Life and History (ASNLH) and establish the *Journal*

---

1. August Meier and Elliott Rudwick, *Black History and the Historical Profession, 1915–1980* (Urbana, 1986), xi–xii.
2. *Ibid.*, 161–238.
3. *Ibid.*, 1.

of Negro History and the Associated Negro Publishers, he also helped to shape the lives and careers of the generation of black scholars who made black history a viable field. Many of those whose lives Woodson touched became, like him, committed to the cause of preserving the record of the Afro-American past and of correcting the errors and distortions in the works of established American historians.

Lorenzo Johnston Greene was a young scholar whose life became entwined with that of Woodson. Fortunately for posterity, Greene kept a diary during much of the time he worked with Woodson; this memoir provides a window into two years in the lives of three of the premier shapers of black history—Woodson, Charles Harris Wesley, and Greene—that is not available from any other source. The diary offers poignant insights into the personalities and relationships of Woodson and Wesley and shows the development of Greene's grudging respect and admiration for Woodson.

Above all, however, the memoir is a window into the mind and soul of Lorenzo Greene. Greene as a young man was a keen and critical observer of people and events. Unlike most of the young scholars who came under Woodson's influence, he was not a southerner. Like W. E. B. Du Bois, he was a New Englander, and he viewed the black subculture of the South and those produced by it through the filter of his New England background. Still, he and the southerners had a common dedication to obtaining an education and making contributions to their chosen professions. The diary reveals the dimensions of the sacrifice and the depth of the commitment made by Greene in pursuit of his goal and in furtherance of the "cause."

Greene was born in Ansonia, Connecticut—a brass, copper, and steel manufacturing town in the Naugatuck Valley—on November 16, 1899. He was the sixth of nine children born to Willis Hamilton Greene and Harriett Elizabeth Coleman Greene. Willis Greene divulged little information to his children concerning his background. They learned that he was born in Pennsylvania around 1850 and that their mother was his second wife. In 1924, when Greene went to New York City to attend Columbia University, he met Bessie O'Pharrow, his father's daughter from his first marriage. From Sis-

ter Bessie—as Greene and his siblings called her—he learned that
other members of the family lived in Newark, New Jersey; but he
made contact with only one of them.

Much more is known about the Coleman side of the family.
Greene's maternal grandparents, George and Louisa Coleman, were
born slaves and went to Arlington, Virginia, as refugees during the
Civil War. In 1880, they were still residing in Arlington, with their
five children. The census enumerator listed the children as Harriet,
fourteen; Emma, eleven; Thomas, nine; Fannie, six; and Savina,
four.[4] Harriett's name was misspelled in the census, and the young-
est child's name was really Louvinia. Several years later, Harriett
met and married Willis Greene. He was twenty years her senior and
had worked as a teamster on the Potomac Canal and for a wholesale
grocer in Washington, D.C.

According to family tradition, in 1888, the year of the blizzard,
Willis moved his bride to Ansonia, Connecticut. There he became
chief teamster for Wallace and Sons Brass Company, which later
became the American Brass Company. Even as the highest paid of
the company's teamsters, he earned only twelve dollars per week.

The Coleman family left Virginia and followed the Greenes to
Connecticut. The son, Thomas, went into the grocery business and
prospered well enough that he was able to retire after World War I.
Thomas had one child, Carrie, who died young. The two children,
William and Estella, born to Emma and her husband, Antipus
Branham, married and left Ansonia. The other sisters, Fannie and
Louvinia, never married. Except for Fannie, the Colemans lived out
their lives in Connecticut. By the time Greene arrived in Washington, D.C., to attend school, his aunt Fannie had moved there,
and he roomed at her home. She figures prominently in the pages
of the diary.

The Greene children grew up in an environment where there
were few other black families. In 1910, Ansonia had 15,152 inhabitants, of whom only 413 were black, and the neighboring town of
Derby, with a total population of 8,991, had but 70 black residents.
The Great Migration during World War I did little to change the ra-

4. U.S. Department of Commerce, Bureau of the Census, *Tenth Census of the United States,
1880*, Virginia, Vol. I, p. 20.

cial composition of the population of this area of Connecticut. In 1920, there were still only 532 blacks in Ansonia and 91 in Derby.[5]

The school population reflected this paucity of blacks. During his years in elementary school, Greene was often the only black child in his class. There were even fewer black children in the high school than in the elementary school. Many children, both white and black, left school to work in the factories after completing the fifth grade.

The older Greene children followed this pattern. Greene's oldest brother, James, left school after fifth grade to go to work. When he was fifteen years old, he was cooking for a wealthy family in another town. Later, he learned auto mechanics, became a chauffeur for a rich nursery owner, and moved to New York City. By the time he was twenty-one years old, James had bought a home for the family, with enough land for the father and the two younger boys to raise food sufficient to satisfy most of the family's needs. Charles, a year and a half older than Lorenzo, dropped out of school to work in his uncle Thomas Coleman's store.

Harriett Greene had hoped that her daughter Careatha, who had musical talent, would remain in school. But the family was unable to provide clothing that would allow her to dress like the white girls. So, much to her mother's dismay and disappointment, she dropped out during her freshman year in high school.

Only Greene, among the five living of the first six children, remained in school. At age thirteen, he had determined that he would finish high school and get a college education. He recalled, however, that his first expression of this resolve came in response to neither a sense of family duty nor a sense of racial responsibility. Rather, it was motivated by his infatuation with an attractive girl his age, who was a year behind him in school. Coming home from school one day, he met her on Main Street and walked her home. "I said, 'Ethel, if you will wait for me, I will go to school and become a doctor and then we will get married. Will you wait?' She said, 'Yes, Rennie.' I believed that I had an oath registered in heaven to

5. U.S. Department of Commerce, Bureau of the Census, *Negro Population, 1790–1915* (Washington, D.C., 1918), 95; U.S. Department of Commerce, Bureau of the Census, *Negroes in the United States, 1920–1932* (Washington, D.C., 1935), 56.

do just that. Ethel married when I was a junior in high school, but I decided to carry on."[6]

In the meantime, other forces came into play to reinforce Greene's resolve to go on to college. There was the inspiration of the other students who talked of going to college and the encouragement of his high school principal and teachers. Above all, however, he was encouraged by the excitement of his mother and the moral support he received from his family and the community in general.

Greene graduated from Ansonia High School in 1917. He was the only black student in his class and the first black person to graduate from that school. He was well liked in school and earned good grades. He was also an active participant in school activities, serving as head of the debating society and president of the first German club organized in the high school. He graduated third in his class and won the history prize. His principal urged him to go to Syracuse University to study law. Others in the town encouraged him to study medicine.

The family's financial situation did not permit him to go to college immediately after high school. Greene worked for two years to help his parents and to save money for college expenses. Although he did not save much money, he renewed his determination to get away from Ansonia before he became a "slave to the factory whistle."[7]

Finally, in 1919, Greene left home to enter Howard University, in Washington, D.C., to study medicine. His mother knew about Howard, and since her sister Fannie had moved to Washington, she and the rest of the family sent him off to school with their blessing. Greene took up residence with his aunt, found a job washing dishes in a boardinghouse to pay his rent, and went to register at Howard.

Since he had refused to take algebra and geometry in high school, however, he was denied admission. Dean Kelly Miller advised him to go to Dunbar High School to take the needed courses. At Dunbar, which was well known for the quality of both its faculty and the students it produced, Greene completed the courses in algebra

6. Editor's interview with Lorenzo J. Greene, March 9, 1986.
7. *Ibid.*

and geometry and began to learn more about black people. He came in contact with black teachers with degrees from the leading eastern colleges and universities, and he became part of a world of black students.

The next year, Greene entered Howard. He completed work for his bachelor's degree in 1924 and was prepared to begin his study of medicine. Up to his final year at Howard, he had not thought of history as a profession he might pursue. During that final year, however, in searching for courses that would fit his work schedule, he found that history courses were the only ones available. He enrolled in Professor Walter Dyson's course in Greek history and speedily learned how much history he did not know. He followed this with courses in English history from Charles H. Wesley and Leo Hansberry. Impressed by Greene's facility in foreign languages, Hansberry advised Greene to return to Howard to do graduate work in history and to assist him with his research in African history. Greene went to New York City and registered at the New York School of Medicine. On the way home, he stopped to talk to Dr. Peyton Anderson, a chest specialist and friend of his family, who advised him to choose history over medicine. He decided to take the doctor's advice and went home to Connecticut with the intention of studying at Yale.

Yale would not accept him in its history program because he lacked sufficient credits. The dean of Yale's graduate school advised him to go to Columbia University to take thirty hours in history in the extension department and then to return to Yale. Greene studied at Columbia for three years. He earned his M.A. degree in history in 1926, and he remained the following year to work toward his Ph.D. His decision to stay at Columbia resulted in part from advice he received from Wesley. During his second year at Columbia, Wesley introduced him to Woodson in the hope that Woodson might be able to offer him financial assistance. Woodson interviewed Greene, gave him an autographed copy of his book *The Negro in Our History*, and promised to get in touch if he could help him. Greene left Woodson, pitying the man for devoting his life to something that Greene did not believe existed, Negro history. Nevertheless, three years later, at Wesley's behest, Woodson offered Greene a job assisting Wesley in making a national survey of the black church. This study was jointly sponsored by the ASNLH and the Institute of Social and Religious Research in New York City.

Wesley, although only about eight years Greene's senior, became Greene's role model in many areas and a lifelong close friend. Wesley was born on December 2, 1891, in Louisville, Kentucky, to Charles Snowden and Matilda Harris Wesley. He attended the public schools of Louisville and went from there to Nashville, Tennessee, where, after a year at the Fisk Academy, he entered Fisk University. He graduated from Fisk in 1911 and, supported by university fellowships, spent two years at Yale University, from which he earned his M.A. degree in history in 1913. He went to Howard University as an instructor in 1913 and, in 1915–1916, attended the Howard University Law School.

Wesley was associated with Howard from 1913 to 1942. Between 1914 and 1921, he rose from assistant professor to professor of history. From 1921 to 1942, he served as head of the history department. In addition, he directed the summer school program in 1937, was acting dean of the College of Liberal Arts in 1937–1938, and was dean of the graduate school from 1938 to 1942. Meanwhile, Wesley continued his education by attending the Guilde Internationale in Paris in 1914 and by spending 1919 to 1921 in residence at Harvard University, working on his doctorate. In 1925, he completed work for and received from Harvard the third Ph.D. in history awarded to a black person.

Wesley and Woodson had much in common, and they undoubtedly met soon after Wesley moved to Washington, D.C. Wesley was vitally concerned about preserving black history and about teaching and writing about the black American experience. He was among a group of Howard professors who pressed for courses in that area. Wesley also called for objectivity in the writing of history. His position was that "the Negro in the United States must be viewed without blind prejudice, and his contributions to American life and history should be included with those of other peoples. When this is done, without doubt some Negroes will appear inferior to some whites and some whites will appear inferior to some Negroes. Any other position is contrary to the facts and their logical interpretation."[8]

8. *Current Biography: Who's News and Why, 1944*, p. 727.

Wesley was also an ordained minister in the African Methodist Episcopal Church. From 1918 to 1938, he served as pastor of the Ebenezer and Campbell A.M.E. [African Methodist Episcopal] Church in Washington, and in 1929, he became presiding elder of the Washington District of the A.M.E. church.

In 1927, Woodson appointed Wesley as a part-time investigator with the ASNLH, and in 1928, he named Wesley to direct the survey of the black church. Woodson complained, however, that Wesley was not devoting enough time to the project. Because of Wesley's ministerial calling, Woodson seemed to have doubts about Wesley's ability to make an objective study of the black church. Therefore, when Wesley accepted the presiding elder position, Woodson abruptly ended the church survey. This caused a rift between the two men. Greene's sympathies were with Wesley. Within a year, however, Woodson and Wesley had reconciled their differences, probably in large part on Wesley's initiative. Wesley was a strong believer in the principle—which Greene also came to espouse—that the cause is greater than the man.

Wesley, like Woodson, was a productive scholar. His history of the Negro labor movement, *Negro Labor in the United States, 1850–1925*, was published in 1927. It was followed by his biography of the founder of the A.M.E. church, *Richard Allen, Apostle of Freedom*, in 1935, and by *The Collapse of the Confederacy* in 1937. Wesley also served as the historian for several black fraternal organizations. The first edition of his *History of Alpha Phi Alpha: A Development in Negro College Life* appeared in 1929, and the twelfth edition was published in 1975. While serving as president of Wilberforce University from 1942 to 1947 and of Central State University from 1947 to 1965, he continued to write histories of fraternal organizations and other works. Books he published during this period include *A History of Sigma Pi Phi, First of the Negro-American Greek-Letter Fraternities* (1954); *History of the Improved Benevolent and Protective Order of Elks of the World, 1898–1954* (1954); and *The History of the Prince Hall Grand Lodge of Free and Accepted Masons of the State of Ohio, 1849–1960: An Epoch in American Paternalism* (1962).

The protagonist in the drama that unfolds in Greene's diary is Carter G. Woodson, who holds the undisputed title of father of Afro-American history. His life story is one of hardship, struggle, and dedication. He was born in rural Virginia on December 19, 1875, to parents who had been slaves and who struggled to support their nine children by farming. There was an elementary school in the area of Buckingham County, where Woodson grew up, but it was only in session five months a year. Since every hand was needed to eke out a living on the farm, Woodson could not attend school regularly even during those five months. He was ambitious, however, and by the time he was seventeen, largely through his own efforts, he had mastered the rudiments of an elementary education.

In order to attend high school, Woodson moved to Huntington, West Virginia, where he worked in the coal mines of Fayette County and attended Douglass High School part time. Finally, in 1895, when he was twenty years old, he became a full-time student and completed his high school work in one and a half years.

After finishing high school, Woodson entered Berea College in Kentucky, an integrated school where all students paid their way by working on campus. In 1900, after two years, he left college to become the principal of Douglass High School. He continued to attend Berea during the summers, however, and received his bachelor's degree in 1903. He earned another bachelor's degree from the University of Chicago in 1907, spent a semester at the Sorbonne, completed the work for his M.A. at the University of Chicago in 1908, and immediately began work on his Ph.D. at Harvard.

Woodson finished the course work for his Ph.D. in twelve months; in 1909, he moved to Washington, D.C., and accepted a job teaching history, English, Spanish, and French at Dunbar High School. This job placed him close to the Library of Congress, where he could do research for his dissertation, "The Disruption of Virginia," which he completed in 1912. Woodson was only the second black person to earn a Ph.D. in history. The first was W. E. B. Du Bois, who received his degree from Harvard in 1895.

Du Bois worked in many fields, wrote history, and was a pioneer in the development of the field of sociology. He was also a founder of the National Association for the Advancement of Colored People (NAACP) and the foremost articulator of black protest thought during the era of Booker T. Washington.

Woodson, however, devoted his life to correcting misconceptions about the history of black people. On September 9, 1915, Woodson and five other people met in Chicago to organize the ASNLH. They incorporated the new organization in Washington, D.C., the following month. The purpose of the ASNLH, as set forth by the founders, was to promote historical research, publish books on Afro-American life and history, promote the study of Afro-Americans in schools, and bring about harmony between the races by interpreting the black race to the white.

To further this purpose, on January 1, 1916, Woodson brought out the first issue of the *Journal of Negro History*. Then, in 1926, he began the celebration of Negro History Week. For symbolic reasons, Woodson picked the month of February for this celebration. He chose the week containing the birthdays of Abraham Lincoln, the Civil War president and author of the Emancipation Proclamation, and Frederick Douglass, the great black abolitionist. From the beginning, the observance was intended to celebrate achievements and to point with pride to the contributions black people made to the nation and to the world. In explaining the reason for the celebration, Woodson wrote, "If a race has no history, if it has no worth-while tradition, it becomes a negligible factor in the thought of the world, and it stands in danger of being exterminated."[9]

Between 1909 and 1922, Woodson held several teaching and administrative positions. He taught at both of the black high schools in Washington—Dunbar High School and Armstrong Manual Training High School—and served as the principal of Armstrong in 1918. In 1919, he joined the faculty of Howard University, where he taught history and served as dean of the School of Liberal Arts. But Woodson soon came into conflict with Howard's white president, J. Stanley Durkee, and had to leave this position after only a year. At the invitation of his friend John W. Davis, who had just become president of the West Virginia Collegiate Institute, Woodson went to that institution to serve as dean and to organize the college department. He remained there for two years. After 1915, while engaged in full-time employment, he was, simultaneously, serving as executive director of the ASNLH, editing the *Journal of*

9. Carter G. Woodson, "Negro History Week," *Journal of Negro History*, XI (April, 1926), 239.

Negro History, and producing an impressive number of scholarly works.

Neither his master's thesis nor his doctoral dissertation was on a subject drawn from the black experience. After completing his Ph.D., however, he began writing in the field of Afro-American history. His books appeared in rapid succession. *The Education of the Negro prior to 1861* was published in 1915; then came *A Century of Negro Migration* in 1918, *The History of the Negro Church* in 1922, *The Mis-Education of the Negro* in 1933, and two books on Africa— *The African Background Outlined* in 1936 and *African Heroes and Heroines* in 1939.

In 1922, Woodson began writing textbooks for use in college, high school, and elementary school courses. *The Negro in Our History*, which was published in 1922, became the standard textbook in the field. In 1928, *Negro Makers of History*, a simplified version of *The Negro in Our History* designed for elementary schools, was published, and in 1935, his textbook for secondary schools, *The Story of the Negro Retold,* appeared. Woodson edited and compiled several other books, including *Free Negro Owners of Slaves in 1830*, which was published in 1924; *Negro Orators and Their Orations,* published in 1925; and the four-volume edition of *The Works of Francis J. Grimké*, which came out in 1942. In 1937, Woodson began publishing the *Negro History Bulletin*, which was designed to reach public school and lay audiences.

Until 1922, Woodson's main task was to find some means of supporting the ASNLH and the *Journal of Negro History*. Although he had been successful in attracting a few donors, he had to teach not only to earn a living but to support his enterprises. In 1922, Woodson succeeded in obtaining a pledge of $25,000 from the Carnegie Corporation, to be spread over the next five years. He used this pledge to obtain a similar grant for research from the Laura Spelman Rockefeller Memorial. These grants and a campaign to develop regular giving from both white and black constituencies permitted Woodson to retire from teaching and devote full time to the work of the ASNLH.

By the time Greene went to work at the association, in 1928, Woodson "had made the study of the Afro-American past a viable enterprise." Greene and Wesley were two of a talented group of

seven black scholars whom Woodson would bring under his intellectual suzerainty. The others were W. Sherman Savage—whom
Greene joined on the faculty of Lincoln University in Missouri—
Alrutheus A. Taylor, James Hugo Johnston, Luther Porter Jackson,
and Rayford W. Logan. None of the others seemed to come under
Woodson's influence to the extent that Greene did early in the process of their intellectual maturation and their definition of a
vocation.[10]

Greene's diary covers two significant years in his intellectual development. Greene came to the ASNLH still skeptical about the intellectual validity of Negro history. The evolution of his respect
and admiration for Woodson coincided with his growing conversion to the cause of studying, preserving, and disseminating facts
about the Afro-American past. Equally important in understanding
Greene's development and his perceptions of those around him are
his engrossing insights about the personal travails of the aspiring
black scholar.

Greene's views of Woodson were shaped, in part, by Greene's relationship with Wesley. In 1928, Wesley, who was thirty-six years
old, was already making his mark as a scholar. He was a family
man, a respected teacher, an administrator, and a minister. He was
also a handsome, debonair figure. Greene idolized Wesley, as his diary shows; in comparison with Wesley, Woodson did not come out
well.

Woodson was in his early fifties in 1928, and he was a man to be
reckoned with in the field of Afro-American history. But he was
married to his enterprises and often exhibited the intolerance and
the impatience of those fanatically committed to a cause. Moreover,
he was introverted, independent, often uncompromising, and
sometimes given to biting sarcasm. Consequently, although Greene
respected Woodson, he did not see him as someone with whom he
could develop a warm personal relationship.

Greene became somewhat disillusioned with both men over the
petty positions they took on discontinuing the church survey. But
initially, his sympathies were all with Wesley. He came to realize,
however, that Woodson was not being vindictive, and he learned

10. See Meier and Rudwick, *Black History and the Historical Profession*, 74–95.

that Woodson had recommended that the direction of the study be turned over to Wesley, without involvement of the ASNLH.

As Greene came to know Woodson better, his opinion of him began to change. Soon after they began working together, Greene, in his diary, characterized Woodson as "rough, plain-spoken . . . but withal scholarly, witty, and even considerate." This last judgment was probably helped along, at the time, by Woodson's giving Greene a ten-day vacation. When Greene learned that Woodson was supporting a sister and her two children, that he was capable of little acts of kindness and thoughtfulness, and that he tried to live by the Golden Rule, he found that Woodson was not the ogre he had been led to believe him to be.

Of course, there were relapses in Greene's growing admiration of Woodson. After some angry incident or a cutting remark from Woodson, Greene would bemoan the abrasiveness of the man. At one point, Greene confided to his diary: "He is dogmatic, conceited, sarcastic, and less than sagacious in dealing with people—particularly his subordinates."

But such moods did not last. Greene began to realize that Woodson was a complex man. He came to understand that the kindness, thoughtfulness, and unselfishness, together with the pettiness, stubbornness, and bitterness, were marks of the man's essential humanness. To understand the Woodson whom Greene came to know and admire, one must read the diary. No single statement or group of statements will provide an adequate understanding.

Woodson's lack of pretension impressed Greene and was an object lesson for him. At first, he was surprised to find Woodson doing janitorial chores around the building or painting the floors. On one occasion, Greene exclaimed to his diary: "A wonderful man! Combined with his marvelous capacity for scholarly work, he cooks, sweeps, scrubs, washes dishes and every other sort of labor."

At this point in his development, Greene seemed to view education as a force that would liberate him from the necessity of doing the menial chores of life and that would, in some respects, liberate him from certain aspects of his blackness. Moreover, Greene, like W. E. B. Du Bois, brought with him into the larger black world of the South and the border area a large measure of New England snobbishness. Greene came into the black world first an American, then a New Englander, and finally a Negro. His association with Woodson, the investigations he undertook, and the contacts he made helped him come to understand, again like Du Bois, the curse and blessing of his "twoness," being an American and being black. He also came to realize the primacy of his blackness.

Some of the most engrossing entries in the diary, however, are those that lay bare the inner turmoil experienced by this sensitive young man who realized the personal price he was paying to complete his education and to begin making a contribution as a scholar. Part of the agony was associated with a fear of failing. Greene had that sense of mission and responsibility characteristic of the generations of black intellectuals who came to maturity before the 1960s. He must not fail, for his failure would not be just a personal failure. He would have failed his family, especially his parents, who counted on seeing one of their children acquire an education, and his brother James, who had sacrificed so much for the family. He would also be failing those who had shown faith and confidence in him. He would have failed Wesley and Woodson. Moreover, he would have failed the race and provided evidence for those who preached black inferiority. This was heavy baggage for a young person to carry.

There was also the price he had to pay in personal sacrifice. The family had assisted him and had asked little of him during his years in school. He owed them financial tribute from the first fruits of his labors, and he intended to render it. But this called for other sacrifices. He could not make a commitment to marry until he could adequately support a wife, and he saw no prospect that he would be able to do this in the near future. Consequently, he led a lonely life. Greene greatly enjoyed and needed the company of women. But realizing that marriage would have to be deferred, he avoided situations in which he might have to make a commitment. Often, though, he exhibited envy of married couples who appeared to be happy.

During his years with Woodson, Greene found his vocation. In the fall of 1933, he went to Jefferson City, Missouri, to take a teaching position at Lincoln University for which he had been recommended by Woodson. He met Thomasina Talley, whose father, Thomas W. Talley, was a member of the faculty at Fisk University. Greene fell in love with her, and they married. They became the parents of Lorenzo Thomas Greene, one of only seven grand-children produced by the nine children of Harriett and Willis Greene.

Greene's first publication, *The Negro Wage Earner* (1930), resulted from the research on Negro occupations he did under Woodson's direction. The work on this project received detailed attention in the diary. Some rancor between him and Woodson developed when Woodson insisted on being listed as coauthor of the publication, but this too passed.[11] Greene co-wrote *Negro Employment in the District of Columbia* (1932) with Myra Colson Callis. He was a member of the Committee on Negro Housing of President Herbert Hoover's Conference on Home Building and Home Ownership. The committee's report, *Negro Housing* (1932), was edited by Charles S. Johnson. His crowning achievement, however, was the study he did for his dissertation at Columbia University, *The Negro in Colonial New England, 1620–1776* (1942). This work has become a classic. Greene also edited the *Midwest Journal* from 1949 to 1955 and did a survey, *The Desegregation of Public Schools in Missouri, 1954–1959* (1959) for the Missouri Advisory Committee to the United States Commission on Civil Rights. He did a similar study in 1962, and after his retirement from Lincoln University, he continued to survey the school conditions of black Missourians for state and federal agencies. In 1980, he coauthored, with Gary R. Kremer and Antonio F. Holland, *Missouri's Black Heritage*.

In Missouri, Greene's scholarly production suffered because he was combining scholarly research with a heavy teaching load and social activism. He became involved with the southeast Missouri sharecroppers during their demonstration in 1939; he worked with such organizations as the Missouri Association for Social Welfare, the Missouri Advisory Committee to the United States Civil Rights Commission, the NAACP, and the ASNLH to improve relations between the races and to fight segregation and discrimination. Greene retired from the Lincoln faculty in 1972.

11. *Ibid.*, 80–82.

As preparation of the diary for publication drew to a close, an era ended. The last two close associates of Carter G. Woodson passed from the scene. After a brief illness, Lorenzo Johnston Greene died in Jefferson City, Missouri, on Sunday, January 24, 1988. His mentor and friend Charles Harris Wesley had died five months earlier on August 16, 1987.

Preface

On the very first day of my work for Dr. Woodson, I began a diary. Since my experiences were so unusual and since I was alone in a strange town, each night before retiring I jotted down the most important events I had experienced and the names of the interesting people I had met or with whom I had conversed. In fact, the diary is a potpourri of the economic, social, and political conditions under which Negroes lived in their communities at that time.

But it is also more than that. Interspersed throughout are the attitudes of prominent white politicians and businessmen toward the Negroes (churched and unchurched) of their communities, and vice versa. Current national and international affairs also find a place in the pages. And I did not omit some of my own health problems and social activities. Uppermost, however, was the Negro and his problems. The diary, then, is a mélange of happenings and opinions, whose author may be criticized for too great a tendency to generalize on the basis of apparently insufficient evidence.

It is clear from what I have just said that the diary is not a scholarly document. It can claim no pretensions to scientific history. Rather, like memoirs, letters, and other records, it is the stuff of which history is made. The diary reflects my private impressions; it contains comments made from day to day. Obviously, another person might have seen things in a different light and have reacted accordingly.

At any rate, I tried to be candid and probably was a little more brash and opinionated than I might have been. That the diary is to some extent biased is to be expected. Nevertheless, I sought to be as true to myself as possible.

To do so was not easy. I admired Woodson's dedication to the cause of Negro history and the sacrifices he endured for it, and I admired his vast grasp of the subject. However, because of his overbearing personality, his impatience, and his acid tongue, we were often at odds. Yet, so much did he teach me that, within a short time, I had become a dedicated convert to Negro history. From Woodson, I received practical training in research, in reading and editing manuscripts, in office management, and in public speaking. I also enjoyed the daily opportunities of meeting prominent people—national and international—who came to sit at the feet of the master. Naturally, there were conversations, not always pleasant ones, between us.

Included, too, are comments about Dr. Charles Wesley, who inspired me and gave me confidence. He was also solicitous about my health and about whether I had the wherewithal to pay for my daily necessities. We traveled, ate, and sometimes shared lodgings. He taught me the art of interviewing. More important, unlike Woodson, he treated me as a member of a team. And, of course, I could not omit our verbal joustings with Woodson.

The credit for publication of the diary must go to Wesley. One day, while recalling one of our experiences with Woodson, I surprised him by saying that I had jotted it down in my diary. I then told him that I had kept a diary during my entire association with Woodson, and I mentioned some of the miscellaneous items contained in the diary. Wesley amazed me by telling me that the diary should be published—that I was the sole associate of Woodson who had kept such a record and that nothing of this nature existed in Afro-American literature. I was astounded. The more Wesley scanned the diary, the more convinced he was that it should be published. Hesitantly, I agreed.

But I had misgivings: What of the numerous people about whom I made harsh comments? What of my reactions to clergymen, educators, doctors, lawyers, prominent white and black businessmen, politicians, storefront preachers, and religious exploiters of the poor? What of my unfavorable observations about Woodson himself? Should I identify the hundreds of people named? Should I use footnotes? What about intimate details of close friends? What about the sexual morality of Negroes as observed by or reported to me?

The diary appears here essentially as it was written. Intimate personal details have been omitted, as indicated by ellipsis points; little attempt has been made at documentation. The style is uneven, as would be expected in such a volume. Editing has been utilized only to make the diary more understandable.

I am deeply grateful to many people for assistance in preparing the diary for publication. My thanks must go to Beryle Moore and Billie Ockleberry, who read and typed certain portions of the diary for the *Midwest Journal*, which I edited; to Jackie Johnson, Cynthia Bonner, and Antonio Holland for encouraging me and helping me to publish the diary; and to Dr. Lynn Loschky, former colleague and professor of humanities, for her careful reading of part of the diary. My thanks also are extended to Dr. Edward Beasly and Enid Mushkin for their invaluable assistance, as well as to Emma Cook and Barbara Mulkey for typing revisions of the manuscript. But my deepest gratitude must go to my good friend, former colleague, and head of the Department of English at Lincoln University, the late professor Cecil A. Blue, who meticulously read the diary and, without altering its contents, made it more readable.

The most credit must go to Dr. Charles H. Wesley, the noted historian, scholar, and author and the former executive director and president of the Association for the Study of Negro Life and History and former president of Central State College. He directed the study to which many of my jottings refer, and he made me realize the value of having the diary published. To him and to Dr. Dorothy Porter (Mrs. Charles H. Wesley), bibliophile, author, historian, and emeritus curator of the Moorland Collection at Howard University, I cannot adequately express my gratitude. They not only spent long hours reading the manuscript and advising me about it, but, equally important, they looked after my health as well.

The Summons

On Friday, March 9, 1928, while pursuing graduate work at Columbia University, I received an unexpected, but extremely gratifying, telegram. It was from Dr. Carter G. Woodson, the outstanding black historian who was founder and director of the Association for the Study of Negro Life and History, instructing me to meet him Sunday afternoon at the Hotel Dumas on 135th Street in New York City.

Its terseness filled me with excitement, for I had no idea what the meeting portended. At any rate, I reached the hotel a half hour before Woodson arrived. Although we had met only once, three years before, he recognized me with ease.

In 1915, aided by four other persons, Woodson had founded the ASNLH for the primary purpose of recovering and publishing the neglected history of black peoples. A year later, he established the *Journal of Negro History* to give Negro scholars an academic vehicle for publishing their findings. To popularize his endeavors, in 1926 Woodson originated Negro History Week. These achievements, together with his voluminous publications, made Woodson the acknowledged father of the systematized history of the Negro.

I had my favorite former history teacher, Dr. Charles H. Wesley, to thank for Dr. Woodson's interest in me. A Harvard Ph.D. in history and a teacher, author, minister, lecturer, and friend, he early became deeply involved with Woodson's association. In 1924, during my senior year at Howard University, I took a course in English history from Wesley. During the following summer, while visiting in Washington, I called upon him. He was glad to know that I was doing graduate work in history at Columbia University. More important, he gave me a letter of introduction to Woodson, the director of the ASNLH. In it, he asked Woodson whether he could grant me some much-needed financial aid to carry on my studies.

Woodson greeted me briefly, read the note, stared at me, then launched into his favorite subject, Negro history. He emphasized the splendid opportunities in the field and stressed his disappointment that so few young Negro students could be persuaded to enter the field. Nervously, I sat while Woodson spoke for two hours of the fascinating rewards Negro history offered. He regretted that the association lacked the funds to help me at this time, but he promised to keep me in mind. As I started to leave, he presented me with an autographed copy of his most famous book, *The Negro in Our History.* "Take this," he said, "read it, and I shall contact you later."

Instead of appreciating the honor the great man had bestowed upon me, I left pitying him. I knew nothing about Negro history and cared less. In my opinion, Woodson was a brilliant scholar who should have been teaching at Yale, Harvard, or some great university. Instead, he was trying to create Negro history—something that never existed. I left him and returned to New York to run elevators; to paint hospital rooms, loft buildings, and houses; and to sell magazines—anything to continue my education. Meanwhile, I forgot Woodson.

Now, here I sat face to face with the man who, three years before, I had secretly derided. He noted I was tense in his presence. Perhaps to put me at ease, he asked whether I had had dinner. Immediately, I warmed up to him; I had not eaten all day and it was now five o'clock. He took me to the YWCA cafeteria on 137th Street. There, over the dinner table, he divulged his reason for coming to New York to talk to me. He was offering me a job—employment with him in Washington, D.C.

Briefly, he told me that the association, in collaboration with the Institute for Social and Religious Research of New York City, was undertaking a national survey of the Negro church. A pilot study was to begin, with Baltimore churches as an example of the church in a large urban community and with Suffolk, Virginia, churches as typical of the church in a rural community. The survey, he continued, would run for three years. He was offering me employment as a field agent. My salary would be $150 a month, plus expenses. I eagerly grasped the opportunity. The offer was all the more attractive because I would be working directly under Wesley, my benefactor and teacher. In accepting Woodson's offer, I had to turn down opportunities to teach at Fisk University and at West Virginia Institute. Within a week, I was ready to leave New York.

With my trip financed by borrowed funds, I arrived in Washington and went directly to the office of the association. There Woodson and Wesley greeted me, and we got down to serious business without further ado.

Woodson was eager to complete the survey as soon as possible. He and Wesley assigned me to Baltimore. After a hasty greeting to my aunt (with whom I had lived while attending Howard University) and to some cousins of my mother, I caught a train for Baltimore. Arriving there, I inquired about a place to stay. Following a disappointment or two, since Negroes could not stay or eat in white hotels or restaurants, I found excellent accommodations.

A Diary, 1928–1930

[1] Answering the Summons

Today marks one of the mile-posts of my life. It is virtually my commencement. For the first time in my life, I am assuming responsibility. Today I begin to draw upon the accumulation of seven years of collegiate and graduate training. Theory must be translated into practice. Words must be resolved into action; in short, Lorenzo J. Greene is on trial—on trial before a critical, unsympathetic public, that measures success or failure by the performance of, or the ability to discharge, the tasks it sets before him. God grant that I may summon every ounce of energy to vindicate my extended training! If I fail, I have studied, sacrificed, and labored in vain.

My job is to act as assistant to Dr. Charles H. Wesley in a study of the Negro Church in America. Its purpose is to show the influence of the present day Negro Church upon the intellectual, moral, social, business, and recreational life of the Negro. Dr. Woodson, the Director of the Association for the Study of Negro Life and History, engaged me for the work on March 9, 1928. At the time I was negotiating with Dr. Thomas Elsa Jones, President of Fisk University, relative to my teaching History there next fall. Because of its international prominence, it had been my fond desire to go there in the role of a teacher, but Dr. Woodson's proposition overshadowed any advantage that Fisk might offer me. With Dr.

Woodson, not only can I earn some badly needed money to help repay loans to Columbia University; but also, more important, I can send my parents regular monthly sums to keep my mother from the backbreaking job of washing and ironing white people's clothes. Finally, in my capacity as research worker, Dr. Woodson has assured me that I could gather enough facts to write the thesis required by Columbia University for the Ph.D. Degree in History.

My job is to travel over the country making a study of the Negro Church. In short, I am an investigator. We are to begin in Baltimore on March 16th. A conference at the office of the Association for the Study of Negro Life and History is scheduled for this p.m. I am to leave New York in order to reach there at that time.

How I hated to leave old friends of years standing! There was Gladys [McDonald]—a dear pal, if ever there was one; [Harcourt A.] Tynes, who struggled through with me to our M.A. degrees at Columbia University; Helen [Notis], the most thoughtful and one of the finest women I have ever known; Marguerite [Skeeter], rock-melting in personality, languid, musical, almost oriental in looks and thoughts; Florence [Bacote], secretary extraordinary, a hometown girl— petite, beautiful, black, and gifted with an unusual sense of humor. She is the cousin of Dr. [Ernest] Bacote and a very unique person, with whom one could not quarrel, and who insists upon styling herself a member of that *sanctum sanctorum*—"the gang"; [Ned] Pope, [Ernest Theodore] Hemby, Muriel [Daniel], [Sidney] Wells, Dr. and Mrs. Vernon Johns, and a list of others I took leave of with a feeling of sadness.[1]

---

1. These persons were members of Greene's close circle of friends in New York City, and many of their names recur throughout the diary. Gladys McDonald, his neighbor and a native of the West Indies, was a librarian at the New York Public Library. Harcourt A. Tynes was a native of Nassau in the Bahamas. Greene met him at Columbia University, where Tynes earned the M.A. degree. He was a junior high schoolteacher in the New York Public School System. Helen Notis, a secretary who lived and worked in Newark, New Jersey, traveled north from Charleston, South Carolina. Marguerite Skeeter, a music student majoring in voice when Greene left New York, was a native of Suffolk, Virginia. Greene first met her at a dance in Hampton, Virginia. She was there on a visit, and he was traveling in the area selling magazines. Florence Bacote was the adolescent cousin of Dr. Ernest Bacote. The Bacotes were from Greene's hometown, Ansonia, Connecticut. Dr. Bacote and

But the simplest leave-taking of all, yet the most significant, was the farewell to one of my best friends, Harry Hipp.[2] We did not even shake hands. We merely raised our hands as a token of "good-bye" and, with a simultaneous "See you later," snapped for a period of two years—Who knows? Maybe forever—an association that had endured unbroken for eight years. It was most appropriate, for no words could have expressed the agony of our separation. Of all my friends, he is my closest and staunchest. But more about him later.

Would have started to D.C. with only $2.00 in my pocket had it not been for Gladys McDonald, who loaned me $5.00.

Missed the 9:05 a.m. train, although I taxied from 66th Street and 9th Avenue to the station. Took the 9:30 express. Travelled as a clergyman. My good friend, the Rev. Johns, very kindly purchased my ticket yesterday, getting it for one-third less. He also gave me his passbook for identification, if necessary. Happily, it was not necessary to display it.

On the way to D.C., I felt both elated and depressed, the former because of the wonderful opportunity presented me for service, and the latter because of the many haunting memories of New York City.

The train was 15 minutes late. Arrived at the conference at

Greene were schoolmates in Ansonia, and they attended Howard University together. Dr. Bacote earned his M.D. degree from Howard in 1926 and practiced medicine in Lawnside, New Jersey, Syracuse, New York, and Newark, New Jersey. He married Victoria Snowden of Washington, D.C. Florence came to New York after finishing high school in Ansonia. She worked as a secretary during the day and attended evening classes at New York University. Later she moved to Washington, D.C., and worked for the Department of State. Greene met Ned Pope at Columbia University, where Pope was working on his M.A. degree in political science. Ernest Theodore Hemby, a 1924 graduate of Howard University, was studying music in New York. He was also a member of Kappa Alpha Psi Fraternity, which Greene would later join. Muriel Daniel, a social worker in New York, married Greene's closest friend, Harry Hipp. Sidney Wells, originally from Washington, Pennsylvania, was a music student in New York but eventually became a social worker. He and Greene traveled together selling magazines for the Union Circulation Company during the summer of 1927. They were one of the first teams of black students employed by the company. Greene met Vernon Johns while selling magazines in Charleston, West Virginia, where Johns was pastor of White Rock Baptist Church. Johns moved to New York, and he and Greene became friends.

2. Harry Hipp, of Jacksonville, Florida, and Greene met as freshmen at Howard University. Along with Ernest Bacote, they lived with Greene's aunt while attending Howard and referred to themselves as "the gang." Hipp earned an A.B. degree and went to work for Standard Oil of New York. He married Muriel Daniel.

3:10 p.m., going directly from the Union Station. The office is located in a three-story house at 1538 Ninth Street, N.W., in a less pretentious section of the city. The first and second floors are given over to office space. The third floor is Dr. Woodson's living quarters. Dr. Woodson was out of town. One of the office girls escorted me upstairs, where I found Dr. Wesley bending over some maps being shown him by one Dr. [R. C.] Woods. Wesley greeted me cordially and introduced me to Dr. Woods. The latter, formerly head of Virginia Theological Seminary, had just come from Baltimore, where he had spent two weeks laying the groundwork for the work which Dr. Wesley and I are to do there. He gave us the benefit of a large amount of diverse information, such as: population, number of schools and churches, number of school children, employment of Negroes in industries, etc. His report was full but not scientifically gathered. He seems to have worked chiefly among a certain group—the upper stratum. The Negro masses must be taken into serious consideration in a work of this kind, for they are the chief supporters of ecclesiastical institutions.

Wesley later expressed to me his displeasure over Woods' ostentation in his work. For instance, Woods had been admonished to secrecy, but, instead, gave out all the details of the study to the *Afro-American*—a Baltimore Negro weekly—with the result that the entire study, together with photographs of Woodson and Wesley, appeared in that paper. Wesley did not conceal his chagrin from me, although he did not mention it to Woods.

Woods is a man of small stature, could be easily mistaken for white, is arresting in his speech and to all appearances a conscientious worker. A pity he has not been trained in this field.

Wesley, on the other hand, is an historian of the first rank. His ability is proven. Already, he has written the best monograph on *Negro Labor*. Wesley is tall, handsome, light brown, almost artistic in mien, a clear, dispassionate thinker. He was one of my favorite history teachers during my Howard "U" days. I believe I shall enjoy working with him. Also, I should learn much from this master.

During the conference it was decided that we should all go to Baltimore. The work was divided among the three of us. I am to check up on the number of churches, fill out questionnaires for all churches, for church members and non-members, and to solicit the opinions of youth regarding the church. Wesley is to take care of the questionnaires for significant churches and pastors; Woods for prominent whites.

Leaving the conference about 5 o'clock, Dr. Wesley brought me to my aunt's home on Swann Street. Knowing that I was just out of school, he was thoughtful enough to ask whether I had enough money to tide me over till next Saturday. I confessed that my total capital amounted to $7.00. He promised to secure some funds for me by Monday, when we meet at the Baltimore Y.M.C.A. To my delight he further informed me that all legitimate expenses will be defrayed by the Association through the Institute for Social and Religious Research of New York City. 'Tis well, else my small pittance would be devoured by expenses.

My aunt [Fannie B. Coleman] certainly is robust.[3] I ate some beans and went to see my cousins on M Street. Saw Bertha [Baylor], who lives with them. She is even more beautiful than when I last saw her three years ago. Attracted by my ball-watch, and chain, she asked me to let her take it. I did so and placed it about her neck. She promises to return it when (or if) I come back to visit her Sunday. Unable to persuade her to return it, I was forced to leave it in her possession. She is the first person who has ever kept that beautiful and unique piece of jewelry for more than a fleeting moment since I found it last year.

3. Fannie B. Coleman was one of three younger sisters of Harriett Coleman Greene, Greene's mother. Fannie was about fifty-four years old in 1928 and had never married. "The gang"—Greene, Hipp, and Bacote—roomed with her while attending Howard University. The cousins, Susie Robinson and Winnie—whose last name Greene could not recall—were his mother's cousins. He met them while attending school in Washington. He also met Bertha Baylor while at Howard, and they developed a very close relationship. The watch referred to was a small spherical watch on a chain that Greene found in New York.

Returned to my aunt's home at 9:50 p.m. Began to recount the events of the day. My aunt was attending services at the "House of Prayer."[4] To me, the latter is only a pretext for extorting money based on religious sanction from poor Negro washerwomen and other common laborers. The movement is identified with one "Bishop" (Daddy) Grace, a portly man of medium height with a foreign accent who wears his hair long, his face wreathed in a beard, affecting the appearance of the Saviour. He hails from New Bedford, Massachusetts, is lemon-colored, and is supposedly of Portuguese extraction. The "Bishop" preys upon illiterate and emotional persons of both races. Both white and black followers are devout believers in his self-declared "healing" powers. In the meantime, he eats heartily, grows sleek and shiny and rides about in a costly, lemon-colored, chauffeur-driven Packard limousine, got from the blood earnings of his parishioners. And, horror of horrors, my cousins and aunt are among his most zealous members!

Called Helen [Grinage].[5] Beautiful, black girl. Seemed surprised, as well as glad, to hear my voice. Was my sweetheart during my last college year here. Tells me Lil, her sister, is married. Rumor has Helen married also. Am still fond of Helen and believe she is not inimical to me. Says she isn't married.

Looks as if the aviators, [Captain Walter G. R.] Hinchcliffe,

4. The United House of Prayer for All People was a black religious cult founded by Bishop Charles Emmanuel Grace, commonly known as Daddy Grace. Arthur Huff Fauset included the United House of Prayer in his study of religious cults of black residents of northern cities. According to Fauset's account, Grace began preaching in the South in 1925, and from there his movement spread northward along the eastern seaboard. The cult was a "Christian sect of the holiness type." Nevertheless, Fauset concluded, "the beliefs boil down to a worship of Daddy Grace. God appears to be all but forgotten. The followers concentrate their thoughts on His 'great man,' Grace." The primary emphasis of the cult was money. Numerous collections were taken during services; at intervals, time was taken to sell Daddy Grace products. They included the *Grace Magazine*—which was claimed to have healing powers—cosmetics, writing paper, emblems, buttons, badges, and even a full uniform with accessories. Meetings were held every night and all day on Sunday. Arthur Huff Fauset, *Black Gods of the Metropolis: Negro Religious Cults of the Urban North* (Philadelphia, 1944), 22–30.

5. Helen Grinage, a student at Miner Teachers College during Greene's student days at Howard University, became a pharmacist and worked for a time in Danville, Virginia. In 1928, she was living in Washington, D.C.

and Elsie Mackay are lost. Left England in an airplane Tuesday for New York and have not been heard from since.

Have they met the fate of [Charles] Nungesser, [François] Coli, Princess [Anne] Lowenstein[-Wertheim] and other daring pioneers who have found untimely deaths in the vast and relentless North Atlantic?[6]

The Teapot Dome oil scandal has tainted many of the most prominent public men: Theodore Roosevelt, Jr., Secretary [Albert B.] Fall, Secretary [Edwin] Denby, Will Hays, William Butler, Andrew Mellon, all have been spotted with the stench of petroleum. Who will be next? The people, however, do not complain, but in face of revealed corruption and dishonesty, go right ahead electing such men to high public office.

6. Captains Charles Nungesser and François Coli were French aviators who disappeared while attempting a transatlantic crossing during the summer of 1927. The sixty-three-year-old Princess Anne Lowenstein-Wertheim, along with pilots Frederick R. Minchin and Leslie Hamilton, was killed in August, 1927, aboard the British plane *St. Raphael* during an attempted transatlantic crossing.

[2] Baltimore

Yesterday was clear and warm. Today it was snowy and rainy when I rose. Bade adieu to my aunt about 11:30 a.m. and left for Baltimore. Had previously warned her against investing too much of her meagre earnings in the House of Prayer. I contend that one cannot buy his way to heaven, even if there were one. I advised her to beware of this man and to make donations to his cause no greater in denomination than she would to any other church.

Arrived in Baltimore at 2:00 p.m. Went to the Y.M.C.A. There I met the director, Mr. Gidgen, and asked him to direct me to the home of some reputable family where I might lodge for a couple of weeks. He referred me to a Mrs. Cornish, 1322 Druid Hill Avenue. I did not like the place but little relished looking for a better one in such weather. Medium sized room in the rear, sort of brownish paper on the walls. Clean enough, but the furniture is of variegated colors. Wanted $5 per week. My exchequer held but four and some change. I handed her $3 saying that I would take it tentatively till Monday, at which time Dr. Wesley could decide where to put me up. Left me with $1.75. Sent a letter to Hipp and Helen [Notis]. Asked Hipp to send me $5 immediately.

Called upon Mr. [Whit W.] Allen, pastor of the Shiloh Baptist Church. Could not see him although he was at home. Have an engagement with him at 10:00 a.m. tomorrow.

My dinner was not at all appetizing—meat half-cooked; vegetables cold.

Came in at 6:00 p.m. Too rainy to do anything. Retired and read for a while.

No trace of fliers yet. Another disgraceful suit in court. Common-law wife, Letitia Brown (colored), suing multi-millionaire [Carleton] Curtis.[1] Hope the details will not be as shocking as those of the Rhinelander case.[2]

Secretary of State [Frank B.] Kellogg still tries to commit the nations to a treaty which will outlaw war. Commendable effort, but believe it just a waste of time and energy. War is too precious a financial and powerful tool to dispense with.

Retired early. Read [Edmund de Schweinitz] Brunner's *Churches of Distinction in Town and Country* till I fell asleep.

Having just completed my report for the day's work, I turn with pleasure to jot down here a few happenings of my first full day in Baltimore.

Because Bertha has my watch, I feared that I had overslept. But when I started out, I found to my surprise that it was just ten minutes of nine.

I had an engagement at ten o'clock this morning with Rev. Allen, pastor of the Shiloh Baptist Church. Having almost an hour before my appointment, I walked about in search of

Saturday
March 17
1928

1. Letitia Ernestine Brown, a black woman, brought suit against Carleton Curtis, a wealthy white graduate of Princeton, to establish that a common-law marriage existed between them. Curtis testified that he had visited her for about sixteen years, until he learned from detectives, in 1926, that she was deceiving him. He denied that he had ever lived with her. The court held that the "relationship between the parties was never anything more than meretricious."

2. The Rhinelander affair remained in the news from 1924 to 1930. On October 14, 1924, Leonard Kip Rhinelander, a member of a wealthy Manhattan family, married a black woman, Alice Beatrice Jones, daughter of a Pelham, New York, taxicab driver. Rhinelander's father disinherited him, and under the glare of publicity, the young couple broke up. Rhinelander brought suit to have the marriage annulled on the grounds that Alice Jones had concealed her racial identity and brought about the marriage by fraud. A jury held for Mrs. Rhinelander and refused to annul the marriage. In 1929, Mrs. Rhinelander filed suit against her husband's father, charging him with alienation of affections and asking for $500,000. In the meantime, Rhinelander established residence in Las Vegas, Nevada, and filed suit for divorce there. The matter was finally settled in 1930, when Mrs. Rhinelander recognized the divorce decree, dropped all actions against the Rhinelanders, and accepted a cash payment of $31,500 and an annuity of $3,600.

additional churches, or to verify the names and locations of those which had been given me.

On Mulberry Street, I found a few small churches and missions, some hardly worthy of the name, but nevertheless all must be included in this study. On Saratoga Street, in the heart of the poorer section of Northeast Baltimore, I found church after church: Baptist, Seventh Day Adventist, Houses of Prayer, Churches of God, and Faith Churches. Most of them were dilapidated, one-story brick structures; some located in small stores; others occupied a room in a house. Made me ponder over so many sects seeking as many diverse routes to an unknown hereafter. I sometimes wonder at the probable consternation, wonder, and disillusionment of any one sect that finds that on the day of judgement every denomination will help to sing His praises. Or that all shall be disappointed in seeking that ethereal haven of bliss and rest.

Found Rev. Allen, a robust, sleek, greasy minister, at home. He was cloistered in his study with a Rev. R. N. Coleman, a young man from Birmingham, Ala., who, I was told, had received his education in Canada. Coleman travels as Corresponding Secretary for the Baptist Educational Board. Has some ideas concerning the Negro which coincide with mine. I advised him to get in touch with the Rev. Vernon Johns when he visited New York.

Rev. Allen corrected some of the errors in the list of churches which Dr. Wesley gave me Thursday. Quite an interesting man. Not well educated. Says "ah" and "heah"; speaks very broadly with a typically Southern accent. Yet he was kind, affable, and obliging. Called several men who could give me information. Also drove me through several streets, where he pointed out more churches. I appreciated, and thanked him for, his interest.

A Rev. [Junius] Gray, referred to me by Rev. Allen, gave me a list of Baptist Ministers—ninety-one in all. My task now is to link them with the churches.

Called upon Rev. [George Freeman] Bragg [Jr.] of St. James Episcopal Church. A wizened, little man, smaller than

I. He declined to fill out a questionnaire at this time but promised to do so and give it to me Monday.

Ate breakfast at 12:30. All eating and lodging places are segregated here. Most Negro restaurants are small, dirty, infested with flies; the service is bad and the food is often ill-cooked or, if well-cooked, lacks variety. Had $1.05. Knit my brow to decide how that amount would sustain me till Monday afternoon, when Dr. Wesley would bring me some much-needed money. After a deal of hesitation, I ordered vegetable soup which contained no vegetables, and drank a glass of milk. Cost me 25 cents. Bought a hot dog later, but it was so tainted I could not eat it.

Filled out three questionnaires for Negro citizens. Most of these people are reticent about answering questions. None of the three replies threw much light upon the facts which we sought. However, I trust that next week the questionnaires will be better received and more revealing.

Later called upon the most interesting man I have yet talked with here. He is a Rev. [O.] Bryant, pastor of the Antioch Baptist Church. It is a small pastorate and I think Bryant too big for the job. A dark, well-built man of average height, with a projecting forehead, he is Secretary of the Baptist Convention of Maryland and holds other offices. His ideas, and the clarity and force with which he expressed them, reminded me of Rev. Johns. Bryant would make the Negro self-supporting. Like Booker T. Washington and others, he strongly advocates the Negro enter the field of business, for therein lies his salvation. His creed for the colored man is to make himself economically indispensable. He will then not only command the respect of the whites but better still, he will be able to employ his own youth. Other ideas which Mr. Bryant expressed I shall not repeat here, but Mr. Bryant needs a bigger and better medium in which to work. Now he must descend to the level of his parishioners. Thus he stultifies his own intellectual growth. In my opinion, he would make an excellent assistant for Rev. Johns.

Worked over a large part of the northwestern section of

Baltimore today. Had to walk, for I lacked the wherewithal to ride. Baltimore is truly a city of churches. Beautiful structures at every turn. If church spires were an indication of the moral and spiritual tone of a community, Baltimore would be ahead by several laps.

Yet Baltimore seems to be an average city. There is not the hustle and bustle of New York, nor the extreme lethargy of a Southern city. Instead, it seems rather complacent.

Wonder of wonders! How cheap are provisions here. I saw bacon 10 cents a lb., fish 15 cents, ham 12 cents. It brought back to me the memories of prewar days. Walked up Laurens Street. There is a large market here, resembling the K St. Market of Washington, D.C. Provisions are much cheaper here than in New York. Could have prepared a fine meal cheaply if a place to cook were available.

Ate dinner at a cheap restaurant. Consisted of fish and bread. My capital was 75 cents. It cost me 15 cents. Unsavory, but filling, especially since the fishy taste necessitated drinking two glasses of water immediately afterwards. Bought four bananas for a nickel. Ate two, left two for breakfast, which, with a pint of milk, will make the total for dinner and breakfast 29 cents. Quite cheap, but an emergency. Reminds me of old school days. Have 46 cents now. If Hipp does not send me $5.00 today, no seeing Bertha tomorrow; neither shall I be able to breakfast Monday morning.

Marguerite's picture gazes upon me from the dresser. A beautiful picture of a sweet and charming girl. I should write her but have no ink nor the means of purchasing it. Last Saturday night I was with her; tonight I am alone while she—?

Hope has been virtually abandoned for the trans-Atlantic fliers. The oil taint still brands men high in offices of public trust. But the people soon forget and prepare themselves for the next plucking.

Sunday
March 18
1928

When I rose today, the ground was blanketed with snow and slush to the depth of almost four inches. It was still snowing though it gradually changed to a drizzling rain.

My breakfast consisted of two small bananas and a pint of

milk. Was nourishing, if not elaborate. My funds total 46 cents. If I do not receive pecuniary aid from Harry today, I shall be penniless by nightfall.

Attended services at the St. James Episcopal Church, Park Avenue and Pressman [Preston] Street, pastored by the Rev. Mr. J. J. Bragg [George Freeman Bragg, Jr.].[3] The church is a small but historic structure, founded in 1827. Dr. Wesley, who is directing the study, suggested that I go there and write up my idea of the sermon and the response of the people to it. 'Twill be an experience, for I have attended few Episcopal Churches.

The services were stereotyped, formal, and ritualistic. First, the acolytes lighted the candles over the altar, reverently crossing themselves each time they passed in front of the crucifix. Then, while a hymn was sung—the congregation standing—the vested choir marched to its place before the altar. Followed then a chant by the priest. After that the congregation reading. Singing again, then a chanted prayer—the people kneeling. Then followed a sermon by the pastor. His subject, "How Can We Escape if We Neglect so Great a Salvation?," was suggested by the second chapter of Hebrews. In its development, Rev. Bragg stressed the value of striving continually if one would gain perfection, whether it be in the moral, spiritual, or intellectual realm. He held there could be no balance, no absence of motion; one either advances, evolves, or degenerates. Man knows but one escape, and that is the cultivation of God in the larger sense. I thought it a very interesting sermon, splendidly delivered.

3. St. James Protestant Episcopal Church owed its existence to the missionary work of William Levington, who began teaching day and Sunday school and holding services in Baltimore on June 23, 1824. After Levington's death, in 1836, St. James had an unsettled history under the leadership of several white and black rectors. In 1872, a group of the younger members broke away and formed St. Philip's Mission. The following year, St. James came under the guardianship of St. Paul's parish; this arrangement lasted until 1888. The affairs of St. James became more stable after George F. Bragg, Jr., became rector, on November 17, 1891. The congregation moved into its first building, at North and Saratoga streets, in March, 1827. In 1890, the church relocated to a structure on High Street in East Baltimore that had formerly housed a white Baptist congregation. The building on Park Avenue and Preston Street visited by Greene was erected in 1901. George F. Bragg, Jr., *History of the Afro-American Group of the Episcopal Church* (Baltimore, 1922), 90–101.

Rev. Bragg seemed to be more concerned with theological values than advocating earthly strivings among his people. Sort of medievalistic, I thought. Still, the fact that this was Communion Sunday may have impelled him to set forth the spiritual in so emphatic a manner. He spoke both to heart and head. However, by his fervid and impassioned oratory it seemed that I was in a Baptist Church. But that impression would have been quickly dispelled, for the usually responsive "Amens," "Hallelujahs," and "Preach it, Brother," were totally lacking. In fact, not one syllable of response emanated from the congregation during the sermon.

Came then the Communion Service. It also was in keeping with the practice of liturgical churches. It was formal, yet inspiring, more so than the haphazard and more simple sacrament as administered by Baptists. The service began with a chant, then responsive reading while the congregation knelt. The partakers of the Sacrament knelt before the altar before partaking of the Lord's supper. The feast was communal, each communicant sipping the sacramental wine from a common cup.

The offering was lifted in an unostentatious manner. Ushers brought it to the priest, who murmured his blessing over it. Rev. Bragg, I should have mentioned, was attired in the cassock and robes of his denomination. After the recessional, he stood in the doorway, shook hands with the parishioners, including me, as I left. Was pleased that I had worshipped with them. The ritual itself was unfamiliar to me, but an elderly gentleman behind me helped me most opportunely.

Returned home, hungry, lonesome, despondent. Finally, Mrs. Cornish brought me a telegram from Hipp. It was a money order for $5.00. I was elated for it meant a good meal. Changed clothes. Went to the telegraph office downtown and cashed it.

Doubted whether I would go to Washington, D.C., although I had promised Bertha I would do so. Called her. She persuaded me to come over.

Arrived there at 5:30. Had been writing Hipp *en route*. Had dinner with Bertha. Aunt Fannie came in while I was eating.

Surprised to see me. I beat her by saying that now since she was here, I did not need to go to her home. She went to Church (House of Prayer) next door.

My mother's cousins tried to persuade me to accept the teachings of the Bishop. Impossible. I do not wish to be tied down by religious dogma. Let each man think for himself and do good deeds for others. That is all the religion that is practicable. Stayed at Bertha's till 11:55. Tried to persuade her to give me my watch. Refused to do so. Finally, offered me a man's watch in exchange for it, but I would not accept it. Seeing, however, that I needed a timepiece, I accepted her watch for the duration of my stay in Baltimore, at the end of which we are to return each other's timepieces.

I left to get the midnight train back to Baltimore. Alas! The train was gone. Bertha's clock was 40 minutes slow. Went to Aunt Fannie's to spend the night. Brought her some ice cream. Knocked for half hour. No response. Went to telephone booth. Called her. She had heard my knocking but was afraid to go to the door.

Chatted till two o'clock, when I retired. Must be in Baltimore by 10 a.m. tomorrow.

Rose at 8 a.m. Caught 8:30 train to Baltimore. Arrived here at 10:00. Landlady thought that I had stayed the night with Baltimore friends. Surprised when I told her I had gone to D.C.

Called upon the Rev. Mr. Gray, pastor of the Psalmist Baptist Church, with whom I had an engagement at 10. Is also a real estate man. Gave me information concerning his church, and threw valuable light upon such churches as First Baptist, Union, Leadenhall, etc. Between him and Rev. Bryant, I ought to secure ample information concerning these churches.

After a futile search for a place to eat, I finally stopped at the Penn Hotel. Clean, appetizing place. But the chef had been fired earlier in the morning, the waiter was drunk, and the pantry practically empty. Besides, the help staged an argument in the kitchen, employing obscenity that was both audible and disgusting to persons in the dining room.

Later attended the Baptist Conference in order to secure

Monday
March 19
1928

questionnaires from ministers. Spoke for five minutes, telling them of the aims of the study and need for their cooperation. Rev. Coleman was there soliciting funds in a speech of Baptist eloquence. A young fellow from the Virginia Theological Seminary delivered a sermon. He spoke with all the fervor of a confirmed child of the faith, shouted, ranted, and railed. I do not even recall the subject. But the ministers—the speaker was superior intellectually to the vast majority—thought it was a masterpiece. In my opinion, it was an oratorical and scriptural excursion. Was amused by the President's stubborn adherence to the letter of Parliamentary rules.

Dr. Wesley came in. Spoke impressively for 10 minutes. Then continued to talk when he should have been filling out questionnaires. Lost valuable time. Received all-told about eight. Woods was there, also.

Wesley took us to the National Cemetery Association. Met Rev. [Elbert H.] Beard, a former classmate of mine at Howard. Is married and preaching in suburb of Baltimore. Also met a Rev. [Samuel] Giles, who promises to find a place for me to stay.

Woods, Wesley, and I discussed best means of obtaining questionnaires from ministers. Wesley proposed that I write them, sending blanks with return postage. I disagreed, arguing that it would be a waste of time and money, for (a) the ministers would give little attention to questionnaires for most would not wish to advertise their ignorance voluntarily; (b) even if filled out and sent in, questionnaires would come in so desultory a fashion that months might elapse before we finished Baltimore; (c) cannot make as forcible appeal in writing as is possible through personal contact. Wesley agreed with me. I suggested that each of us take one denomination or more: Woods the Methodists, I the Baptists, and Wesley miscellaneous. Again Wesley assented.

We agreed to meet Thursday at 2 p.m. at the office of the Cemetery Association. Located a few churches. Had dinner. By the way, I have yet to find a decent place to eat here. Because of segregation, restaurant conveniences for Negroes are deplorable. If the food is good, the place is dirty, or they are out of every meat except pork chops. If they have them, and one asks for them, they are usually badly cooked, or cold. Have had no green vegetables yet. Only one lunch room served milk. The prices are high, yet one gets little for his money. Must find a place to eat.

Wrote Harry, Marguerite, Columbia University, Ansonia (Conn.) *Evening Sentinel*, Mother, Ruth, Gladys, Tynes, and Lena.[4]

Retired about 11.

My first official act was to go to the Cemetery Association, where I was to be directed to a comfortable stopping place. While talking to Beard, Dr. Woods entered. I received a few questionnaires from him and also promised to call upon him between 6 and 8 p.m.

Tuesday
March 20
1928

Rev. Giles, an interesting young fellow who holds an M.A. from Edinburgh University and is working for a Ph.D. degree from that school in Church History, has found a place for me to stay. He took me up to a Mrs. [Annie or Anna] Hitchens, 1530 McCulloh Street in the upper class Negro section of Baltimore. Mrs. Hitchens is a handsome, motherly type of woman. She is a social worker, has a beautiful home, and immediately made me feel as if I were one of the family. Gave me a splendid room with day bed, desk, books, etc. Told me I may even use the kitchen for preparing my breakfast if I desired. Also found me a place a block away where I could get real homecooked meals with a friend of hers, a Mrs. Fernandez [probably Mrs. Sarah C. Fernandis, 1427 Madison Avenue, an investigator for the health department and society editor for the Baltimore *Afro-American*].

Walked considerably today. Went to a barber shop. Received interesting questionnaires from barbers and patrons. Both have unfavorable ideas of the church. Think it should promote Negro business. Questioned a man on the street.

4. Ruth Beverly was a student at Miner Teachers College during Greene's college years. In 1928, she was teaching in Maryland and lived in Anacostia, a suburb of Washington, D.C. Lena, whose last name he could not recall, was a native of Plainville, Connecticut. Greene met her around 1925 when she was visiting New York City.

Told me that the "old time religion is lacking. Money is God." Met a most interesting man, a Mr. Johnson, on Carrollton Avenue. Believes emphasis on money overshadows all else in the church. Preachers are exploiters. Should build business instead of buying churches. "Ministers," he told me, "are morally lax. They alone are to blame for bad conditions in the community. They are the leaders, but have lost the confidence of the people."

Did not eat dinner till 8:20. Best Negro restaurant here, in Hotel Penn. Had no vegetables, only canned spaghetti and peas. A deplorable place, Baltimore, as far as dining conveniences for Negroes are concerned.

Received a letter from Helen [Notis] this morning. Was delighted to hear from her. She could not believe that I could be lonesome. Helen is one of the finest, best all-round girls I have ever met.

Called upon Woods about 9 p.m. He was reading the *North American Review*. Rev. [Willis J.] Winston, where he is stopping, has a fine library.

Unpacked my things before going to bed and put everything away tidily. Even Hipp would be surprised to know how well I keep my room.

Wednesday Went to breakfast this morning at Mrs. Fernandez [Fer-
March 21   nandis]. First enjoyable meal in Baltimore: grapefruit, oat-
1928   meal, ham, eggs, buckwheat cakes, and milk. Nicely cooked, nicely served, and just 35 cents.

Called upon Rev. Taylor, 804 Laurel Street [Rev. Alonzo W. Taylor, 804 West Lanvale Street]. Swore he was too busy to see me. Persuaded him to give me two minutes to fill out questionnaire for pastors. Did so reluctantly. Not only filled out his questionnaire but also gave me additional information concerning himself. Thinks people should "shout" if they want to. Claims no decrease in membership of youth in his church. Considers greatest need of his church to be money. Rather uninformed man to be leading people, but then his parishioners probably are of the intellectual level to appreciate him.

Left him. Went to a Bible conference at Shiloh Baptist Church, 816 Laurel Street [listed in the Baltimore City Directory at 823 West Lanvale Street], to see Rev. Allen. He is a big, black, hearty, well-fed fellow. Found him in company with two other ministers, one, the young fellow who had delivered the sermon at the Conference Monday. A small, sour-faced man . . . who was reading, scowled as his listeners greeted me. As I made ready to note some ideas from a young fellow beside me, the minister called out: "Mr. Greene, pardon, but you are delaying the Bible class!" Whereupon I strode out without further ado, apologizing as I did so. Scant appreciation of this work he has!

Met a Mr. [William W.] Colbert, an A.M.E. Evangelist. Accosted him, noting his ministerial garb. Asked him to fill out a questionnaire. He pleaded lack of time; had to return to the Conference. Walked along with him while he talked. On way, he stopped and bought lunch: 5 cent head of lettuce, can of salmon, and a sweet potato pie. The latter purchase stamped him as a real "Ethiop." How he excoriated the colored preachers! Railed against them as "immoral drunkards, grafters, and the enslavers of the people." He invited me to his home. I wrote as he cooked and ate. So bitter was his invective against the preachers that I suspected he nourished some private grievance against them. "They are exploiters, son. Yes, we've done come from one slavery to a worse slavery. The Church is getting worse and worse. Why? Because the preachers are grasping for money. They do not want the truth. Told the people the truth one night during revival meeting. The minister got mad. Later wanted to fight me in his own house where I was staying. He would have done so, too, had it not been for his wife." He was illiterate, and probably as great a scoundrel as those absent ministers whom he now berates.

While walking along with Colbert, a man rushed out of an office and grasped me by the shoulder. I looked up onto the face of an old classmate of mine—Dr. [Ernest C.] Melton. What a surprise for both of us! He has been practicing medicine here two years. Insisted I come into his office. Doing well, he told me. Has bought two houses and a car. Married but regretfully so. Two other classmates of mine, Drs. Frazier and Hall, seeing me, came into the office.[5] Spent a couple of hours in happy recollections. All of them filled out questionnaires. Ideas a little radical. Were exasperated with practice of Church, though still adhering to Christianity.

Melton's office girl, a Miss Hynsmaid, and her friend, Miss Colona, also filled out questionnaires. Miss Colona, third year high school student, is pretty, and well-formed. She is 19. Wanted to peruse a book on Gynecology. "Why," I asked her, "to look at the pictures?" She rewarded me with a blush, remarking that it was something she should know. I could not gainsay her.

Both girls, while stating they were at variance with the Church's prohibitive attitude on amusements, nevertheless admitted that the church had the right to ban such diversions. They added, however, that it did not mean that they were constrained to obey them. In fact, both maintained that they had the *right to dance, play cards, and attend the theatre.* How narrow of any church today to attempt to force such an obsolete restriction upon young people, or older people for that matter! It but breeds hypocrites and a non-church-going public, creates disrespect and disgust for the church and its devotees. The Negro church, especially the Baptists and Methodists, are too ignorant or too stubborn to yield to the irresistible onward surge of civilization. It is a hundred years behind the times. Tries to hold a 20th Century civilization by 19th Century doctrines.

Melton introduced me to a Mrs. [Maybelle] Weaver, a pharmacist, married to a Dr. [Jesse B.] Weaver, a dentist. Left questionnaires to be filled out.

Enjoyed dinner. Rev. Giles left note to call him when I came in, i.e., between 6 and 7 p.m. Called at 7:15. No answer.

Giles called later. Told me Wesley would see me Thursday at 10:30 a.m. instead of 2:30 p.m. Informed Woods of the change of time.

5. William H. Frazier earned his B.S. from Howard University in 1923 and his M.D. in 1926. The Dr. Hall mentioned could have been either Philip Nathaniel Hall, who earned an M.D. in 1926, or William Samuel Hall, who received his degree in 1923. Both men were Greene's contemporaries at Howard.

Secured interesting information from Rev. Bryant of Antioch Baptist Church. Asked him if there existed statistics on Baptist Churches, giving name, location, pastor, value of church property, number of members, etc. Told me minutes for such were now at the printers. I asked if I could see proof sheets. Referred me to Rev. [Daniel G.] Mack of Macedonia Baptist Church, head of Publications Committee. Could get permission from him.

Oh, yes, received letter from President Jones of Fisk University. Offers me $2,000.00 a year to teach history in place of Mr. A[lrutheus] A[mbush] Taylor, who is leaving for Harvard to work on Ph.D. in history. It never rains unless it pours. When I had no prospects of a job, Jones informed me he could not use my services until next year. I would not give up this work now for a teaching position. It is too fascinating.

Wrote Jim (my brother), and Julia Moore.

Called upon Rev. Mack about 10 a.m. Was just rising. Dark brown man, middle age, of medium height, intelligent looking, of kindly mien. Willingly gave me permission to use proof sheets. Also gave me pictorial history of Macedonia Baptist Church, of which he is the pastor. The church started above a stable prior to 1876 under the direction of Leader Jones and Charles Lawson of Union Baptist Church. Building was later converted into a church; stable was floored and seats installed through the philanthropy of one Mr. West. Organized September 29, 1874, church took name of Macedonia, ordained and installed Lawson as first pastor. Built new church costing $3,000 in 1889. Now has one of the most beautiful Negro churches in the country. Attractive grey stone edifice. Cost $80,000. Literally given as present to church by large, white congregation who formerly worshipped there. Negro encroachment on the section made former white neighborhood black belt.

Met Wesley at 10 a.m. Woods and I made report. Told Wesley about Minutes. Hopes I may get them by Saturday.

Chanced upon a Spiritualist Church located on Stricker Street in the 600 block [Moses Spiritual Church, 508 North

Thursday
March 22
1928

Stricker]. Just for a lark, I rang the bell. It was a private house. A dark woman of medium height and build responded. She looked at me timidly. I told her my business, but she seemed loath to admit me. I insisted. Finally she let me in. I walked into the Church proper and seated myself. She excused herself, ostensibly to tidy up. Meanwhile, I jotted down a description of this Spiritualist temple.

The room was of ordinary size, with portable chairs sufficient to seat 18 persons. In front was an altar, made of a table, covered with a white cloth. In the center stood a statue of Christ. All about it were candles, large, small, and indifferent—some whole, some half-burned—white, yellow, green, and pink. Statues of the Madonna, and vases of flowers all upon the altar. On one side of the altar was a barber's chair. This I imagine, was the throne—the seat royal from whence the Rev. Alberta Wallace dispensed her healing powers. On the other side of the altar a reed organ reposed. The walls were literally covered with pictures of Christ, of the Madonna and child, the crucifixion, the disciples, cheap heads (plaster) of Hindus, Indians, horns of rams, goats, oxen, tin cups, and a large cross fashioned from artificial roses. The mantle piece was hidden by vases of decayed material, and of artificial flowers. A sickening odor of incense pervaded the room. Seeing nothing burning, I surmised it to have been induced by aromatic powders that the Rev. had sprinkled about. My head ached, for the place was devoid of air.

Just then the "Reverend" entered. She had put on a light blue apron over her black dress. She responded freely to my questions: No, she had no members. They came only as they wished to be healed. She had more young folks than older ones. The educated Negro, she thought, held the same opinion toward the church as his illiterate brother. "Co's sometime dey get stiff necks and shoved out chests. Den they falls." Money, yes, she could always use that. She had a diploma. It hung on the wall. Poor, deluded woman! It was an authorization certificate from three scoundrels to set up a spiritualist church to feast off such people as she. I did not disillusion her.

She might have stoned me. She had taken a course in healing from a Dr. Kennard, who was undoubtedly a quack.

She owned the house (worth $3000), worked as a domestic along with her healing, for which she received no special renumeration. She likened herself to Christ, healing *gratis*. Ah, fools! There are those who would make mockery of religion and, still worse, there are those sincere, but benighted, faithful who are bled of their little substance by professional bamboozlers.

This woman, I believe, is sincere. Everything in the church, she informed me, had been donated. Did she heal? No, I say. Perhaps what happened is this: the devotee caught up in such an atmosphere in which both the mind and the physical eye are met, upon every side, by images and pictures which connote the spiritual, with the unearthly odor of incense pervading that air-tight room, and with a dozen shrieking, half-hysterical folk, moaning some incendiary hymn—the devotee is carried to such a high pitch of emotional frenzy that he forgets, for the moment, his physical disability and his earthly or bodily pains are momentarily forgotten—drowned in his religious ecstasy.

I bade this woman adieu, glad to reach the fresh air again.

Went to Rev. Bryant's, who allowed me to peruse a very valuable book entitled *The History of Baptist Churches in Maryland*. Secured valuable information upon the founding of the following Baptist churches: First Baptist, 1834; Union Baptist, 1852; Leadenhall, 1872; Macedonia, 1874; Perkins Square, 1880; and Sharon, 1885. This information carried the Church to 1885, from which date, according to Dr. Bragg, pastor of St. James, who knows more about local Negro churches than any other man in Baltimore, no subsequent history is to be found.

Stopped by Melton's. Secured questionnaires Miss Hynson [Hynsmaid?] had filled out for me.

Had to wait till 10 a.m. for breakfast. Spoiled edge for day's work. Felt rheumatic pains in knee. From bad teeth. Took salicylates.

Friday
March 23
1928

Went to Maddix Printing Shop to secure proof sheets. Not available till tomorrow.

Strolled down near Orchard and Franklin Streets. Poorer section of town. Interviewed two Negro laborers—one Catholic, the other Methodist. Catholics here give little or no information concerning their Church.

Left questionnaires at Provident Hospital (colored) to be filled out by nurses. Promise to call for them tomorrow. By the way, a new Provident hospital is being built at a cost of $3,000,000 raised partly by the community chest and churches. Will partly care for medical needs of Negroes in Baltimore. Ordinarily, white hospitals do not admit Negroes and, if so, only to wards. This exclusion adds to the health problems of black people. Mrs. Fernandez [Fernandis], Negro social worker, tells me Negroes cannot secure private rooms in hospitals, regardless of their ability to pay.

Met a Mr. Wilson sunning himself on doorstep. Beautiful, balmy spring day. Told him of my project. He invited me inside. Excused himself. Soon returned, bringing armful of literature. Told me his views on church were in his lectures.

Informed me that God had sent me to him. He believes in healing, yet denies he is a healer. The room looks as if it might be an improvised Church, but he assured me he was just a harmless lecturer. Expressed some unique opinions. Holds Negro church losing its grip because it is not doing its job. Has commercialized religion. No such thing now as consecrated ministers. Calls churches "builders of hypocrites and a vise squeezing the life blood out of the people." Read at great length until a Reverend Brown came in.

Latter looked like a street laborer in khaki trousers, sweater, coat and workshirt, with an old hat jammed on his head. I marvelled how he drawled . . . so boisterously. Yes, he was a preacher and 42. Had no pastorate. Church has not the spirit, he said, in substance. "Dey needs no Christ in de Church; dey moves . . . in the big white churches and gibs you dis 'shake hand' religion so dat dey can pay for de church and get bigger salaries." Illiterate though he was, a blind man leading the blind, still I must admit there was not a little truth in his statements. He preached a sermon to me before he left. In broken English, true, but the spontaneity of his words, which at times assumed a grandeur, similar to that of a Demosthenes or a Webster, convinced me that this man was sincere in the thoughts he expressed. I was moved. Told Mr. Wilson I'd appreciate his writing a few paragraphs explaining his beliefs on religion and ideas about the Negro church and I would collect them Monday. He agreed.

While crossing Druid Hill Avenue, met Drs. Wesley, Woods; Reverends Beard and Gray. Wesley took us to a Methodist conference. There I met Dr. King, Hipp's old pastor from Asbury Church in New York City; Rev. Williams, a classmate of mine at Howard, now pastoring at Wheeling, W.Va.; and Mr. Ashbie Hawkins, a lawyer, who knows considerable about the church.

Later secured questionnaires from High School student and from two men.

Returned home about 4:30. Received letters from Hipp, Bertha, and Mother.

What a friend, Hipp! Never another like him. Went out at 12 midnight to send me money order. Perhaps last money poor fellow had. And Florence, she will be one of the "gang" in spite of all. A self-constituted member. And she a female! And 'tis said, "If you wish to spoil anything masculine, inject a woman into it." But this little girl (17) has such a wonderful spirit. Feeling she belongs because she is the cousin of the third member of our inimitable trio, she added $2. Yet, perchance she will not even have the wherewithal to return to school. What a spirit! It almost makes me weep, as well as happy, that one has true friends to whom he may turn in time of stress.

Beautiful day. Seems as if spring is here.

Met Wesley at 12 p.m. Rendered both report and expense account—$36. Includes railroad fare, etc. Seems as if my expenses will be cared for, which will practically give me $1,800 per year clear. Must give folks a third. They rightly deserve it and I am glad to do it. Don't know whether to start account for them or whether to give it to them in hand.

Saturday
March 24
1928

Woods informed me that he is allowed a dollar a day for all expenses. But then my preparation is greater than Woods' and he may receive a larger salary (which I doubt). Wesley asks that I try to keep expenses as close to $2 per day as possible. Shall certainly try.

Gave Woods my information on colored churches to 1885. He is working on that material.

Left him to peruse minutes at printing office. Told they could not be found. A Rev. [Robert] Johnson of Mt. Carmel Baptist Church, residence 1603 McCulloh, had them. Called him several times but was unable to catch him at home.

Wesley asked that I look into St. Katharines Church. I hear it is high Episcopal, with white and colored parishioners. I shall go there tomorrow. Suggested also that I try to see Father Duffy of St. Thomas Catholic Church.[6] Went to the latter Church. Father Duffy was hearing confession. Could not interview him. Another task for Monday. Will have full day; then too, I am to meet Wesley at 2:30.

Met a Dr. [Bernard] Harris (Howard alumnus of 1923) at Provident Hospital. Invited me to his home Monday at 5 o'clock. Would have some folks come in to tell me just what the church is doing. Tells me I must put my morals away for a while lest they be rudely shocked. Guess I can stand it, at least momentarily.

Saw [Samuel] Murray, classmate of mine. Called him about 3 p.m. Filler expensive, cost 65 cents. No mail today. Thought Marguerite would have written by this time.

Sunday
March 25
1928

Rose at 9:30. Mrs. Hitchens invited me to breakfast. Was late for church, but those delicious muffins were worth it.

Attended services at St. Katharines Episcopal Church, Pressman and Dunson Streets.

When I arrived, the congregation was singing a hymn. The

6. George F. Bragg, in his *History of the Afro-American Group of the Episcopal Church*, said that St. Katharines and another black congregation, St. Marys, were chapels of Mt. Calvary, a white parish. The two chapels were served by the clergy of Mt. Calvary. The St. Thomas Aquinas church and school were at 1000 West 37th Street. The Father Duffy mentioned was probably Father Thomas J. Duffy, who in 1930 was pastor of St. Francis Xavier Church.

church seats almost three hundred people. A large painting of the crucifixion hung over the altar. The walls were studded with pictures of the journey of Christ to the cross, ending up with a crucifix standing upon the altar table. A vested choir furnished the music. In my opinion, about 200 souls, two-thirds of them children, were in attendance. About five whites, including 3 sisters, were also in evidence. A white man sang in the choir.

After the singing, notices were read by the priest. The church, I understood, was in debt. In a drive to raise money a Mrs. Benson, captain of a team, brought in $16.00, thereby winning a prize of $5.00, which she magnanimously turned over to the church. The priest appealed for a more liberal Easter contribution. The mark set was $200.00, $60.00 more than last year's offering.

I noted while the priest spoke that the crucifixes were enveloped in a transparent purple cloth. Why?

The text of the sermon, "Godliness is Profitable unto all Things," was taken from the fourth chapter of St. Timothy, 8th verse. Taking such a text, the priest demonstrated that since man ever seeks to gain by his own efforts, he should not forget to seek the greatest of all prizes, *Godliness*. This, above all, should be sought, for Godliness is profitable for us individually, physically, financially, morally. Also it is profitable for the family and the nation.

The sermon was interesting and enjoyable to me, but I daresay four-fifths of the audience lacked interest in what the priest said. Some of the children slept. Some of the older folk slunk back in their seats as if resigning themselves to the tediousness of listening to what they were accustomed to hear but could not understand. That there followed no response for the sermon was matter of fact. It struck the head, not the heart. A practical sermon in my opinion.

Chanting and music followed the sermon, then the collection was lifted.

An altar boy swung a censer containing burning incense before the altar. The priest then took it, wafting the fumes before the crucifix and the entire altar as if it were a live thing.

The collection was then blessed and held up before the altar by the priest. An incense burner wafted the fragrance among the congregation.

Followed then the chanting of a hymn, the congregation kneeling, the priest facing the altar. Two acolytes took positions on each side, a little behind him. Then came two taper bearers, assuming positions equidistant behind them. Then the choir sang, the congregation still kneeling. The priest drank from a silver goblet. From a bottle a liquid was poured into the goblet held by the priest (Did he wash his hands?). The candles were extinguished, the altar cleared, and both choir and priest chanted the benediction. The priest then passed to the door to greet the congregation personally as they passed out. I shook hands with the priest, Father [Oliver W.] De-Venish. Told him my mission, that I should like to secure information concerning his church. Assented readily. Gave his address as 816 N. Eutaw Street; Tel. Vernon 6140. Informed me I could also secure information concerning St. Marys Episcopal Church.

After dinner, Mrs. Hitchens suggested to "Bazom," her nephew, that he bring me downtown in her car. I was overjoyed, for it enabled me to see quite a bit of the city besides meeting some nice people and securing information in addition. Took me out to Towser [Towson?], Maryland. Beautiful section but restricted to whites. Magnificent homes.

Meant to go to church tonight to hear Rev. McMillan, a former classmate of mine. [This was probably Lewis Kennedy McMillan, who received an A.B. from Howard in 1922.] Was preaching at First Baptist. Came back from Towser [Towson?], Md., too late. Wrote Hipp, Florence, and Bertha.

Modest "Lindy" (Lindbergh) may retire from aeronautics. Can't stand the crowds. Marvelous fellow. Been before the public 11 months. Fine to be a hero, but even that palls at times. Has worn his honors well, however.[7]

---

7. This comment shows that Greene was caught up in the American idolization of the nation's premier hero of the 1920s, Charles A. Lindbergh. Lindbergh's solo flight across the Atlantic in 1927 from New York to France and his modest and dignified conduct thereafter made him almost an object of public worship. Of course, this

Britain offers a new naval suggestion. Wishes to restrict ships to 30,000 tons, no guns over 13 inches. Foxy old John Bull. He already has the two most powerful battleships in the world: *Rodney* and *Nelson*, 35,000 tons each, and mounting 16 inch guns. Must give her statesmen credit. They are trained diplomats of the first rank. While I decry a naval armaments race between the United States and England, I do think that our country should take care that it is amply able to withstand the force of any naval unit in case of war, even if that enemy be England.

Today has been quite warm, 67 degrees. Many have discarded overcoats. Spied three girls coatless and hatless promenading about 6 p.m. Will regret it later perhaps. Warmest March 25 on record.

After breakfast, journeyed to the Rev. [Robert] U. Johnson's, 1603 McCulloh, to inspect the Baptist Church minutes. Rev. Johnson had left them for me. While looking them over, he came in—jovial, big, and fairly well educated, judging from what he said. Shook hands with me and hastily departed. These ministers, many of them have congregations ranging from 7 to 50, are "so busy." Perhaps they *are*, "making eyes" at the "sisters."

Monday
March 26
1928

Minutes were woefully incomplete. Some churches omitted Sunday schools entirely. Others failed to give seating capacity, expenses, and other pertinent information. The larger churches refused to divulge the minister's salary. That the latter was so, may be ascribed in great part to the fact that the minutes were prepared either by or under the personal eye of the pastor. Then, too, the unorganized state of the Baptist Church renders any such effort optional on the part of the church and, therefore, results in lack of uniformity in the information obtainable from such records.

Of the many Baptist churches here, only about 35 in Baltimore proper were listed. Yet there are approximately one hundred Baptist churches here. Disappointed in the report.

comment was written before Lindbergh's pro-Nazi, anti-Semitic, and racist views were publicized in the 1930s.

Returned home. Drank a pint of milk I had bought Saturday afternoon. Kept it out-of-doors. Ate raisins with milk.

Went to Conference with Wesley and Woods after writing up report of services at St. James Episcopal Church. (Rev. Bragg, March 18) and St. Katharines Episcopal (Father De-Venish, March 25).

Wesley, as I, was disappointed over inadequate information in Baptist minutes. Decided we must see these ministers individually.

Wesley informs us that, to date, he has only thirty (30) questionnaires from churches, six questionnaires from youth, about nine from prominent citizens, and six from prominent whites. We must secure a hundred of the first, the same of the second, 300 of the third, and 200 from the fourth.

Wesley handed me $24.00 re-imbursement for my expenses, less $12.00 which I had borrowed from him. Also gave me check for $75.00, my first bi-monthly payment. Was not due till March 31, but Wesley realized that my fiscal standing was more than precarious. From Wesley went to Y.M.C.A. Received two letters, one from Helen [Grinage], other from Ruth [Beverly].

Went to Dr. Bernard Harris, 30 S. Caroline Street, East Baltimore. Harris is a Howard man, graduate of '23. I remembered him. Promised him Friday I would pay him a visit in order to learn something about East Baltimore.

What a sink of vice and ignorance is East Baltimore! Most Negroes live in dilapidated houses. Brazen, lewd, and unkempt women; sly, evil-looking men.

Harris was out. Wife and friend (lady) entertained me till his arrival. He suggested we go to see a man named [John E.] Smallwood, who runs a soup kitchen feeding hungry and homeless men.

Not finding Smallwood at home, we called upon a Rev. Charles Brown, pastor of [People's] Christian Church. (It was the largest building tenanted by that denomination that I had yet seen.) He was presiding at a trustee meeting but made an engagement to confer with me Wednesday morning. Dr. Harris tells me his views on religion are quite radical.

We returned to Harris's home. Table was spread for dinner. Ham and eggs, peas, tea, butter, bread, and pie. I felt overwhelmed with gratitude, for I knew this was done solely for me, since they had already had dinner. When the doctor first broached eating, I demurred, although hungry, saying that I did not care to put his wife to any undue trouble. "We live quite simply here," he assured me. "And you're a Howard man, aren't you?" That dispelled all barriers, real and apparent. The doctor joined me, although he had previously eaten. Patients coming in caused him frequently to excuse himself. Then, a Miss Nichols seated herself at the table, carrying on a spirited conversation with me. Pretty, I thought, and quite young to be the mother of three children. I felt quite at home.

Suddenly, Rev. Smallwood came in. A tall man with searching eyes, an affable and almost obsequious expression. Yes, he had been a Methodist preacher. Had been humiliated at the convention. Lacked $10.00 of the $110.00 which his parish was to bring to the General Conference. Was ridiculed by his Bishop. Told that he was too small for the charge. Smallwood said he resigned, but kept the $100.00.

Asked how he had conceived the idea of a mission, he responded that one night while on his way home he stumbled across a Negro man lying in the snow. Helping him to his feet, he sobered him enough to ask where he lived. The fellow answered he had no home. In a few moments after leaving him, Smallwood said, he heard a crash and, turning, saw an officer running toward the man. The latter had thrown a stone through the plate glass window of a jewelry store. Naturally, the man was arrested. Next day, Smallwood went down to the Court to inquire into the disposition of the prisoner. He had been sentenced to six months in jail. Upon Smallwood's plea for clemency, the sentence was commuted to 90 days.

Later Smallwood informed his wife that, since nothing was being done to feed and house colored vagrants, he himself would start a mission. He opened it in his own church. Having done so, he then went to a bakery, and asked the proprietor for any stale bread he might have daily, citing his purpose for doing so. The baker cheerfully assented. A butcher, likewise, gave him meat scraps and bones, from which he made soup and hash. Charitable-minded people gave clothing. Cards were distributed at police stations and other public places stating that homeless men would be housed at Smallwood's mission, and also fed till they could find either employment or a means to leave the city. That was in 1923. Now the mission has become an institution in East Baltimore. Smallwood occupies a position here equivalent to that of the Urban Leader of New York City, called Mr. Zero, whose famous bread line is an institution in that city.

But Rev. Smallwood is astute. He exploits, but hides his exploitation under the garb of charitable and unselfish administration. His is a subtle sort of self-seeking. Certainly, a less infamous sort than that of many orthodox Baptist preachers. Smallwood has a restaurant which yields a nice income, runs a farm which he works with vagrants in summer for room and board, and also a wood yard where wood is sawed by the same kind of labor. To the world at large, the wood constitutes a legitimate means by the sale of which the mission can be carried on. But Mr. Smallwood is making a handsome profit himself.

And he is far-sighted. His entire family—says Mr. Harris—belongs to at least four different insurance companies. The Reverend gentleman, himself, has a $10,000 life policy.

Last year he attempted to buy a steamboat, paid $2,000 on it, then discovered that the whites with whom he had purchased the steamer had defrauded him of his portion. On its first excursion, the boat leaked so that it barely made port on the return trip. His white partners then obligingly declared Smallwood the owner. He was arrested but, through the aid of influential white friends, managed to squeeze out of the clutches of the law.

Anything that he desires in reason, Smallwood informs me, he can get from the whites. He showed me letters from police chiefs, desk sergeants, and other white persons directing men—floaters, vagrants, and drunkards—to Smallwood's mission. His is the only colored organization which is permitted, like the Salvation Army, to beg on the streets. At

Christmas time he pays men $2.50 a day to stand on street corners, garbed as Santa Claus, and solicit funds. They are equipped with a bell, and an iron pot. Of course, he remarked, "quite a lot of income comes that way," some of which, I was informed, goes into his own pockets.

Smallwood confided that he pays $11.00 per week for his mission. Informed me how he was opposed by the "orthodox religions." Preaches on the street at times, says Dr. Harris. (Profitable.) Raises about $15.00 after ten minutes preaching. Has only such mission in Maryland. Whatever the vices of the individual, the mission is rendering a distinct service. Were Smallwood as solicitous for the upbuilding of the mission as he is for the fattening of his own purse, he could have developed an institution that would not only render a larger service to the community but also constitute a source of pride and satisfaction to the owner. But self-preservation, I suppose, "is the first law of him who gets it."

From Smallwood, I went to First Baptist Church, McEldery and Caroline Streets, to Sunday School Convention. Hoped to gain all necessary data upon Sunday Schools. Representatives here from all over Maryland.

Woods, who had suggested coming here, did not arrive until 9:30. I sat in the rear of the church. Woods, introduced by Dr. Weston, who presided, took a seat up front.

The program had much of interest for me. I learned that the Sunday School started in Gloucester, England, in 1781. Its leader was Robert Wicks. Bible instruction was not a novel idea; the Catholics for a long time had taught the Catechism. Women at first were employed as teachers. London established its first Sunday School in 1803.

New England, ultra-conservative at the time and fearing anything which smacked too strongly of Episcopacy or Romanism, for a long while frowned upon the Sunday School. Puritan leaders considered it a violation of the rights of the home to have the children in Sunday School upon the Sabbath and also a most ungodly infringement upon the Lord's Day. (Remarkable how those Puritanic elders and their descendants could split such amazingly fine hairs.) Philadelphia was more receptive. The first Sunday School convention took place in New York in 1832. The first World Convention of Sunday Schools occurred in London in 1889. This information alone was worth going there for.

Rev. Mack of Macedonia Baptist then spoke upon the "Importance of the Denominationalization of Sunday Schools." His address was along the main Baptist lines. He would make and keep the world Baptist; I would make it more Christianlike. He believed that the progress of Negroes was due to the fact that older generations believed implicitly in God. Of course, the younger Negro differs in that he believes implicitly in himself. Mack recommended that children should be brought up in the faith of their parents, that the Sunday School must be controlled by the Church, since it is the offspring of the Church. The doctrines of the Baptist must be indoctrinated into youth. They must not read liberal Union literature, but Baptist literature only. How could any minister be so bigoted, so narrow? Woe unto Sunday Schools, Baptist, Methodist, or what not, if they had to follow the absolute dictates of the illiberal group such as Dr. Mack represents. It is difficult in the face of such to be reconciled to the fact that we all serve the same God.

A septet (female) rendered a very pleasing number. Then the chairman introduced our good friend and co-worker, Dr. R. C. Woods, former president of Clayton Williams Seminary and also of Virginia Theological Seminary, now engaged in work upon the Negro Church. A roseate opportunity, I thought, to secure a large number of questionnaires from Church and non-Church members, and those of any preachers who were present, and there were not a few. Woods, I supposed, would speak for five minutes, then ask permission to pass out the questionnaires, which would then be collected within another five minutes. But, alas! much to my disgust and to the intense annoyance of the audience, who resented his taking so much time from their pre-arranged schedule, Woods spoke for forty minutes. Furthermore, he spoke with as much importance, confidence, and complacency as if he had been the speaker of the evening.

When he sat down, the people heaved a sigh of relief. Especially was this evident among those who had places on the program, and who feared lest they be denied the privilege of displaying their talents by the garrulousness of Woods. Oh, yes, he did take enough cognizance of poor me to tell the people I was in the audience with questionnaires. In his excitement he even granted me a Ph.D. degree, which I certainly would desire to have, but unhappily do not now possess. Woods had nullified by his loquacity the purpose of our going there. Told of our mission first, then beclouded it with a rambling discussion of Church History here, in Norfolk, and of diverse other things. (Palpable errors in much of it.)

When the convention adjourned for refreshments, Woods remarked, smiling with smug satisfaction: "Well, I certainly convinced them." "You might have used that time in filling out questionnaires," I replied.

My landlady, Mrs. Hitchens, and dear friend, if I may call her such, after so short an acquaintance, was similarly bored, and heartily agreed with me.

In the dining room the Mistress of Ceremonies invited Woods, others, and me to supper, but I had just had dinner, and could not "oblige" them. Later, "just to keep the peace," I did eat some ice cream. Would have enjoyed another plate, but was called to share a ride home with Rev. Allen of Shiloh.

Secured four questionnaires before leaving.

Quite a full day, and it was hot, too. Shall have to divest myself of this coat, shortly.

After breakfast, phoned Father DeVenish at St. Marys Episcopal Chapel, 806 N. Eaton Street. Arranged conference for 11:15.   *Tuesday March 27 1928*

Arrived there, was a little disappointed in the Chapel. It was rigidly simple in furnishings. The table in the reception room was dust covered. Father DeVenish greeted me as he entered, drawing upon an old black pipe. Thank goodness, it was not too strong, for he sat close beside me. He is a white priest administering to a Negro congregation. A throwback to the pre–Civil War days.

I told him, in brief, what I desired. He responded there was little information he could divulge. He was rector of St. Katharines, a mission of St. Marys congregation, composed chiefly of boys from their school. Church held 300. Membership was about 200, about 100 active. No church debt, he said; no salary was paid him. Current operating expenses $1,600.00. Sunday School? Yes, a graded one—100 students and one teacher.

DeVenish thought Negroes were progressing. Against "shouting" in the church. Would answer nothing else. DeVenish is an elderly, stoop-shouldered, meek-looking man. Close-lipped. Told me the rector of St. Marys would be able to enlighten me further.

I went there. Rector was out, but the assistant-rector, a pleasant-faced young man, Father Leveritt, attired in cassock and hat, came in. I warmed up when I saw him. We discussed college, etc. Gave me what meager information he could about St. Marys. Yes, both these churches, St. Katharines and St. Marys, were for "colored." Both were administered by white priests. Said he enjoyed working among Negroes. (I wondered whether he really did.) Told me that I would find all the information I desired by inquiring at the Diocesan House at 408 N. Charles Street.

I asked Father Leveritt's opinion about the Negro Church. Held dim view of it. Thought it too commercialized; the ministers mostly ignorant; and the people impoverished because of pouring their meagre substance into churches, new and old. I was forced to agree. Even the old church members of the race complain today that their very life's blood is being drained by these parasites in ministerial garb. As one old man remarked, "Son, dey's keepin us 'po.' We done come from one slavery into a worser slavery."

Leaving Father Leveritt, I stopped at Mr. Watson's, spiritualist ballyhooer, who earnestly insists that he is *not* what he *is*. Was to have written a couple of paragraphs for me, giving his idea of the Negro church. Hadn't done so; nevertheless, would have kept me talking for a long while, had I not taken leave of him. Promises to have a summary of his views for me Friday.

Went to a little Christian Church on Orchard Street near Franklin. A woman is pastor. She invited me in. The church was a single room in a private house. Twelve chairs, barren walls except for oil lamps. The odor of fish pervaded the place. No, she had no real congregation *yet*. Had no salary, but she collected $20.00 last month and put it in the bank. Her greatest needs were money, members, and books. Filled out questionnaire for me.

Went then to Washington's Monument, on Washington Square. Looked inside. Said to be the oldest monument to Washington in America. High tower surmounted by figure of Washington 285 feet high. Also saw a shot tower built by Charles Carroll of Carrollton, Maryland, in 1801. Said to be the last one standing in the country.

Went to Diocesan House, 408 North Charles Street, as Father Leveritt had suggested. Received *Journal of Episcopal Diocese of Maryland* for 1926. Woman asked whether I wanted to use it for school work. When I explained my purpose, she corrected certain errors in it before giving it to me.

Returned home, dressed for dinner. Sam Murray came for me before I was ready. Miss Groom entertained him till I was ready.

Murray took her to the library then sped back to his residence at 2400 Madison Street with me.

Had enjoyable evening. Dinner excellent. Found Mrs. Murray very sociable and amiable. Sam has a nice home, which can be made into an excellent one with a little time and labor. Sam plans to do extensive renovating later. He teaches art. Mrs. Murray also teaches. Murray and wife brought me home about 10 p.m.

Arrived home, intending to bring my diary up to date. Interrupted by Mrs. Hitchens calling me. Talked with her in her room for a half hour, then showed her one of my poems on *The Unknown Soldier*. [See Appendix II.] Thought it excellent. Liked *The New Negro*. [See Appendix II.] Laughed heartily.

But don't think she approves of my doing away with God in entirety.

Went from breakfast to Dr. Harris, on Caroline Street. Both of us were tardy. I, because of waiting for Woods to bring me questionnaire, then taking the wrong street car; and Harris, because of unexpected appointments.

Reached Rev. Brown's by 11 a.m. . . . The Rev. was just returning home as we arrived. Liberal regarding church. Doesn't believe that dancing or movie-going is injurious. One of the most remarkable pastors here. Started church in house in 1913. Later bought the house, then three more. Sold them and bought a $35,000 Church. Latter now debt-free. Bought adjoining house. Will turn it into a nursery. Intends to open Community Center soon. Other denominations refused to help. Afraid they would lose their congregations. (That is one of the curses of denominationalism. Each one distrusts the other and very little cooperation between them is effected for general uplift. Each is a group within itself—a sect apart.) Rev. Brown hopes to buy the entire block of houses in which the church is located, rent them, and use the rent to pay the church expenses, thereby lifting some of the burden from his members. He has started Bethany College in Penn County. Thinks "shouting" alright, if sincere. Admits members give him splendid support, but claims he needs "more cooperation" in his church.

Rev. Brown is a dark man of medium height and build; talks fast but clearly. Very modest. Longs for the training necessary to achieve his hopes. Doesn't believe he can do so. Says "someone else must follow me and bring my plans to fruition." I considered it a great privilege to meet such a man. He is earnestness personified.

Dr. Harris later took me to Eager Street in an effort to find Rev. [Simon W.] Williamson of Faith Baptist Church. His wife, stuttering horribly, informed me that he was not at home. Set out then for Fountain Baptist Church. Met Mrs. Fernandis on way.

Walked down Monument Street to Fountain Baptist

Church. Crossing the street, I espied a black-coated gentleman emerging from a barber shop. I asked where I might find Rev. Cole [he is listed in Baltimore directories as James R. Coel], and to my surprise he answered he was the man. Filled out questionnaire for me. Has quite a large church, valued at $35,000. Owes $10,000 on it. Also "owns" another $25,000 church. Cole is unlettered. Believes in "shouting."

Left him and went back to Dr. Harris to leave blanks for Rev. Smallwood, who is to have them filled out by prominent whites. Left them with Mrs. Harris.

Went to St. Thomas Catholic Church. Arrived there, I did not know whether to bow or cross myself upon entering, so I did neither. Happily, the priest's back was turned. Did not know whether to sit or kneel when I entered a pew, so taking the course of least resistance (habit) I sat. Father Duffy, the priest, was busy rehearsing an exercise with Negro boys for Easter. Waited an hour, then left to see Father Call in lieu of Father Duffy, at St. Thomas Chapel on St. Paul's Place. But Father Call was resting, so I returned to the Church. Was tired. The boys had gone when I returned.

Sent my card to Father Duffy by a youngster who was polishing a sign. He told me that the priest would see me in a minute. True enough, out came the Father, a scholarly, pedagogical-looking, middle-aged man, well built, with a tinge of sternness underlying the kindliness of his face. His hair was nearly white.

Informed him of my mission. He gave me some information of importance about St. Francis Church. It is the oldest colored Catholic Church in the United States (1863). Also an historic building. Henry Clay was nominated for the Presidency there in 1832. The Democratic Convention of 1846 met there, and in 1861 the Maryland Convention to decide whether Maryland should secede from the Union convened there. Present St. Francis, built in 1837, was first a Universalist church, then a meeting place. It was given to Negroes as a Church in 1863. Came under the Order of St. Joseph—priests who pledged themselves to teach Negroes—in 1871. All other colored Catholic churches—St. Barnabas and St. Monica—

are offsprings of St. Thomas. It seats approximately 1100. Has 1200 communicants.

Father Duffy assured me no prejudice existed in Roman Catholic churches here. (I have heard reports to the contrary, particularly about the Church of the Immaculate Conception, where Negroes are said not to be desired. Not given palms on Palm Sunday.) Duffy believes that Negro Church is commercialized. I agree with him. Some colored ministers, he states, are well-educated, in part, but the majority are unlettered, blindly trying to lead the blind. Felt that because of Negro migration, the entire Northwest section of Baltimore would soon be colored. Ten years ago, there were no colored there. Fine, he thought: the Negroes should seek better homes. Yes, the Catholic Church encouraged Negro youth to prepare for the ministry. Did have two: one—Father Divantegelos—died (prejudice broke his spirit); the other was sent to teach in the Seminary at Newburgh, New York. (Christianity, for all its high-flown ethical concepts, is purely an abstraction where racial things are concerned. It must bow in shame before Mohammedanism and Buddhism, where all of the same sect and of the same social status are treated as peers.) Father Duffy's answers show how those in authority will cloak the truth in order to uphold the honor of their church.

He thought mutual lack of confidence was keeping the races apart. Education would help, but Christianity must effect it, though he doubted whether the latter ever shall. Agreed with my statement that Christianity had helped to justify and maintain racism.

I came home, stopping first at St. Joseph's Seminary, where Father Duffy had told me I might secure a booklet giving information on Catholic churches of the city. Failed to secure it.

Rev. Giles came in. Invited me to lunch with him tomorrow. Promised to do so.

Returned home. Went to fashion show at vocational school with Mrs. Hitchens. It is a night school located at Lawrence and Colburn Streets. An exhibit of work done by the students was on display. I was touched, inspired by the splendid samples of shirts, hats, lingerie, dresses, beautiful lampshades, painted scarfs, scrap books, and other work of these students, ninety percent or more of whom had recently come from the South. All are serious-minded. Most of them work during the day and welcome this opportunity to educate the head and hand at night. Majority—many of them middle-aged persons—have just learned to read. Mrs. Hitchens, my host, introduced me to the principal and teachers.

After the exhibit, we went downstairs for the program, fashion show, and awarding of diplomas.

The Director of Colored Schools, Mr. Hines, a big, jovial fellow, but a wretched speaker, said a few words. He lauded the students for their good attendance and their work, and praised them as the best-behaved students he had ever seen in the city. A salvo of applause greeted his remarks. I almost resented the allusion to good behavior, inclined to construe it was a means of creating a favorable atmosphere for the speaker. Later learned of my error from one of the teachers. Mrs. [Estelle] Arnold informed me that they were the most serious-minded students she had ever taught. Mr. Hines then read a preamble from the manual of the Board of Education in which the latter was pledged to offer the same educational advantages to all citizens regardless of color, creed, or previous conditions of servitude. He desired to do even more and stated his willingness to give the school any course for which there was a demand. The words were later substantiated by the principal. However, my cursory observations of white and Negro schools left me unconvinced, since separate schools are the rule here. And separate schools mean inferior ones for Negroes.

Mr. Hines then asked the audience to sing for him. Having charmed him at first, they now proceeded to overturn the proverbial pail of milk by singing, or attempting to sing, "Hail, Happy Springtime." Poor song was massacred, and many in the audience giggled. Thought they might have done better by singing "The Star Spangled Banner," which they all knew.

In the fashion show those who had made dresses marched

across the stage wearing the same, halting in the center and turning slowly so as to afford the audience a good view of their handiwork. They came—old and young ones; black, yellow, and brown ones; thin, medium, and fat ones; tall and short ones—all self-conscious, yet all keenly elated. Followed next an exhibition of hats. I was interested in the introductory remarks of the lady who introduced the hat wearers. Said she, "there were three types of faces: the round, which should avoid curves, the square which should avoid all lines, and the oval, or perfect face, which might wear any style." The lady personifying the perfect face could have passed for Nannie's double. [Nannie Hagans was a seamstress from Rocky Mount, North Carolina, who lived in New York City; a friend of Harry Hipp introduced her to Greene.] I was astounded.

Came now some youngsters—some shy, diffident, sleepy little things. Others, bolder, strutted before the audience with all the nonchalance of an experienced grownup.

Director F[rancis] Wood, who was to have awarded the diplomas, was unhappily absent. Mr. [Hammond J.] Briscoe, a school principal, substituted for him. He walked upon the platform wearing a shabby brown overcoat. He was tall, thin, brown, sickly looking. But where were his social graces, where his culture? Mrs. Hitchens was shocked. After giving out the diplomas he essayed to speak, drawing a highly colored figure of speech far above the comprehension of these simple people. They were laborers, people from the alleys of Northwest Baltimore, perhaps from other sections. Everyone seemed relieved when he sat down.

Mrs. Hitchens was then called on to speak. What a lovely woman! Her smile, as she stepped upon the platform, won her audience, and for ten minutes she held their undivided attention. She congratulated them upon their success, but cautioned them that they were but entering upon the beginning of life, that they must keep "polishing the brain" in order, by continual striving, to grow strong in their vocation. Emphasized the benefit of work and the value of having confidence in themselves. She also praised them for their good behavior, exhorted them to double their numbers next year. Above all, she urged them to strive to make better citizens for God, for country, and for their race by endeavoring to educate themselves. She sat down amid a storm of applause. She was well liked anyway, but the pertinency of her remarks, the simplicity in which they were couched, and her ability to appeal to the best in these education-hungry people elated me.

I felt affected myself. These graduates, after two years' work, receiving diplomas normally granted from the High School in four years, were singularly happy. Brought back memories of receiving my first diploma. How extremely exalted I felt. This diploma was certainly as much appreciated by them as my college diploma was by me. (Remembered two years ago, when my girlfriend, Nannie [Hagans], received a diploma from the Y.W.C.A. in New York City at the completion of a course in stenography. At first, I did not intend to go, feeling that the occasion was of no real consequence. However, when Bea, our mutual friend, made me realize that this was a crowning event in Nannie's life, I did go, giving her a gold pen as a present.[8] She was so happy when I arrived in time to see her receive the Diploma that later she confessed she could scarcely sleep for crying for joy.) Perhaps some of these women and girls did the same.

Later I spoke with Mrs. Arnold, friend of Mrs. Hitchens. Very charming woman. Told me how great a pleasure it was to work with these people.

Arrived home about 12. Met Miss Groom, young lady who lives upstairs. Joked with her. She invited me to see her tomorrow. Promised to do so.

Received a letter from Harry. Desires to know when I expect to come to New York and whether I need money. No, the latter is assured now.

8. Bea was Beatrice Burbridge Tinney. She and Greene grew up on the same street in Ansonia, Connecticut. She married Clarence Tinney, and they and her mother moved to New York City. Hipp, Ernest Bacote, and Greene—"the gang"—roomed with Mrs. Emma Burbridge in a brownstone on Edgecombe Avenue while attending Columbia University. Bea and her husband and Florence Bacote also lived there.

Late for breakfast, making out report. Was to meet Dr. Wesley at 10 o'clock, but he did not arrive till near 11. His little girl is ill with bronchitis. Was quite worried about her. He looked haggard and drawn. I fear he is trying to do too much. He assured me he will relinquish his ministry in Washington. Has been engaged in that profession along with other duties.

He desires to finish work in Baltimore by Saturday. Would like to secure more questionnaires for "youth" and citizens.

Woods reported his final data. May leave us to go to Alabama for Dr. Woodson. The Association for the Study of Negro Life and History is short of funds. Exists largely from royalties from Woodson's *Negro in Our History*, his speeches, and small amounts of money raised by faithful workers. Woods is needed to raise money.

When Woods had gone, I made my report to Wesley. Latter was gratified over information concerning Rev. Brown's Christian Church and St. Thomas; also concerning the Episcopalian Church.

Spoke to him concerning my tendency for details. Highly to be desired, he informed me. Told me if we did a good piece of work on this study we might work together at Howard University. Latter school does not appeal to me so strongly now. Would prefer Fisk, if I would teach.

I am leaving Baltimore Saturday noon for New York. Am to be initiated into Kappa Alpha Psi Fraternity. Have fought against joining fraternities for seven years. Capitulating now because I have nothing tangible to gain by going in. No axe to grind. Do not need it as a symbol to impress people with my college affiliation. Nor shall I be enabled to perform my tasks one whit better for being a "frat" man. "Frats" breed snobbishness, clannishness. I could acquire neither now because my "undergrad" school days are over. In my opinion, Greek letter organizations on college campuses ought to be prohibited. Non-Greeks are made to feel "left out." I joined a literary society.

Shall go direct from New York to Washington, D.C. Am to meet Wesley there at 9 a.m. Monday. Entrain from there for Suffolk, Virginia.

Went to St. Joseph's Seminary. Failed again to secure information. Tried to communicate with pastor of Seventh Day Adventist Church. In vain. Came home, found sweet letter from Helen [Notis]. Tells me she misses me more than anyone she has ever known. And I miss her. I look forward eagerly to her letters. So modest. Asserts she has not the ability to express herself as I. Would that she only knew of the great gift that is hers, and which I fondly desire: simplicity and directness of expression. Surely, Helen is one of the most splendid girls I have ever known. She and Helen [Grinage] have much in common.

Took things to laundry. Must get them Saturday.

Came back, wrote in diary. Dressed for dinner. Rev. Giles came to dine with me. Radiates sunshine and color. I admire him very much.

After dinner, we recounted experiences. Later he took me to see a Miss ———. Pretty little lady about my height, very intelligent with roguish sense of humor. Also has most engaging ing profile. Enjoyed her.

Mrs. Hitchens and Miss Groom returned about 12. The former brought me ice cream. So thoughtful of her. She has made me feel so much at home that I hate the thought of leaving. But such is to be my portion in this work; as soon as I become adjusted to a place, I shall have to leave. Had another charming repartee with Miss Groom. She told me I had disappointed her. Had dressed before dinner for me, then I did not come up. Told her she had gone out at 8. "Yes," she replied, "because you had company." Am to see her later tonight. She has a nice sense of humor which is refreshing.

Woods came by this a.m. before I had risen. Told me was going to D.C. (Washington). Stopped on way for $1.25 I had borrowed from him. I had received the amount in silver but gave him a bill and five nickels. Woods would return at 5 p.m., he said. Asked him to bring back some questionnaires for citizens.

*Friday
March 30
1928*

Entered notes in diary till breakfast time. After that, went to Zion Cemetery Association. Rev. Giles was to meet me there at 10 a.m. to intercede in getting a check cashed for me (my first one on the job). He arrived about 10:30. Secured endorsement of Bishop Davies easily. Rev. Beard will cash my check.

Walked with Giles to McMechen Street. Bade him farewell there. He is going to the Eastern Shore of Maryland, a predominantly rural section on the other side of Chesapeake Bay. He calls it the "wilderness." Does so because it is the training ground preparatory for a more important charge in the A.M.E. Church. Told me last Sunday he sweated, fumed, and roared in the pulpit in one of his three churches, and was rewarded with the handsome offering of fifty-cents, ten cents of which he donated himself as a "starter." The total congregation consisted of 8 persons—(5 cents each). I advised that next time he start the collection by dropping a dollar in the box and the congregation would probably respond by contributing a half dollar apiece. I assured him, however, that if he had visions of a nicely furnished home, an automobile, and all the other appurtenances that go along with the typical Negro preacher, namely: broadcloth suits, a slick and greasy countenance, and a well-filled stomach, then he must abjure his present faith, for he had hitched his horse to the wrong wagon. He must be baptized instead of being sprinkled; become, in other words, a Baptist preacher. He laughed, but said he could not deny the mocking truth in my words.

Sorry to leave Giles. Splendid fellow with remarkable capacity for successful leadership.

Stopped at Urban League. Mr. [R. Maurice] Moss, the Director, was out. Called at the grade school—Dolphin Street and Pennsylvania Avenue. Collected questionnaires for citizens left for teachers to fill out yesterday. Two refused to answer the questions. They are afraid, I suppose, of losing their positions, fearful that I shall publish their names in a colored newspaper, or afraid to express their opinions about the church. Poor Negroes! They are often so negative to something worthwhile. Thanked Mr. [Perry D. G.] Pennington, the [vice-]principal, very much for his cooperation. He also filled out a questionnaire.

Went to Douglass High School. Immense edifice; larger

than Dunbar High School in Washington, D.C. Has every convenience. About five years old. Left about 80 questionnaires for youth to be filled out by students, preferably juniors and seniors. Was allowed to stand in Principal's office for five minutes before any notice was taken of me by the clerk, who was engaged in only routine work. One hardly expects such bad manners in an institution of learning. Would never have happened in a New England school.

Later I stopped by Dr. Melton's on way to Cemetery Association. Latter drove me there. Wants to take me to a party tomorrow night. Wagered I'd have time of my life. Anything might happen, he confided.

Arrived at the Association, found Rev. Lee and Rev. Gray (Methodists) arguing about origin of first colored Methodist Churches (C.M.E. and A.M.E.). I had seated myself in an adjoining room since I expected they were in conference. Their disagreement was my gain, for while they argued, loudly, I was busy jotting down information.

Lee promised to buy a ticket (New York and return) for me on his clergyman's passbook. Will cut my cost in half. I gave him $10.00 to buy ticket. He promised to secure ticket and meet me at office at 5 p.m.

Called upon Rev. [Michael S.] Banfield, pastor of the Third Seventh Day Adventist Church. Largest Church of that denomination I have seen. Banfield is thin, dark man, about 35 years of age, tall, fairly well educated. Is a graduate of Atlanta University. His church started here in 1912 in an undertaking establishment with 10 members. Now he has 250 members, a church worth $50,000, and a school worth $12,000. That bespeaks both program and cooperation among the members. Although the increase in church membership is painfully slow, the church disburses about $10,000 for salaries and expenses, pays $2,000 annually on its debt, and has a large Sunday School with 175 members and 23 teachers. This is the largest Sunday School teaching force yet reported to us. In order to attract the young folk, courses are offered in nurse training, dietetics, and practical nursing. Despite the excellent work which this church does, its attractions must be manifold in order to draw people to it, since the fact that they observe the Sabbath on Saturday is a powerful factor in keeping people from joining the church. I frown upon the idea of denominational schools. They are biased, poisoning the children's minds and indoctrinating them with partisan teachings. I believe the public school system, despite its obvious shortcomings, produces the best citizens and the more liberal and sympathetic minds. There are 85 children receiving instruction in the school. The teachers are Normal School graduates. The head of the school is a Columbia University graduate, holding the Master's Degree.

According to Rev. Banfield, the Seventh Day Adventist Church was founded in Rochester, New York, in 1846. In that year the church was organized under the leadership of Joseph Bates. The total membership in the United States now stands at 2,000, indicative of relatively slow growth. There are four churches here, Rev. Banfield told me, with a composite membership of only 500.

The church is doing a good job, yet I deplore the necessity of so many sects, each of which seems confident that the road to salvation is by their way alone. Some must be right. If all are right, then the end must be something different from the generally held conception.

Collected questionnaires from 60 Douglass High School students. Replies interesting on the whole. Crux of the student questionnaire lies in the attitude of the church toward harmless amusements. Where the church frowned upon these amusements, majority of the students differed, but did not materially change their attitude towards the church. A few remained non-committal. Others were more assertive: one styled the Church's attitude as "dumbness"; some stood for "innocent pleasures"; a few agreed with the attitude of the church. But the majority were clearly at variance with the church's stand on amusements.

From the high school stopped by Dr. Weaver's. Wasted one and a half hours while they talked. Secured their questionnaires. Said goodbye to Dr. Melton. Rushed to Cemetery Office. Closed.

Came home, stopping by "Y" on way, where I picked up letters from mother and Bertha.

According to mother's letter, the Morris Loan Co. wants me to send an installment on my loan. I shall send it Monday.

Called Dr. Bragg. Arranged to see him between 5:15 and 6 p.m. Wonderful old man. Storehouse of all kinds of knowledge. D.D. from Wilberforce. Has read voluminously and has marvellous library. Gave me historical setting of all Negro churches here. Thinks majority of preachers (Negro) are "ignorami." Called buying churches "foolish."

Told me first Catholic sisterhood was founded here in 1829. Centennial will be held next year. St. Thomas Academy housed them. This was before the establishment of St. Thomas church.

Went to dinner. Mrs. Fernandis' niece played piano for me afterwards.

Home, where I found the adorable Mrs. Hitchens. Chatted with her a while.

Went to barber shop. Returned, read, wrote, talked with Mrs. Hitchens.

Miss Groom, with whom I pass many a quip and receive the same in return, just returned, bringing me a letter (special) from Dr. Wesley. He decides that we must stay here for another week. Text of letter follows:

> 1538 Ninth St. N.W.
> Washington, D.C.
> March 30, 1928

My dear Mr. Greene:

I am writing to inform you that it will be necessary for us to remain in Baltimore for another week instead of going to Suffolk, Virginia, on Monday. After looking over the questionnaires, I find that we do not have enough of citizens, pastors, and youth in order to make a good showing. There are 46 pastors who have reported out of more than a hundred. We have 63 churches, which is a sufficient number, but we must concentrate on those mentioned above. Therefore, you will return to Baltimore on Monday a.m. and I will meet you at the office at noon. In order that you may have this change of program, I am sending it special delivery.

> Yours sincerely,
> Charles H. Wesley

I am to go to New York tomorrow for initiation, at night, into Kappa Alpha Psi Fraternity. May "Allah shrive me!" Long and vehemently have I withstood joining fraternities only to capitulate now. But at least I am hoping for nothing. Neither is my "brother," Harry.

I was to have gone directly from New York to D.C. Planned to see Bertha on Sunday. Had I known this, could have communicated with Helen [Notis].

Two Germans are preparing to fly the Atlantic from East to West, which has never been accomplished before. Hazardous. They are brave, resourceful, undeterred by the deaths of nearly a dozen others. That is why the white man rules the world today. He is a pioneer. The Negro sits back, lets the white man open the way, then he comes in to enjoy it. 'Tis the main reason our estate is so low. We are consumers not producers.

[3] New York: Renewal of Old Acquaintances

Today clear and cool. Breakfasted late, 9:00 a.m. Informed Mrs. Fernandis that I would be in the city another week. She professed delight either because she found me tolerable or because of a pecuniary interest in my staying. Maybe a combination of both. Won't say which is uppermost.

After dinner, went to Zion Cemetery Association to inquire about tickets Rev. Lee was to purchase for me. Latter was not to be found. I was perturbed lest he should fail to get here before train time. Told Rev. Beard I would return before 12.

Took suit to tailor. Mrs. Hitchens directed me to hers. I promised to return at 12:00 p.m. Got shaved, secured laundry, bought few necessities, returned to office. Lee still had not appeared. I became apprehensive, but found Beard had left a note directing Lee to call me. Impossible to communicate with him because he has no phone.

Went home to dress. In the midst of it, Lee called. Told me to stop by the office on way to station. I was certainly relieved.

Secured ticket and his clergyman's pass. Gave him $1.00 for the favor. Cost $8.00 all told. Round trip saved me $7.00.

Uneventful ride to New York with the exception of a fright that was given the passengers between Newark, New Jersey, and New York. Motor trouble caused the train to stop with a sudden grinding of brakes, nearly catapulting us out of our seats . . .

Went to the "widow's" (Mrs. Burbridge's), where I formerly roomed. Certainly glad to see Harry [Hipp] again, who opened the door for me. We are always happy to see one another. Looks as if we shall have to carry on, since "Rabbit" (Dr. Ernest Bacote) seems to have lost the desire or ability to communicate with the "gang." Sure sign he is getting along well in Syracuse.

"Captain's" (Florence Bacote's) eyes bespoke how delighted she was to see me. It certainly filled me with gratitude to be so warmly welcomed. She swears she will still remain a member of our "gang."

The "widow," Mike, "Bus," Pollard, even my "traditional enemy," Mrs. Gross, were all glad to see me. ["Mike" was Clarence Tinney, the husband of Mrs. Emma Burbridge's daughter Beatrice; "Bus," Pollard, and Mrs. Gross were all roomers in Mrs. Burbridge's home.]

Found a letter from Kappa, giving me preliminary instructions concerning the initiation. Harry, [Ernest] Hemby, and I went to the "place of execution" designated.

Initiation left me a trifle sore in spots. Yet understood the fellows were lenient with us.

After the ritual went to Darktower, where we communed and regaled ourselves till about 3 a.m. Beautiful place, but not the type to inspire artistic strivings. In my opinion, just a nice place to meet and dine.

Met Countee Cullen and Langston Hughes, outstanding young Negro poets; also [Richard] Bruce Nugent, and Aaron Douglas, artist.[1] The latter's covers for the *Crisis* magazine are well-known. Nugent affects the Bohemian. Sits around with shirt open at neck. After all, man is an imitative animal; therefore I should not censure too severely the black literati's emulation of white artistic strivers.

Well, I am a "fratman." Glad to be one because of the permanent bond of comradeship now between these men whom I have known and admired for over a year and me. Some I have taken as personal friends. The joy of being a "fratman" for the

1. Richard Bruce Nugent was a writer and one of the founders of *Fire,* the literary magazine of the "New Negro" movement.

sake of receiving a "pin" does not excite me. Had it not been for the petty politics, the snobbery, the boorishness, and the low intellectual standard of "frat" members at Howard, I should have been a member long ago. It may seem that I am supercilious, egotistic, and biased against "frats"; but I came to Howard a young idealist, and the actions of the "frats," their attitudes toward certain social things, shattered my idealistic conceptions of what such a brotherhood ought to be. To me they were sterile, barren, bereft of any uplift movement, yet posing as an aggregation of the race's finest. New York's Omicron Chapter of Kappa seemed to me the best of the lot. It appeared to be an active force, attempting to ameliorate conditions for Harlem's Negroes economically, socially, politically, and intellectually, not an extinct, lifeless form.

I am happy to be with the boys, but not elated. Elation would have been my reaction during "undergrad" days. I shall do nothing which will not redound to the honor of Kappa. But I wish to see the organization stand for something significant and strive to achieve it. There is so much to be done before we achieve full citizenship.

Six of us later piled into a taxi and rode home. It cost me a quarter, although the meter read but that. Lost a glove getting out.

Rubbed with liniment before going to bed.

Alarm clock woke me at 6:30. Could not go back to sleep. Rose at 9:00.

Sunday
April 1
1928

Went to St. James Presbyterian Church, 141st Street at St. Nicholas Avenue. Did so especially to hear Rev. [Lloyd] Imes, who, I hear, is an excellent speaker. Disappointed. Church crowded. Pastor, Rev. Imes, will preach funeral at 1:15 p.m., but no morning sermon because of Communion. Disappointed, I left about 12:13.

Called on Nannie [Hagans], native of Rocky Mount, North Carolina, pretty, ingratiating personality, very light-skinned. At one time thought I was seriously in love with her. Was at Church (St. Mark's). I called on Harcourt Tynes, one of my best friends. He was suffering from nose-bleed. Still in bed. Is dear pal of mine. Took M.A. degree in History with me at Columbia in 1926. Married charming Helen Jones, legal secretary. She invited me to breakfast. First declined, then accepted. After breakfast, Tynes loaned me his frat pin till I should receive mine. Had previously given it to his wife, Helen. She, who has a refreshing sense of humor, looked at me and remarked: "Alas, so you are going to take my breast pin away from me." Splendid of Tynes, but more remarkable of his wife to part with it for me.

Went from Tynes to Mrs. B.'s, which for two years I called home. Harry was out. Found him at Hemby's. Latter is acting Polemarch of Kappa. Instrumental in getting us in. Classmate of mine from Howard University. Sidney Wells there, also. Had loaned Hipp his pin. We decided to let $3.50 (for plain pin) go upon more expensive one to be bought later.

Went to dinner at Mrs. Daniel's (Hipp's prospective mother-in-law). Muriel [Daniel], his intended, matched wits with me by asking whether I could sit down yet. Knew of last night. Fine dinner; hospitality excellent. Had to leave as soon as I ate. Mrs. Daniel is nice old lady, though despotic and ruling her home with a hand of iron. She is, nevertheless, kind, efficient, and hospitable. I like her. She knows and understands my weaknesses.

Called upon Nannie (Miss Hagans) again. Found her with Miss Clara Twine, preparing to go out. Nannie was the girl whom I almost persuaded myself that I loved in 1926. We are friends now, nothing more. Both of us have recovered from our "folly." She thought she loved me and told me so. I answered that I loved her not. I believed later, since she had vowed not to waste further time with me, that I loved her. Then she turned the tables on me. I believe we both were insincere.

Walked out with her and Miss Twine. Told Nannie of my offer from Fisk, and asked her if her fiancé could not take it. Would pay $2,000 a year. He is a marrying man; she desires to be wedded. They could make a start. But he does not take his degree this year. Nannie is becoming buxom. When I told her so, she asked me what the word meant. Told her; she blushed.

Added she did not wish to become fat, yet was becoming stouter every day.

Called on the Skeeters. Glad to see me. Leslie embraced and kissed me. Carrie did the same. I believe I like Carrie. Has engaging and likeable personality. Marguerite was surprised. Could not recover from seeing me. I think she felt a little embarrassed, because she had not written me; was about to say I am disappointed in her, but I am not. She came over and embraced me. Apologized for not having written.

Went to see the Rev. Vernon Johns. He was not at home. I returned to Skeeters. Chatted. I talked about the Church. Did not feel like being sentimental with Marguerite. Felt as if I should have given some time to Helen.

Two fellows came in, both to see Marguerite. Leslie and Virginia grinned. One was Lawyer Perkins. We became engaged in a discussion on the Negro. I called the professional class—lawyers, doctors, teachers, etc.—parasites. He, feeling that his legal dignity was likely to suffer, confronted me with his logic. Tried to prove by Socratic reasoning that bankers then must be included as parasites. I stoutly maintained that now they did work upon the dollar by investing or loaning it, causing the dollar to reproduce itself. The discussion waxed hot. The point in question was aroused by my saying that more of our young men should go into business, for a race without a business foundation is a shaky vehicle upon which to rear an unwieldy super-structure of professionals and litterateurs who earn their bread and ease by sucking the life's blood of the masses, thus weakening the prop that supports the super-structure of which they are a part. The argument apparently terminated in my favor through the decision of Mr. ———, a businessman. The lawyer was Mr. Perkins, who seems proud of his legalistic training and is ever ready to "mouth." I had noticed that trait in him frequently at the intercollegiate club.

I was going to take the girls to my brother's apartment. Did not think they could leave, so I did. Marguerite came out of the room to kiss me good-by. Asked me to write her soon. Was sorry the group could not go to Jim's. The girls asked me when I would leave. I told them tonight. Had I said in the morning, they probably would have come to Jim's later. But I wanted to go, for I had not intended even to come here.

Went to Jim's. He had been walking. Had hurt his ankle in a fall last week. Supported himself with a cane. Told me of accident to Emma's (our sister's) husband, John. Lost two fingers in the brass factory where he worked. Also that dad was found by mother upon her return from church in an unconscious condition. Dad is old, but he has hitherto borne his years well. I was alarmed. A wonderful father. Would give anything in the world for his children. Unselfish, unstinting, self-abnegating, with a sense of humor which renders him youthful and good company always. Hipp thinks him wonderful. Dad has been taking aspirin tablets of late. Believe they have weakened his heart. Must go home as soon as possible. In two weeks, I shall be able to begin sending him and mother their bi-monthly payments.

Left Jim at 11 p.m. Rushed home. Packed. Prepared to take 12:40 train. Hipp was asleep. "Cap" also. Former had left note: "Came home ill at 10 p.m. Wake me if you are going tonight." Shook him three or four times, but he did not wake up. I left for the Pennsylvania Station.

Reached station 12:30. Passed as clergyman. On the train, did not look at conductor, read, and handed him clergyman's ticket.

Train was full of Negroes who acted disgracefully. Embarrassed me, yelled, ran from coach to coach, laughing boisterously, drinking, fussing, and passing coarse jokes. Ought to have been in a cattle car. Were I a railroad executive, I'd segregate them myself. There are some Negroes who should be segregated, but it should not be made general. There are some who are intelligent, well dressed, and orderly. They should be given consideration, but there are some who are not fit to sit with hogs. The same applies to some whites also.

Uneventful trip to Baltimore. Arrived 5:25 a.m. Tired out. Went to bed.

[4] Baltimore Again

Rose at 11:00. Met Wesley at 1:30. Waited for him an hour and a half. Detained because of trouble with car. Little daughter is improving. Had been ill with severe attack of bronchitis.

Wesley told me we would spend additional week here. Needed more questionnaires on youth, citizens, and pastors.

Was gratified to learn of my securing 75 questionnaires from students of Douglass High School.

I mentioned Woods. He had gone to Alabama to raise funds for the Association. Ought to be proficient at such for he is a good speaker. But, as a historian, he is terrible. Wesley had been asked by Woods to allow him to work with us. Wesley had put the matter up to Woodson as far as Woods was concerned. But Woods would be taken aback, I know, to find out that Wesley told Woodson he might have Woods, for he is everything else but a historian. Is no researcher. Gives no details.

Discussed method of writing up our findings. Wesley suggested the topical method; I, the sectional. He disagreed with me, and I was made to see the motive in his reasons for so doing. Said Negroes not scattered uniformly enough for such a method.

Wesley glad to know I had received the reduced rates by virtue of Lee's clergy ticket. Gave him my expense account of

$16.00. Thought it o.k. Told me I would secure reimbursement next week. Asked me to meet him Thursday noon.

Went to St. Joseph's Seminary to gain information about colored Catholics. Received bulletin containing same.

Coming up Penn Avenue, espied second hand bookstore. Had bought a briefcase for $3.00 a few minutes before. Bought *Personal Memoirs* of U[lysses] S. Grant, Vol. III; *The War of the Rebellion,* Vol. LXXIV, Series I; [Semen Markovich] Dubnow's *History of the Jews in Russia and Poland,* 2 volumes; [Norman DeMattos] Bentwich's *Hellenism*; [Joseph Bay] Esenwein's *Art of [Public] Speaking*; and *Story of 100 Operas* for the incredible price of $1.00. The *Memoirs* of Grant and the *Records of the Rebellion* alone would have cost $20.00 at least. I have a mania for books, and to amass a library is one of my paramount aims.

Came in early. After dinner wrote Helen [Grinage], Helen [Notis], Harry, Florence, Mother, and Mr. Johnson.

Mrs. Hitchens came in and chatted for an hour. Brought me an apple. Told me she heard me tripping up the steps about 5:30 this morning.

Had delightful tête-à-tête with Miss Groom. Is conscientious about her school work.

Tuesday
April 3
1928

After breakfast, went to Samuel Coleridge Taylor School on Preston Street near Druid Hill Avenue. It is a Platoon School; i.e., half of the pupils are receiving academic training while the remainder are engaged in vocational work. The building is of brick, new (just a year old). Has every modern convenience, even to showers for boys and girls. The structure also is fireproof.

The principal, Mr. [W. Douglas] Johnson, is quite a remarkable man. He taught for three years at West Virginia Collegiate Institute, then for six years in a High School in Baltimore. When the new school was completed, he was given the principalship.

He told me of his sojourn at West Virginia Collegiate. Taught there with Mr. Alrutheus Ambush Taylor, author of *The Negro in the Reconstruction of Virginia* and *The Negro in*

South Carolina During the Reconstruction. The latter is now head of the History Department of Fisk University.[1] I once expected to substitute for Taylor while he went to Harvard to begin work on his doctorate. Mr. Johnson asserted that the life of a professor at West Virginia Collegiate was virtually one of slavery. Teacher must attend all church services, chaperone young folks, attend nightly meetings and all assemblies. In addition, each professor had one room. He was married. At first, he and his wife had two rooms. Later, only one. Two professors in one room. He congratulated me upon not being there. Told him I had been offered a position there last year, but refused to teach English along with History.

Johnson is of brown complexion, medium weight and build, with a kindly eye, back of which, however, lurks the power to be stern if sternness is needed. He has a square, strong jaw, beautiful teeth, and wears gold-rimmed glasses, which he took off and put on nervously. Talked in a clear, deep, pleasant voice.

I related my mission. Told of my desire to leave questionnaires for teachers. He agreed readily. Left 25 questionnaires with him. Promised to call for them tomorrow.

Met Sam Murray. Teaches here. Took me through the school. I was impressed with the fine vocational work of the youngsters. Murray showed me footstools, tables, lamps, floor lamps, and numerous other articles, all the products of these children. I sighed, for when I was in the grades such manual training in our primary schools was unheard of.

Left two questionnaires with Rev. [John M.] Harrison. He is pastor of Wayman A.M.E. Church, as well as janitor of one of the shower rooms. At first, the worthy doctor told me he

1. Taylor joined the faculty of Fisk University in 1926. He was dean of men during the 1927–1928 school year, became acting dean of the college in 1929–1930, and was dean of the college in 1930. Before going to Fisk, he taught at Tuskegee Institute (1914–1915), was a social worker with the National Urban League and New York Urban League (1917–1919), and taught at West Virginia Collegiate Institute (1919–1922). From 1922 to 1925, he held a position comparable to the one Greene had with Carter G. Woodson at the Association for the Study of Negro Life and History. Woodson published Taylor's books on Reconstruction in South Carolina and Virginia through the association. Greene was invited to teach at Fisk when Taylor went to Harvard during the 1928–1929 school year to continue work toward his doctorate, which he received from Harvard in 1936.

could not fill them out this week, for time would not permit. I told him, in disgust, it would take but five minutes. Promised to give them to me tomorrow.

Went from the school to Provident Hospital. Met Drs. [Ernest C.] Melton, [John Wesley] Gaines, and [Bernard] Harris. Melton told Harris that one of his (Harris') patients desired to change physicians—to come to him. Of course, he told her that such a practice among physicians is unethical. Whatever that meant to her, she desired to get well. Said Harris had discharged her.

Hospital questionnaires are not filled out yet. Been here two weeks. Head nurse gave me permission to talk to nurses if I cared to wait. Waited with pleasure. After 20 minutes, met class of 15 girls. Passed out questionnaires. Received the best lot yet. Questions answered clearly and in detail. Not flattering to the church.

Left hospital, after asking Harris about questionnaires Smallwood was to have filled out. He replied Smallwood had not seen questionnaires. Wife must have forgotten to give them to him. Harris promised to take care of that and also to secure questionnaires from Rev. Williamson of Eager Street.

Went to Melton's. Received one questionnaire there. Came home. Dressed for dinner. After dinner went with Mrs. Hitchens to call on a Mr. [Miles W.] Connor, principal of Normal School. Was playing whist with wife [Mattie], a sister-in-law, and a Miss Williams—school teacher. Had southern accent. Quite noticeable.

Speaking of school, and particularly of Columbia, I found that we both received M.A. degrees in the same year, 1926. That was the year when the initiation of an outdoor commencement was ruined by a downpour of rain. Both Mr. and Mrs. Connor remembered it.

Played whist. Connor and I were beaten by Miss Williams and his sister-in-law. Miss Williams is from Florida, almost my height, brown, slim, with a thin face. Has fine disposition. The other lady was plump, of same complexion as Miss Williams, and attended school in D.C.

Met another lady, Mrs. Henderson, and daughter, Mrs.

Williams. Mrs. Hitchens tells me the mother has a color psychosis. She is fair, but no one could mistake her for white. When she took her daughter to Ohio State University, she told the dean that she did not bring her daughter there to go about with colored youth. Poor Negroes! They make so much distinction among themselves. Still, in the eyes of the whites, "all Negroes look alike."

Spent a pleasant hour. Left about 9:20. Called upon Dr. [W. Tyler] Coleman on same street about five blocks down on McCulloh. Enjoyed talking with him. Daughter, who teaches in Homestead, Pennsylvania, not at home. Mrs. [Veola] Coleman was also out. Son in hospital.

Talked for 40 minutes. Dr. Coleman, who treats both the body and soul—he became a minister before studying medicine—threw some interesting light upon the "Over Controversy" of Union Baptist Church.

Asked me to return. Left about 10. Met Mrs. Coleman in street. She certainly appeared likeable.

Returned home about 10:30. Mrs. Hitchens gave me some cake and pudding. Read in bed till my eyes hurt, then retired.

After breakfast, called upon Rev. [William W.] Walker, pastor of Madison Avenue Presbyterian Church, for questionnaire. Though he has had it for three weeks, he has not filled it out yet. Asked me to return tomorrow. Don't believe he means to give it to me. That's the sort of attitude the majority of ministers manifest towards us. He impresses me as being a little man. Spends a deal of his time at the YMCA playing checkers. **Wednesday April 4 1928**

Stopped at Urban League to see the Secretary, Mr. Moss. Was out. His secretary assured me he would return in a few minutes. He returned as I was about to leave. Is alert fellow of slight build, my height, lighter in complexion. Well informed upon things generally. Has had eight years' experience in social work. Organized Urban League in Toledo, Ohio. Moss has been here three years. Also organized the present office here. Is a cousin of David Moss, a classmate of mine, now studying for the ministry at Yale University. The former is a graduate of Columbia, '19, and School of Social Work, '20.

His idea of Negro Church was aptly expressed in two words, "damned rotten." He was overjoyed to know we were undertaking such a work. Had planned to do some himself. Had even begun the survey when he learned we were doing so. Told me of his jousts with ministers and how one had threatened to run him out of town because Moss dared to expose his chicanery. Seems to be a fearless young fellow. Has data upon Smallwood. Thinks latter doing fine piece of work. Other material in his possession I asked him to lend us that we might peruse it when we begin to write up Baltimore study. He agreed. Decried buying of white churches by Negroes. Told me of six hundred thousand dollars expended for churches in 2 years by eight congregations, with per capita tax of $51 annually for next ten years.

Walked with Moss as far as Preston Street. He went to church; I to the Platoon School. Arrived there, saw groups of pupils outside. Mr. Johnson, the principal, stood on the steps awarding prizes for races. How the faces of the youngsters beamed with joy as they got their little trinkets: a medal or a badge. Both boys and girls received them. Such was unknown in my primary school days. We knew not of it, therefore never missed it. After the prizes were awarded, I sought Mr. Johnson in his office to receive the questionnaires I had left there yesterday to be filled out by the teachers. Were not ready. Went down in basement to see Rev. Harrison, who is janitor of the shower room. Before I could secure his questionnaire, however, Mr. Johnson came to inform me of a play being given by the kiddies which he thought I might be interested in seeing. The little skit was quite well done by the pupils of the 2nd and 3rd grades.

I secured the questionnaire from Rev. Harrison. Again Mr. Johnson came to tell me that Rev. [Walter A.] English was speaking and to know whether I'd like to hear him. Of course, I had heard much of Rev. English, but did not know him. As I arrived in the assembly room, Rev. English was just concluding his remarks, exhorting the youngsters not only to be good in their attendance and in their school work and deportment but to be careful of their health, their teeth, face, hands, etc. He urged them to always do their best, that they might become a credit to their race, to the nation, and to God. Rev. English is a tall, dark man with natural ability and a fine carriage. Is an intelligent man, thank heaven!

Finally secured ten questionnaires. Oh, I had almost forgotten! Mr. Johnson said a few words after English spoke, then introduced me. I made a few remarks.

After securing questionnaires, met Miss Williams, who stays at Mr. Connor's. Walked with her up to the 2000 block of McCulloh Street. Fine company. She beat me at whist last night.

Mr. [Eugene H.] Carter was out. . . .

Came home, dressed, went to dinner. I am wrong there; walked over to North Fairmont Avenue to Dorsey Printing Shop, there found classmate of mine, Charles Dorsey. Is married. Introduced me to wife and baby. Father has retired. Charles runs the shop. Two brothers assist him.

Met Mr. Dorsey, Sr. Man of about 60. Intelligent, affable, willing to give freely of the full store of knowledge he has accumulated throughout the years. Dr. Bragg told me he knew more about the Catholic Church than any other man in Baltimore.

Said there was prejudice in the Catholic Church. His brother, Father Dorsey, had experienced it. Is segregated, too. Told of case at St. Mary's Parish in Ridgby[?], Maryland. Negroes sat in rear or upstairs. Arraigned priest because of it. Said, "Father, every Catholic is supposed to go to church at least once on Sunday, isn't he?" "Yes." "Well, if one is colored and has to stand or sit upstairs in the gallery, does that still apply to him?" Replied the priest, very arbitrarily, "Under normal conditions everyone is expected to attend church on Sunday." (Of course, it was for the Church to say what it considered normal conditions.) Says he has eaten, lived, and slept with priests. Will write me an account and give it to me Saturday.

Returned home, went to dinner, back home. Read, wrote, went out to mail letters for Mrs. Hitchens. Took topcoat, but tailor shops closed. This is not New York.

Bought Phospho-Lithia; take it as aperient as well as contrarheumatism.

After breakfast, interviewed Mr. Carter of 2005 McCulloh Street. Mr. Carter is the son of the late Rev. Nathaniel Carter, former rector of German Lutheran Church of North Eden Street of this city. A unique study. Here in Baltimore exists the first colored German Lutheran Church that I have yet seen. It is pastored by a white minister, a Rev. [Leo] Tecklenberg.

Mr. Carter, anticipating my arrival, had prepared an outline of pertinent facts connected with the Church. He is a man of rather short and thick stature, about thirty-five, prematurely greying. Affable, obliging, and informative. He is a teacher in the Junior High School here. According to him the Lutheran church was begun as a mission in 1896 by one Moses Hayes, a pious German jeweller and missionary. He started a mission for Negroes in Ivy Mill Lane, Laurainville—now an incorporated part of Baltimore. Morgan College is situated on this site. Through Hayes' influence a most remarkable thing happened. He persuaded a little Baptist congregation to forsake their faith and become Lutherans. (Extraordinary, because the Negro is primarily an emotional being, and to relinquish a faith which permitted the indulgence of the warmest fervor, for the cold ritualistic ceremony of the Lutheran Church, appears to me little short of marvellous.)

Through Hayes' influence, Carter was sent to a Lutheran Seminary, and was ordained in 1894. Confronted with the urgent need of a church for his congregation, Rev. Carter travelled through the West for two years in order to raise the needed funds. After a long struggle, he built the church in 1898. To secure funds from the Lutheran Churches proved a difficult task, for the Germans were very parsimonious in giving to churches.

A word about the Rev. Carter's life. He was born in Hanover County, Virginia, and received private instruction in Randolph-Macon College. Quite exceptional, for this was a white school. He taught school in Ashland, Virginia, for 13 years, coming to Baltimore in 1892, where Hayes was con-

ducting his mission among the Negroes. Through Hayes' influence, Rev. Carter studied for the ministry in order to prepare himself to interpret the tenets of the Lutheran Church to
his people. While studying for the ministry, he taught at
church and mission schools in Ohio. There, schools were under the jurisdiction of the Mission Board of the Ohio Synod.
Starting with approximately eight members, the number
grew to 100 in 1904, when Rev. Carter died suddenly from an
attack of acute indigestion. He had come to be beloved by his
parishioners. Zealously, he had striven to interpret the word
of God to his people. He acquired German to such an extent
that he lectured fluently in the language and even taught German lessons on week days. After his death, Rev. Pfiefer took
over the church. His stay was short. Two other men held the
pulpit before the advent of Rev. Leo Tecklenberg, the present
pastor.

The church is located on North Eden Street on the fringe of
the former red-light district of Baltimore. Seeing a German
Lutheran Church reposing in the midst of a colored settlement, I had made a mental note that the church would shortly
fall into the hands of a colored congregation, never dreaming
for a moment that it was already colored.

Mrs. Carter, the widow of the late pastor, gave me bits of
her recollections of the church. They were quite unconnected
and hazy. Her husband had died when the eldest child was 12
years of age, but through her untiring efforts, she had educated all of them. They were now engaged either in ministerial
or pedagogical pursuits. I felt proud of her and she has every
right to feel proud, too. One son, Rev. Marmaduke Carter, is
pastor of St. Phillip's Church on Evans Street, Chicago, Illinois. From what I learned of the requirements for the Lutheran
priesthood, he must be well educated.

The Church falls under the Ohio Lutheran Synod. It was
this Synod that prepared Rev. Carter for the pastorate of the
Eden Street Church. Subsequently, there arose a Missouri
Synod, the result of a schism inside the Ohio Synod, induced
by a dispute on the doctrine of predestination.

Leaving Mrs. Carter, I went to meet Dr. Wesley. He had

left word for me to come to Grace Presbyterian Church. Arriving there I found Kelly Miller in the midst of one of his characteristic speeches.[2] Negroes, of all groups, should uphold the Constitution because they have most to gain by doing so. (I agree with him there.) Further, he stated Negroes should engage in politics in order to secure their civil rights. He cited President Hoover's segregation policy in the Department of the Interior as an example of discriminatory practice which could be wiped out if Negroes would utilize their full political potential. He likewise favors the Negro minister entering the political arena. I think so, too. I am also in favor of collective bargaining by Negroes as the best method of extracting privileges from the party in power. However, I think that we must first develop ministers capable of understanding the political game before expecting them—ignorant as the majority are— to fight intelligently for the rights of the race. The suave and efficient politicians of the other race will but pull the wool over their eyes. I believe that if we develop business, we will of necessity develop politicians, who will have interests to be guarded and, in protecting their own, will be securing the rights of their co-entrepreneurs.

What especially disgusted me with Miller was his conviction that the Negro had a special genius for religion and that he should abjure the material realm and bend his every effort to the furtherance of the spiritual. Holds Negro's power lies in this area. Whites, he went on, have a monopoly on the things of this earth. In concluding, he sounded a dismally pessimistic note: It is futile for the Negro to strive for material things. Urged that the Negro allow the white to take the world and say as the old colored woman: "But, 'jes' give me Jesus." The ministers loudly applauded him. Had it been anyone else but Kelly Miller, I should have considered him a smatterer, a jug-

2. Kelly Miller was considered one of the more conservative black leaders of the early twentieth century. In 1906, he called the manifesto issued by W. E. B. Du Bois and members of the Niagara Movement during their meeting at Harper's Ferry "a wild and frantic shriek." Miller earned both his undergraduate and graduate degrees from Howard University and also did graduate work in mathematics and physics at Johns Hopkins University. He joined the Howard faculty as professor of mathematics in 1890 and became dean of the College of Arts and Sciences. Miller lectured and wrote extensively on race relations and the education of blacks.

gler of words, attempting merely to please his immediate listeners. But this man is regarded by all as one of the leaders of
the Negro people. As such his remarks carried authority.
Practically the entire congregation were ministers, and the
majority of them illiterate. Moreover, Miller's remarks coincided with their medieval concept of religion. I was alarmed,
for such sentiments as these uttered by Kelly Miller, for whom
all present had the profoundest respect and admiration, would
be inculcated into the people by these ministers from their
pulpits, thereby serving the vicious purpose of inoculating a
large segment of Baltimore colored people with the lethal
germ of economic inertia.

Kelly Miller's sun of leadership has set. The philosophy of
men of his kind belongs to an earlier day. He would have us
develop but one side of our nature. Would not have us emulate
the white man. In my opinion, the white man has everything
that conduces to progress. Not only that, he has religion too,
probably a thousand fold more sincere and practical than that
of the Negroes. How vain for even Kelly Miller to delude
himself into believing that the Negro alone has a monopoly
upon the spiritual values. I, for one, will take the world and as
much of Jesus as I can get, or *vice versa*, if you please. At least, I
would rather ape the white man than wallow in the slough of
artificial spiritual fervor and unprogressiveness that Kelly Miller proposes to his followers.

Nevertheless, the ministers rose and tendered Kelly a rous-
ing vote of thanks for his speech. (Humorously enough, they
had to spend five minutes before such a vote was decided
upon, while Miller sat before them highly amused at their
feebleness.) Rhapsodic comments were made concerning the
speech. One minister even went so far as to suggest that the
Negro ministers adopt Kelly's views by resolution and pledge
themselves to carry them out. Was not done, however, much
to my joy.

The question was raised why colored youth did not study
for the ministry, there being but 100 preparing for that vocation in all the seminaries in the country. Various answers were
offered, but the best came from a Rev. J. E. Lee, whose rea-

sons might be summed up as follows: 1) Because after securing a religious education, young preachers find that their intelligence *cannot* be *utilized* in the ministry, since the Negro masses do not *appreciate* a trained minister. 2) That the older ministers are *hostile* to youth who enter the field. I believe he was referring especially to the Methodists, where the young minister is put on a probationary period to prove his fitness. No such barriers handicap the young Baptist preachers. Case of Rev. Johns will illustrate this point.

Conferred with Wesley after meeting. Tells me to stay here till Monday, meeting him in D.C. at 10:50 a.m. Desires more citizens' questionnaires. Also informed me of an attempt by Professor [Monroe Nathan] Work and others at Tuskegee to undermine us in this study.[3] They had written a letter to the Institute in New York which is helping underwrite the study. But the Institute, much to their chagrin, referred them to Wesley.

Went to Mr. Dorsey to secure information about Catholics. He promised to write his views and deliver them to me Saturday.

Came home, dressed for dinner. Wrote couple of letters. Took laundry and shoes to shop. Returning, found Miss Thelma Coleman here. Had come to repay our visit of Tuesday. Daughter of Dr. Coleman, physician, Howard "grad" '25. We recognized each other. She is teaching in Homestead, Pennsylvania. Invited me to her home. Interesting to talk with.

Went out about 9 to mail letter for Mrs. Hitchens. Met Theodore McMillan, former classmate, in drug store. "Mac" does not have that prosperous look which he manifested when last I saw him. Face is thinner. Has had a rough time of it, chiefly because, in my opinion, of his lack of tact. Graduating from the Yale Divinity School, he accepted a position as Instructor of Theology at Shaw University, a colored school in

---

3. Monroe Work, who received his education at the University of Chicago, was director of the Department of Records and Research at Tuskegee from 1908 to 1939. He developed the Bureau of Information, which collected materials relating to black Americans; and in 1912, he began compiling annually the *Negro Year Book*.

Raleigh, North Carolina, and Baptist at that. "Mac" tried to instill his newfound dogma, imbibed at Yale, into his students here. They were shocked at his "modernism." The faculty became alarmed, saw in "Mac" a subversive influence tending to corrupt their time-honored, hide-bound Baptist tradition. Worse, the administration, failing to induce "Mac" to see the light as they saw it, turned him adrift. "Mac," now a confirmed radical, then came to Baltimore, having soured on all the Negro pedagogical powers that be, and began writing scathing exposés of the Church in the *Afro-American*. He is still employed there.

In my opinion, McMillan should be more diplomatic. I believe he first should have built up a strong and independent congregation, and only after having strongly intrenched himself, set about to reform the Church. The reformer usually has a light stomach, and "Mac" illustrates that well. Promised to call on me at 7 p.m. tomorrow.

Mrs. Hitchens is making preparations for her trip to New York tomorrow. I fixed a light for her. Surprised myself while gratifying her.

This is Good Friday, but as such it means nothing to me. My work goes on notwithstanding. Beautiful summer-like day.   *Friday April 6 1928*

Sammy (Rev.) Giles came over about 9. Wanted to say farewell to Mrs. Hitchens, but she had already departed for New York. I had risen early in order to bid her good-by. Promised I shall be gone when she returns Monday. She invited me to stay with her whenever I return to Baltimore. Assured me it was a pleasure to have me in her home. It was mutual. Her sense of humor, motherly interest, lack of affectation, plus a warm friendliness and a charitable disposition, will always cause me to remember her with extreme pleasure.

After breakfast, called Dr. Harris. Sent a young fellow for me in his car. Met him at the hospital. Took me to see one Dr. [John T.] Avery, a slow, colorless, sluggish person. Refused to fill out questionnaire, yet was dull enough to answer my questions, this enabling me to secure his opinions of the Church in spite of himself. Miss Gee, a school teacher, quite talkative and quite settled-looking, although she gave her age as 25, filled out a blank. Is an enthusiastic worker in Rev. Tecklenberg's Lutheran Church. Could or would not tell me where he lived, however.

Called on a Dr. Fisher. Has spirit, éclat, all that Avery lacks. Mrs. Fisher reminds me of Mrs. Hitchens. Has that way of speaking which makes one feel right at home. Also has an adorable smile which makes her almost beautiful. The Dr. was in a hurry, but he took time to fill out a questionnaire. She asked to be excused. Says she adores Madison Avenue Presbyterian Church and her pastor, Rev. Walker. I told her of my inability to persuade her pastor to fill out a questionnaire, although he has had it for three weeks. She promised to tell him about it. I hope her mentioning the matter will impel a little diligence on his part in filling out the blank.

Went to a Miss Tillman's. Dr. Harris left to keep an engagement at the hospital. Promised to see me at 2 p.m. Took me to see Rev. Tecklenberg of the colored Lutheran Church on North Eden Street. Was not at home. I left my card with a housekeeper, promising to call tomorrow at nine. She spelled the name "Chlereberg." I had asked her for the information, stating I had looked in vain for his name (according to my spelling of it) in the telephone directory. She could not help.

Went back to Dr. Harris. Filled out questionnaires for Mrs. Harris, her father, and others. Was beautiful balmy day. Sat outside on porch. Dr. Harris finally came in about 5 p.m. Took me to Miss Nichols, where I secured interesting questionnaires from her father. While waiting for Miss Nichols and her sister, who were going for a ride with us, a Rev. Williams came over to speak to the doctor. Williams is a rough-looking, unintelligent man. Allowed me to fill out questionnaire for him. Miss Nichols and her sister came out in the interim and entered the car, the latter with two children. How young the latter appeared! After the minister had departed, I turned to Miss Nichols (Dorothy) in order to get her opinion of the Negro church. The appearance of the girl astonished me. I had seen her before at Dr. Harris'. Now attired in a blue suit with a sport sweater of a greenish mixture and a little black hat, she appeared the very incarnation of delicate beauty, as frail and lovely as the slender lily. Her smile disclosed even white teeth which literally lighted up her face. Her hair was of a reddish hue, but it blended perfectly with her complexion. I gazed entranced upon her, then upon her sister in surprise, for I had believed Dorothy to be married. Yet I found her sister, Mrs. Evans, though scarcely twenty, to be the mother of the children.

No, the church was not progressive, according to Miss Nichols. The preachers, in her opinion, were responsible for bad conditions, for they did not set an example for the members to be guided by. Of course, she said, they are human, but they should have more self-control than the laity, because they were endowed with the greatest of strength—the "inspired word of Christ." She railed against the ministers as immoral, hypocritical, and overfond of women. Why, she exclaimed with indignation, "a minister even kissed me two years ago, as I was dozing in a chair in the kitchen." Asked who it was, she responded, "It was Rev. Williams, whose questionnaire you just received." She believed the churches would be better if the ministers were better trained, more consecrated to their tasks, and if the unadulterated doctrine of Christ were preached instead of the eternal clamor for money, which robs the sermon of its vigor.

I had an engagement with McMillan at 7 o'clock. Harris asked me if I desired to go to Havre de Grace to play cards with him and Miss Nichols. Of course, I replied, I should be delighted, if I could possibly cancel my engagement with McMillan. By the way, I had seen "Mac" this evening on South Caroline Street and had given him ten questionnaires to have filled out by the employees of the Baltimore *Afro-American*, to be sent to the Association's office in the District by him. He assured me he would do so. Asked my opinion of East Baltimore. Told him what little I knew about it.

Dr. Harris drove me to Mrs. Hitchens'. No one had called for, or upon, me. I changed my clothes and went back to the car, where the girls and Dr. Harris awaited me. Back to Dr. Harris' home. In the meantime, I had lots of fun with Dorothy.

After dinner, we played whist. Were horribly beaten by Dr. Harris and Mrs. Evans. Dorothy was my partner. She became sleepy and tired after three games were played.

Mrs. Harris, who had gone to choir rehearsal, returned at eleven and we set out for Havre de Grace. I was shocked because I had not shaved. Girls assured me my beard was not discernible.

Ride to Havre de Grace was delightful. About 36 miles. Arriving at the friends of Dr. Harris, we found them just about to retire, having given up hope of our coming out there. However, they invited us in and we played a game called *Pit*, where the object is to secure, by trading with the other players, nine cards, or all the cards specifying a certain commodity. The person first securing nine cards of a given staple, i.e., corn, wheat, etc., cries out (laying them down at the same time), "I corner the market on 'corn,' 'wheat,' or whatever it happens to be," wins the game. What excitement! The most stimulating game I had ever played. Mrs. Evans won.

We left about 2:00 a.m. Unusual for me, I drank a little beer. Don't know why, unless it was to keep from appearing like an "oddball." But then I had appeared odd before and didn't mind it.

On the way home, Dr. Harris asked us to sing. I was dozing; Dorothy and Mrs. Evans were asleep; but I joined in the Howard *Alma Mater* with Harris. Then we had a regular plantation show. Spirituals galore, the woods reverberated with them, and oh, what "harmony"! My voice sounded like an old dishpan upon which someone was standing. The singing, or better noise, perhaps enabled us to reach home safely, for Dr. Harris was falling asleep at the wheel. I recalled he stopped short once while traveling about 30 miles per hour. He was in the middle of the road, and no obstruction was in sight. It did not dawn upon me at the time what had caused the sudden stop. However, Harris confessed he had dozed momentarily and waking had slammed on the brakes, not knowing where he was.

Arrived home safely at 4 a.m. Only late hour since my advent in Baltimore. Seemed suspicious. While Mrs. Hitchens was home, I was always in at night. Now on her first evening away from home I remain out virtually all night. But that's life.

Rose quite tired at 9:30 a.m., having retired only five hours earlier. After breakfast called on the Rev. Tecklenberg of the St. Phillip's Lutheran Church located on South Eden Street. The minister proved to be a young, flaxen-haired man, about 30 years of age, almost boyish in appearance. Found him quite affable, frank, and willing to talk. Spoke with little or no restraint. Once he apologized for what he believed I might consider an aspersion upon the Negro. He was referring to a keg of beer which the German founder of the mission (which ultimately developed into St. Phillip's Lutheran Church) had to kick out of his path on his way to services there. He told me that the beer was being rolled down the street by Negro men to a group of their people who were holding a picnic near Ivy Mill. I told him such an apology was unnecessary, for as a research worker I was concerned neither with personalities nor with racial consciousness. My business was to collect the facts. Thereafter he spoke more freely. He admitted that when he took charge of the mission he knew absolutely nothing about work among Negroes. He had enjoyed little contact with them, having been born and reared in a section of Ohio where there were few colored people. Here, however, he had found an interest which gave him a good deal of satisfaction. Assured me the church was growing. He resorted to ingenious methods in summer to hold his congregation, even holding the meetings in the street, where he would have 75 listeners instead of 4–5.

Has a Bible class which meets daily. The Sunday school, he assured me, was growing by leaps and bounds with the staunch assistance of Miss Gee. He also informed me that he puts emotion into his sermons in order to hold the attention of the people. It is practical, he added, if not according to the strict letter of Lutheranism.

The work at St. Phillip's, he went on, was under the supervision of a Board of Colored Missions, consisting of 3 clergy and 2 lay members, all residents of Baltimore. The mission itself is directly under a Superintendent (Richards) who is responsible to the Board.

From the point of information, I considered my time with Rev. Tecklenberg well spent. He gave me a picture of the church, the Sunday School, and the Bible Class. I then bought two 25 cent slides of the old mission from which the church sprang, and the old school, which formerly was a saloon. The Reverend then presented me with one of his pictures, in which he had the appearance of a college freshman, endeavoring to look profound. Was favorably impressed by this young pastor. Felt that he is giving his best to the task before him. It is a difficult one for, in my opinion, he cannot relate to his parishioners as freely as a colored man could.

Went to Miss Nichols' at 1573 Jefferson Street. Yesterday she had appeared almost divine. Today, I beheld her as she was. With hair unkempt, kimono half-open, bare legs, she looked like anyone except the Dorothy Nichols of last night. Spent two hours talking. Told me of her love affairs.

Went to Dr. Harris' to get my pen, which I had left there. From there dropped in at the office of the *Afro-American*, a Negro newspaper. Could not get questionnaires. McMillan had forgotten to have them distributed to the staff. Still had them in his desk. Promised to send them to me in D.C. I pretended to be sorely disappointed about last evening. "Mac" begged profuse apologies. Had he known how I tricked him last night! Here he was, mind you, apologizing. Tried to see Mr. Carl Murphy, owner of the *Afro-American*, but he was busy. *Afro-American* has very nice offices. Business-like, too. Finally got to talk with Mr. Murphy just as I was about to leave. Gave me interesting news about the paper.

After dinner, went to Mr. Dorsey to obtain his article on "Colored Catholics in Baltimore." Did not have it ready.

Promised to send it to me. Told him I would be in town till Monday and would call for it then. I half-way believe he thought better of giving me his opinions on Negro Catholics and was trying to squirm out of doing so. Was determined, however, that he should not.

On the way home got my shoes from the repair shop and bought some razor blades. I wish I did not have to shave. Must do so almost daily, however, which renders my face quite tender. Gillette blades do not seem to shave me adequately.

Oh, yes, Rev. Lewisstall called on me. Could easily divine the reason. Wanted money to found a religious seminary. Some Negro is always founding a school and, worst of all, frequently is no better equipped for such than a porter in a first-class educational institution. Lewisstall wanted a dollar. Told him I had it but not to spare. Asked about his questionnaire. Told me he had sent it to D.C. Replied I would send him a dollar after my arrival there, meaning if his questionnaire were there, I would, or might, send him the money.

A beautiful, warm day. Rained about 7 p.m.

Tried to catch up with my diary but was too sleepy. Retired at 9 o'clock.

Rose at 9:30. Got to breakfast an hour and a half late. Afterwards went to Bethel A.M.E. Church. It is said to be the oldest A.M.E. Church in the country; at least I understand it vies with St. Thomas of Philadelphia for that honor.[4] Bragg gives it to St. Thomas; Bishop [C. M.] Tanner to Bethel. Disappointed in sermon preached by Bishop [Sampson] Brooks. Has magnetic personality, but his sermon was discursive. The church was beautiful, with a profuse display of lilies

Sunday
April 8
1928

4. Here Greene became somewhat confused in his black church history. When Richard Allen, Absalom Jones, and William White led the black members out of St. George Methodist Episcopal Church in Philadelphia, they organized the Free African Society. Some of the members of this organization, including Absalom Jones, organized St. Thomas African Church, which affiliated itself with the Protestant Episcopal Church and became the first black church of that denomination. Richard Allen and others remained in the Methodist Church, but they purchased a building and established Bethel Church, which was dedicated in 1794. In 1816, Allen led in the founding of the African Methodist Episcopal Church, and Bethel in Philadelphia became the first church of that denomination.

before the altar and canaries singing from cages. The church was crowded with people in Easter finery, with adults predominating. Rev. Brooks surprised me by exhorting the congregation to "shout."

Met Miss Pauline Stewart of D.C. Slim, cute woman of about 30. Unsophisticated, charming, interesting. Had lots of fun with her and Miss Nichols, whom I jokingly named "Bridget." After church, dinner at Dr. Harris'. Dinner was deliciously cooked and served, and very enjoyable. The Harrises certainly know how to make one feel at home.

After dinner Dr. Harris took me out to interview people in regard to their attitude toward the Negro church and its ministers. The information I gleaned was not flattering to the ministers. They were called everything, blamed for bad conditions in the church and community, also accused of many things, most of which, I regret to say, are true. Said one fellow, "A minister cheated me out of $7 in a crap game." Another added, "Rev. Williams drinks just as much liquor as I."

Most of those interviewed considered the ministers to blame for the bad conditions in the community, ascribing such to their selfishness, hypocrisy, sexual laxness, and greed for money. They all considered the greatest need of the church to be "more Christian Spirit," whatever that means. The majority said that the church had nothing to offer them.

Went to a club next door to secure information. It was so disreputable that I had to find a sponsor to get in. Found it in Bill, a boy whom Dr. Harris looks out for. While I was filling out questionnaires, a group of girls ranging in age from 15 to 21 came in. They were shown upstairs and told that the boys would be up later.

Dr. Harris came by to take me to church. His little boy was speaking on the Easter program. The exercises took place at Centennial Church. It was Fred Douglass' old church and is 143 years old. Reverend [Charles S.] Briggs is pastor. The children spoke their pieces well. Little Junior Harris drew forth muffled laughter and applause by his unique way of bowing. Although but 3 years old, he told the people that he was there to proclaim "the Lord is risen."

After church, we went to the Club Arabia. Harris paid $7.50 for our fare. Would not let me spend a cent, although I did pay an extra half dollar for checking wraps. The Club Arabia is on the top floor of three three-story buildings. Dining and dancing. Tables all around with a square of about 16 feet for dancing. Draperies hid walls and ceilings, making it almost impossible to secure air. But in this conservative Catholic city night clubs are closed on Sunday. Enjoyed dancing with Miss Stewart. Became quite friendly with her. She asked me to come to see her in Washington. Danced with Dorothy twice. The last time I kissed her. Could not help it. She threatened to slap me, but her anger was short-lived. A girl danced and sang; so did a fellow. Might have spared their pains. But then a girl danced such as I had never before seen a girl dance in public. It was past the stage of suggestion. If she did nothing else, she certainly succeeded in awakening the fires of desire in all the males present. She did things I had not seen even in the "speakeasies" of New York City. We left at 5 a.m. My! my! what would Mrs. Hitchens say? Had a fine time, though tired out. Don't believe I like Miss Nichols as much as formerly.

After breakfast succeeded in getting questionnaire from Rev. Walker of Grace Baptist Church. Certainly had a job obtaining it. Walker doesn't impress me. Asked another man to help answer the questions intended for him.

Monday
April 9
1928

Went from Walker's to Rev. Taylor. Could not find him at home. Secured valuable opinions from two men standing on a street corner who were arguing with a third about religion. Old man, 89, voiced opinions on the church that astounded me. In essence, it was "rotten."

Stopped at Dr. Coleman's. Thelma, their daughter, had gone back to the University. Missed her altogether. Nevertheless secured two very interesting questionnaires from the Colemans. The doctor then drove me out to Dorsey's printing plant. Secured typewritten statement from Mr. Dorsey concerning Negro Catholics which he had promised me. Returned home, found Mrs. Hitchens had returned. Glad to see her. Told of my escapades during her absence. She laughed, told me I waited for her to go away "before turning them on strong."

Thought I had lost my pen. Had much writing to do. Called Dr. Harris. Wife told me Dorothy had it.

Went after it. Dorothy's sister had put it away. Could not secure it till she returned. Played Black Jack, fan tan, and whist. Dorothy was so sleepy, she could not keep awake. Bade them farewell. Left at 10:30, went home. Dead tired.

Tuesday
April 10
1928

Last day in Baltimore. Stopped by Mrs. Fernandis' to say good by. Assured me her house would always be open to me. I hated to leave Mrs. Hitchens. Invited me to stay at her home whenever I came to Baltimore.

Picked up other questionnaires. Went to Harris' to get my pen where I had left it. Seems that I am constantly forgetting it. From there went to Zion Cemetery Association. Talked over a number of things with Dr. Davis, such as advisability of taking out insurance, getting out laundry, saving money, etc. Must take out about a $2,500 insurance policy. Davis is an unselfish man, always trying to help someone. Losing his church, I hear.

Caught 4:35 train for Washington, D.C. Arrived at Aunt's on Swann Street, N.W., about 6 p.m.

To my surprise, Ernest Bacote, one of my dearest pals, was visiting there from Syracuse. My aunt told me to look in the little room at the top of the steps. Did so and discovered speedily that the effects therein were Bacote's. He was out, but returned shortly as I was eating. Surprised to see me. We were both overjoyed. If only Hipp were here now, the "old gang" would be intact again. Bacote does not like Syracuse. Business is not so good. Told him he owed me a letter. Gave no good excuse for his failure to write. Same as most of us, I presume— procrastination. He went out, promising to return at 10:30. Of course, he was going to see Vickie (Miss Snowden), his fiancee. Presume they will make it after all, although once I thought it was all over with them.

Called Helen [Grinage]. Not at home. Left word for her to

call me. Waited till 8:30, then called Bertha. She asked me to come down.

Refused to give me my watch. Told me that she was never selfish where I was concerned. Would give me anything— always thought of me, never of herself. Yet, I would not give her my watch. Asked if there were anyone else to whom I had promised it. No. Was there anyone else to whom I would rather give it? I told her I meant to give it to no one. When she told me that she desired the watch because it reminded her of one whom she loved, after she had recounted her unselfish love for me, I felt unable to persuade her further to return the watch. Incidentally, she had already exchanged with me a man's watch in lieu of mine. I was wearing the former at the time. I finally left her still in possession of that unique watch.

Ernest opened the door for me when I arrived home. We talked till about 3 a.m. Discussed Hipp. Bacote, a logical thinker, believes Hipp is wrong in contemplating marriage now. Thinks he should accumulate something first. Bacote expresses my sentiments as far as Hipp is concerned. The latter is dear to both of us, but then, one can express his opinion and no more. Bacote asked me to secure a bulletin of the Census for him. Promised to do so.

Bacote left at 9 a.m. I went to the Association for the Study of Negro Life and History at 9:30. Wesley came in at 10. We worked, looking over papers from Baltimore till lunch time, when I stopped in to see Virginia, an old girl friend of mine. Is married now and has a little boy. Does not look as attractive as formerly. Lost her mother in December. Not much of a loss, for she was less than a mother. Spent the afternoon at the office. *Wednesday April 11 1928*

Arrived home about 5:30. Aunt told me Helen had called. Called her. Not home. Lil, her sister, answered. Would have Helen call me when she came in.

Tried to write in diary. Too sleepy. Waited til 9 for Helen to call. Called Bertha. Told her I was leaving tomorrow for Suffolk, Virginia. Went to bed.

[5] Suffolk, Virginia, and Environs

Arrived at the office 9:25 a.m. Dr. Wesley was already there. Is a fine fellow to work with. Never forces an opinion on one arbitrarily. Considerate. Always willing to ask advice. So different from Dr. Woodson!

Wesley suggested that we secure our tickets for Norfolk, Virginia, at noon. We go to Suffolk by ship. He drove to ticket office. We paid $6.65 apiece for passage. Included stateroom. Discrimination here as always. Bunks over the wheel and engine room especially reserved for Negroes.

Returned to office. During the afternoon I tried to figure out per capita debt of Negro church-going population in Baltimore. Know it must be high but need more data—i.e., wages. Sending to Mr. [R. Maurice] Moss of Baltimore Urban League for it.

Left office about 4:00 p.m. Gave aunt a dollar before leaving. Promised to send her some money from Suffolk.

Arrived at the pier at 5:00 p.m., an hour before boat departs. Dr. Wesley came down later. We sailed down Potomac to Chesapeake Bay. The river was beautiful in the late afternoon sunshine.

Dr. Wesley and I chatted informally, while sitting in the waiting room: History, business, my banking of funds, etc. were among the matters discussed. Dr. Wesley even took me into his confidence about various personal matters.

This is my first experience aboard ship. When I saw the porters "rushing" bags, it reminded me of my pal [Harry] Hipp, and his work on the Hudson River Day Line. Yes, the boat indoctrinates one with the "germ of servility." Both Wesley and I agreed it is the basest and lowliest of all means of making a livelihood. It was degrading to me, these men bowing, grinning, and "scraping" before the white patrons! My, I could never do such! I told Wesley that I had never known the experience of "waiting," although I had done nearly everything—running elevators, washing dishes, windows, walls, toilets—anything to earn an honest dollar to secure an education. Nor had I "hustled" bags on board ship.

Wesley assured me I was fortunate, for it was the most degrading work he had ever done. The servility of it! "Why," he added, "a man asked me to request the orchestra leader to play a certain piece, then asked: 'Can you remember that or shall I write it down for you?'" Wesley said he replied, cuttingly, "I presume I can," and strode off.

Soon it was too cool to remain on deck, so we retired after an interesting conversation of four and a half hours.

I slept on the top bunk in order to mitigate the jarring effect of the bunk caused by the wheel. Window rattled so I had to get out of bed to close it with paper. That stopped it effectively. Got very little sleep.

Rose about seven. Wesley was already up.

Beautiful morning on the water. We stopped at Old Point. Passed a warship in the bay en route there. Arrived at Norfolk about 8 a.m. Could not find a place to eat. Discrimination everywhere. Waited till we came to Suffolk.

Went immediately to find my classmate. Dr. [Richard Henry] Bland, to see whether he could accommodate us. Could not do so due to Dental Convention meeting in town. White hotels, of course, will not accept Negroes, so poor Bland had four dentists quartered in his home. Took us across the street to Mrs. Skeeter's house. She is the mother of Marguerite, Carrie, and Leslie, who live in New York City. A kindly, middle-aged woman. So happy to know that I was a

Friday April 13 1928

friend of her daughters. Received us cordially. So sorry she could not lodge us. Asked again about her daughters. Of course, I praised them to the skies. Mrs. Skeeter has a large, well-appointed home, surrounded by a porch on two sides. A beautiful hedge encloses the yard. Again she regretted she could not accommodate us.

Dr. Bland then told us he would take us to a Mrs. [Odella] Peele, who he was quite certain could receive us. He had already called two other places, but both were filled with convention guests.

Found Mrs. Peele a pleasant-faced woman of perhaps forty-five. Has finely furnished home. Just opposite Booker T. Washington School on Lee Street.

After depositing our baggage, we made ready to go to the school while waiting for Mrs. Peele to prepare breakfast. Had a fine breakfast. Mrs. Peele is a kindly, friendly woman.

Met Mr. [Edward D.] Howe, a kindly old gentleman who is principal of the school. He knew Dr. Wesley. Invited the latter to speak to his eighth grade class. Wesley did and it bore fruit, for we distributed 46 questionnaires among the pupils, and, more important, collected them. Some of the answers were quite humorous.

Mr. Howe showed me a booklet containing pertinent information of Suffolk. I asked him to procure one for me. He readily promised to do so. Incidentally, he asked Dr. Wesley to return at 11:30 and speak to the entire school. The latter graciously consented.

There is no assembly hall in the school. The children had to stand in the lower hall with stairs as an improvised platform. Altogether different in the white schools. But then that is how segregation works. I saw about nine teachers, one so fair we took her to be white, so much so that Dr. Wesley changed the tenor of his talk. (Children and teachers showed marked effects of racial mixing.) What an inspiring speaker! I had to marvel at his rapidity of thought, and his fluency in translating it into words. Eloquence personified! He drew upon his rich store of knowledge and experience, yet couched his thoughts in such simple language that I felt positively certain that the students and teachers alike both understood and enjoyed his words. (Of course, Wesley is a minister—A. M. E.—as well as a scholar, which explains partly his ease of holding the attention of his audience.)

Later, we went to grade nine and secured 40 questionnaires from the pupils. While distributing them, I mistook a teacher, Miss [Helen?] Estes, for a pupil. She was so petite. She waved aside the paper. I apologized and substituted one for "citizens."

The school is small and not well ventilated. There are two buildings, each containing about eight rooms, both inadequate for the children. Many of the latter, as well as the teachers, are of very light complexion.

From the grammar school we went out to Nansemond High School in East Suffolk. There we met Professor [William A.] Huskerson, principal of the school. He is a man whose very mien bespeaks indomitable courage and unflexing will, a man of bulldog tenacity. In fact, he gives the appearance of one of those tenacious animals. Undoubtedly he is all, or partly Indian. Is a former friend of Wesley's, a graduate of the Engineering School of Howard University. Prejudice kept him from working at his profession in the United States. Had spent nine years in the jungles of Brazil and Panama.

Huskerson showed us through the partially completed building. It is roughly 50 × 100 feet. Huskerson says that he drew the plans, supervised construction, and in some cases even aided in the actual work. It seems almost incredible that such a building, two stories high, could be built at the extremely low cost of $15,000. The second wing of Booker T. Washington School cost $52,000. Either Huskerson's figure was impractical or there must have been enormous misappropriation of funds in the latter case. Of course, the need of compensating an architect etc. for Nansemond was obviated by Huskerson's filling that role.

The dentists were holding a meeting here. Could not use the hotels. I met Dr. [Elwood Davis] Downing of Roanoke, Virginia, and his brother. Remembered me from last summer, when I sold magazines.

Luncheon was served in the Assembly Hall in the rear by
Drs. Bland, [Edwina Mae] Reeves, and others. Dr. [Clarissa
C.] Wimbush, a Howard classmate, insisted that Dr. Wesley
and I join them. We did so, while the school glee club sang
spirituals. A shame, I thought, to stultify the musical knowledge of these students by relegating them to hymnals and
spirituals only. The singing was atrocious. Wesley commented upon it. Huskerson was disgusted but looked at me
with a gesture of impotency, for the ministers of the various
churches demand just this thing. The Glee Choir wailed "Old
Black Joe." Hope I never hear it sung like that again!

Dr. Wesley was persuaded to speak, following remarks by
Mr. [Robert] Williams, one of Suffolk's leading Negro business men, and also by Dr. Cobbega of Norfolk [this was
probably Dr. S. F. Coppage, who presided at sessions of the
Dental Convention]. Again, Wesley astounded me by his fluency and ability of extemporaneous rapid thinking upon his
feet. The man is truly eloquent! He lauded the dentists for their
meeting in probing for scientific data in order to better fit
themselves for their professional duties. Praised the fine work,
their standing in the community, etc. Spoke upon the need of
disseminating the facts of Negro History. Referred to inci-
dents of Negro achievement, peopling of Southern Europe by
Africans, probable discovery of America, and other contributions by the race. In the presence of this modest genius, I
desired only to be seen, not heard.

Dr. Bland gave me two tickets for the dentists' banquet.
Formal. And I left my tuxedo in D.C. Wesley, however, is in
the same fix but says he shall go. So shall I.

Mr. Huskerson, after adjournment, took us for a long ride
into the country. Went in the direction of Holland. Showed us
Negro farms along the roadside. Returned to Mrs. Peele's
about 6:30.

Sent a suit to the tailor to have pressed. Had it back by 8
o'clock. Mr. Huskerson promised to call for us at 9. Did so,
but we three chatted until eleven o'clock.

Arrived at the Elk's Auditorium, the scene of the banquet;
everything was in full swing. Saw Elizabeth Colden there,

friend of Leslie Skeeter. She introduced me to some friends, and her husband (was he drunk?).

Met Miss Ira Skeeter. Picked her to be Marguerite's sister without an introduction. Similar complexion; taller than Marguerite. Face not as full. Ira introduced me to her aunt, Mrs. [Grace] Finch. In turn, I introduced her to Dr. Wesley, who seemed to intrigue the eyes of more than one lady by his masculine beauty. I danced with Miss [Hortense F.] Phrame, music director of the High School. Is stout and taller than I. 'Twas a duty dance, for she was a member of Mr. Huskerson's party. Also danced with Mrs. [Lillian] Huskerson, even though she is much taller than I. Wesley proved a good mixer, although he danced only once. Both of us were tired. Made excuses. Left about one o'clock. Both agreed we had an enjoyable time. Thus ended the first day. Quite a bit crowded into it.

Wesley and I shared the same bed at the Peeles'. Chatted until we finally fell asleep.

After breakfast we walked out to see what information we could gather. Met Rev. [J. J.] Posey, deposed Episcopal minister, who is now pastoring in Newport News, Virginia. He informed us Suffolk whites found him a little obnoxious. Was advocating better school facilities, parks, etc. for Negroes. Was also guiding spirit in the erection of Nansemond High School (there being no High School in the county for Negroes). Whites irritated. Found he had been in Suffolk but a short while and, perceiving that in his capacity of an Episcopal clergyman, he could be removed at the discretion of the Bishop of the Diocese, enlisted the aid of the Bishop's son (also a pastor in Suffolk) to have Posey removed from his charge here. Thus was dismissed one of the most public-spirited men of the Negro group in Suffolk. His departure was a great social loss to the community. Dr. Wesley had a questionnaire filled out by his (Posey's) former church.

Leaving Rev. Posey, we went to the Tynes Street Baptist Church. It looks as if the building would fall over for little or nothing. Reverend Anderson Boone, the aged pastor, was

Saturday April 14 1928

away on vacation, we were told by a man living next door to the church. Said Rev. Boone had pastored the church for 47 years. Consequently, the people were devoted to him.

Going into the church we met the sexton, the honorable Mr. Moses Dixon. Is an expressman when not engaged in shouting "hallelujahs" and "chasing" devils. What a world of common sense and philosophical sayings he possessed! Recited a parable to prove how some people accept Christ and his doctrines till they had negotiated a difficulty then straightaway dropped him. Told a story of a man who, lost in the jungles, was met by a lion who licked his hand, showing signs of friendship, and finally became attached to the man, shielded him from all danger by the other wild animals. But, after many days of struggling, during which the lion was his devoted companion, the man, one night, saw the lights of the long-sought city shining in the distance. Now that his journey was practically over, he said to himself, as he lay down to sleep, "Well, I am in the city gates now. There is no further danger from wild animals. Therefore, the lion is of no further use to me. I cannot take him into the city, so I shall shoot him." And, as the faithful lion slept at his feet, the man raised his gun and dispatched him. Upon entering the city, he told about his experience, and the people asked him what had become of the lion. He told them, and straightaway they began to abuse him. "Just so," added the narrator, indicating the moral, "do people act toward Christ. They stay with Him while in need, but as soon as that is past, they get rid of Him." Both Wesley and I were astonished at his logic.

We spent an hour there with him.

The church was a tiny frame structure with benches, the pulpit extraordinarily low. It was heated by two stoves; each stood about equidistant from the ends of the building. A stovepipe from each ran across the room, converging at the wall. The church was whitewashed inside. Outside there was no telltale evidence of paint.

Leaving Mr. Dixon, regretfully, Dr. Wesley and I returned to Mrs. Peele's for dinner. Wesley packed and made ready to leave on the 4:30 train for Washington. Suddenly, it dawned upon us that Mr. Huskerson had invited us to dine at his home at 2:30 that same day. And we had accepted. 'Twas three o'clock now. Nevertheless, although just having eaten, we went (could not afford to offend people as important as Mr. Huskerson and his family). Food—food—chicken salad, peas, potatoes, and a host of good things. We could do little more than mince with the food and hope our hosts were not offended. Miss Phrame, the music teacher with whom I had danced last night, was there. She and Mrs. Huskerson are anti-types. Miss Phrame is plump, fleshy, and dimpled. She also possesses a charming disposition. Mrs. Huskerson, on the other hand, is thin, bony, and wiry—if that term can be applied to a woman. She is likeable, however.

Mr. Huskerson is brusque, lion-like or bear-like, as you will. Impresses me with the idea of brute strength. Must be wholly or partly Indian, as I said before. Is deeply tanned by his work in Brazil and Panama. Mrs. Huskerson accompanied him. Amused us by telling story of once finding a deadly snake coiled under her bed and shutting the door, as she fled the room, upon the man who, answering her screams, came into the room and killed it.

Huskerson related stories of malaria fever, prejudice, and his work as an engineer in Brazil. Were highly interesting. With all this, dinner passed off fine. Later Huskerson took Wesley to the station. Before leaving, Dr. Wesley asked me to work chiefly among citizens and pastors. Said he would be down within another ten days. Would arrive so that he might study the country churches.

Later Huskerson drove me out to Holland. Saw Negro-owned farms, homes, and churches. Of great interest to me.

What a splendid fellow—Huskerson. He can't do enough for me. Told me of the niggardly way in which most of the people acted toward him as principal of the high school. Excoriated Mr. Howe of Booker T. Washington School for his "littleness." Finally, brought me home at 6:30, but only because I requested it.

Oh, yes. I had taken Dr. Bland's hat by mistake last night. Was better than mine, but too large, though the shape and

color were the same. I returned his hat and received mine. I
had told Bland about the mix-up this morning.

Stopped at Ira Skeeter's. She was out. Had gone to the dentist with Miss M——, who lives two doors up the street.

Went home. Wrote letters; mailed them. Returned home to
read and write. Finally retired at eleven o'clock.

Sunday   Went to church this morning with Mr. [James] Peele, who
April 15   owns a fine barber shop. He took me in his car. Attended First
1928   Baptist Church. Is small building. Rev. Harrod [James A.
            Harrell], the pastor, is a pompous, middle-aged man. Has
average education. Rev. [John] White, wholly and pitifully
illiterate, attempted to preach. Poor fellow—that such as he,
well meaning as he might be, should presume to lead these
people. The blind are never safely led by the blind. I worried
through the sermon while Mr. Peele apologized profusely for
the man's ignorance.

The minister, having been given my card, must needs call
upon me to speak. I had attended without any intention to do
so. My mission was to listen.

I said a few words about the Association, which gave me the
opportunity to introduce Dr. Carter G. Woodson. First, however, I congratulated them upon Nansemond High School,
which the church helps support. In conclusion, I told them of
the study being made by Dr. Wesley and me. Everyone commented favorably, but, of course, that means nothing. I was
introduced as "professor," so, of course, they expected something, and it took little effort to convert my "nothing" into
"something."

Secured speaking engagement for Dr. Woodson for next
Monday.

After church Mr. Peele drove me to a section of the city
which I had not seen. Boston, I believe it was. Returned home
about 2. Stayed in. Mr. and Mrs. Peele are very solicitous for
my welfare and comfort. Can't do too much for me. Southerners certainly are in a class by themselves when it comes to
hospitality, and Virginia surpasses them all.

I am called "professor" now. What can I say or do to avoid

such a title? It is onerous, much too much so for me. I prefer to be Mr. Greene to strangers and "Rennie" to friends.

After breakfast called upon Rev. [Davis F.] Gladney of the A.M.E. Church. His wife, who answered the door, mistook me for book agent. Angrily told me of one Mr. McNeil, who, a few years ago, had secured $2 from her as a deposit upon a book which she never received. Upon writing the company she found that he had given her a false address. Reverend Gladney, incidentally, was not at home.

Called upon a Rev. [G. F.?] Powell, who keeps a grocery store in Philadelphia, a Negro section of Suffolk. Has no church. Is a tall, dark, unemotional man of 60, though I confess his looks belie his age. I thought him 40. Answered questionnaires reservedly. Some ministers are "good," some "bad." Asked whether ministers or church members were to blame for bad conditions in the community, he replied noncommittally, "Those who do not keep God's commandments, whether ministers or church members, are at fault." What the churches needed, in his opinion, was "more Grace."

Went to Booker T. Washington School to secure questionnaires from teachers. Professor Brown, for everyone who teaches school here is a professor, invited me to watch the pupils line up at recess and talk to them for a while.

What an unruly set of children! Their actions seemed to portray lack of proper home training. They showed respect for neither teacher nor guest. Mr. Brown, a kindly, indifferent, old gentleman who teaches because he needs money—and has been doing so for 32 years—was powerless to preserve order. I was astonished, then disgusted. This would never have happened in a New England school. We should have been severely chastised. Furthermore, we always stood upon our best behavior when visitors came to school.

I did not need to wonder what I should speak about, for seeing their utter lack of discipline, I exhorted them to be obedient and orderly, stressing obedience as the first law of God and nature. Moreover, I attempted to show them that obedience to their teachers *now* would be appreciated by them when they grew older, while their disobedience to authority but sowed the seed for future regret. I then told them something of prominent Negroes that they might have the lives and achievements of some of their own race to inspire them to greatness, but ended by stressing most forcefully the need for obedience. Met Miss Estes, one of the teachers. Invited me to her home.

After lunch called upon Rev. Harrell, a small, pompous, slightly grey-haired man, pastor of First Baptist Church. Was eager to help me. When I asked him for a few facts about his life, Dr. Harrell took down a volume of the *American Negro* and showed me a chapter concerning his life and achievements together with his picture. Seems to be fairly liberal in his attitude toward amusements. Also well-educated in comparison to most of the Negro preachers here. Told me he would like to build a new church but the less intelligent of his congregation oppose it. The more affluent and enlightened members have moved to a better residential section, and the present site of the church is unfavorably located for them. They, of course, want the church moved into a more desirable neighborhood—that is, closer to their homes. While the divergent opinions of these two groups threaten to "split" the church, Rev. Harrell diplomatically "sits on the fence," seeking to hold his congregation together. He deplores the "splitting" of churches, and advocates a Baptist Conference as the only means of preventing it. Aided by giving me much information about Suffolk and its Negro churches. I appreciated his spirit of cooperation. Told him Dr. Wesley was bringing Dr. Woodson here to speak next Monday. He considered it excellent and offered to throw open his church for the meeting.

Thanked him and promised to notify him when I ascertained definitely whether Dr. Woodson was coming, and whether Dr. Wesley would accept his kind offer to use his church.

Rev. Harrell is also quite active in the community. He told me that he founded the Phoenix Bank here. He also teaches Latin and Bible at Nansemond High School. He gives his services *gratis*. Poor Southern students! No wonder they lag so far behind Northern students. Generally, they do not have properly prepared teachers to instruct them, because of the segregated educational system.

Finally succeeded in interviewing Rev. Gladney, pastor of the only A.M.E. church in town. The latter is a frame build- ing, seating about 250. Is debt-free. According to Rev. Gladney, he has 280 members, all active. I remarked that such was unusual; active members rarely exceed 60 percent of the membership. Gladney replied that he did not count inactive members. Has Young People's Society of 70 members. I was agreeably surprised to learn that it is non-denominational. Anyone can join. Rev. Gladney appears to be doing an effec- tive work among young people. Has literary and other pro- grams for them. Has $500 in the treasury. Gladney says they expect to build a brick church. I suggested they build a com- munity center. One is badly needed and would be feeder for church members. Gladney agreed it would be.

I later found out that Gladney had served as pastor of a church in Abingdon, Virginia. Knew Sophronia Harris, whom I met in Bluefield last summer. Gave Mrs. Gladney her address. Rev. and Mrs. Gladney told me that a Rev. [Howard S.] Hardcastle, a white pastor, might give me his views con- cerning the Negro Church. Gladney offered to call him for me. I promised to call Mrs. Gladney to find out whether the Rev. would meet me.

Coming home, found Mr. Peele. Offered to take me out to help me secure information. Told me to see a Rev. [William A.] Cobb. I did and secured valuable information from him. Mr. Peele invited me to go to Nansemond High School, the Negro high school for the county, to see a play of some kind. I had planned to call on Ira Skeeter. Promised him I would go, however. While he went to Saratoga, I called on Ira. Found her correcting papers. Resembles Marguerite, her sister. Very pleasant. Invited me to go out with her tomorrow evening. Would send brother to notify me. Met Ovieda, her fat, little sister.

Hear there is a "Skeetertown" here. Populated chiefly by Skeeters who have inter-married. Quite a dangerous thing, provocative of insanity, I understand. (Marguerite had told me her father left Skeetertown and married outside the "clan.")

Returned, found Mr. Peele awaiting me. The play was nothing, and to make it worse, it was preceded by a series of hymns led by a seemingly illiterate Baptist minister from Portsmouth. I noticed the look of disgust upon Huskerson's face. A prize was to be given to the neatest dressed woman and the most ragged man. Mr. Huskerson called upon me to present the prizes—a dollar to each winner. The woman won by mistake, or because the judges could not see, for though none of the women were models, the neatest, in my opinion, was a lady in blue. A good night wasted, but I suppose all such experiences make up life. Told Huskerson about Woodson's probable visit here. He thought either the school or the First Baptist Church acceptable. He was certain people, if they were interested, would go to hear Woodson wherever he spoke. Some would not go at all, regardless of where, or how many times, he spoke.

Quite cold today.

Tuesday
April 17
1928

Had my first experience today of interviewing the Southern white man. Found him cordial, polite, and just the same as the Northern man, except for the single exception that he would forget and say "nigger" in referring to colored people. Called upon "Col." [Richard L.] Brewer, a lawyer. Seems that every white man is a "Colonel." Southerners like it. I don't mind addressing them as "Colonel," if I can wheedle out of them the information I desire. That is the way the old time Negro secured so many favors from the white man. He feeds upon the latter's vanity, bows reverently, obeisantly, before "Mr. Charley" to make him think he is the greatest man in the world. Poor Negro! He does not fool the white man, for the latter takes tenfold from him; as for the white man, he is deluded into believing that the Negro "loves" him. Yet that same genuflecting "darkey" would be his worst enemy were their respective situations reversed.

Col. Brewer was out. I called upon Lawyer [S. Edward]

Everett. Middle-aged and Southern through and through. His Southern drawl is characteristic of the people here—singular, lazy. I heard him conversing with his secretary before I entered his office, and had I not seen either, from their expression I would have guessed that both were Negroes. Such provincialisms as "taters," "down yonder," "ah reckon," and "deed ah" brought to my ears a decidedly Southern twang. Never having approached one of these "Colonels" before, I met him just as I would any other man. Since he was a lawyer, I addressed him accordingly. He was affable, talkative, willing to give his opinion as he saw it. Did not believe there was any real difference between the Negro and white churches. If any difference existed, he stated, it was that the Negro infused more emotion and "spirit" into his devotions than white people. Everett believed that the Negro preacher was doing fully as much for the Negro as the white pastor for his group. Negro ministers, he added, were active in charitable work. Yes, there had been some interracial cooperation. He had even officiated at a colored church and had lifted the collection. Told me he had felt proud to do so. On the whole, his replies were quite favorable to the Negro church. Yet I wondered whether his sentiments were genuine, whether he was careful not to say anything derogatory concerning the Negro church because it might injure his practice among Negroes, or whether he was sincere in his convictions, but did not really *know* the Negro's Church. He believed in the old cliché that Negro church members made more dependable and honest employees than nonchurch members. Told me he once gave one of his workers some money to buy groceries and the fellow walked three miles to his office in order to return his change of 5 cents. Sounds like one of those fairy stories about Abraham Lincoln. One of his tenants (a Negro woman) came in. He permitted me to use his desk to fill out her questionnaire. Mr. Everett is the first white man I have interviewed here. Although somewhat paternalistic in his attitude to Negroes, he impressed me favorably.

From lawyer Everett, called upon Col. Brewer, Speaker of the House of Representatives, whose office is just across the hall. Was not in. Neither was Lieut. Governor [Junius E.] West, an insurance man, at his office on Main Street. Left a questionnaire with his secretary.

Stopped at Mr. [Luther] Colden's, who owns the largest barber shop in town. Has lunch room, rest room, and kitchen in the rear, and a large auditorium upstairs. Talked with him for at least one and a half hours. Believes that the Negro church is "sleeping," that the immorality of the ministers is to blame for bad conditions in the Negro community. Thinks the greatest need of the church is trained ministers. Criticized Rev. Harrell as pusillanimous and vacillating. Has outlived his usefulness, Colden thinks. Is a "yes" man. (Harrell had already admitted that he seeks to please all factions.) Literate and better economically circumstanced members of First Baptist Church desire to move. Older ("Shouters") members wish to remain at present site. Colden believes that the church is badly located for its largest group of members. Naturally, since Colden belongs to the "have" group, he thinks the church *should* be moved. However, Reverend Harrell probably realizes that the main support of the church will come from the *masses*, not from the *elite* of his congregation. Therefore, he does nothing.

Met a Rev. [Tyler F.] Fenner in the barber shop. An old man who resigned his church in January. Offered to take me to ministers' conference. I gladly assented. What a pitiful spectacle! To witness these benighted men who are seeking to lead our people. About seven were present. Rev. Powell, a storekeeper who manifested considerable common sense, presided, but the entire average intelligence of their group could not have been much above the third grade. The ministers spent three hours in useless talking that, to my mind, was of no real benefit to them. One old man, chewing tobacco with great gusto, with brown rivulets of juice running out the corners of his toothless mouth, and arrayed as if he had just left the plow or the feeding of his hogs, repeatedly interrupted the meeting by inarticulate and nonsensical comments. The strain upon the English language was terrific. So great was the havoc wrought thereon that several times I wanted to laugh outright, but was forced to restrain myself even though I nearly choked trying to do so. Rev. [Willis T.] Faulk, of the Christian Church, who, I believe, with education could develop into an excellent minister, pled for more cooperation between the churches for the protection of the ministry, by eliminating denominationalism.

Later, Rev. [William R.] Taylor introduced me. I told the ministers the work in which I was engaged and asked them to cooperate by filling out questionnaires for me. Everything was going splendidly until certain suspicions, aroused possibly by my being an outsider, arose among the members. A man who considered his knowledge and experience vastly superior to the others' rose to ask who was behind me in this work, which entailed the expenditure of large sums of money. I replied that the Institute of Social and Religious Research of New York City, together with the Association for the Study of Negro Life and History, were its sponsors. Aha! He could see some ulterior motive in the whites aiding such an enterprise. All the information I sought concerning the Baptists, he went on, could be got from the Baptist Publishing Co. It was already collected. I was somewhat exasperated, but I answered, saying that this information could not be utilized by us: (1) because we could not take another's word for our information, but must hear and see for ourselves; (2) that the material to which he alluded, even if published this year, was already out of date, the data for such having been collected over the period of a year; (3) our study concerned the contemporary church, and the only practical, scientific fact-gathering method for our study lay in interviews etc.; and, finally, (4) that most Negro church groups, especially Baptist, were notoriously poor keepers of records. He sat down, more silenced, I believe, than convinced. But he had infused such a spirit of suspicion in the members around him that four ministers refused to fill out questionnaires.

After the meeting had adjourned, one Rev. [William] Turner, an insurance man, asked me the same questions as my former inquisitor, saying he could discern a hand behind this study. I realized that he had been influenced by his colleague. However, possessing a higher degree of intelligence than the average minister there, he soon accepted my explanation. I asked him the name of the minister who had objected so strongly to the study. He replied, it was Rev. Ferguson, an Evangelist, who had travelled all over America and part of Africa. I thought he was quite stupid for all his travel. While I was talking with Rev. Turner outside the church, Rev. Ferguson came up. He joined in the conversation, having first shaken hands with me. He is a tall, peculiar-looking individual, with an air of importance. His hair was curly, closely cropped, cut to simulate a wig. He reminded me of an Indian. I took his measure morally, very quickly, for he was so interested in every girl or woman who passed that most of the conversation escaped him. It was "Who is that woman, Rev.?," or "That's a good looking sister," while his eyes sparkled. My dislike for him now turned to disgust.

Left Rev. Turner. Stopped at office of Lieut. Governor West. He was in. West was of medium height, stockily built, with white hair—although, obviously, not an old man. He received me graciously. Asked if someone who "knew" the Negro better could not fill out the questionnaire. Assured him that no one probably "knew" the Negro better than he. Then, too, I told him of the weight his opinion would have. Agreed to do so. I am to call for it Friday.

After supper Mr. Peele took me to East Washington Street, where I obtained questionnaires from Lawyer [J. H.] Fulcher, Dr. [Archie R.] Fleming, and Mr. [W. H.] Crocker, brother of the real estate dealer. Very kind of Mr. Peele. Does everything possible to forward my work, as well as for my comfort.

Returned home at 8:30. Dressed. Went to Miss Ira Skeeter's. Very charming girl. Chatted with her a while, then went over to Miss Moody's. Remained there till 12:30. Enjoyed myself. Went home. Received letter from Helen [Grinage?], notes with questionnaire and letter from Dr. Wesley.

Wednesday
April 18
1928

Arrived at Nansemond High School at 9 a.m. to speak to the assembly. Tried in my talk to encourage the students to prepare themselves for some useful work in life. Spoke upon achievement. Gave what I considered the steps to it: Inspiration, or the vision of what one wishes to do or to be, then consecration in preparing one's self for that goal. Then, when success ultimately comes, it should be used, not selfishly, but for the uplift of one's fellow men. Cited examples of Toussaint L'Ouverture, Frederick Douglass, and Edison. Told them of work of Association for Study of Negro Life and History. Was well received, I thought. It was so cold, though, I shivered while speaking. Mr. Huskerson, who sat behind me, must have been amused. However, those in front did not realize it, because I stood behind the podium.

Went to the various rooms afterwards and distributed questionnaires. Received some very stimulating answers, although Rev. Gladney, who teaches Latin and English here, tried to, and actually did, tell the students what to write in answer to some questions. For instance, when I looked over the questionnaires of those students in his Latin class, response to the question: "What is your belief about Christianity?," all had the same answer, "Christ is Divine." It provoked me that this man of the Gospel would encourage these youthful students to falsify by giving *his* opinion as their own and also by stifling in them the impetus to original thought. However, Mrs. Huskerson and I soon destroyed the result of his influence by having the students answer that question afresh. For what has the divinity of Christ to do with the tenets of Christianity?

Going into another class, I found the same answer on the papers of some of the students regarding that particular question. Seeing a reply that struck me not only as showing originality, but also of comprehending the entire scope of Christianity, I held up the paper before the class. "Listen," I said, "to the best reply to the question, 'What is your belief about Christianity?.' Some of you no doubt have been influenced either by what has been told you, or by someone else's answer, for I note that there are several identical answers: 'Christ is Divine.' It is doubly misleading, first, because the definition is faulty, and secondly, because sentiments have been expressed as yours which are not yours, and hence constitute a falsehood. Were I, say, a Confucianist who desired to change his faith, and asked what your religion was and in reply received such information, I should never relinquish my own religion, regardless of how little I had, or how faulty it had proved, for the definition 'Christ is Divine' tells nothing of what Christianity really is." "Now," I said, "listen to this answer," and I read: " 'Christianity really is Love and will save all.' That, in my opinion," I remarked, "embraces the real essence and motive of Christianity. I cannot easily conceive of divinity, but I do know what love is." Of course, Gladney, the culprit, was profuse in sanctioning my statements. "Oh, yes," he responded, "Mr. Greene is correct." (Had I my way, however, no preacher would teach in the public schools.)

The essence of the students' replies to the questionnaire was contained in their answers on dancing, card playing, attending movies, etc.

About 85 per cent declared that their churches forbade such amusements. Generally, they did not approve of the attitude of the Church on diversion. Asked if this affected their attitude towards the Church, they responded "Yes."

Evidently, the ministry is not a popular vocation for these youth. The question, inquiring of the boys whether they planned to study for the ministry, brought mostly negative replies. Some said the salary was too small, or that they desired some other profession. Asked would they marry a minister, most of the girls returned emphatic "*No's.*" Why? Generally, ministers would curtail their pleasure.

The girls ranged from 16 to 20. The average age for high school students here seems higher than in New England. The average age for a high school graduate in New England is 17. It is not wholly the students' fault. The segregated system is to blame. The faculty is weak. With the exception of Mr. and Mrs. Huskerson and Miss Phrame, who teaches music, no one else has a right to be on the faculty. Mr. Huskerson is a former engineer who built roads in Brazil. He built the high school virtually single-handed, although he still suffers from the ravages of malaria. He takes quinine tablets regularly.

Secured about 80 questionnaires in all. Highly pleasing. Mr. Huskerson was amused at the action of Gladney. Vows he will get rid of all ministers as teachers at the school. Told of woeful weakness of the English Department under Gladney. I promised to speak to students on Shakespeare and Milton next week.

Had lunch at Huskerson's, following which he took me downtown, where I met Rev. Staley of the Christian Church, white. He is a kindly old gentleman of distinguished appearance and enjoys the distinction of being the only man in Suffolk who wears a silk hat. Mr. Huskerson introduced me. Told him my mission. Consented readily to give me whatever information he could. Told me of sterling qualities of some colored people whom he knew and "loved." Gave an instance of the confidence which he reposed in an old colored woman here. Last Saturday night, a Negro knocked at his door and informed him that Aunt ——— needed $7.00. Staley gave it to him, only to find out later that the woman had sent for no money. She, however, fearing lest her son, who lived ten miles away, might be guilty, went into the country and brought him before Staley as proof that it was not he. Staley was convinced that one who knew of her good reputation with him had taken advantage of it to defraud him of $7. That is an example, he mused, of a person's reputation being too good. Showed his vindictive spirit towards a bad "nigger" when he suggested that the culprit should be forced to work on a chain gang. Quite a talkative old man. Gave him two questionnaires, one for himself and one for Rev. Hardcastle. Told him I would call for them Saturday.

Went back to school with Mr. Huskerson. Called upon Rev. Low, the pastor of the Apostolic Church. He is a carpenter by trade. Says the tenets of his church forbid laziness. (Good denomination, I'd say, for all Negroes to join.) Has small church of about 50 members. Fundamentalists. Members interpret Bible literally.

Called upon Rev. [Edward] Evans of the Sanctified Church. This man is a bricklayer. Believe he is more proficient at former than at pastoring. Is woefully ignorant. Has a handful of followers.

Later called upon Rev. [Thomas] Johnson, pastor of Pine Street Baptist Church and principal of the East Suffolk

County School. He is the most enlightened minister I have met so far. Of medium height, middle aged, heavy set, dignified in appearance, and, without a doubt, better trained than any of the Negro ministers whom I have met here. I have been told that he frowns upon emotionalism in the church. Told me there were too many churches. Blamed the illiteracy of the ministers for bad conditions. Told me of his vain attempt to start a playground. He now has a boy's organization called the Knights of Christ's Kingdom, who are recruited chiefly from pool rooms and whose ages vary from 16 to 18. Johnson advocates a combination of churches. Tried to get Tynes Street Baptist Church to unite with his, but failed. Both church groups in part were responsible: Johnson's, because no provision was made for old Anderson Boone, for 30 years pastor of Tynes Street Church; and the latter congregation, because they opposed the Pine Street congregation as being too "dickty."

Johnson is in advance of most churches here. Holds Junior church every Sunday morning. Preaches to children for fifteen minutes. (Children certainly need juvenile sermons. In my opinion, they get little, if anything, from the regular services. How can they, when most adults don't?)

On the way home, stopped at Lieut. Governor West's office. West is a middle-aged man of medium height and stocky stature. Either was, or affected to be, busy. Told me he did not know anything about Negro churches. Told him all I desired was his opinion. Asked me to come for it Friday. Col. West seems to be the type of man who, though he treats the Negro with due respect, does so with an air of condescension. But so long as I accomplish my purpose, I can overlook that temporarily.

After dinner Mr. Peele took me to see some of the Negro businessmen—Mr. [Eugene] Boykins, the undertaker; Mr. Archer, the realtor; Drs. [Daniel C.] Fleming, [John] Pierce, and [Ederton] Rance; Mr. [John W.] Richardson, the banker [Phoenix Bank of Nansemond]; and others. Their questionnaires had much in common. They blamed the ministry and desired a better trained pastorate and more practical sermons.

Later went to Mrs. Finch, aunt of Miss Skeeter, where I not only spent an enjoyable evening but, in addition, secured two very thoughtful questionnaires.

Spoke at 9 a.m. to the students of the county school in East Suffolk. Teachers and students expressed their approbation. Rev. Johnson seemed to be gratified.

Thursday
April 19
1928

Later, I secured about 40 questionnaires from the pupils of the 7th and 8th grades. They average in age from 15 to 18. Quite a high average for grammar school, but then these pupils are the victims of segregation and do not have New England scholastic opportunities.

From Dr. Johnson's school, I called upon Rev. [Arthur] Wood, the only A.M.E.Z. [African Methodist Episcopal Zion] minister in the town. He lives on Division Street next door to the Church. Only church here that owns a parsonage. He entertains some splendid ideas. Rev. Wood blames the ministers in part for bad conditions. Not dedicated to their work. Believes there are too many churches. Feels two large Baptist Churches, one Methodist, one Christian, and one Episcopalian would be sufficient for the needs of the community. I agree that his basic idea is sound. However, I believe that even that number is too many. The population, by race, is almost equally divided, and the whites have only one Baptist, two Methodist, one Episcopalian, one Christian, and one Catholic church here.

Rev. Wood believes that the Sunday School should be organized upon the same basis as the public school. Also believes teachers ought to be trained and compensated for their services. His is most advanced sentiment on this subject I have yet heard from any Negro minister. He scored the petty rivalries between the colored ministers. Stated that during his one-year tenure here, he had invited every colored pastor to speak at his church, but had received similar offers from but two of them. With Rev. Faulk of the Christian Church and Rev. Johnson of Pine Street Baptist Church, Rev. Wood started a religious survey of Suffolk, the prime purpose of which was to induce the people here to attend some church. Most of the ministers refused their support. The people, while admitting the necessity of the survey, considered the time unseasonable, feeling that the traditional August Revival would be the most opportune time for it. The survey, of course, failed to accomplish the results that the sponsors had hoped for; nevertheless, it was at least a start in the direction of united interdenominational endeavor. As such, it also marked a milestone in the development of interchurch cooperation among Negroes in this community.

Rev. Wood, likewise, is a firm advocate of an organized Baptist Church in order to prevent "splits" from increasing inordinately the number of Baptist congregations. Every discerning individual who beholds Baptist Churches springing up overnight like mushrooms cannot help but applaud such a suggestion. In fact, many of the better educated Negroes believe such an organization must come in order to render Negro Baptist churches more efficient in the performance of their duties.

I must say that Rev. Wood's ideas impressed me favorably. He is not what one might style a formally educated man. He has had no theological training, but, evidently, he is a man who has supplemented a large vision with considerable reading. His views upon young people were especially interesting. He would build community centers where youth could have their amusement under church supervision. In his opinion, the church at present does not offer sufficient attraction to youth, therefore is in danger of dying at the roots.

Arriving home about 4 p.m., I found a letter from Dr. Woodson, who was scheduled to speak at Nansemond High School Wednesday evening, April 25. His communication authorized me to make arrangements for him according to my letter to Dr. Wesley—that is, for either Monday or Tuesday night at First Baptist Church. I was in a quandary. Should I arrange the program for First Baptist or for Nansemond High School? Mr. Huskerson, principal of Nansemond, had received word from Dr. Wesley on Tuesday to arrange for Dr. Woodson at his school. I did not want to cause friction between Mr. Huskerson and Rev. Harrell, although I believe the former too big a man to stoop to anything so petty. Furthermore, Huskerson had gone to the trouble of having tickets and programs printed for Wednesday. I rushed to the Booker T. School first, informed Professor Howe of the change of date, and asked that he announce it in the local paper tomorrow. Mr. Peele took me then to Nansemond, where I found Mr. Huskerson. We would have time, he assured me, to change the date of the program, although tickets were perhaps ready to be printed. The next thing now is to placate Rev. Harrell, who had expected Dr. Woodson to appear at his Church. Believe we could have done better there, since it is more centrally located. However, I hope for the best.

Called upon Mrs. [Betty S.] Davis, the child welfare nurse. Miss Skeeter arranged the interview for me. I had seen some shocking living conditions and desired to know how general they were among the Negro masses. Feeling that my visiting homes alone would cause more or less suspicion, I asked if she would take me along on some of her professional calls. She readily consented. Told me of terrible conditions among Negroes in Jericho and Saratoga—suburbs of Suffolk—1–2 rooms, filthy and full of uncared-for children, who were little more than skin and bones, the result of malnutrition. Related story of home with one room and a jump (attic room) in which lived 43 persons of all sexes and ages. Said she went there one day and found the grandmother ill in bed with two babies beside her and 23 children sitting about upon the floor.

Told me of another home which she visited last July, where three half-naked women ironed before a fireplace, about which sat no less than 15 irons. The room was like a furnace, she declared, making it impossible for them to wear more than enough clothing to cover their extreme nudity. These reports, plus my own observations, make me suspect that McKinley's reports need a little checking. [According to Woodson's annual report for 1928, John J. McKinley, working as an investigator for the Association for the Study of Negro Life and History, studied the social and economic conditions of Negroes in North Carolina, South Carolina, Georgia, and parts of Virginia.]

Stopped by Miss Estes'. Cute little school teacher. Enjoyed chat with her. She took me to her aunt's, a Mrs. Hunter, where I spent a few moments. Called upon Miss Skeeter, to thank her for securing interview for me with Mrs. Davis. Stayed there an hour longer than I had planned.

All colored Suffolk is agog today over the teachers' convention which meets here tomorrow in Booker T. School. I saw enough potential potato salad to feed 800 people. Teachers and pupils were assisting in preparing the food.

O yes, received a letter from Carolyn Worrell today. Informs me she will be here tomorrow. Have not seen her since last August. It dawned upon me last Sunday that she lived in Portsmouth (about 20 miles away), and I sent a letter to the High School where she told me she was teaching. Was quite surprised as well as gratified to hear from her so soon.

[6] Suffolk, Virginia, and Environs (Continued)

Interviewed Col. [Richard L.] Brewer, Speaker of the Virginia House of Representatives, today. Very liberal and kindly old man. Received me cordially enough. Thought Negro Church improving; could see progress. Positive that influence in community was salutary. Saw no difference between white and colored churches so far as worship was concerned. Said if one were taken into better class of Negro church blindfolded and compelled to listen to the services, he could not tell whether he was in a white or colored church. Thought some Negro church members good; others indifferent. Negro a little more religious and emotional than the whites. Of course, he added, the colored church member makes the more desirable employee than the unchurched. He observed that although Negroes contributed more freely to their churches than white people did to theirs, the Negro had too many churches. The greatest need of the Negro church today, he believed, is trained ministers. He stated the congregations are far ahead of the pastors. I was forced to agree with him. In his opinion, the only difference between the races was one of education.

"Educate the Negroes," he said, "and the problem disappears, because there develops, as a result, mutual understanding." As example, cited misunderstanding on the part of Negroes during typhoid epidemic here. Everyone had to be vaccinated. Illiterate Negroes refused to take the needle, fearing the white folks were trying to "fix" them. Mrs. [Betty S.] Davis, the Negro nurse, told me the same thing last evening. [Lieut. Gov.] West thought the South best place for Negroes because the white man "understands them best here and is their best friend." (That may be true, but the facts prove otherwise. At any rate, I'll take the North for my place of residence.) Says Negroes have trouble only with lower elements of whites, who are largely uneducated. I asked him whether whites considered all Negroes alike. "Certainly not," he answered, "we make distinctions between classes, even as you do." But it is the mass of the whites who do not. His private opinions, as expressed to me, signify virtually nothing, for he could not afford to state them publicly. Yet, I believe there are many broad-minded Southern men who might feel kindly disposed toward Negroes, but who must yield to the racial sentiment of their environment in so far as things Negroid are concerned. Of all the white men here, Mr. Brewer, I understand, perhaps is the best liked by the Negroes of Suffolk. He is a member of the Christian Church, a church worker himself, a large contributor to Negro churches, and also a lender of money for the building of Negro homes, for which he doubtless exacts a high interest. I count it a pleasure to have met him. My interview lasted for fully two hours. Incidentally, Brewer also owns a real estate and jewelry business.

Secured questionnaires from Lieut. Gov. West. He is an aspirant for the Governorship of Virginia. Believes Negro Church in good condition "for the race." He also believes that there are different race levels and standards, with the Negro at the bottom. Thinks the Negro Church differs from the white Church because *Negroes* are *different*. Although white churches, in Col. West's opinion, improve the colored ones by contact, this influence Mr. Brewer discounts as negligible. He [West] thinks the Negro's religion is spiritual only "if he really has it." He disagrees with Mr. Brewer by denying that the Negro connects morals with his religion. I should have to lean in West's direction, for the Negro generally does not reconcile religion and morals. Religion to him generally is some high-flown spiritual or abstract thing to be shouted at, prayed at, and sung at, but not to be applied to daily living. It is for Sunday only and just for the length of time he is in church. Unlike Brewer, too, West does not feel that being a church member makes the Negro more efficient or dependable as a workman. In fact, he knows of but one exception. Thinks, on the other hand, that the Negro Church should impart higher standards of honesty and loyalty by the Negro worker towards his employer. I presume West would like to see the old slave regime in operation again, where all deference and obedience, body and soul, was given to the white man by the Negro. Disgusting!

Returned to Mr. Peele's. The school grounds across the street were filled with automobiles and teachers who are attending the Tidewater Teacher's Conference. Walked over to try to locate Miss [Carolyn] Worrell. Passed her on the street. Miss McDowell, a classmate of mine from Howard University, called to me as I did so. Then Miss Worrell grasped my hand, blushingly remarking that I did not desire to recognize her. We were old pals; my sister-in-law's niece. Almost became a match. Met her first in Connecticut in 1921. Saw her again in 1923, then in 1926. Saw her last in August, 1927, at Petersburg, Virginia. She is now teaching in the High School at Portsmouth, Virginia. Sought to persuade me to come to her home for the week-end. Said her mother told her to bring me back with her. Her mother has been in poor health for a couple of years.

Spent about 10 minutes with her while she ate lunch. She then went to a departmental meeting, promising to see me later.

Met Mrs. [Lillian] Huskerson, Miss [Hortense] Phrame, and Miss Jordan. Went to a Language Conference with them. Ways and means were being discussed of increasing the students' proficiency in grasping foreign languages. A Mr. Lee proposed to improve it by giving "exams," say of 10 questions, 5 easy and 5 more difficult. He believed that the bright students would not only answer the 5 easy, but also 3 of the other five, giving them 80%. The more backward, he believed, might answer two of the more difficult questions, plus the first five, for a percentage of 70. Most disagreed. Seemed to be unable to determine what caused students so much trouble in grasping a foreign language. I took the liberty to attribute it to the fundamental lack of knowledge of technical English grammar. Most high school students cannot define gerunds, gerundives, participles, cannot decline nouns, and know practically nothing about conjugation of verbs. I cited the case of a New York City College Negro student who found Spanish difficult. Asked me to aid her and then upon investigation disclosed to me the fact that she did not know English.

Went to the City Auditorium for the afternoon session of the Conference, where Lieut. Gov. West and Dr. [W. E.] Starke of Hampton were to be the chief speakers.

When I arrived, Mrs. Cashion White (Child Welfare Nurse) was speaking. Told of ravages of tuberculosis here. County in which Suffolk is located has highest tuberculosis rate in the United States. Over 25,000 active cases in Virginia. Highest among Negroes. May be many more unaccounted for. Urged plenty of air, milk, rest, and good food to combat it.

The Lieut. Gov.'s speech resolved itself into just a flow of words. A lot of "hokum." Poor fellow, he has neither eloquence, nor wit, nor brain. Made a pitiable muddle of his speech. Advocated that Negroes stay in Virginia. Lauded state as most progressive, richest, and most fertile in its production of great men. A lot of "bunk" to relegate his speech to vulgar parlance.

Dr. Starke of Hampton was an improvement. His subject was "Aren't Folks Queer!" He spoke upon the need of appreciating the other fellow's point of view, with referrals to the teachers in regard to the eccentricities of their pupils. He exhorted teachers to study their pupils' hopes, aspirations, and also their state of mind at their age, in order to best use those methods which would be beneficial to each student. His tone was conversational, easy, yet filled every corner of the room. His wit was ready but not offensive. Everyone applauded vociferously when he finished.

A band from Huntington High School of Newport News furnished the music, and a quartet from the same school sang delightfully.

Miss Phrame, teacher of music at Nansemond High School, was to have rendered a violin solo, but the petty antics of Prof. [Edward D.] Howe of Booker T. Washington School prevented it. He neglected to provide a piano for her accompanist, Miss Jordan. I was disappointed, for knowing Miss Phrame to be a graduate of the New England Conservatory of Music, I had anticipated quite a delectable number from her.

Professor Nurse, who has a grievance against Nansemond High School, refused to announce Dr. Woodson's appearance there from the platform. Exasperated, since the people were beginning to leave, I prevailed upon Mr. [L. P.] Palmer [of Newport News], President of the Conference, to do so.

Met Miss Skeeter (Ira). Walked home with her. She introduced me to a Miss Langston, who teaches in Whaleyville. I had promised to take Miss Skeeter to Colden's Auditorium. Don't know why I thought it was free. Cost 35 cents per person. I bought tickets, although Mr. [H. P.] Reid demurred.

Enjoyable evening. Band played well for High School students. Young fellow did acrobatic stunts. Picked up chair with back, walked on his hands, and while lying upon his back, picked up a glass of water with his knees, placed it upon his forehead, assumed an upright position with the glass and contents still balanced upon his forehead, lay down, and with his knees replaced the glass from his forehead upon the floor. He received much-merited applause. Another young man gave three excellent imitations of an Italian.

Took Miss Skeeter home at 9:50. Chatted till 10:45.

Received special delivery from Carolyn [Worrell] at breakfast time. Related how sorry she had been not to see me before leaving for Portsmouth. Said mother expected me to return with her. Wanted me to come over for week-end. Asked me to telegraph. Don't know what I shall do. Wanted to go to county churches.

Saturday
April 21
1928

Went to have check cashed. Called upon Drs. [Richard] Bland, [John] Pierce, [Daniel] Fleming, and a Mr. Bingham for their questionnaires. Secured all but last two. Received one from Dr. [Edwina Mae] Reeves, female dentist.

Met a Mr. Robert Williams in the Phoenix Bank. Owns more property than any colored man in Suffolk. Widely travelled. Knows Dr. E. P. Roberts, outstanding New York physician, Eugene Kinckle Jones, ex-Secretary of National Urban League, and host of other prominent Negro men. Had fine chat of $1\frac{1}{2}$ hours with him. Williams is a stockholder of the bank. Told me Negro businesses in Durham, North Carolina, are interlocked and colored people's money circulates through Negro banks and building and loan associations, but ultimately lands in the Negro bank. Churches, lodges, wage earners, business and professional men, he continued, support the Negro banks there. All above factors account for success of Negro business in Durham. Not so here in Suffolk, he complains.

I had my first haircut today since March 30. Not pleased with it. Could not complain; my landlord, Mr. Peele, did it. Returned home with some placards announcing Woodson's appearance which Mr. Huskerson gave me. Bland wishes to take me to Portsmouth tomorrow. May go, although we (Mrs. Huskerson and I) had planned to work with four colored ministers at the school Tuesday evening in order not to offend any of them, thereby insuring the support of their congregations for Woodson's forthcoming talk here. I suggested Rev. [Willis T.] Faulk of the Christian Church, Rev. [Arthur] Wood of the A.M.E.Z. Church, Rev. [James A.] Harrell of First Baptist, and Rev. [Thomas] Johnson of Pine Street Church, respectively. All, we hope, will do a little, which will gratify their sense of importance and also yield a larger attendance, for Negro congregations generally follow the lead of pastors.

Sent mother fifteen dollars, also $15 to a Loan Co. in my home town. That debt is now reduced to $25, thank heaven! Received letters from Bertha [Baylor] and Helen [Grinage] today.

Attended Pine Street Church. Rev. [William] Turner spoke,
or he fumed, railed, and sang the church from this material,
temporal earth and placed church and members figuratively
down at the foot of the sanctified throne of God in that blissful
land of milk and honey. It was a shame, in my estimation, for a
businessman (Rev. Turner is an insurance agent during the
week) to give a congregation such spiritual "clap trap." I
brought nothing away from the service. Quite a few people
shouted and screamed, much to the amusement of the children, who could not keep from "grinning." Wretchedly
planned sermon, worse grammar, and no content. No wonder the Negro Church is losing those persons who could be its
best workers. Mr. [W. H.] Crocker assured me that some
Negro churches had better services than this. Of course!

Rev. Turner introduced me, asked me to say something.
Spoke upon Dr. Woodson and his achievements. Desired to
make his importance stand out so boldly that they would
come to hear him Tuesday night. Told things about his coming appearance. They seemed to be interested.

Called upon Dr. Bland. Is leaving for Portsmouth at 3.
Happy to hear I shall accompany him. Called upon Ira, who
lives across the street. Mother ill.

Left for Portsmouth at 3:15. Passed several colored farms
and churches on the way. Were pointed out to me by Mr.
Evans, barber and friend of Bland's, who accompanied us. We
passed bridge over Nansemond River, scene of near auto fa-
tality last Wednesday, when a large limousine, heavily laden
with teachers on the way to the conference at Suffolk, crashed
through the guard rail and hung perilously with its human
freight suspended over the river.

Reached Portsmouth only to find that Hobson Street was in
Truxton, a suburb.

Found Carolyn at home. She was surprised to see me.
Mother ill in bed. I spent over an hour chatting with her.
Bland promised to call for me at 6:30. At that time a Mr.
Johnson entered; later a Mr. Davy came in. Interesting fellow.
I left Mrs. Worrell to help entertain Mr. Johnson downstairs.
We enjoyed a stimulating discussion upon the church. All

gave personal opinions regarding it except me. All I did was gain the attitude of others.

We left for Suffolk at 10:30, with a Miss Harris, school teacher from North Carolina. She and Carolyn are buddies.

I kissed Carolyn goodbye. Miss Harris saw and twitted me about it, although she was in the car at the time and should have been looking elsewhere. Must visit Mrs. Worrell again before leaving Suffolk.

By the way, learned that Nannie [Hagans] was in Portsmouth. Asked Carolyn if she knew a Mrs. Smith. Did, but told me she was now in the hospital and her sister had come down from New York to see her. That sister, I knew, was Nannie. Shall see her when I visit Carolyn again.

Arrived home about 11:45 after a very delightful trip. Bland is so solicitous for my welfare. Hope I shall be in position soon to return some of these favors.

Peculiar weather. Warm, then rains, then clears up to darken and rain again.

Monday
April 23
1928

Received a telegram from Dr. Wesley this morning inquiring the date of Woodson's engagement here. I believed that was perfectly clear to both of them. Still Woodson might have changed the date without Wesley's knowledge. I hear he is quite willful.

Sent the following telegram to Wesley. "Engagement Tuesday night as per Woodson's instructions of April 18th." I hope that removed all doubts. My conscience is clear, for Woodson alone is to blame if any conflict of dates occurs. I still have his letter of April 18th as proof.

A very rainy day. It has rained intermittently now since Friday. Today the downpour was both heavy and prolonged. Could do little.

Met Mr. W. H. Crocker. He bewails the hard times here. Is a realtor of considerable prominence. Says creditors are pushing him and he may have to foreclose. Will give me interview tomorrow.

Took laundry to shop today.

Wanted to go to theater tonight. Started to take Miss Skeeter with me. Changed my mind and chatted with Mr. Peele. He has a large store of information. Told me of shocking conditions that obtained at Booker T. Washington colored school here, just across from his home. He complained of laxity of teachers as regards care and supervision of children. Latter danced in school after hours till 5:30. Janitor upstairs. Boys come around in cars, blow horns, and girls come out at recess and ride about with them. Instances of punishment of girls by male teachers were cited. He brought these grievances before the School League, made up of colored citizens. Discanted on inefficiency of Mr. Brown, a teacher here, for 40 years. Principal is a white man's Negro. A "Yes suh" man. Things were always in good shape. Would have had high school here for Negroes but for Brown, says Peele. Whites left him in because he would ask for nothing; Negroes because he had been teaching for such a long period. Woefully inefficient. Can't even keep order.

Howe, present Principal, is a little man. *Very little.* Opposes the building of public high schools for Negroes. Why? I don't even suppose he can tell. Huskerson could have had the job. Would not take it although more money and prompt payment assured him. Preferred to stay at Nansemond and develop that school according to his ideas. Howe is a man of 65, at least. Is inefficient. A high school graduate. Should not be principal. Another "Yes man."

According to the newspapers, Wilkins has flown across the North Pole. Did so yesterday. Now ice bound on island near Spitsbergen. First time feat has been accomplished. Nothing is impossible now. *Bremen* fliers still marooned on Greenly Island.[1]

Expecting Wesley and Woodson tomorrow.

1. Captain George H. Wilkins and Lieutenant Carl B. Eielson completed their Arctic polar flight on April 12, 1928. The flight from Alaska to Spitsbergen, a group of islands in the Arctic Ocean, took just over twenty hours. The men spent five days, however, on the island of Dead Man's Point, where they were forced to land because of a blizzard.

The German Junker plane *Bremen* left Baldonnel Airdrome in Ireland on April 12 on a transatlantic flight to Mitchell Field in New York. Captain Hermann Koehl and Commandant James E. Fitzmaurice of the Irish Free State Air Force were copilots. Baron Gunther von Huenefeld, the backer of the flight, was also aboard. The *Bremen*

Called upon Mrs. Davis at 9:30 a.m. She is the Colored Child Welfare Nurse here. Promises to take me with her to inspect some of the homes in Saratoga and Jericho in Nansemond County.

Spent most of the morning in Saratoga. This is a colored settlement and reflects it. There are no sidewalks; the streets are unpaved and, after the heavy rains of the last few days, were almost impassable. There is no sewage disposal system out here. Ditches, varying from one-half to a foot wide and about two feet deep, catch the water from the roadbed, which stagnates and gives rise to noisome odors. The stench of pig sties, cows, horses, and chickens combines with that of the ditches to make this section extremely unsanitary and unwholesome. This is one of the evils of segregation. Though Saratoga is technically a part of Suffolk, the "city fathers" evade any responsibility for conditions by refusing to incorporate it. Reason: It is a Negro community. Boston, Williamstown, and Philadelphia, all black areas, suffer likewise. Whites refuse to incorporate them within the city limits of Suffolk; therefore they have neither running water, paved streets, schools, nor other civic improvement. Saratoga does boast a county school, made possible by the combined endeavors of the county, Mrs. Ida Easter, and Julius Rosenwald, who gave $1200 toward its erection, which was probably as much as the school cost.

Wherever the Jew goes, business springs up; wherever the Negro settles, churches rise. In this little settlement of perhaps five hundred people, there are four colored churches, only one of which is worthy of the name. That is Lakeview Baptist Church, a small, neat-appearing, frame structure, located on Third Street. It apparently had been given but one coat of white paint, yet looked fairly representative of the churches of

---

crew was forced to land on Greenly Island in an icebound region just off the southern coast of Labrador. A Canadian relief plane reached Greenly on April 15; but the *Bremen* crew decided to wait for parts, repair their plane, and complete the flight. They finally gave up on this plan, abandoned the *Bremen*, and flew out in a relief plane. They arrived in Quebec on April 26 and a few days later reached New York City, where they "received the welcome that city reserved for heroes" (New York *Times,* May 1, 1928).

this community. The pastor, Rev. Sharp, I was told, lives in North Carolina. He holds services here once a month, then other itinerant pastors visit and carry on.

Our people will build churches, or so-called churches. Seems as if they delight in calling anything a church, so long as it has a cross at the top or a sign to that effect. Some of these churches would not even make a respectable chicken coop. But, as Kelly Miller says, and gloats in saying so, "Our people have a genius for religion." He might with more truth have said, "Our people have a genius for building churches." At least three of the five Negro Churches here apparently are standing by the Grace of God alone. One, the Antioch Christian Church, is a small, unpainted structure, the belfry of which leans at a crazy angle toward the southwest. Looks as if it might fall any moment. In the last stages of dilapidation.

A little hut that I passed, thinking it to be a deserted one-room house—if the latter term can be applied to anything so tiny—I was informed bore the imposing title of the First Baptist Church of Saratoga. To be sure, it looked to be the "first" one built and the first one to fall to pieces also.

The church contained only two windows—both on the same side. To make it more comical, a bell hung upon a pole in front of the building. A gentle wind, in my estimation, would blow the church over to Jericho—another little Negro section of Suffolk. On the same street stood the Wiggam Sanctified Church. Looked to me like a barn that had been overstuffed with hay and whose sides were about to burst asunder. Unpainted boards put on perpendicularly. Hardly had I ceased to contemplate this "imposing" structure when across the street I chanced to see a cross on top of a little hovel. Latter had been whitewashed. I dared not to believe that this, too, was a church. Our people would build churches, but, I bethought me, they had not yet arrived at the point where each family had its separate house of worship. Out of curiosity, I had to delve into this religious clannishness or exclusiveness. Entering the yard, saw the name of Reverend [Frank] Ford on the front door. I knocked. No one responded, though a little tot assured me the Reverend was at home. I started toward the

rear of the house and the unmistakable odor of pigs met me,
but I persisted till I saw a large black woman carrying a pan of
rats. I hailed her. Putting down her burden of rodents, she
returned me a cheery "good morning," ending with "God
Bless You." I inquired whether Rev. Ford was in. "Yes, he is
in the pig pen. Just cleaning it out." "The rats?" She had put lye
in corn for them last night. Had become a menace. I asked
what she intended to do with them since she had the rats so
carefully laid out in a large pan. "Oh, nothing." "Yes, that is
the 'Church of God and Saints of Christ,' and Rev. Ford is the
pastor." She called him. A man, past middle-age, pungent
with the odor of the pig sty, ambled over and shook my hand.

To my queries concerning the size of the church membership, cost of the church, etc., both answered that they had
"retired from the world." "Would have nothing to do with the
devil's work." Mine was the work of the devil. I attempted to
show them that this survey aimed to aid the well-being of the
people by correcting the faults of the church. Therefore, it *was*
God's work. They could not see the light in that way. The
woman then began to speak. Illiterate, but eloquent, she
quoted from *Jeremiah* and *Job* to show that their precepts could
not be followed. They believed "men would die and wake
not." Based her faith upon I Corinthians, XV: 51. "Behold!
We shall all not sleep but we shall be changed." She then had
me read from St. John I: 51, VI: 51; Ezekiel XVII: 27, 28, 29, 30
to prove that man will not die. Held Baptists and other orthodox denominations preaching wrong doctrine. Saw light 20
years ago, when husband was critically ill with influenza. Told
God, with Bible in her hands, to make manifest his sayings
that men should not die. Husband recovered. Started church
then. Have 25 members. Church cost about $250. Husband
receives no salary. (Of course, if the worshippers desire to
donate something, he would not offend by refusing it.) There
is no choir. Have Sunday School of 20 members. Rev. Ford
and wife are the teachers.

Poor Negroes! How can they prosper in worldly necessities
when such well-meaning, but ignorant, people stifle every
initiative for better living by inculcating such enervating doc-

trines in the guise of religion. They believe that one should shun all things of this earth. Their point of view can never be reconciled with that of the younger or more intelligent Negroes. As had been said many times, death alone can rid the Negro race of these well-meaning, but misguided, advocates of this pernicious doctrine. Don't believe that either Rev. Ford or his wife—she seemed more versed than he in the Scriptures—can be classed with that large band of predatory Negro ministers who prey upon a gullible and ignorant race for their own self-aggrandizement.

Went to the Minister's Conference, abetted by Rev. Turner. I asked the ministers to give over their most important meeting tonight, where they were to discuss "whether Eve or Adam was responsible for the first sin," in order to hear the famous Negro historian, Dr. Woodson. I pointed out that they could derive much spiritual and intellectual stimulation from the lecture of Dr. Woodson, which, as leaders, they might secure and then dispense to their people. I seemed to have carried them until an old man, Rev. Ferrier—who has no church—made an eloquent plea that they go along with their original plan. "The church is slipping," he shouted, "especially the Baptist church, and we ministers are to blame. We must get together. This man (meaning Woodson) might preach interdenominationalism. Now it is far more beneficial to us that we discuss our topic than hearing this man." I was dumbfounded but was saved by the Rev. [William A.] Cobb, who reminded his ministerial colleagues that they "could come together at any time to discuss, fuss, etc. Let us all turn out en masse," he concluded, "to hear this learned man tonight." His words took hold, and the discussion was postponed indefinitely.

Had an engagement with Mr. Crocker at 3:00. Reached there at 3:10. Mr. Crocker, Suffolk's leading Negro business man, sees the Church in a deplorable condition due to ignorance and lack of strong leadership. Finds the ministers immoral, untrained, ignorant, and selfish, lacking in civic sense. Says church has done very little for uplift of the Negro community. The ministers, Mr. Crocker added, catered to the masses; hence no progress can be made by the more intelligent group. (Minister knows where his suits, his coal, wood, automobile, etc. come from.) Thinks greatest need of colored church is trained ministers with ability to do things. Needs strong men, better Sunday Schools, practical sermons which one can apply to his daily needs. Also believes ministers should have the concern of the Negro community at heart, should be the leader in all things. They should not condemn worldly progress and uplift, nor harmless amusements, but should seek to obtain better schools, hospitals, wages, and living conditions for Negroes, also aid, abet, or even advocate Negro enterprise. In other words, the Negro Church must practice the social gospel. I agreed with Mr. Crocker in every detail.

From Mr. Crocker's went home. Drs. Woodson and Wesley had not yet arrived. Mr. Peele took me to the station, expecting they would arrive on the 6:10 train from Richmond. When they did not appear, I assured him they must be motoring. Mr. Huskerson also came to the station, looking worried. Desired to know whether he should secure extra seats for the people. I told him most assuredly that Woodson would be there.

Mr. Peele, meanwhile, took me to Kingsbridge, a part of Suffolk where Mr. Brown of Booker T. School has a farm. Quite a valuable piece of land, situated between two railroads. Old Brown is land-poor; mortgages, I hear, have practically eaten up the farm.

Went through Williamstown, a colored suburb. Homes sitting on the side of hills, in gullies; pumps not far removed from privies. No sewage system, no running water. Similar to the Saratoga section. Poor Negroes! Segregation is an insidious, vicious thing. Here in this disease-breeding area, it can only mean one thing—*elimination*.

Returned to Mr. Peele's. Found Woodson and Wesley had arrived. Had gone to the school. I started to dress. Engaged in it when they returned to Mr. Peele's.

Woodson is quite a comical fellow. I experienced that in New York last March when he took me to see *Porgy and Bess*.

Evidently someone had told him about Miss Skeeter (Ira), for he began teasing me about her.

Started for Nansemond High School at 8:30. Arrived there, learned that only a handful of people were present. Waited outside in the car until the crowd gathered. Rev. Terryman came over to shake hands with Woodson. Affected to know the latter intimately although he had only heard Woodson speak once. A conceited scoundrel. Don't care for him. Looks sly. Is quite fond of the fair sex, too.

Some 250 people had gathered by 9 o'clock. Mr. Huskerson acted as master of ceremonies. He would make a better mechanic. My, how he did wobble through the introduction of Wesley. Forgot all about announcing a violin solo by Miss Phrame. Poor lady had to do so herself.

Wesley was as eloquent as usual in introducing Woodson. Latter spoke generally on various aspects of Negro history and culture. Started off humorously. Cited his seeing a Negro leaning against a pole one day. Felt depressed for future of his race. Passing on, saw whites doing same thing. Felt greatly relieved. After all, no difference, he concluded, between the races. Pleaded for Negro enterprise. Urged cooperation on part of race in patronage of Negro business. Enjoined Negro business man, need of "square deal" with people. Urged the Negro to become familiar with his past in order to prepare for a more brilliant future. Condemned aping of white man unless we imitated his virtues. Gave illustrations of progress of black race. Among others cited Antar, Arabian poet and warrior. I was thrilled by his words. Not eloquent, but forceful, clear, and endowed with a sincerity which carried conviction. Woodson put his speech over "big." A collection of some $20.00 was raised.

An awkward silence ensued after Woodson finished. Huskerson looked straight ahead, not realizing that after the speaker had finished, some remarks are usually forthcoming from the master of ceremonies.

Rev. [Davis F.] Gladney and Rev. Johnson were to lift the collection. Gladney threw a cold and wet blanket over the opportunity of securing a reasonable collection by placing a dime upon the table as a starter. It was bad psychology. Wesley immediately addressed the people, stressing the monetary requirements of the Association and imploring their aid. Collected $20.00 or a little more. A far cry from $60.00 that I had promised Woodson from First Baptist. Don't believe Woodson was satisfied.

We had three copies of *Negro in Our History* by Woodson. A Mrs. Warren, wife of Dr. [Herbert] Warren, wanted to buy one but the price evidently made her change her mind. Many of the people came upon the platform to shake hands with Dr. Woodson.

Glad when the day was over. Wesley and I are roommates tonight.

Wednesday
April 25
1928

Mr. Huskerson arrived in his car for us before we had finished breakfast. He was to take us out to Holland and the surrounding farming community to show us the colored homes, farms, and churches.

We passed several insignificant frame churches on the road to Holland. Passing a farm on which stood a dilapidated house where a Negro woman and two children peered out of the only window visible, Dr. Wesley got out of the car and snapped the picture. I thought that the woman might view his doing so with ill humor, but she only grinned and waved to us.

A Mr. [T. L. G.] Walden, according to Mr. Huskerson, owns a general store in Holland, but we did not take time to stop there. What a wonderful farming country! Folks plowing or planting corn, cotton, peanuts, wheat, etc. Boys and girls plowing or planting. Little ramshackle, unpainted farm houses leaning crazily in the midst of a plowed field; little children playing about the house as the mothers did their chores while the father devoted his time to the farm. Dr. Wesley snapped pictures of farm houses and churches as we passed by them or as Mr. Huskerson pointed them out to us. We arrived in Holland (or shall I say four miles from Holland); there sat, practically in the woods, the only brick church owned by the Negroes in Nansemond County. It was an imposing edifice which would have done credit to any city. Marble pillars supported a portico over the door. The door of this remarkable country church was open. We entered. Its seating capacity I judged to be about 500 including the balcony. It had seven separate Sunday School rooms. Was heated by a stove. Had oil vapor lamps, but the general interior was one of beauty. An old Sunday School book showed that the number of pupils was about 135. This was the Mt. Sinai Baptist Church. Mr. Huskerson, when asked where the people who supported the church were, told us that they came from miles around. The church sits in the midst of the most prosperous staple crop section of Nansemond County. The Negro farmers in this vicinity are relatively well-to-do.

Eager to secure some information regarding the cost and membership of this Church, we inquired of a woman next door; but she could tell us very little, other than to estimate that the Church cost $24,800. Dr. Woodson humorously accosted her by asking whether lunch was ready, to which she replied in all seriousness, "No."

From the Church we called upon Mr. Walden, who owns a farm of 140 acres nearby. His home is a large, white building about a hundred feet from the roadside. Mr. Walden is about seventy years of age, whitehaired, yet hale and hearty.

According to him, there have been several Mt. Sinais. The first church on the present site, the original Mt. Sinai, was a brush tent. Later, a log-cabin was built as a home of worship, then a slab-top building. Following that was a "right nice" frame building, then the present brick structure. The money was raised among the church people. The Church cost $21,000. There is now a debt of $6,400; $2,400 was paid last year. At that rate, in less than three years the Church will be completely free of debt. Mr. Walden's figures for membership are about 500–600. The great bulk of them, he says, are children; the old folks are dying out.

Mt. Sinai, according to Mr. Walden, owes its origin to a Rev. I. Cross, Ph.D., to whom a memorial shaft is reared in front of the church, bearing the inscription: "Rev. I. Cross, born 1839, ordained 1876. For 40 years pastor of the Mt. Sinai,

Morning Star, and Piney Grove Churches. Died May 23, 1911. His favorite words: 'I am a sinner saved by Grace.'" He baptized more than 3,000 souls. The church was organized in 1868 by Rev. Cross and rebuilt in 1921 by Rev. L. J. Alexander, the present incumbent. The church has both piano and organ. The Sunday School has 122 pupils and 13 teachers. Under the trees in front of and to one side of the church was a roofed pavilion, which I presumed was used either as a picnic ground, or as a place for people to eat their lunches in summer after having traversed the long distance to the church.

Cross was born a slave about three miles from the Church. Went to school three months. Argued with teacher about the Scripture. Teacher did not know as much as he. Left. Built three churches in his lifetime. Pastor of all. Remained in all till he died in 1911. According to Mr. Walden, who is by no means illiterate, Rev. Cross, in his own way, could preach as well as anyone has ever heard.

There are no Methodist churches, curiously enough, in this vicinity. All the work on the church except the actual contracting was done by colored men of the church. Nothing donated but sand, which was hauled free of charge.

Other prosperous farmers in the community are Mr. Walden, Jr., J. H. Lewis, and Mr. Axum Holland.

Went to the County School not very far from Mr. Walden's. Nice brick building—a Rosenwald school. It has seven rooms, goes as high as second year High School. Rosenwald gave $1,500 to the building, four schools raised $2,000, and the County gave the materials for the building. The principal told us there is a domestic science as well as a vocational department. Will have 9 months of school next year. Naturally these students are all generally over age for these grades.

Went to see the Corinth Chapel Christian Church near Holland, located further in the woods. A large frame structure. Will seat 400. Has an organ. Heated by stove. The cornerstone reads: "Corinth Chapel Christian Church. Established 1868. New building erected 1918." The exterior is whitewashed, although Dr. Woodson insisted that it was paint. I, who have painted for some little while, feel as if I should be able to detect the difference between paint and whitewash.

Mr. Huskerson insisted that we visit the Church of God and Saints of Christ at Belleville. On the way there, we stopped to take pictures of other churches which Mr. Huskerson pointed out along the road. He informed us that we were in the midst of a truck-farming district, and I could see immense fields of kale, spinach, collard greens, peas, etc. In some fields, baskets and crates for shipping this produce stood in great heaps. Near Drivers, Mr. Huskerson had told us of the prosperity of this district, but its opulence was not reflected in the churches. Most of them were crazy, old, dilapidated, frame structures, some of which seemed liable to topple over at any moment. Especially was this true of the Oak Grove Church. Passed Canaan Baptist Church on Norfolk Road. A hall stood nearby. Both were dilapidated, tiny frame structures. Of all the miserable looking churches which I have yet beheld, the Tabernacle Baptist Church surpasses every other one in dilapidation. A small, frame affair, torn and battered by the elements until it remained little more than a shell, it stood, an eloquent testimony of the unprogressiveness (church-wise) of the Negroes of this truck-farming section. Unpainted, with shattered windows and a belfry that leaned at a hazardous angle, this little church presented a marked contrast to the beautiful, rich structure of Mt. Sinai outside of Holland. The door, or what was left of it, stood open. Dr. Wesley, Woodson, and I entered. A stove stood in the center of the room. Light was furnished by lamps. A small organ occupied one corner. The seating capacity of the church was approximately 100. This church emphasizes only too strongly the necessity of union among Negro Churches, especially the Baptists. To make this spectacle all the more impressive, a deserted two-story house whose windowless exterior made it resemble so many gouged-out eyes, leaned at a dangerous and crazy angle not more than ten feet from the church. Interestingly enough, this church stood in the richest truck-farming section of Nansemond County.

Passed Union Baptist Church, built in 1852. At Sholes Hill, Virginia, Dr. Wesley took pictures of this and all other churches. Passed through another beautiful section. Flat country; gardens are well kept, and tended chiefly by Negroes.

Belleville at last! This is the headquarters of the Church of God and Saints of Christ. Bishop [William H.] Plummer, "Grand Father Abraham," is the head of this sect. Mr. Huskerson told us Belleville is almost a self-sufficient community. Upon entering it, Mr. Huskerson pointed out the Bishop's home, a unique structure with a square house built on a square of the roof. Mr. Huskerson was acquainted with the Bishop's son, who gave us permission to view the colony, withholding, however, permission to take pictures.

What a place! Virtually self-sustaining. These people have their own saw mill, laundry, barber and tailoring shops, general store, and studio. Also have their own mechanics, carpenters, brick masons, engineers, electricians, etc. A guide pointed out the new Tabernacle which was in course of construction. Its architecture defied description—a combination embracing ancient Assyrian, Babylonian, and Egyptian styles. There is also an industrial building, a two-story frame affair; the old tabernacle, a long, narrow, yellow frame structure about 200 feet long and 50 feet wide; and a primary school, presided over by one Professor Coleman of New Jersey.

We were escorted by the son of the Bishop into the sacred presence of that exalted personage, the Bishop himself. Latter is a tall, dark, spare man of about 65. He seemed to be in feeble health. In striking contrast was the richness of his apparel. But I should not have wondered, for is he not Grand Father Abraham? He was quite affable; invited us to his private office. The "Bishop" had just left the baseball park, where he had been watching a group of boys at play.

The office was a beautiful brick structure, which had just been completed. Its purpose was to insure the Bishop the necessary privacy commensurate with his exalted station. He told us that he was the successor to Bishop William S. Crowdy, who had held the office from 1908 to 1917. He,

Crowdy, was also the founder of the Order in 1896. Crowdy died in Washington, D.C., having previously convinced his followers that, like Christ, he would be resurrected upon the "third day." Staunch in their blind faith in his words, the people left their dead prophet's body unburied, waiting for his promised resurrection. It did not come, and perhaps feeling that the good Lord had seen fit to postpone this second miracle, they refused to bury the body. They were finally forced to do so, however, by the Health Department. Needless to say, they did so with great reluctance.

Bishop Plummer, the present incumbent, had been a storekeeper in Roxbury, Massachusetts. He had risen to the chief lieutenancy of Bishop Crowdy. Upon the death of Crowdy, Plummer was elected his successor, notwithstanding that Crowdy, before his death, had conferred upon Plummer the headship with the title of "Grand Father Abraham." Crowdy passed over his own son, whom we met—a man now about 52, handsome, well-built, and of admirable carriage. The choice of the new Bishop apparently was a wise decision. When Plummer succeeded Crowdy there was 5 cents in the treasury. Now under the guidance of Bishop Plummer the church owns (or Plummer owns, for the property is in his name) 810 acres of excellent farm and woodland, all of it contiguous by reason of judicious purchases. The total property valuation is $250,000, with only $13,500 mortgages upon the entire property.

The venerable Bishop pointed to a fine map illustrating the location of the purchases, their size, date of purchase, and from whom purchased. An admirable piece of drawing. The Bishop's private car—a Packard—also had been drawn upon the wall. We had to marvel at the skill of these people. This place, which now is a garden spot, as well as a hive of industry, was weeds 20 years ago. It is not only the headquarters of the Church of God and Saints of Christ but also a widows' and orphans' home.

The women here! How woe-begone and bedraggled they look! To me they seemed lifeless. With their long hair and old fashioned clothes, high neck waists, long, dragging skirts with flounces, and high laced shoes, they looked like phantoms out of a departed era. They seem to have reconciled themselves to the inevitable, and are a part of something which they must feign to have an interest in and derive pleasure from, but, in reality, from which they apparently receive neither.

We were escorted through the Bishop's home. It is palatial. Everything reminiscent of Africa, the walls, ceilings, curtains, and some of the fittings all suggestive of the art of Ethiopia. The Bishop's son informed us that his father is making an effort to recreate the lost Ethiopian art. What beautiful birds, flowers, and other animals were crocheted in the curtains! Beaded work, basketry, and other things in profusion hung upon the walls. And the Bishop controls everything. All is his. The results of their labor all come to him. And he doles out subsistence to his people. A patriarch!

But he does things in a way which brooks no denying. Called for $25,000 one week in May. On the next week he had it. Taxed every church $25.00. There are other churches of this denomination in South Africa (4), Cuba (1), Jacksonville, and Deland, Florida. The Church of God is a split from the Church of God and Saints of Christ.[2]

2. Greene's account of the history of the church agrees in some essentials with other histories, but no two accounts agree in all factual details. The Church of God and Saints of Christ is one of the sects composing the Black Jewish Movement. William S. Crowdy, who had been a cook on the Santa Fe Railroad, founded the church in 1896 at Lawrence, Kansas. Crowdy said that he had a series of visions that revealed to him that black people are descendants of the "Lost Ten Tribes of Israel." The doctrines set forth by Crowdy are a mixture of Judaism and Christianity. The Jewish calendar is followed, and the Sabbath is observed. Such Jewish rites and customs as circumcision and the Passover are observed, along with Christian rites.

Accounts of the succession to leadership vary widely. According to *The Encyclopedia of American Religions*, in 1900, Crowdy moved to Philadelphia; and in that year, he convened the church's first annual assembly. Crowdy was head of the church and held the titles of bishop and prophet. When a prophet dies, the office remains vacant until another receives a divine call.

When William Crowdy died, in 1908, the office of prophet remained vacant. Bishops Joseph N. Crowdy and William H. Plummer assumed joint leadership of the sect. Joseph Crowdy died in 1917, leaving Plummer, who was called "Grand Father Abraham," as sole leader. The same year, Plummer moved the headquarters to Belleville, Virginia, and established the communalistic colony; those who chose to settle there could withdraw from the world and engage in economic experiments. Other local churches, however, were not organized in this way.

William Plummer died in 1931, over two years after Greene's visit. He was suc-

We also saw some high powered automobiles near the Bishop's home. Of course, they were his. Also, we were shown the passenger busses, two large commodious vehicles, each capable of seating 25 people. We could get no pictures because the Bishop feared the prejudice of outsiders who had made several attempts to quash the association. We arrived home about seven o'clock after a marvelous day. It was certainly worthwhile. Dr. Woodson seemed enthusiastic over what he had seen. I was glad, because the trip had been a failure financially.

After dinner, Mr. Peele took us out for a walk. We called upon Mr. W. H. Crocker. He was not at home. Mrs. Crocker, we found quite affable and charming. Stopped at Mr. [George C.] Bryant's. Mrs. Bryant and her son came downstairs to greet us. They have a well-furnished home. One of the Miss Bryants came downstairs also. She, as well as her sister, is a school teacher. Her father has just recently inherited $35,000. I jokingly told her I would try to find her a wedding "ring" at Woolworth's tomorrow, whereupon she blushed roundly. I told Dr. Woodson I should prefer her to Miss Skeeter, about whom he "kids" me, because of the former's dowry making her so much more attractive. We walked past Miss Skeeter's home. Dr. Woodson suggested that we stop, saying in response to my fear that it was too late, that he was quite sure I would be received.

We were all glad to retire after a very busy day.

When I awakened, Dr. Woodson had been for a walk through Saratoga, a Negro section of Suffolk. His survey, cursory though it was, confirmed the reports which I had given him

Thursday
April 26
1928

---

ceeded by Calvin S. Skinner, the last of the leaders appointed by the founder. Skinner died three months later, however, and the leadership then passed to Howard Z. Plummer. This was probably the son of William Plummer, who had extended such warm hospitality to Greene and his companions during their visit to Belleville. The Church of God and Saints of Christ remained a relatively small sect. In 1926, the movement had 112 churches and 6,741 members located largely in the upper South and in the East. In 1959, there were 217 churches and 38,217 members. *The Encyclopedia of American Religions* (2 vols.; Detroit, 1987), II, 330–32; Albert M. Shulman, *The Religious Heritage of America* (La Jolla, Calif., 1981), 312–13; U.S. Department of Commerce, Bureau of the Census, *Negroes in the United States, 1920–1932* (Washington, D.C., 1935), 538–53.

and Dr. Wesley respecting sewage, drainage, homes, etc. of that section. We went out there and took pictures of the various churches; the Lakeview Baptist, a decent-looking frame church; First Baptist, a weatherbeaten, little shack with a bell on a pole; the Wiggam Sanctified Church; the Antioch Christian Church; and the Holy and Sanctified Church, which sat in a man's back yard. All of the above named are more shacks than churches. They can hardly be dignified by that name.

Went from there to the Planter Peanut Factory, but were refused permission to go through. Had better luck at the Bell Hosiery Mills. They employ all colored girls. Most of the spindles are not running. None of the girls looked healthy, but hollow of jaw and glazed of eye. They work by the piece. Our guide, the son of the owner, Mr. Bell, told us that by hustling they could make $2.50 per day. I am inclined to believe, however, that they cannot earn more than $1.50 per day. We saw the process from the thread through the manufacture of each portion of the stocking—that is, the leg and foot are made separately, then sewn together—to the dyed, pressed, and packed article ready to be shipped. The immense dye vats color the stockings, freeing them of the fine cotton fuzz. Then they are washed and ironed in steel forms, corresponding to the various leg sizes, through which steam passes.

From the factory we went back to Peele's. Dr. Wesley, Woodson, and I went over to Booker T. School. We visited the rooms. Dr. Woodson told an African fable of the Dog and the Jackal to the students, much to their delight.

We stopped in Miss Skeeter's room, where Dr. Woodson twitted her about me.

Drs. Wesley and Woodson left for D.C. about 11:30. I went down to see about some questionnaires. Saw Miss Skeeter about 11:30 as she was going home to dinner. Walked home with her. Made an engagement to take her to the movies tonight. Met Miss Estes on the way back. Was chatting with her as Ira passed.

Went to the Easter Grade School in Saratoga. Talked to the

kiddies, as I was supposed to do this a.m. Met a Miss Nevells, a cute little girl.

Took Dr. Warren a copy of Woodson's *Negro in Our History*. I called upon Mr. [Robert] Williams to see if he could use his influence to secure me entrance into Planter's Peanut Factory. Said it could not be done. Believes they wish to tidy up before admitting visitors. Must know month in advance, as was the case with the dentists' convention. All hope of viewing the interior of the place now vanished completely, for I knew if any Negro in Suffolk could procure admittance for me it would be Williams, for surely no colored man in Suffolk wields the influence among whites that he does.

Mr. Williams' home is elegant. Filled with antiques. He has a portrait of Abraham Lincoln that is almost lifelike. Promised to take me to see Lawyer [Bradford] Kilby tomorrow to show me map of battle for Suffolk during the Civil War.

Returned. Took Ira to movies. Charming companion. Enjoyed the show immensely.

Went to Nansemond High School at 9 o'clock with borrowed camera which Ira had kindly procured and sent over to me. Mr. Huskerson promised to take me to see churches in a different direction. Waited two hours for him. Did not appear.

Friday
April 27
1928

During the interim, Mr. Crocker came by in his car. Hailed me. Told me how he started a Fair Development Corporation, etc. Also informed me that time after time he has come to aid of Nansemond High. Impressed me as highly efficient business man. Took me to Mr. Williams, who brought me to Lawyer Kilby's. Latter showed me a map with detailed explanation of struggle for Petersburg during the Civil War. Suffolk played only incidental role in it.

Going into the Post Office met Mr. [H. P.] Reid, county farm demonstration agent. Was going to Surrey. Offered to take me. I demurred at first but, upon hearing of the historical nature of country, decided to go. Passed farms owned by Negroes and others worked by Negro tenants. Schools for colored are poor in contrast to well-appointed white schools.

Latter have playgrounds and busses to carry their children back and forth to school. Most people adhere to staple farming, which Reid thinks weakens the soil.

In Isle of Wight County, we passed Old St. Luke's, the oldest Protestant Church in the United States. It is a brick structure, the bricks of which were brought over from England. Church was built in 1632, two years after the Puritans landed at Boston. It stands practically in the woods, with a little graveyard surrounding it. The church itself is small, the bricks all turned green and yellow with age; fissures have appeared in the walls but have been cemented together.

The church was erected under the direction of Joseph Bridges. Is a famous edifice. George Washington and Patrick Henry used to worship here. It is quite small; the altar has been rebuilt within the last 20 years. I brought a little hymnal away as a souvenir of this historic church. As I stood within it, I could conceive of those hazardous days of 1632, when one went to church with his ever-ready musket upon his shoulder, always alert for the red foe who bided his time to strike at the purloiner of his hunting grounds. In the little cemetery I made out on an iron slab the words "Sacred to the Memory of Mary Eason. Died June 1767. Born 1729." There was the Todd family plot, which included a large number of graves of persons from Southhampton, Isle of Wight, Nansemond, and Surrey Counties, the leading peanut sections of Virginia. If slaves were among the deceased, their graves were unmarked.

At Smithfield, the home of the celebrated ham by that name, we stopped at Mr. Shiver's store. It is the best stocked Negro store that I have ever seen. Shiver has a meat market and provision store. Also owns a wholesale fish market and ships barrels of fish to Baltimore, Washington, D.C., and New York. Employs a cashier and four clerks. I rejoice in all such signs of Negro progress. In addition, there is a colored furniture store here and other businesses. In such a small town, perhaps the Negro has more business per capita than any other community that I know of. Street fronts the James River.

In Surrey County saw the celebrated Bacon's Castle. Home of Nathaniel Bacon, hero of Bacon's Rebellion of 1676. It is a large brick house sitting in the midst of an immense farm. The muddy James River flows in the rear. The bricks have turned green and yellow with age; the foundation has been strengthened with concrete, and an addition, made of stucco, has been erected. The old slave quarters are still visible in the rear of the home. Iron cannon balls are strewn about the lawn.

The house was built by Arthur Allen in 1635. During Bacon's Rebellion, a party of rebels seized and fortified it. On December 29, 1676, it was captured by a group of sailors from a ship in the James River, who aided in putting down the rebellion. Nearby stand the ruins of an old brick church attended by Bacon. How I revelled in the sight of this old house. I could visualize the ship, with its quaintly clad sailors firing hot shot into the house. Frail as it was, it withstood the ravages of the heaviest shot of that day. What would but one small shell of the 20th Century have done to it!

We passed Pleasant Creek, where Gov. [Sir Edwin] Sandys, the treasurer of the Colony, made a settlement in 1625.[3]

We also passed near John Smith's fort, built by him soon after he founded Jamestown. The land descended from an Indian King, Opechancanough, to James Rolfe, son of Pocahontas. His house, built in 1652, is one of the oldest in Virginia.

How glad I was that I had come with Reid! He pointed out everything of interest. Wanted to take me to Jamestown, but it was cold and rainy on our return, so we decided to forego it. Too bad, but at least I could say I have been within four miles of Jamestown. Shall see it yet.

We got back to town by 4:30. Kilby *could* not fill out the blank for *Prominent Whites*.

After dinner took camera to Ira's. Went to Mrs. Davis, a nurse, for information she had promised me. I was to speak at Nansemond High School. Arrived there, but it had rained so hard, practically no one came out.

---

3. In 1619, Sandys was elected treasurer or president of the Virginia Company, which owned and ruled the Colony of Virginia. He served only one year. In 1624, at the behest of King James I, the Company's charter was annulled and Virginia became a royal province.

Bade farewell to Mr. Huskerson. He has been an indispensable aid to us. Could not thank him enough for his kindness.
Asked me about cost of Woodson's *Negro in Our History*. Told
him I would give him a copy, which I considered little enough
compensation for his cooperation.

Mrs. Huskerson and Miss Phrame brought me home. They
told me they had seen me last night with Ira Skeeter. That was
the reason, they said, that she failed to come to rehearsal for a
play.

They took me to see a large fire in a five and ten cent store on
East Washington Street.

Bade Mrs. Huskerson and Miss Phrame farewell. Went to
Ira's. Remained until twelve thirty. She hugged and kissed
me. Told me she hated to see me go. It was mutual; I did not
want to leave her.

This was my last night in Suffolk. I would that it were not.

Saturday   My last day in Suffolk. The work has been enjoyable here. I
April 28   have cultivated acquaintances. Just as I became acclimatized,
1928   so to speak, I must go elsewhere. But I shall remember
               Suffolk.

Did Suffolk make its impression upon me? Assuredly. A
surprising community. I had expected to see a rural settlement, with Suffolk as its center, boasting of a general store.
But on the other hand, I beheld a thriving industrial center
possessing nine peanut factories, candy factories, two hosiery
mills, lumber mills, five banks, stores of all kinds, a thriving,
wide-awake little town of 10,000 persons in Suffolk proper.

Now as to Colored Suffolk. There are about 11,000
Negroes in Suffolk and its environs. Really out-number the
whites. As to business, they have a bank capitalized at $50,000;
an active development corporation headed by an able business
man, Mr. Crocker; a drug store, barber shop, hotel, two first
class lunchrooms, grocery stores, fish markets, dance halls,
and taxis. Quite commendable.

Professionally, there are teachers, two lawyers, three doctors, two dentists, and two undertakers.

Laborers: Both men and women are employed in the factories. Unskilled male labor receives between $2.50 and $3.00 per day as an average wage for 10 hours. Skilled laborers earn $4–$5 per day. Waiters and butlers $10–$12 per week, exclusive of tips.

Women in industry, who form the bulk of the workers in the peanut factories and hosiery mills, receive $1.25–$1.50 per day, the latter being the top wage. Ten hours is a working day. In the hosiery mills laborers are paid by the piece. But one never makes over $2.00 per day, in my judgment. Domestics receive $5–$8 per week.

Working Conditions: In the peanut plants, very bad, on account of dust, which becomes a potent factor in the large tuberculosis death rate. Most of the workers I saw appeared to be sickly.

Living Conditions: Very good among the best people. Mr. Peele, the Crockers, the Bryants, Skeeters, Estes, Hunters, Dix, Finches, and others have homes which would be a credit to any community. Good, among say 60% of the people. Remainder live in unpaved, low sections of Philadelphia, Saratoga, and Jericho. Streets, especially in Saratoga, unpaved; drainage poor; rains turn streets into quagmires. Ditches, varying in width from 1 to 1½ feet and from 1 to 2 feet feet deep, line each side of the road. There is no drainage, and the water stagnates, giving off foul and disease-breeding odors—another fertile source of tuberculosis. Many of the homes in these sections are poor, inadequately furnished, and unclean. There is little or no sanitation. Privies all outside. So, too, is the water pump and, in some cases, no more than twenty feet away from and on the same level as the privy. It is marvelous that the death rate is not higher. As Carter Woodson remarked in his speech in Suffolk Tuesday, "Segregation is an insidious thing, for it aims, if practiced widely and rigorously enough, at the entire extermination of a people." Despite these conditions, however, I must say that about 60% of the homes would pass muster. About that same number of Negroes own or are purchasing their homes.

Race Relations: Very good for a Southern town.

Segregation: In living quarters, although there are certain districts for Negroes, it is a common occurrence to find Negroes living on one side of a street and whites on the other. Wellons Street is a case in point. One can always tell, however, for the pavement stops abruptly where the Negro section begins. Wellons and St. James Streets are good examples.

Schools: Disparity here. County school tax in regard to Negro education used unfairly. Whites have two grade schools and one high school. Colored have one grade school, Booker T. Washington, which is inadequate, although Negroes outnumber the whites. Have no public high schools. Negroes themselves built Nansemond High School. Rosenwald Schools in East Suffolk and Saratoga help to take care of the education of Negro children.

Teachers: Younger ones seem competent. Older, not as well prepared. Most ought to be retired.

Churches: Much too many. Eighteen Baptist churches alone here. Whites have but one. Negroes have not one representative edifice in town. Most of the churches are barnlike structures like the Christian Church, Tabernacles, etc. Others are in last stages of deterioration, notably, Antioch Christian, Tynes Street Baptist, etc. The two Methodist and the First Baptist churches are fairly respectable frame structures. Pine Street Baptist is building a brick Church on Washington Street. Will be only colored brick church in Suffolk. Outlying churches surpass them. Mt. Sinai Baptist Church, near Holland, is beautiful brick building.

Ministers: Not one really educated. Mostly self-centered, narrow-minded men. Ignorant as a whole. Indifferent to racial progress. Of the "Hallelujah" type. Only worthwhile man seems to be Rev. Wood of A.M.E.Z. Church. Desires cooperation of ministers to sponsor community projects. Decries narrow denominationalism. A voice "crying in the Wilderness."

Outlying Districts: Include well-to-do Negro farming communities—Holland and adjacent districts grow staple products: corn, peanuts, cotton. Some farmers cultivate 100–150 acres. Some magnificent and well-kept farms are owned by Mr. Walden, Sr., Mr. Walden, Jr., and Mr. Lewis. Average for Negro farms about 70 acres, according to Mr. Reid and Crocker. Toward Norfolk truck farming predominates. Spinach, kale, peas, beans, fruit, etc. raised in abundance.

State and County agents render farmers advice as to what to plant, how to plant it, and when to plant it. Farmers receive instruction as to what crops thrive best in certain soils, according to Mr. Reid. A county farm demonstration agent serves each county.

County Schools: Whites are consolidated; invariably brick, with playgrounds. Colored: usually frame, except for a Rosenwald School here and there.

Diversion: Three dance halls; Elks and Colden's Auditorium are best. No community centers. One theater which colored may attend. This is the Photosho, which can scarcely be called a theater. Even here they must sit upstairs. Lack of clean amusements is a hardship to young people, especially those who attempt to be decent.

Morals: Very low, on the whole, especially among the factory workers. All people in Suffolk decry, but know not how to remedy, these conditions. I do. Let the churches unite and found community centers, something to interest these workers in clean living and harmless amusements, rather than concentrate on sex. But then both white and blacks exhibit sexual laxity.

Conveyance: Entirely by bus or taxi. Very expensive because they are segregated. Negroes do not ride in white buses. Therefore, to prove they thrive under oppression, Negroes organized bus lines of their own. Davis and Smithhall Bus Lines have large modern buses making trips at stated hours between Portsmouth and Suffolk. Davis Company alone operates seven large buses.

Miss Skeeter (Ira), Miss Estes, Miss Bryant, and Little Miss Wards leave their impression upon me. Mr. Robert Williams, Dr. Bland, Mr. Crocker and his brother, Mr. and Mrs. Huskerson, Miss Phrame, Prof. Howe (for his narrowness), Mr. and Mrs. Peele, and others I shall always remember.

Miss Estes sent me her aunt's questionnaire, while I was eating breakfast. I asked Mrs. Peele to return Miss Skeeter's umbrella, which she had loaned me night before. Bade farewell to Mrs. Peele and daughter. Enjoyed staying there. They had left no stone unturned to make my stay pleasant. Food good and plenty of it. Refused to charge me extra for milk. Paid $28.00 for my stay.

Taxi, hired yesterday in advance, came for me. Paid driver and sent him off. Mr. Peele offered to take me to station, and I had accepted.

Went to say goodbye to Miss Estes. Very interesting young woman. Has a refreshing frankness that is extremely charming. Bade farewell to Mr. Peele. Assured me his home was, and is, open to me, at anytime. I was touched by his hospitality. He took me to the station. Had to ride to Washington in "Jim Crow" coach.

[7] Washington: Great Expectations

Arrived in D.C. at 2:30 in a driving rain. Went to Association Office. Worked on Baltimore questionnaires till 6:00 p.m. Incidentally, told Woodson I had given one of his books, *The Negro in Our History*, to Mr. Huskerson. Woodson had brought three to Suffolk last Tuesday with him, and presented one to the Bishop of Belleville. Huskerson, who had been so kind to me and to him, also, who had spent the entire day, Wednesday, driving us about, heard him make the offer to the Bishop. When Huskerson told me later he would like a book for the school library, I gave it to him. Told Woodson I would pay for it, but he refused to accept the money.

Saturday April 28 1928

Went to dinner. Returned at 7:30 p.m. Wesley was out. Woodson shocked me. Told me that he did not intend to give Huskerson a book. Had spoken for his school. That was sufficient. "But," I replied, "it was not Huskerson's school." Again I offered to pay, for I saw he was brooding over the matter. He again refused to accept the $5.00 which the book cost. Could have done nothing less, in my opinion, than to give Huskerson a book.

Worked until 10:00 p.m. Wesley brought me home. Advised me to pay no attention to Woodson. Asked him how he and Woodson got along so harmoniously. Said he followed his own ideas; would not argue with him.

We will work Sunday, starting at 11:00 a.m.

To our surprise a lady called Woodson about 9:30 p.m.
Gave her name to Wesley only as Etta. We laughed. Woodson
had been "kidding" me about Miss Skeeter. Now I shall have a
comeback.

Sunday
April 29
1928

Beautiful Day. Went to office at eleven. Remained till 2:00
p.m., working upon citizens' questionnaires from Baltimore.
Later went to baseball game at Griffith Stadium. Saw Yankees
beat "Griffs." Ruth hit a home-run out of the ball park. Returned home. Went to see Bertha at 8:00. Returned home at
11:00. Fliers [Hermann] Koehl, [James E.] Fitzmaurice, and
[Baron Gunther von] Huenefeld attended church in New
York today.

Monday
April 30
1928

Dr. Wesley and I went to Baltimore at 9:00 to secure pictures
of churches for our survey. Dark, gray day. Sun shone fitfully.
    Arrived in Baltimore, called Dr. [Bernard] Harris. Not at
home. Was at hospital (Provident). Went there but he was
preparing for an operation. Took pictures of Bethel, Sharpe
Street Memorial, Trinity, Union, Metropolitan Baptist, and
other churches.
    In afternoon met a Mr. ———, who seemed to be imbued
with a desire to help me. Took me to Sarasota Street. Paved
with large cobblestones. Poor section.
    Wesley and I went to home of old colored lady. White-
haired and invalid, she took care of the house while the housewife worked in service. The sight of her in such surroundings
was pitiable. There she sat in the midst of squalor and poverty
and her own uncleanliness. The room was small, walls unpainted. The furniture consisted of a battered and tattered old
couch, a broken down settee, an old side board that was lit-
tered with every describable sort of article—combs, brushes,
dishes, hair grease, pictures, clothes, etc. A small stove furnished heat. No curtains at the window. The floor alone was
fairly clean. But everything else was dirty and dusty.
    In the midst of this squalor sat the old woman. Her clothes
were in the last stages of deterioration from both age and dirt.
Her arms were coated with dirt, and deep scars (from burns, I

judged) showed upon them. She was barefoot. As I entered she was wringing out a rag from a dishpan of water as black and dirty as I have ever seen. Whether she was washing the floor or her arms with it, I shall never know. She had been a Church member for 50 years, we were informed. But now, in her old age, the Church had forgotten her. Each of us gave her a little mite. It is to be hoped that this study of the Church will bring out the defects in that institution, thereby impelling it to show greater concern for the community. A Church home should be caring for this old woman. Some of the neighbors brought her to the door in a chair so that I could take her picture. In this house there was neither gas, electricity, bath, nor privy. It rented for $2.50 per week. Such is the case in a large section of Baltimore, even in the best Northwest residential section.

Wesley left for Washington an hour later.

I took more pictures of missions, etc. Called upon Mr. Moss of the Urban League. He could or would give no information on wages for colored in Baltimore. Referred me to Mr. Saunders of the Y.M.C.A. Employment Bureau. I believe Moss expects to make a similar survey for Baltimore and does not desire to give out his findings.

Saunders readily gave me what he knew about wages. Industrial workers, he said, are fairly well paid: 40–45 cents per hour. Domestics are not so well compensated, receiving $4–$5 per week. A day's work brings $2.00 here. In the North $4–$4.50 per day for women. Skilled laborers received $20–$35 per week.

Felt quite tired. Had been walking since 10:30 a.m. About 4 o'clock now. Went to Dr. Harris's. Not at home. Walked up and took pictures of First Baptist and People's Christian Churches. Saw Dorothy Nichols and her sister. Took sister's picture.

Dr. Harris finally came home at 5:30. Took me to take pictures of St. Francis, Ebenezer, Leadenhall and Bragg's Churches.

Left for Washington, D.C. at 5:30. Arrived there at 9:50. Called Wesley. Neither at home nor office.

Koehl and other fliers honored by New York today. Herbert Hoover and Governor "Al" Smith of New York State look like Presidential nominees of their respective Republican and Democratic parties.

Tuesday
May 1
1928

Went to the office today. Worked on questionnaires for "citizens" in an effort to secure a line on the trend of their attitude toward the Church in Baltimore. Finished, then began on "pastors." Wesley is writing up the "community attitude" concerning the Negro Church. Is handicapped by paucity of information secured by Woods, whose job it was to gather such.

It was quite a surprise to me when, after having completed his first typescript of the community attitude, Wesley brought it to me for my criticism. I read it, noting several instances where I thought corrections should be made, i.e., "bathing in laundries" or explanations given, such as "independent movements of Baltimore Negroes in religious and several fields." Disagreed with him as to whether people "followed" the Church. In most instances, the Church has had to "follow the people." It was an honor to me that a man like Wesley should bring his manuscript to me for corrections and criticisms. All my comments were well received; the result will be another typing of a revised account.

Am leaving for Chicago, Saturday, 3:00 p.m. on Capitol Limited. Dr. Woodson secured reservations for me this p.m. Am writing to Baltimore to see if I can get reduced fare.

Received letter from Helen Notis today. Quite lengthy, but as enjoyable and interesting as the lady herself. Contained some shocking news. Informed me of the death of little Frances, the niece of Rubye Bingham of Greenwich, Connecticut. The little girl was mysteriously burned to death. What a pall must hang over the family! Rubye and the little girl's mother had gone to the dentist. Mrs. Blackwell, the grandmother, was asleep upstairs. The little girl had just gone to bed. After a while, two of the other little tots awakened the grandmother, telling her the child was on fire. Arriving there, the grandmother found she was dead, burned beyond recognition.

Called Miss [Pauline] Stewart, whom I met in Baltimore. Invited me to call before leaving the city.

Wrote Harry [Hipp] for first time in a month, also Mother.

These are surely busy days. Drove to the office this morning at 8:30. Could not get in, however. Miss [Hazel Powell], the stenographer, came up while I stood there. Beautiful and well-formed, is from Kentucky. Had not met her before. Chatted till Mr. Wells, the all-round man, came and opened the door. I had been working upon questionnaires for "citizens," culling the gist of their opinions. Today, having completed those, I concentrated upon the "pastors." How amusing to read their opinions. Of the 50 ministers whose questionnaires we have, over 31 listed themselves as theological school graduates and a similar number as college men. I personally know that this is a gross exaggeration, for, having interviewed most of them, I feel that I am competent to say something on this particular score. There are only four or five well-trained Negro ministers in Baltimore: Rev. R. H. Green, who studied for the bar as well as the ministry; Beale Elliot, pastor of Sharpe Street Church; Dr. [Ernest] Lyon of [Ames Memorial Methodist Episcopal Church]; and Rev. Samuel Giles, graduate of Drew Seminary, who is doing work for the Ph.D. degree at the University of Edinburgh. Judging from their conferences, particularly among the Baptists, I dare say not 25% of the Baltimore ministers of all denominations are educated men.

Dr. Wesley is working feverishly. Shows signs of strain, too. Dr. Woodson asked if I had made reservations for Chicago this a.m. I told him "No." He made them for me on the Capitol Limited.

Will be my first ride in a Pullman. Woodson advised my securing a place to stay, if I was acquainted in Chicago. I had the secretary, Miss [Dorothy] Revallion, send a letter to Mrs. Ida Johnson of 4616 Prairie Avenue, Chicago, where we— [Sidney] Wells, Martin, and I—had stopped last year. Asked if she could accommodate me and said to telegraph at my expense if she could.

Read over several sections of the survey as Wesley completed them. He accepted my criticisms graciously.

Left at 5:30. Called Miss Stewart. Would see me about 8:30. Also called Helen [Grinage]. Would have gone out there, but she had promised Lil, her sister, to help her entertain the latter's club. Arranged to see her tomorrow noon. Spent enjoyable evening with Miss Stewart, although a doctor, who seems to be smitten by the lady, put in an appearance. However, he did not stay overly long. I asked her why she had not married. For two reasons, she said: First, her fiance had been killed in the World War. Secondly, because she did not enter into the social life of Washington to the extent of other girls. She had been allowed to bloom unseen, so to speak. Asked me to write her from Chicago.

Thursday
May 3
1928

The same hubbub at the office. The work saw a little progress, but we still have a long way to go. Wesley has finished the "Church in the Community." I read it over and corrected, with his approval, several of his mistakes. Gave it to the stenographer, Miss Revallion. Poor girl. She is certainly being rushed with this work. Don't see how we can finish by Saturday.

Saw Helen [Grinage] a little later, at noon. Went to the laboratory where she was preparing an experiment. She looked at me seemingly with her soul in her eyes. What a girl! Can be no more like her. We chatted concerning Bea Shorter's marriage. To my query, whether she had been accused of persuading Harry to change his mind about marrying Bea, she answered, "No." Said she had never regarded such profound educational differences as the sole cause of Harry's change. I knew she was correct, but did not admit it. We sat together in a study room, she with a laboratory book in her hands tapping her teeth with the butt of her fountain pen. I hardly knew what to say to her. During the silence, her professor walked in. Saying nothing, he disappeared. I went back to the office to my task. Meanwhile, Helen promised to write me before I returned from Chicago. She will do so, too.

Back to our task. I wrote down opinions of Prominent White Persons. Opinions varied: One thought the Negro Church equal to the white; others thought it differed, even as Negroes and whites differ. Another thought it a cross between the lore of Africa and Christianity. Most considered the Negro minister uneducated. The consensus of opinion among Baltimore whites interviewed by us is that little relationship exists between the Negro's morals and his religion. The white Church has helped colored churches, but the influence of white upon Negro Churches has been negligible, a fault ascribable to both races. One man claimed that Negroes were suspicious of whites. (Can't blame them.) Another stated that the Negroes desired the whites' *money* but not *them*. (Can't censure Negroes for that either.)

Worked tonight. Went from there to bid Bertha good-bye. We both were tired. She refused to return my watch.

The task of writing up our findings, relatively speaking, is no nearer completion. Wesley looks haggard and tired. So am I. It is terribly hot, but still we work, hoping against hope to be able to finish the manuscript soon. I have completed the "Prominent Whites" questionnaires. Dr. Wesley now asked me to write up the "citizen's opinion of the church." I had not expected to do any writing at all. What a wonderful experience for me. Only wish this had come before I did my residence on the doctorate.

In the afternoon, Dr. Wesley received a telegram from Mr. Fisher of the Institute. Had been looking for a reply all week respecting our proposed trip to Chicago to attend the A.M.E. Convention. Mr. Fisher approved of Dr. Wesley's going to Chicago, but not of my accompanying him. Naturally, I was disappointed.

Woodson believed that our having exceeded the budget limit on expenses for the first seven weeks of the survey was responsible for Fisher's decision. Woodson wishes to put us,

Friday May 4 1928

or me in particular, on the same expense plan as his men, namely, $1 per day, which he believes to be an equitable amount over the normal limit of expense if one were living at his own home. Woodson's argument is that everyone has a normal living expense. Said when his workers are traveling he pays them the excess over and above their normal expenses. I could see the logic of his position but did not wish to admit it. Then, too, after a man has spent so much time in preparation, he cannot be expected to work under the same conditions as a man would who is not a trained student of history. Wesley is diplomatic, cool, unruffled. Believes that if we have gone over the estimated figure, then the budget should be enlarged to include it. Woodson held that his estimated travel budget was not too low, despite the objections of the Institute that it was. Now let Woodson admit he was wrong. If Wesley has his way, things will go on as before. I hope so.

I am not to go to Chicago, but shall stay here and complete the report. Sorry and glad. The former because I had looked forward to the trip; the latter because it proves that Wesley is confident that I can do the work. I shall try to vindicate his confidence.

Saturday
May 5
1928

Still working on the citizens' questionnaires. Dr. Wesley started upon the pastors' questionnaires but soon turned them over to me, instructing me to include them in the "Opinion" section. I am to forward them to him in Chicago for correction.

I went to lunch. When I returned, Dr. Wesley had gone. At least I saw him drive past the lunch room just as I was finishing my meal.

Stayed at the office till 4:30. Went to barber shop. Reached home about 6:00. Terribly hot. But a storm is brewing which no doubt will cool things off.

Took Miss Stewart to the movies. Was my first trip to movies here since 1924.

Woodson is a *bête noire* to the office force. They all declared a holiday after he left.

Rose at 12:30. Breakfast at 2:30. Went to Rosslyn, Virginia, to see Mother's cousins, Rose [Alleyne] and Grace. Was my second home while attending Howard University in Washington, D.C. The rendezvous of our "gang" (Hipp, Bacote, and I). Unfortunately, there was no one home. Today was probably their communion Sunday. Sunday May 6 1928

Went to Hall's Hill [Virginia] to see another cousin, Almira [Streets], and her mother. She has a very attractive little bungalow. While there a Mr. Nickerson came in. The folks began telling stories suggested by a cut upon Mr. Nickerson's hand, into which my cousin desired to pour a little Sloan's liniment.

He wisely refused, telling her of a time when, after having injured his foot as a result of a stone falling on it, he poured a bottle of liniment over it, rubbed it in well, and went to bed. Then the fun started. The foot burned so terribly he jumped out of bed and plunged it into a basin of cold water, thereby succeeding only in intensifying the pain. It was eight weeks, he told us, before he could again touch the floor with his foot.

Again, he told of the old-fashioned remedies which his mother and her contemporaries employed for various accidents such as a bad cut, a sprain, etc. Once, having cut his hand badly, he stated that his mother took cobwebs and soot, stuffed the wound with those crude, unsanitary remedies, and bound it up. The hand gradually became worse until the doctor was sent for. He told his mother that he had come just in time to prevent gangrene. When he was seventeen, after having cut an ugly gash on the top of his foot, his uncle clapped a plug of chewing tobacco into the wound, tied it up, and sent him home. His mother did nothing. From Saturday to Friday he remained in bed, the foot swollen, ugly, and paining dreadfully. His mother finally sent for the doctor, who promptly notified her that the foot must be removed. For nine months he was unable to walk, when a little medical care would perhaps have prevented such pain and agony.

My cousin told of toothache remedies. A favorite one was to secure some substance such as scale from a horse's leg. It was called *nighteye*. One would smoke it and blow the smoke into the mouth of the toothache sufferer. Mr. Nickerson said he saw his mother sit up half the night on one occasion smoking a pipe and blowing the smoke into the ear of his sister, who was suffering from an earache.

He told, also, of using a little pinch of Red Seal lye for an aching tooth. Put just a pinch into the cavity. Said for a few minutes he felt as if he could have pulled the world over. Then the pain subsided and the tooth has never bothered him since. Subsequently, however, it broke off and he pulled out the particles. A pal of his tried it upon his recommendation and nearly went crazy as a result. A woman did the same thing, added my cousin, and it nearly ate her jaw away. She also told of putting lye on a corn and being disabled for six months.

I was amazed and horrified at the old-fashioned remedies used by Negroes, some of whom had been slaves. They seem so childish and dangerous now. But then, those were the best and only resources they possessed and they used them. How much might be ascribed to their African heritage I could not venture to speculate. Or to the dictates of the master, who did not consider slaves as human beings.

I promised to come back Wednesday night to a whist party.

From Hall's Hill went to see Bertha.

Monday
May 7
1928

Mrs. Wesley called about 10:30. Told me Dr. Wesley had telegraphed her asking her to have me send him the manuscript on the Negro Church. Sent what I considered to be the correct one, along with some other matters.

My first day here alone. Hope the girls don't run over me. Miss Revallion is friendly.

Finished "Opinion of Citizens." Started on "Pastors."

Thought I found what Dr. Wesley really wanted at approximately five o'clock. But Miss Revallion had gone home. Took manuscript with me. Could not mail it for I did not have Wesley's address.

Went to see "Seventh Heaven." Excellent picture. Came near weeping.

Wrote Helen Notis.

Sent Mother money today. Banked $50.

By dint of hard labor, Miss Revallion and I succeeded in finishing the first part of Chapter III, entitled "Opinion of Citizens." Majority of them believe that the church is in bad condition and suggest 23 different remedies for it. The most important suggestions, as might be expected, came from the more intelligent group. They, as a whole, desire a more practical form of Christianity instead of loud and empty preachments. Tuesday May 8 1928

Sent the other manuscript to Dr. Wesley in the morning, together with my expense account.

Went to see Bertha in the evening.

Poor Miss Revallion. My wretched scribbling will surely ruin her eyes. Today the poor girl had to get a magnifying glass to aid her in deciphering my writing. I felt sorry for her, and yet I am doing the best I can to make my handwriting legible. Wednesday May 9 1928

Am working now on the questionnaires for pastors. Their opinion is important. Are doing little more than preaching, praying, and singing.

After work, went to Hall's Hill to see Almira. Played whist, etc. Stayed overnight. Cousin Jane was not very well. Almira is very attentive and devoted to her mother.

Received bulletin from Census Bureau this morning. Sent it to Bacote in Syracuse. Am a trifle behind in my plans. Aimed to have all "Opinions" finished tomorrow. Can't do it now. Thursday May 10 1928

Miss Revallion still struggles heroically with my writing. However, I manage to keep her in good humor by a timely joke once in a while. When she laughingly complains of my evil penmanship, I tell her deciphering it increases her value to the establishment, which causes her to laugh in spite of herself.

Finished "Pastors" questionnaires today. Started on "Prominent Whites." Hope to finish them tomorrow morning. Shall start then upon "Youth," which I anticipate will be quite a task.

Miss Revallion is tired out, but I asked her to humor me in an effort to finish "Prominent Whites" that it might be sent to Dr. Wesley tomorrow.

Did not go out tonight.

Met [Albert Woods] Dumas today. Was a classmate of mine at Howard U. Is now a medic student. Asked if he knew [Maurice Montera] Wesson. Told me latter was a freshman at the Medical School. Gave him my card for Wesson, asking him to inform the latter that I was in town and desired to see him. Wesson was my closest pal during my first year in D.C. at Dunbar. He, however, failed to enter the University the following year and thus our ties grew weaker due to the fact that [Ernest] Bacote, then [Harry] Hipp, came to color my life as no other association has.

Friday
May 11
1928

Woodson came in from Chicago this morning as I was dictating a letter to Columbia University. One of the girls stayed out. Miss Revallion remarked that Woodson would be savage. My, he must be a *bête noire* here! Miss Revallion tells me that she has endured him for four years but cannot imagine how. In her opinion, he is unsympathetic in his attitude toward his employees. He is willful, eccentric (I suppose the latter word may, with propriety, be applied to him since he is a recognized scholar). I jokingly told Miss Revallion his scholarly achievement gives him every right to act as he does.

He is despotic in a way, although I have not yet felt the weight of his Czaristic temperament. Yet, it may be on account of his tremendous responsibility. But under it all, I believe that Woodson is a fine fellow. Comical and very human. Makes an excellent traveling companion.

Finished "Prominent Whites" shortly after dinner. Could not get started on "Youth." Just couldn't write. Too tired.

Miss Revallion was given a manuscript on manufacturing to type by Woodson. She was exhausted, poor girl. I had tried to give her a rest during the p.m.

Wrote Carolyn [Worrell] and Hipp.

Upon returning home, thought I would go out to Anacostia. Rain threatened. Decided I'd stay in. Phone rang. Aunt called me. Ruth Beverly was on the phone. I did not expect to hear her voice. She is a dear pal of my school days. Perhaps she loves me, or shall I say she does love me? Asked me to come out. Did do. She looked well, although tired from a forty-mile bus trip. A fine girl. She pained me when she told me I would have loved her more were she better educated. I replied that she should not entertain such thoughts. She twitted me about a letter which I had written her two years ago.

Left about eleven thirty.

Tired. Did practically nothing all day. Miss Revallion was out. Took an exam, I believe. It was lonesome upstairs without her. Saturday May 12 1928

Walked out with Miss Powell. A real Kentucky lass. Pretty, russet-brown, well-formed. Her speech is quaintly amusing. Says "haid" for head, etc. Is a Wilberforce girl. Admits she is "too lazy to work." I told her she had better go back home.

Went to Rosslyn. Cousins out. Saw Mr. Fitz [Alleyne], Cousin Rose's husband. They now have electric lights in the house, a cellar practically dug, and will soon put in a furnace. Upon reaching home, Ruth [Beverly] called. Invited me to dinner tomorrow. I called Bertha. Am to see her this evening.

Rose at 10:30. Sent Mother this telegram for Mother's Day at 11:00 a.m. "Love to you and Dad on Mother's Day." Sunday May 13 1928

While waiting for a taxi to go to Ruth's met Lee. She is Ruth's cousin. Married about four years ago. She was quite surprised to see me. She looks quite well. A trifle stouter. Detained me for a while to ask me about my work. Introduced me to the mother-in-law of [William Brooks] Edlin, a Mrs. White. Edlin was a classmate of mine at Howard. Lee took me to Ruth's, where I dined and remained till 4 o'clock, when Ruth and her sister Vashti left for Maryland, where they teach school.

Ruth, I believe, loves me. In fact, I ought to know so without being conceited. A fine girl. But??? Saw them off. Kissed her good-bye. Ruth asked me to write her from each place I visit. I promised to do so.

Went to Mrs. Hood's. She is the lady at whose home we used to have such wonderful parties. Was our second home while in D.C. How glad she was to see me. Mrs. Adkins, her daughter, was visiting a friend. Failed to see her. I used to make her laugh so. Left about six o'clock. Met Mr. Adkins while on the way to Pennsylvania Avenue and 21st Street. He is a cripple—poor fellow. Has a curvature of the spine which causes him to stoop almost at right angles. So glad to see him. Told him I would drop over later.

Went to Bertha's. Not finding her home, stood outside for a while. Heard a rhythmical knocking and thumping. Could not explain it. Finally realized it was coming from the [United] House of Prayer [for All People]. This is a large brick house converted into a church. Curiosity prompted me to go in. What I beheld almost made me weep. Surely, I told myself, these people could not be civilized. A swirling, jumping, dancing, shouting mass of human beings filled the place to overflowing. Screams, laughter, songs, and groans broke from this gyrating, frenzied, perspiring throng. I looked on in amazement. Women shouted—jumped up and down. Men did the same. Some of the men held the women's arms in the air and swayed to a monotonous but stirring hymn. A girl with hair and clothes dishevelled stood up, shook her head, then uttered a piercing cry and collapsed. Another, after crying out "Glory to God," screaming, and jumping, fell prostrate over a chair, mumbling incoherently. This inarticulate muttering these people style "talking in tongues," which is evidence that the devotee has been visited by the "Holy Ghost." The stamping of feet, the cries of "Lord have mercy" and "Hallalujah," the wild shouts and mutterings of these people awoke in me a profound feeling of pity. This is their conception of Christianity. Empty "mouthings." Emotional frenzy and manifestations of barbaric dancing and primitive religions in the midst of civilization.

I looked for Bertha. She sat not the least disturbed, and I could not but realize how much out of place she was in the midst of this semi-savage throng. Finally the cause of this emotional storm appeared—a steaming bespectacled man of about fifty years of age, whom they called "Elder." I could not but wish—of course, secretly—that he might be jailed for exhorting these people to this great waste of energy that could be better applied to racial uplift. I look upon him and Bishop

Grace, the head of this organization, as the vilest type of miscreants—seducers of the weak and illiterate, parasites who suck the life's blood out of a people, already bled white, so to speak, by 300 years of servitude. They talk of teaching a race to die before teaching it how to live. I believe in religious toleration, but I think it would be a fine idea for the state to inquire into the intentions of those who found such cults as these that prey upon the weak and emotionally susceptible classes. I saw no intelligent persons there. If they were present, they probably attended for purposes of exploitation. I left more saddened, however, than disgusted. If this be religion, deliver me from it! Yet whites and blacks participated with the same fervor.

The same crowd who had been shouting in that ill-ventilated church could be heard in loud "mouthings" upon the street.

I told Bertha about it later. Remarked I was surprised at her, intelligent as she was, to be taken in by anything like that. She told me I did not understand. I tried to show her that religion did not consist of loud mouthings, shouting, dancing, and epileptic fits, that it was best exemplified in service. Christ's doctrine, I continued, was simple, perhaps so simple that the majority overlooked it in the search for it. It is *love*. She repeated that I did not understand. These people had the spirit, she went on, therefore knew what to do to serve God. I contended every man has in him a bit of God that guides him aright, if he will but hearken unto it. She said I spoke irreverently. Spoke to me concerning salvation. Told her religion was a personal affair between man and his creator, that one should exemplify his Christianity by his life, not "mouth" it. She agreed with me. Yet, told me that there was something in this faith which strengthened her. Told me of the great work of the Bishop. I replied his religion was a vicious doctrine, which lulled in the Negro every desire for economic betterment here on earth, not only for himself but for his children. She responded that I scarcely believed in God. Asked her could any man behold the stars at night, the sun at dawning, the coming and passing of the seasons, and a thousand other manifestations of God's omnipotence and then doubt the existence of a Supreme Being? Ah, no, each time I see a leaf or the tiniest insect it connotes God. Go out in the open, I told her, get out into the woods where one can contemplate God and see God, then realize as never before how near we are to Him and how personal religion is after all.

Advised her she could render more service in a more intelligent church. No, she retorted, they needed her here. She would stay. Told her she should not handicap her son by foisting this strange faith upon him. Reminded her that as soon as he could think for himself he would renounce it.

My words only seemed to make her reassert that she would stay there, so I withdrew from arguing with her. 'Twas a delicate subject. Believe I hurt her, but God knows I did not do so purposely.

Monday May 14 1928	Worked on "Youth" questionnaires today. Practically finished. Went to Congressional Library to borrow *How to Study the City Church* by H[arlan] Paul Douglass. Failed to secure it.

Youth of Baltimore for most part attend church regularly; like the services, although some feel they are too long. Most youth are orthodox in religion, but desire practical sermons. Few wish to study for the ministry. Most go to the church of their parents. When this is not the case, youth is swayed by preferences rather than circumstances.

Tuesday May 15 1928	Wesley's letter came to my hand this a.m. Advised I cut allowance down to $1.00 per day while in D.C. Halfway expected such. Takes about $8.00 a week from my expense account. Wants me to start upon Suffolk questionnaires after completing Baltimore. Sent vouchers to New York as *per* his instructions.

Woodson wrote for *How to Study the City Church*. Miss Revallion started upon "Youth" this p.m. I started upon the "Citizens" questionnaires of Suffolk.

Walked home from work with Miss Powell.

Went to see "Old Ironsides" at Republic Theatre. Segregated, of course. Met Edwards and wife. He was formerly Dot's sweetheart. Liked the picture.

Received letter from Helen Notis. She met Miss [Beatrice] Shorter, Harry's old sweetheart. Helen wrote she nearly collapsed upon learning it was she.

Started this morning in earnest upon Suffolk questionnaire. Finished the "Citizens" manuscript. Find there are three distinct groups: (1) business, professional, and a more intelligent group, which is also a church-going group; (2) business and professional and intelligent non-churched element, which also includes a few less enlightened persons; (3) more illiterate churched group. As a whole, citizens believe the condition of the Negro Church is bad, blame the ministers chiefly for bad conditions, although the more enlightened members censure both church and non-church members. They believe that the churches have had some influence upon the community for good, especially in the case of schools. They do not believe the ministers are the right type of leaders. Accused them of immorality, hypocrisy, and ignorance. Feel that the Sunday Schools are inefficient, that the church is not run on a business basis, that the ministers do not take part in politics, although, in the opinion of the more enlightened groups, they should do so for the betterment of the race. The greatest need of the Negro church, in their opinion, is educated ministers. The majority are not satisfied with the services they hear, desiring a more practical sermon from an educated ministry. They believe that the church is doing something for charity but not as much as it should, nor as efficiently as it could be done.

Left description of services at First Baptist Church in Suffolk, and account of Baptist Minister's Conference, also of Suffolk, for Miss Revallion to type.

After dinner called upon Bertha. Is still the same Bertha.

Wednesday
May 16
1928

Prominent Whites and Negro Pastors of Suffolk absorbed my attention today.

Went to Congressional Library to get *1000 City Churches* by

Thursday
May 17
1928

H. Paul Douglass. Contains valuable information concerning how to study the Church. However, Woodson does not feel that it will be of much assistance for the study of the Negro Church. But, I hold it will at least give me a hint now and then, which may be applied to the survey of the latter.

Woodson has a low opinion of white magazines and journals. Says he spends 20 minutes per month reading white periodicals. Calls most of it trash. Includes *Current History*, which I consider a good magazine. Of course, I feel that he can afford to read up on the things which concern him most vitally, but for me to attempt the same now would hardly be practical. I must read everything in order to be broadened. Woodson claims that he is interested in *the Negro*, and that his ingesting the white point of view, which is propaganda in favor of white domination, would vitiate his outlook and his work. Says he reads colored newspapers, etc. religiously. I told him his great knowledge, coupled with extensive travel and wide experience, permitted him to do so, even constrained him to, if he would achieve what he considered his all-important life's work. I must wait until I can afford to be a one-sided genius, for that is what any specialist is.

Have completed tabulations of "Citizens," "Pastors," and "Prominent Whites" of Suffolk. Shall begin upon "Youth" tomorrow.

After dinner called Helen Grinage. She was my sweetheart when I attended the University. But I did not write her often. Many times six or seven months passed before I would write her during the years I spent in New York. So presumably she turned to another man who loved her. I do not know whether she loves him.

Last night when I walked into her living room, a young man sat playing the piano. He wore no coat and appeared very much at home. He greeted me coldly, and I returned the same in kind. He appeared to me as if he were the man of the house.

Finally, Helen came in. She blushed, greeted me warmly, and sat down beside me on the couch. We talked about my work concerning the Church Study. Meanwhile, the gentleman went to the kitchen to get his coat, returned, and resumed playing the piano.

Lilly [Lillian], Helen's sister, came into the room. She greeted me warmly and made ready to play whist. She and I played together against Helen and her "boy friend" or husband. They beat us two games out of three.

As I was leaving, Helen came to the door with me. She asked me to call her by "phone" tomorrow, but, not knowing what the situation was, I did not reply.

I wondered whether I should visit her again. Was she married? Her boy friend, or whoever he was, remained after I left. He appeared as if he belonged there.

Lilly asked who was my sweetheart now. I told her no one especially. She laughed. Perhaps she still believed that I might yet marry her sister. But Helen seems lost to me forever.

Lilly suggested that the old gang meet after five years. She is to go to Fort Madison, Iowa, in June to join her husband, who will practice medicine there.

Her cousin brought me home.

Worked today on the churches of Suffolk. Found that the Baptist Churches (six of them) claim one-fifth of the entire Negro population of Nansemond County as their members. Their church valuation is roughly $68,000.

Friday May 18 1928

Started writing up the "Opinions of Citizens of Suffolk" concerning the Negro Church. Miss Revallion, I know, will be pleased to begin upon them tomorrow.

Would be quite lonesome here without her.

Walked home with Miss Powell. She is a true "Blue Grass" [a reference to her being from Kentucky] maiden. Sat beside her outside her house talking with her. As we sat there, she caressed my hands and fingers. It gave me a peculiar feeling. For two hours we sat there. She invited me inside, but I declined, not wishing to become involved with her, since we both work in the same office and I as her superior. She appeared to be a very passionate individual, agitated by slumbering fires. She does not interest me in any way except to joke with her. Wanted to know whether I liked Miss Revallion. Told her "No." Asked why I did not visit her or take her to movies. Told her I was too busy. Finally left her; arrived home at 7:30.

Miss Revallion brought me two letters this morning. One was from Columbia, acknowledging my pledge of five dollars to their alumni drive. The other was from H———. It contained astounding news. For a moment I was stunned. His letter—I had not heard from him for three weeks—informed me that L ——— was about to become a mother. In order to prevent it, he had engaged a doctor—a former classmate from the University—who promised him that he could handle the case easily. Then H——— became ill with influenza. Meanwhile, the girl also became ill and had to go to bed. The doctor— wonderful to relate—had loosened the afterbirth, but not the fetus itself. Naturally H——— is greatly upset over things. Then, God forgive us, the girl's mother found out everything. She wept, the girl wept, and perhaps H——— did also. The mother said that they both should have told her. Things did not please her. Now they must marry, perhaps within the next three weeks.

I feel very sad about the whole affair, for H——— has neither money nor a job to earn money. It is unfortunate that he will be rushed into this union. In this situation, he will be under the domination of his mother-in-law. This is what E——— and I feared. He needs money. I am glad that I have something to send him. He has always been a true friend to me. I shall send him some money on Monday.

Worked all day upon "Opinion of Citizens." Developed sore throat with fever.

Despite the soreness of my throat and fever, I felt that I must see Cousin Rose and Grace in Rosslyn. That was our second home while in D.C. We were always welcome. Many was the meal we ate over there. To their everlasting credit, may it be said that, though they had never been to college, they understood college men. When my hungry tribe would descend upon them without warning, they never asked, "Will you have dinner?", but "Come boys, dinner is served." How I made Helen Tynes [the wife of Harcourt Tynes] laugh concerning our weekly pilgrimage there for our Sunday dinner, and how we would sometimes arrive after they had gone to Communion. Nothing abashed—although we had not eaten all day and it might be about three o'clock before they arrived home—we would sit patiently on the porch, waiting. How woe-begone we would look! Each one—as his stomach acquainted him with the fact that all was not well below—would raise his bowed head slightly and look at the other. And reading the same message in the others' eyes, we would forget our hunger and burst into a prolonged roar of laughter.

Soon, however, the Ford would roll up to the door and my cousins would exclaim, "Oh, here are the boys." Theirs not to question whether we were hungry; that embarrassment was spared us, for perhaps they saw in our lean faces that we needed food uppermost of all. At any rate, into the kitchen they would go, and in a few minutes we would be sitting down to an elaborate dinner. Weekends we spent here, and those incomparable holidays—Christmas, Easter, Thanksgiving. We had a room that they reserved for us at all times. There were only three in the family—one cousin, her husband, and her sister, who is a divorcée. They are my second cousins. They have a ten room house, therefore could easily accommodate us.

Arrived there today just as they were eating dinner. Just told me to sit down and gave me a napkin.

Discussed a thousand things after they had recovered from their surprise at seeing me. They think very little of the House of Prayer and its leader, "Bishop" Grace. Aunt Fannie, Cousin Winnie, and Cousin Susie [Robinson] belong to it. Told me James, Susie's boy, died chiefly from lack of medical attention because of "Daddy" Grace. Parents did not believe son would die. His mother was trying to heal him with a handkerchief. The "Bishop" told his mother that the Lord wanted James; therefore, he would not go contrary to His wishes; neither should his Mother. (The "Bishop" should be put in jail.)

Went down with them to look over the new Ford.

Went to Bertha's. Told me she had given up insurance upon both herself and her son, Wilcie [Wilson]. Asked her why. Replied she had so much trouble in securing the premiums. I believe, however, she was dissimulating. Probably gave them to "Bishop" Grace. Persuaded her to reinstate Wilcie's policy with the insurance company.

Monday
May 21
1928

Spent a miserable day in the office. My throat was so sore, could hardly swallow. Felt feverish. Yet the work must go on. Miss Revallion also is sick. So is Miss Powell.

Worked on "Opinion of Pastors." Half finished it today.

Went to Dr. Dumas at night. Told me to get an atomizer, spray my throat with *Dobell* solution.

Almost forgot. Sent Harry $50. Hope it will help him over his financial difficulty.

Tuesday
May 22
1928

Felt better this a.m. Took Epsom salts. Nasty dose. Rushed to office; finished "Opinion of Pastors." Shall begin "Opinion of Prominent Whites of Suffolk" tomorrow.

The chief need of the Negro church, according to the ministers of Suffolk, is *money*. Most Churches, they believe, have no peculiar hindrance. They believe that the attendance, or rather membership, of youth is increasing faster than of the older members (which I am inclined to doubt). Negro Churches, with the exception of four instances, offer no attractions for youth, save the Sunday School and some form of young folks' meeting. Some lack even the latter. They do little or nothing in an interracial way. Most Negro pastors feel that the white church has little influence upon the Negro church. Very few of the former involve themselves with community affairs. With the exception of Revs. Johnson, Harrell, Gladney, and Wood, none belong to the Parent-Teacher's Association. Even they are largely inactive or manifest a spirit of noncooperation. They, as a group, believe that "shouting" is decreasing, although most of them approve of it.

Ruth [Beverly] called after dinner. Wanted me to say that I

love her. But I did not think that was a wise thing to do, especially since I do not feel that way towards her.

I am concerned now with how to write up the "Community Background." Wretched weather here. Raining intermittently since last Friday.

Wrote up "Opinion of Prominent Whites" of Suffolk today. They believe the Negro Church is in good condition, that the Negro minister is a sincere and upright individual. On the whole, they consider the Negro's religion the best there is, feel he is more liberal in his gifts to the church, yet is in some way influenced by superstition. They believe that the white church has influenced the Negro church chiefly through the imitativeness of the Negro. Although they have given some aid to Negro churches, white individuals of Suffolk, contrary to those of Baltimore, do not believe that the Negro connects morals with his religion. In fact, Lieutenant Governor West states the failure to do so is the weak point in the Negro's religious armor. It is significant that two of the most influential white men here feel that Suffolk Negroes have too many churches.

Naturally, whites believed Negro employees with church connections make better workmen than the unchurched Negroes. The churches do not function interracially here, and, in the opinion of whites, there is no need for such. Race relations here, they contend, have always been excellent. Presumably the Negro knows his place and stays in it.

After work, walked home with Hazel [Powell]. Asked me in. Accepted for a few moments. Told me there was something she desired to say to me. Then changed her mind and decided not to tell me. Finally persuaded her to do so—I was shocked. She told me that Woodson informed her that she must leave me entirely alone so that my work might not be interrupted. I was astounded. I asked her when Woodson had said this to her. She told me that it was yesterday. Then I remembered the occasion. Monday noon, Hazel came into my office during lunch time. She leaned "dangerously" over the table and tried to read the paper which I held in my hand. She bent down closer to me, but I paid little attention to her. Nothing that either she or I was doing ordinarily would have called for what followed. At this moment, however, Dr. Woodson came out of another room and into the office where we were. I did not look up from the paper. Hazel quickly went downstairs. Woodson said nothing to me, but during the afternoon he spoke to Hazel about it. He reminded her that I was young; so was she; that we must be careful, for he had been forced to discharge a young man and woman several years ago. Naturally, I was angry, for he had no right or cause to attribute such to me. Had he mentioned the incident to me, hot words between us would certainly have followed.

Called Bertha about 8:30. She persuaded me to visit her. I did so. Back home at 11:00. Have mapped out my day's work for tomorrow.

Miss Revallion takes up much of my time, talking with me.

Thursday
May 24
1928

Worked assiduously upon "Youth" all day. Miss Revallion noted that I was grouchy today. Perhaps for two reasons: (1) because I wanted to finish the work on the "Opinions of Suffolk Youth," and (2) because I kept thinking of what Woodson had told Hazel.

Found that Suffolk youth attend church more regularly than the Sunday School or Young People's Meeting. They enjoy the music but neither the sermons nor the services as a whole. The sermons are "unintelligible, too long, or too emotional." (I don't blame them.) Their churches for the most part forbid harmless amusements. They disapprove of the church's attitude, and as a result, their outlook towards the church is changed. Yet many are orthodox in their religious beliefs. More than one-third believe in Jesus Christ as the mainspring of their religion. Most youth report they go to their particular church because they like the sermons there. An overwhelming majority of them are found in the churches of their parents, but their religious ideas differ more from their parents' than from those of the church. This difference they ascribe to the greater ignorance of their parents. In Baltimore, the reverse was true: The ministry has fallen into disfavor with young Negro men. Don't study for it because of social restrictions upon the minister, inadequate salaries, and preference for other professions. Most girls say they would not marry ministers because it would interfere with their social pleasures.

Youth constitutes the best educated element in Suffolk. Church had best find some means of reconciling itself to some of the innocent demands of youth, for the future of the Negro Church largely depends upon the active adherence of youth to the institution.

Remained at the office till 6:30.

After dinner went to movies.

Dr. Wesley walked in unannounced this morning. Had just returned from Chicago the night before.

Friday May 25 1928

Told a story of sordid bargaining and corruption at the A.M.E. Quadrennial Conference in Chicago. Liquor, drunken women (white and black), cursing, fist fights, and other disgraceful procedures which one would ascribe to a political convention rather than to a church conference. Why, he said, there were men who offered to supply any number of women, white or black, for the pleasure of these ministerial gentlemen. Others had every brand of whiskey, gin, and other liquors at hand for distribution. Drunken ministers—flasks in their hip pockets—were a common sight. One even offered Mrs. Wesley a drink. God, it is no wonder that the sensible person who has any insight whatever has pulled the mantle of pretense from these so-called men of God and exposed their weak and entirely human frailties. Some Negroes, as a result, renounce religion along with the ministers, or else set up their own private conception of religion. Poor Wesley was disillusioned. He had heard of such doings but said he had not actually believed them. Sometimes it is best, he remarked, that one be not disillusioned. The reaction may prove too great. His feelings, as expressed to me, bordered on disgust.

Saturday
May 26
1928

Still working on "Community Background for Suffolk." Do not believe it is going to please Wesley. It certainly does not please me.

I can easily understand now why the girls who work in offices often fall in love with, or are loved by, their bosses or other men who work in the same office. One necessarily, by close proximity, becomes friendly. This I have discovered since I have worked with Miss Revallion. We are both young and, in spite of our different positions, are becoming more and more friendly in a platonic way.

After dinner called upon Mrs. Hood. No one at home. Went to movies.

Sunday
May 27
1928

Meant to go to church in Rosslyn, but it was raining when I rose. Changed my mind. Left home about 2:30. Called upon Miss Powell. Not at home. Called upon Almira [Streets], distant cousin of mine. Is a graduate of the Cornell School of Music. Conducts a music studio on Vermont Avenue, N.W. Has forty-three pupils. Haughty, pretty, self-conceited, although not directed at me. From Almira's went to Bertha's.

Monday
May 28
1928

Still at work on the "Community Background." Does not seem to satisfy me. Dr. Wesley is reading my manuscript on "Opinions of the Church" for Baltimore. Presume he will have a very poor opinion of my ability as a writer when he finishes. Literarily speaking, I seem to have no style at all. Hear [Sidney] Wells is to leave on Thursday to take a teaching position at Downingtown. Poor fellow, he is deathly afraid of Woodson.

Dr. Wesley went to Baltimore to get more pictures of churches there.

Called upon Hazel [Powell] after dinner. What a girl! She is a flame of fire!

Tuesday
May 29
1928

Finished "Community Background" today. About 35 pages. What a report we will have. Will be over 200 pages in all. Wesley is elated. I hope it will please him, especially the portion on Suffolk done by me. Baltimore will pass muster, I believe, because of Wesley. The latter still works upon "Opinions in Baltimore," revising, excising, including.

Went to the movies tonight.

Decoration Day, but just another day to me. Could not stay away, knowing that the work must be completed as soon as possible. Arrived at office at ten. Wesley came in at noon. He remained till 3:30. Dr. Wesley started reading the "Community Background of Suffolk," which I had written. What a job he will have correcting *that*. He must read my wretched writing.

Went to Bertha's. Teased her about her watch.

Later went to a party at Thelma Duncan's. Classmate of mine at Howard. Is teaching now in North Carolina. She used to be very clever at play writing. Has one included in Alain Locke's book on Negro plays. Miss Revallion was there. Looked sweet and charming. A picture of loveliness. Played whist with her, but her mind was centered on music. Danced with her. She joshed me about my shortness of stature. I retaliated by railing against her height. Agreed that it was embarrassing for both of us to dance together. Had enjoyable evening. Returned home about 1:30.

I am working on "Significant Churches and Pastors of Suffolk." Only four significant churches in Suffolk: First Baptist, Pine Street Baptist, [Willis T.] Faulk's Tabernacle (Christian), and Macedonia Methodist.

Two girls came to the office today seeking employment. Wesley and I marvelled at their uncouthness, also at their lack of information. Woodson asked them questions to which they returned sharp replies. Nevertheless, he is so pushed with work, he had to engage one. She is to report tomorrow. Lives at the YWCA. Woodson called her during the afternoon. Her references were so disappointing that I felt Woodson would inform her in his blunt way, when she arrives tomorrow morning, that her services are unacceptable.

Wednesday May 30 1928

Thursday May 31 1928

Dr. Wesley finally finished reading the "Community Background." Made no comments, though he asked me a few questions about it.

Received a letter from Columbia offering me a position at Howard University as Professor of History and Political Science. A year ago, six months ago, I should have welcomed it. But now? No! Especially after I turned down the Fisk offer. Also received an offer from [North Carolina] A.[gricultural] and T.[echnical] College at Greensboro, North Carolina. Wrote Columbia Appointments Office informing them of my inability to accept positions. Told Wesley of it. Informed me he needed a man at Howard and that Professor [Walter] Dyson had written to several schools in regard to the matter.

Coincidentally, I had just sent $5 to Columbia Alumni Fund this morning.

Friday
June 1
1928

Received three academic blanks from Columbia this a.m. Desired me to send one to Dyson at Howard Univesity after filling them out. The other two were to go to Columbia. Wesley evidently has seen my record sent to Howard. Told me I must have done a high grade of work there, judging from the recommendation. Would release me if I desired the position. Told him "No" flatly, that I did not desire the position. Would prefer to teach at Fisk, but since I declined the latter, the former holds no attractions for me. Furthermore, no offer from any Negro School now could lure me away from this work. I am with Wesley as long as he allows me to stay with him.

Too bad Hipp is not qualified. Could get him in. Perhaps Tynes will take it. Wish he would. Wrote him, asking whether he would accept position.

Wesley went to Baltimore. Woodson engaged the girl after all.

Have nearly finished "Significant Churches and Pastors of Suffolk."

Sent Columbia $20, Mother $25.

Today I practically finished "Significant Churches and Pastors of Suffolk." Took the First Baptist, Pine Street Baptist, Macedonia A.M.E., Allen's Temple A.M.E.Z., The Tabernacle Christian Church of God at Belleville, and Mt. Sinai Baptist Churches as significant organizations. Are chiefly so because of their interest in local Negro education. Among the pastors, the Reverends [J. J.] Posey of a little Episcopal Mission and [Arthur] Wood of the A.M.E.Z. impressed me the most. These churches deserved mention because of their active participation in Community projects or on account of their broadmindedness or advanced notions of church organizations.

After office took Helen [Grinage] to the movies. The "Baltimore Report" is complete in four copies. Dr. Wesley and I each took one home to edit tomorrow.

Saturday
June 2
1928

While correcting the manuscript, the doorbell rang. I was astounded to behold [Harcourt] Tynes. Had no idea he was in town. He had just come from Lincoln University (Pennsylvania), where he had been on Kappa business. Would not teach at Howard. Did not consider himself sufficiently prepared now.

After completing manuscript, I took him to dinner at Thurston's. There we met Ned Poe, local Polemarch of Kappa Alpha Psi. Quiet, unassuming, gentlemanly, and in all probability efficient. Visited the Kappa House. A large, three-story building with about fifteen rooms, concrete basement, an arbor, garage, and favorably located.

Went up the hill to Howard University for the first time since October 1926. Returned, took Tynes to station, where he caught the 7:45 train back to New York City.

Afterwards I went to Anacostia to visit Ruth.

Wrote description for C———.

Sunday
June 3
1928

Finished "Significant Churches and Pastors" and started upon "Education in the Suffolk Churches." Found that Negro pastors have always been interested in Negro education there.

Monday
June 4
1928

Had to be, for state and municipal educational facilities for Negroes are far below par on the elementary level, and entirely lacking on the secondary level. What price segregation!

Yet, in striking contrast to their interest displayed in extra-church education, the pastors themselves are most illiterate. Negro citizens, youth, and even prominent whites are of the same opinion. So, too, is the best educated Negro pastor of Suffolk. The Negro ministers take almost no interest in secular reading. There is a question as to whether the educated or uneducated minister makes the better type of pastor. Surely the illiterate minister can hold some congregations better than the enlightened one. But his tenure is insecure, temporary, for with the rising level of education among his members, the latter tend to fall off and affiliate themselves with the more lettered clergy.

Woodson advised that we send the two reports to New York simultaneously. Shocked me by saying that Suffolk should be written up as if we had never heard of Baltimore. Neither Wesley nor I agreed with him. We both felt that as soon as possible the Institute should have something tangible to show for the money which it is expending regularly upon this work. The report, even now, is almost two months overdue. Concerning Woodson's opinion that the reports should be written without any relation to each other, this would, in my opinion, destroy or tend to defeat the very purpose of the study—namely, to compare the Negro Church in two divergent communities, with Baltimore as the Urban and Suffolk as the Rural.

Wesley went to Baltimore in the a.m. Did not return. Woodson did not have time to look over a copy of the manuscript. Took a copy with him to Charleston, South Carolina, where he is to make a Commencement address. Asked me to see that the door was locked, the windows fastened, to take care of the mail, and to supervise the typing of a valuable manuscript which is being done by a typist especially engaged for the purpose. He left at 6:30 p.m., stating that he would telegraph Dr. Wesley concerning the *Report*, if it was not "too bad."

[8] Blasted Hopes

Tuesday
June 5
1928

When Dr. Wesley arrived today, a telegram was awaiting him
from Dr. Woodson. Wesley read it and smothered a gasp. He
then passed it to me. I read with astonishment: "*Report* worthless to page 58. Remainder fair, but style rough. Too much
repetition. Too much sermonizing." I could hardly suppress
my surprise. To think that he should call the *Report* worthless
up to page 58! That included all save ten pages that Dr. Wesley
had written. I had expected that the full brunt of his unfavorable criticism would fall upon my section dealing with
opinions.

Dr. Wesley immediately decided to ignore Woodson's telegram and to send the *Report*, notwithstanding. We both felt
the tone of the dispatch was calculated to discourage us so that
we might hold the *Report* until Dr. Woodson returned either
Thursday or Friday. He is so self-opinionated. Makes little
allowance for the point of view of the other fellow. I can
readily see how the unfortunate assistant, coming under his
supervision direct from college, would either have to break
with him, as Dr. Alrutheus Taylor and others did, or else
permit themselves to become completely subservient to him.
And to think, I narrowly escaped that fate last fall, when he
offered me room and board to work with the Association until
he could arrange a salary for me. As Wesley stated, I "got a
break" when I was employed to assist him (Wesley).

We remained at the office till 5:30. Made a final check of the report. Sent it off about six o'clock.

I wrote the two Helens, then went to movies.

Wednesday
June 6
1928

Wesley came in this a.m. Told me that in a letter from the Institute, received while he was in Chicago, the officials had taken the pains to assure him that no one could possibly supersede him in the work as Director. Why, I asked myself, this need of such reaffirmation? Obviously, someone had communicated with the Institute, either suggesting a man "better qualified" or else offering himself as a probable Director. Wesley thinks it may have been Monroe Work of Tuskegee, Editor of *The Negro Year Book*. He left at 11:00 a.m. Was to examine two candidates for M.A. degrees in History at Howard.

Miss Revallion was piqued at my lack of amiability this a.m. She thawed out later; however, I was worried.

Wesley returned about 4:30. Miss Revallion had gone. The other girls also. Wesley said they must have left a little ahead of time. True, a few minutes earlier.

Wesley told me that one of the candidates flunked her M.A. exams. According to him, she knew practically nothing about her subject.

Wesley delivers Commencement address at Downingtown tomorrow.

Called Bertha. Later called Thelma [Duncan]. Dorothy [Revallion] was there. Took them both to movies.

Thursday
June 7
1928

Finished Taylor's *Reconstruction of Virginia* today. Gives much information concerning Reconstruction otherwise omitted from the average book on the subject. Most important was his refutation of the old [William A.] Dunning [author of *Reconstruction, Political and Economic, 1865–1877* (1907)] and others' thesis: The Negro was responsible for all the ills of the South during Reconstruction; therefore, his disfranchisement by the white Southerners was justified. But book is not well proportioned. Read half of [Arthur Meier] Schlesinger's *Political and Social History of U.S.*

Walked home with Hazel. Called upon Bertha. She has bad cold.

Coming in from lunch, found Woodson dictating letters to Hazel. Asked me if anything had happened. Assured him nothing untoward had taken place, to which he replied: "Something *has* happened, but nothing *untoward.*" I wondered what he implied, but said nothing. Later asked me whether we (Wesley and I) had received his telegram. Responded in the affirmative. He said nothing more. Neither did I. We have thwarted and angered him, I believe, by sending the report against his advice.

Went to movies.

Friday
June 8
1928

Wesley came in. I placed two parts of the "Suffolk Report" on his desk for him to peruse. Asked me if Woodson had said anything concerning the report. Informed him that Woodson had inquired only about receipt of his telegram. Woodson entered a little later but said nothing to Wesley about the report. Yet, I felt that something ominous was about to happen regarding the study. When a letter lending encouragement to us came from the Institute today, the officials acknowledged receipt of the report. Considered it promising. Would read it over and let us know results later. Wesley now intends to send the "Suffolk Report," without allowing Woodson to read it. Thinks latter's comments worthless. Wesley left office at 1:30. Had to attend a funeral.

Saturday
June 9
1928

Rose too late to go to church. Bertha called at 3:00. Went there. Left at 7:30. Attended movies later. Saw Ruth Thomas. Also Dotson.

Sunday
June 10
1928

Wesley went to Baltimore today. Took two parts of "Suffolk Report" with him to peruse en route.

After correcting two sections which Miss Revallion had typed, I began reading *A Tropical Dependency* by Lady [Flora Louisa Shaw] Lugard. A truly remarkable book. Treats of Nigeria. She develops the astonishing thesis that the home of

Monday
June 11
1928

civilization was not the valley of the Euphrates, but the Sudan. Holds thesis Negroes gave civilization to world. I had noted references to this book in [Parker Thomas] Moon's *Imperialism and World Politics*.

Called Bertha about 8:00 p.m. Just wanted to talk with her.

Tuesday
June 12
1928

Spent most of the day reading *A Tropical Dependency*. Interested in the theory of Mrs. Lugard that civilization in Africa spread from West to East. Also, that contemporaneous with European ignorance and superstition in the Middle Ages, the light of education, culture, and refinement, also science, was burning brightly, not only in Spain under the Arabs, but also in the black Sudan, in Ghana, Mali, and other states.

Called on Bertha to borrow my little watch to show to the folks at the office. Mr. Yarborough [Bertha's suitor] was there. I promised to return the watch on Thursday.

Wednesday
June 13
1928

Spent the day correcting parts of the survey and reading.

In the evening went to Thelma's, where Dorothy, I, and others were to play cards. Dorothy did not appear. Spent an enjoyable evening with Thelma. Was a classmate of mine at Howard. Came away with her class ring and my "Stylus Key," which I had long desired to repossess. Left my book of poetry there.

Republican Convention opens in Kansas City tomorrow.

Thursday
June 14
1928

Corrected the last portions of the essay today, and Miss Revallion started upon the final typing.

Read further in Lady Lugard. Took watch back to Bertha tonight. Teased her by telling her I had forgotten it. She thinks as much of the watch as she does the owner. Perhaps more?

Friday
June 15
1928

Wesley informed me that the A.M.E.Z. Conference at Union Wesley Church last night voted affirmatively for union with the A.M.E. Church. Good news! This would bring into oneness the largest groups of organized Negroes in the Country. It is a union which should have taken place over a century ago, for there exist no doctrinal differences either in theory or in practice between the two churches. Richard Allen and James Varick, the founders of the A.M.E. (African Methodist Episcopal) and A.M.E.Z. (African Methodist Episcopal Zion) Churches, respectively, would have combined early in the 19th Century—about 1806—had it not been for personal ambition on the part of both men.[1]

Wesley asked me to cover the Conference. He believed it was being held at the John Wesley [A.M.E.Z.] Church, 14th and R Streets. Instead the sessions took place at Union Wesley Church, 23rd Street, near L Street, N.W.

When I arrived at the Conference, reports were being read from the various churches. It was stated that Dr. Hampton Thomas Medford, pastor of the John Wesley A.M.E.Z. Church at 14th and R Streets, had been endeavoring to adapt that church to the changing economic, social, and educational needs of the age. He feels that such a program is imperative if youth is to be retained in the church today. I fully agreed. Dr. Medford is now General Secretary of Foreign Missions for the church.

1. It is unlikely that Allen and Varick were discussing union in 1806. Neither the African Methodist Episcopal Church (A.M.E.) nor the African Methodist Episcopal Zion Church (A.M.E.Z.) existed as separate denominations in that year. The A.M.E. Church had its beginnings when the white members of St. George Methodist Episcopal Church in Philadelphia decided to segregate the church's black members. Richard Allen, Absalom Jones, and William White led the black members out of the church; and in 1787, they formed the Free African Society, which was more a fraternal than a religious organization. In 1791, some members of the society joined with Jones in organizing the St. Thomas Protestant Episcopal Church; but the majority remained with Allen, who in 1794 established Bethel Church as an independent black church within the Methodist denomination. Blacks in other cities followed this example and organized separate churches. Finally, on April 9, 1816, sixteen delegates met in Philadelphia and founded the A.M.E. Church.

The A.M.E.Z. denomination had similar but different origins. The black members of the John Street Methodist Church in New York City withdrew amicably and began worshiping separately in Zion Church. For a number of years, the members of Zion Church remained under the supervision of the John Street Church. Between 1816 and 1820, Bishop Allen tried to attract the New York independents into his movement, but he had only limited success. In 1821, the Zionists completed the organization of the A.M.E.Z. Church as a separate denomination.

Both denominations were basically Methodist in their polity, but there were differences between them. The A.M.E.Z. Church assigned a more prominent role to the laity; and from the beginning, the Zionists placed no restrictions on the ordination of women. Benjamin Brawley, *A Social History of the American Negro* (London, 1970), 68–70; E. Franklin Frazier, *The Negro Church in America* (New York, 1966), 25–28; Carter G. Woodson, *The History of the Negro Church* (3rd ed.; Washington, D.C., 1985), 61–73.

The Church Schools were reported to be well organized. All the reports were shot through with references to youth. It is commendable, for it at least demonstrates that the Negro Church is awakening to its problem of retaining youth within its bosom.

Bishop [J. S.] Caldwell, a striking figure, tall, well-made, with clean-shaven head, presided over the session. He impressed me as being an efficient parliamentarian. He needed to be such, for, at the time, the hubbub would have overwhelmed a smaller, less competent individual.

The following receipts were collected during the year from the churches included in the Washington District:

CHURCH		RECEIPT
Galliopolis		$14,276.00
Union Wesley		17,212.17
Union Wesley, S.S.		1,849.26
Metropolitan		11,483.56
Lennox		2,899.00
Britain		2,089.86
Roah		1,089.75
Fox		184.47
Oak Grove		204.07
Ger M		243.48
(?)		647.58
	TOTAL	$52,179.20
Property Valuations		$703,700.00
Members		5,080
Total Enrolled		3,552

Rev. Howard, the presiding Elder of the Salisbury, Maryland, District, an irrepressible man of medium height, read a report so full of "flowers" and so lengthy that the Bishop had to admonish him to shorten it. He began by saying, "The Great day of the Bishop has came," which convulsed his hearers with laughter. He had not done so well financially because of the hard winter and lack of employment among his membership. Spoke of a revival held in Delaware, which won no converts. His report was replete with extraneous matters and anecdotes. How these people waste time!

Finance! Finance! Finance! It transcends everything else here. Woodson commented similarly about the A.M.E. Conference in Chicago.

Rose early to get to Metropolitan A.M.E. Church at 11:45. Father's Day. Speakers, speakers, speakers—all reiterating the same general thought. The church is large, too large for the congregation, if two days' attendance can be taken as a criterion. The auditorium was not wholly filled and the spacious gallery was empty.

A Mr. —— of the Victory Insurance Company spoke. His entire talk was punctuated by "uh-ruhs." The pastor's sermon, however, was short, concise, logical, and well-delivered.

The music was appropriate to the occasion and rendered by a large, well-trained, vested choir.

As usual, there took place a multitude of collections. So many, in fact, that the spiritual content of the services was practically nullified by the clanking of silver.

The recessional of the choir was very impressive.

Met Dorothy and Thelma after church. Went home with them.

Mrs. L—— "forced" me to dine with the girls, even though I demurred for a long time.

It was insufferably hot, yet we went out to take pictures. Arrived at Thelma's; we sat in Mr. Jeter's car and talked till 7:30. I had a tea engagement at Mrs. Mahoney's [Mahony's?]. Leaving the girls, I arrived at the tea at 7:55 p.m., just in time to secure a glass of punch. Saw no tea.

Called Ruth Beverly. Wanted me to come out; but considering it too late, promised to see her next Saturday.

Wesley is still in Wilberforce. Miss Revallion plans to finish the typing of the Suffolk manuscript by Tuesday. I will then send it to New York. Edited as much as she had completed.

Mrs. Lugard in her *Tropical Dependency* makes the statement that Meröe, now Abyssinia, was the cradle of civilization. A most remarkable book. For the first time I have been able to

secure an impartial account of the ancient and medieval glories
of the Negro. Yea, even his modern splendors!

Went to Dr. Dumas to see him concerning a cold. Gave me
capsules.

Tuesday
June 19
1928

Miss Revallion has completed the final typing of the manuscript. Corrections will be the order of the day for tomorrow.
She is working diligently to help me get this off. A fine typist.

Bertha called tonight. Desired to know why I did not call
her last night. Made engagement to take her to the movies
Friday.

After Dr. Woodson sent his ill-starred telegram from Danville, Virginia, two weeks ago, Dr. Wesley decided then and
there to ignore Woodson as far as the "Suffolk Report" was
concerned. Wesley believed (and I confess I did too) that
Woodson did so in order to coerce him (Wesley) into delaying
the sending of the report. Whether we have accused Woodson
wrongly or not, Wesley, through Miss Revallion, instructed
me to forward the manuscript, when completed, to New
York. Not having received specific orders to submit the report
to Woodson, I made no effort to do so, despite the fact that
today Woodson asked whether the Suffolk manuscript was
completed. I replied negatively.

Wednesday
June 20
1928

The report will assuredly be sent away tomorrow. Miss Revallion and I made herculean efforts to get it off today. There
were, however, about nine pages to be typed and numerous
corrections to be made. Remained at the office till 6:00 p.m.
Left some pages for correction upon Miss Revallion's desk.

Took Thelma Duncan to the movies tonight. How attractive she appeared in her sporty, pin-stripe suit. She is just
about my height, slightly plump, russet-brown complexion,
with jet black hair and a pair of striking eyes. Tonight, her hair
parted in the center, she looked very charming. Her disposition is so winning that I asked her how I happened to spend so
little time in her company at Howard. She blushed. I did not
really know Thelma.

Leaving the movies, I invited her to stop and have some ice

cream. Joshed her about it, by telling her I had done so only to afford her an opportunity to decline. After doing so several times, she finally accepted, laughingly informing me that she was doing so just to "call my bluff." Upon leaving the ice cream parlor (Brook's), we found it was raining hard. We took a taxi to Thelma's, for she must not get her hair wet. Spent delightful evening with her.

By dint of hard work, I finished editing the manuscript and packed it for shipment at noon. Mailed it after dinner.

Thursday
June 21
1928

While correcting the manuscript, Dr. Woodson asked to speak to me privately for a moment. Could not imagine what he wanted. He invited me into the private *sanctum* (the kitchen), and asked me to take a seat. He then proceeded to unfold to me a devastating bit of news. First he began by informing me that the Association, in joint cooperation with the Institute of Social and Religious Research of New York, was bearing half the expense of the Church Survey. I already knew that. Then he shocked me by saying that Wesley had agreed in his contract to give up all connections with the church when he accepted directorship of the study. Instead, he had resigned one position only to accept another—the Presiding Eldership of A.M.E. Church for Washington, D.C. By so doing, continued Woodson, Wesley automatically abrogated his contract. Therefore he considered it "advisable" to withdraw the support of the Association from the study, since the survey, in his opinion, could not be completed, in such a "leisurely manner," for at least five years. Furthermore, he stated that he had already written both the Institute and Wesley informing them of his action. From the point of view of the Association, *the study was over*, he added, unless Wesley resigned his Eldership. He had suggested to the Institute officials that they might set up the study independently of the Association, defray all expenses, and allow Wesley to "prosecute" the work along with his other duties. But from his point of view, "the study was over."

I was dumbfounded. I saw all my hopes of three months crumbling about me like a house of sand. But then a larger issue loomed before me. What would the Institute officers, Messrs. Fisher, Bowen, and Frey, think of Woodson and Wesley? Would this not exasperate them, confirm the general belief in the unreliability of the Negro, strengthen the prevalent idea that Negroes are incapable of concerted action, and render them all the more hesitant about putting such projects in the hands of Negroes in the future?

Wesley, how I admire him! He has been so kind, so inspiring; had allowed me to write practically half of the Baltimore and all of the Suffolk Report. But Woodson states that Wesley is actuated by self-interest. Told me that two years ago Wesley came to him. Asked him for a job. Woodson agreed to pay him at a rate of $1,500 a year during the school term, while Wesley agreed to give up his church while in the employ of the Association. He was to produce a monograph on Negro occupations. Woodson, in disgust, told me that Wesley not only retained the pastorship of his church but also taught summer school at Howard, with the result that at the end of the year Wesley had collected a mere handful of information. At that time, says Woodson, these combined duties paid him a salary of about $6,000. Then he secured the directorship of the church study for Wesley, obtained for him a salary of $4,000— $3,000 from the Institute and $1,000 from the Association— the latter just to help out. Yet, Wesley, he continued, refused to give up church work. He accepted the position as Presiding Elder with a salary of $2,400 per year, making, in all, $6,400 per year. Woodson claims that he called Wesley's attention to his breach of contract upon his accepting the church office last April. I had specifically asked Woodson the question, for I did not believe that Wesley would deliberately break his word. Even if he did, I had faith in him that he would rectify it immediately, upon his attention being called to the fact.

Woodson felt that Wesley was perfectly capable of "prosecuting" the survey and paid tribute to the latter's scholarly virtues. But, he added, Wesley is primarily interested in "the making of dollars." Then, probably reading my thoughts, he assured me, "You will be taken care of. I got you into this study, and I shall see that you do not suffer even though the survey will be discontinued."

I was too amazed, too dejected, to reply. To me, it was inconceivable. This study upon which I had based so much, to come to such an untimely end. The potentialities of this survey: contact, travel, experience, during two years of research! Then a reputation which would be mine through the association of my name with Wesley's in this study. Also the prospects of other studies in the event that we made a creditable showing in this survey. I saw all the advantages, all the fond expectations, all the mental pictures which I had been constructing since January—in short, all my fond hopes—dashed by this interview. My castle of dreams destroyed! And Wesley, stabbed in the back!

I left after having been closeted with Dr. Woodson for nearly two hours. Dejection was my companion during the afternoon. Miss Revallion noticed it. Tried to cheer me up. Impossible. I wondered whether Woodson had been impelled to this action by our total ignoring of his telegram of two weeks ago. Was he jealous of Wesley?

Read till 4:30. Miss Revallion desired to know whether I would continue to work for the Association. Advised me against it. Doubted my ability to get along with Woodson. I doubted it, too, after his treatment of Wesley.

After dinner went to Carrie's. Started to movies. Changed my mind. Returned home at 9:30. So depressed, could not sleep.

Wesley came in this a.m. He seemed worried about something. Told me he had just returned from Wilberforce. Asked me about the Suffolk manuscript. Told him I had sent it to New York.

Friday June 22 1928

Wesley then told me that Woodson had written the Institute people in New York telling them that, because of his (Wesley's) acceptance of the Presiding Eldership, he (Woodson) had withdrawn the support of the Association from the study. Wesley added that on his arrival home, he had found a telegram from the Institute directors, desiring a conference with him and Woodson on Monday in New York and directing him to bring the Suffolk Manuscript with him. He also found a letter from Woodson telling him of his action in severing the connection, that is, that of the Association, from the project. Wesley was indignant because Woodson had stated in his letter to the Institute that he had repeatedly informed him (Wesley) that his acceptance of the office of Presiding Elder would automatically sever his connection with the church study. At least, Woodson was pleased to construe it in that light. I asked Wesley whether this was the condition upon which he accepted the Church Study.

In reply, Wesley told me that Woodson had never mentioned the incompatibility of his assumption of the church office with the directorship of the Church Study. In fact, the only references to it, he continued, were a few jocular statements by Woodson, some of which were made in my presence. I can clearly recall one occasion in the office when Woodson jokingly remarked that Wesley would soon be Bishop and that I would be his assistant.

Wesley seemed as badly smitten by the turn of events as I. And why should he not? He admitted that he had broken his contract by accepting the other office, but justified it on the ground that he realized the insecurity of his position while affiliated with a project with which Woodson was connected. Wesley recalled to me a loss of $21,000 which he had sustained in an unfortunate business transaction a few years ago. He had apprised Woodson of that fact. Though he admitted his error, he felt aggrieved because Woodson had not spoken to him about the matter first.

Then he crushed me by informing me that *he* had resigned as Director of the Survey. In fact, he added, he had sent in his resignation from Wilberforce, even before coming home. At the time, he knew nothing of Woodson's letters. I was hopeful that he and Woodson would thrash out the matter before the conference with Messrs. Bowen and Fisher of the Institute on Monday.

Wesley took the telegram from Fisher which he had shown

me to Woodson. Returning, he told me that Woodson could not find it convenient to go to New York on Monday. In fact, Wesley believed that Woodson had literally stabbed him in the back. He could not justify Woodson's waiting till he (Wesley) had gone to Wilberforce to write such a letter either to him or to the Institute. I myself considered the letter to Wesley perfunctory, even superfluous, for Woodson could easily have talked with Wesley at the office. Yet, relations between the two had been a trifle strained since Woodson's telegram from South Carolina.

I could imagine how Wesley felt, for my own depression was great enough. In fact, he sat there at times silently drumming upon the table or balling up tiny pieces of paper. What to say to comfort him I knew not. I finally left about 1:45 to go out to Brightwood. Just as I was leaving, Mrs. Wesley telephoned a telegram to Wesley, informing him that Messrs. Fisher and Bowen of the Institute would come to Washington Monday for a conference with him and Woodson. Ominous! Little to be hoped for now.

As if that weren't enough for Wesley to bear, Miss Revallion called and told him she could not live upon her salary. Threatened to accept other offers. Poor Wesley! Replied that he would be able to give her an answer by Monday, that then he would know definitely whether the work would go on. In the meantime, he advised her to speak to Woodson. Wesley, with an air of complete resignation, told me of Miss Revallion's demand. It only deepened my gloom, for I did not think she could have chosen a worse moment to apprise Wesley of her seeming ultimatum.

I went out to Brightwood. Saw Helen Grinage and Julia. Had not seen the latter since 1924. The former insists she is not married. Still, she will not permit me to call upon her. Brought her a box of candy. She must have been surprised, for it is only the second time in four years that I have done so. Spent enjoyable time with the girls. Lillian, Helen's sister, came in as I was leaving. She is going to Iowa to join her husband, who is just beginning to practice medicine there.

I returned to the office about 4:10 p.m., just in time to

receive another telegram for Wesley from the Institute. I telephoned its contents to his residence, it being too late to expect his return to the office. Telegram referred to coming to Washington of Messrs. Fisher and Bowen of the Institute of Social and Religious Research, which is bearing half the expense of the church study. Time of their arrival was 9:00 a.m. I am not at all optimistic over the outcome.

Took Bertha to the movies. Looked beautiful in white. Reminded me of other days. She, with her wit and laughter, aided immeasurably in dispelling my gloom.

Saturday
June 23
1928

Did not reach the office till eleven o'clock today. Miss Revallion informed me that Wesley had come in and gone. I remained till 1:30, at which time I went to lunch and from there to the ball game.

Returned home at 6:00 p.m. Miss Revallion called. Informed me that Woodson promises to give her $1,200 a year after August. She is happy. She deserves it. Is a competent secretary.

Remained in tonight. Cannot fully compose myself after the shock suffered yesterday. Heard that two men from Suffolk were in town looking for me. This means that I shall either be forced to secure new quarters or else have renovated these where I now live.

Sunday
June 24
1928

Went to Metropolitan A.M.E. Church. Too late to hear sermon, but in plenty of time to be greeted by a series of collections. According to my usual custom, contributed a dime to one of them.

Went to Thelma's with her and Dorothy. Chatted till 3:30.

Called Bertha. Went to her home. Remained there till 8:00, when Yarborough called.

Later took Miss [Pauline?] Stewart to the movies. She wore a beautiful large black hat. Looked stunning in it.

Monday
June 25
1928

When I arrived at the office, Woodson and Wesley were closeted with Messrs. Fisher, Frey, and Bowen, the three leading men in the Institute. I went into Miss Revallion's office next door.

I overheard part of the conversation, although I made no conscious effort to do so, and purposely sat as far removed from the door as possible.

Woodson claimed that he had spoken to Wesley relative to the consequences of his accepting the Presiding Eldership of the A.M.E. Church here, which would automatically cancel his position as director of the Church Study. Wesley contended Woodson had not done so. Woodson held that "the survey, as Wesley was now leisurely pursuing it, would take about five years." Wesley countered that we could have made better progress with the study had the men assigned by Woodson to cover the community background discharged their duties effectively. This was especially true in the case of Woods, whose work in Baltimore was of practically no consequence. Woodson then confounded Wesley by stating that the latter had written from Baltimore requesting that Woods be left there another week. Also, Woods had written to the same purpose, stating that Wesley needed him there. Wesley denied it but Woodson, in a loud and confident tone, offered to adduce written evidence, stating that he had the letters on file.

Woodson then brought forward some of McKinley's reports to prove to the gentlemen of the Institute that the reports of McKinley were satisfactory in every way. Wesley did not contradict him. At least, I did not hear his efforts to controvert Woodson's sallies. The latter was merciless; his words dropped vitriol. Several times Bowen had to admonish him to silence.

Woodson related that he had advised Wesley to go to the Conferences at Chicago (A.M.E.), Kansas City (A.M.E.Z.), and St. Louis (Baptist) in May, for there he would reach a great number of men whom it would be very difficult to meet otherwise. Instead, he concluded, ruefully, Wesley spent three weeks in Chicago and came back with nothing. Woodson also reminded the men that he had suggested to Wesley that he cover the Baptist Conference meeting in New York. The latter had not done so. Just what retort Wesley made to these sallies, I do not know, for the drumming of the typewriter drowned out his softly spoken words.

It was evident to me that Wesley was being worsted. Woodson dominated the conference. His voice, exultant, boomed out his sentences, acrid with sarcasm and irony, and pungent with evil.

Messrs. Bowen, Frey, and Fisher then went into a conference to decide whether they would continue or not with the survey. Woodson had suggested that they do so independently and still retain Wesley as Director, but the Association would be relieved of bearing half of such a "leisurely prosecuted" study. He reiterated his belief in Wesley's ability to do the work. Finally, Wesley and Woodson withdrew, leaving the three men from New York to decide the ultimate fate of the Negro Church Study.

Both Miss Revallion and I had lost hope completely. She attempted to interrogate me, but her queries only irritated me. I desired to be left alone. Woman-like she sought to cheer me.

Finally, after what seemed a millenium, Mr. Fisher called Woodson who, in turn, summoned Wesley. When they entered the room, my hopes rose anew at Mr. Bowen's exclamation that this was the first clear day they had had in some time. It augured, I thought, well for the study in which my heart was wrapt. But, just as one struggling through the arid and torrid wastes of the desert mistakes the mocking mirage of the sun, sand, and atmosphere for a well of refreshing water, and sinks disillusioned into despair and despondency, just so was I doomed to utter disappointment when I heard Mr. Frey say, "the survey will be discontinued." After a few other perfunctory remarks, they withdrew about eleven thirty.

Wesley came in to tell Miss Revallion and me what we both already knew. Our connection with the work would cease on June 30, when we would receive our final checks.

Wesley told me that Mr. Bowen asked about me. Told him to write concerning me. Wesley intimated that he might demand that the Institute honor its contract of February, which stated that two (2) months' notification is required of each party in event of its intention to discontinue the study. At that rate, I felt that the Institute itself must make good two months' salary. However, I would not press the claim.

Wesley realized fully the tremendous opportunity which he and I had lost. He regretted now that he and Woodson had not thrashed the matter out before meeting the men from New York. I agreed with him. He accused Woodson of distorting the truth. Said he almost lost his temper at one time. And I assured him he had every reason to do so. Doubt whether, in face of Woodson's badgering, I could have kept mine. Wesley had been asked by the Institute to send all the materials on Suffolk and Baltimore to its office.

I helped him collect them. I knew not what to say. Wesley expressed sympathy for me, especially since I had turned down so many teaching offers for the Church Study. I told him that Woodson had promised to take care of me employment-wise. He was glad of that.

I felt commiseration for him, knowing that he was bearing the brunt of the storm and that, because of broken faith, he would have to forfeit this monumental opportunity. He was plainly dejected when he left a little after noon.

Later in the afternoon Woodson called me into his private "sanctum"—the kitchen. We sat at the white-enamel-topped table, stained with food, the black undercoating showing where the enamel had been worn off. On the table were remains of his luncheon—the reamed out halves of six or eight oranges, a tall glass of water, and a pitcher about a quarter full. Dirty dishes filled the sink. The stove was heavily coated with grease, and here and there a roach ran up the wall or over the floor. Woodson swept one off the table with a flick of his hand. Surely a woman was needed here. Said he desired to speak with me for five minutes. He was sorry that the Institute had seen fit to call off the survey. Believed they would set it up ultimately under Wesley, or someone else. Told me that Wesley had injected the personal element in the discussion by stating that the two of them had had frequent quarrels, and also that he (Woodson) was attempting to secure the directorship of the study for himself. He ridiculed that idea. "Why," he asked, "why should I seek to supersede Wesley when I worked so hard to secure the appropriation and the position for him?" He labelled Wesley "an inveterate money seeker."

Then adverting to me, he offered me either one of two positions: (1) to do field work such as I had been doing, or (2) to "develop a study of Negro Occupations." Would give me the same salary. I could use the study, he assured me, for a doctoral dissertation at Columbia. Told me to think over his proposition. I reminded him of the two-months' notification clause in my contract. Replied that the Institute was morally obligated "to take care of me for that period" but advised against suing them. Asked me what I conceived to be the attitude of the Institute men when they left. I retorted, "one of exasperation and disgust, also the growing conviction that Negroes cannot be relied upon to work together harmoniously." He laughed and agreed that perhaps it was true. Said Wesley should not have resigned. I withheld a reply, for, in my opinion, it was Woodson who had precipitated the crisis. The latter sank in my estimation.

Left Woodson. Read for a while. Wesley returned about 4:30. Gathered up all papers and material (notes) bearing upon our surveys and took them out to his car.

Thinks Woodson played a nasty trick on him. So do I. Says no one can get along with him. I talked with Wesley a long while outside the office. Is going to Hampton tomorrow, then to Norfolk. Would have taken me with him, but the events of the morning changed all that.

Have been morose all day. Miss Revallion has tried vainly to hearten me.

Could not stay in at night. Took a walk and ended up at the movies. I saw Woodson there, but we only nodded to each other. My sympathies were all with Wesley.

[9] Hope Renewed: New Duties

Tuesday
June 26
1928

Rose at 9:30. Went down town. Bought a filler for my diary, an autograph book for Dorothy [Revallion], and had shoes mended. Expect to go to New York in the morning. Almost noon when I arrived at the Office.

Woodson asked to speak to me again for a few moments. We went into his *private of privates*, the kitchen. He reiterated his promise of yesterday that he would write the Institute regarding me, recommending that they include me on a subsequent staff, if they decided to resume the Church Survey. I had told him that since I had already begun the survey and was attuned to it, I should prefer continuing in it, even though under a different Director.

Again Woodson reminded me of his proposition. Told me if I were tired, to take a couple of weeks' vacation with pay. I certainly could use a vacation, for I have not had one since 1917. He wants me to write a monograph on Negro occupations. Here again he struck a verbal blow at Wesley. "We paid Wesley $1,500," he said, "and haven't a darn thing (snapping his fingers) to show for it." Told me that if I did not do the work, he would have to sign someone's name to it. Told me he would take me to the Library of Congress, get me a cubicle there, and assist me in beginning the work. I told him I would think it over.

Startled me by showing me [Alrutheus Ambush] Taylor's

Reconstruction of Virginia and *The Negro in South Carolina During the Reconstruction*. Said he practically wrote them. Also, he added, "don't tell me you will do the work, then accept a position at Howard University." I assured him that once my word was given him, even though something more remunerative were tendered me, I should refuse it. I left Woodson's presence with mixed emotions. Could I, should I work with him? Should I accept his offer, or Wesley's? I had spent over two hours with Woodson. Spent the rest of the afternoon in a state of bewilderment.

This was the night of Dorothy's party. I started to dress but lay across the bed till after nine. Had just completed dressing when the phone rang. It was Dorothy. Desired to know whether I was coming. Joshingly told her no. Responded that I must come.

Arrived at the party about 10:15. Just four couples. As usual, I acted the buffoon. Dorothy said the party was dead until I got there. It reminded me of other parties in D.C. (Washington), New York, and elsewhere. Guess I am slated to play the fool for others' enjoyment. Well, it is better than crying.

Dorothy looked lovely in her little flowered dress. Thelma [Duncan]—by the way, I called her "Fifi"—had all the appearance of a maiden from the South Sea Islands. Her disposition is exceedingly charming. I have often wondered why I saw so little of her socially at Howard. 'Twas my personal loss.

Drank a little punch. It seemed to put me to sleep. I am the weakling in that respect. Have no taste for liquor, but hide the fact from all but my closest friends.

Had a fine time. Danced and played cards. Each one took home a piece of Dorothy's birthday cake.

Senator [Joseph T.] Robinson caused a fist fight among the delegates at the Democratic Convention at Houston, Texas, today. The participants reacted in that bellicose manner after listening to a plea by the Arkansas Senator for religious tolerance. What would they have done had he, like [J. Thomas] Heflin [of Alabama], advocated the drawing of sectarian lines in order to exclude Catholics from the Presidency? His (Robinson's) fervent exhortation for religious tolerance was delivered for the benefit of Al Smith, present Governor of New York, a Catholic, who is virtually assured of the Democratic nomination for the next President of the United States. Were Smith opposed by any other man besides Hoover—whom, God forgive me, I believe to be an honest man—I should certainly cast my vote for him. He is one of the most popular governors New York has ever had. Is a man of the people.

After spending the morning in leisurely reading, I informed Dr. Woodson about one o'clock that I had "prayed" over his proposition and was ready to give him an answer.

Wednesday
June 27
1928

For the third successive day, we spent about two hours in his "sanctum."

He told me that the Institute of Social and Religious Research, which organization, in conjunction with the Association, had been sponsoring the ill-fated Church Survey, disclaimed any responsiblity for my contract. He read from a letter of Mr. Bowen—that such a contract was made between Wesley and me alone. That, I reminded Woodson, was a highly erroneous statement, with which the latter agreed. I felt, and so did Woodson, that the Institute legally owed me two months' salary. However, he stated that he should regret my suing them for such. I told him that so great was my mortification and embarrassment over the abrupt termination of the study that I should not think of pressing my legitimate claim.

Woodson read me a letter from the Institute in which the officials expressed regret at my predicament caused by the sudden termination of the survey. They expressed pleasure, however, that Dr. Woodson had offered me a position and at the same salary. They also, to my satisfaction, stated that the reports which we submitted to them on the Negro Church in Suffolk and Baltimore demonstrated the wonderful potentialities of such a survey. I was grateful to hear that.

Woodson, in response to a statement in the letter which he was reading, remarked, "Wesley is perfectly capable of making the survey; the only question is *will* he do it?"

He then read me a letter which he was sending the Institute, in which he recommended Wesley as the head of the same Church Study, set up independently of the Association. "This ought to prove conclusively," he stated, "that I do not covet the directorship of the study of which Wesley accused me. Why should I," he asked with some heat, "when I went to all the pains and trouble of securing the study for him?"

He brought me back to my engagement with the Association. I told him I would accept the position to make a study of Negro Occupations, but that I would need at least $2,000 per year to live here. He acquiesced with very little opposition. I am sensible enough to realize what this study will mean to me.

We chatted informally upon different topics, school, the writing of history, etc. I asked him if he would consider the writing of a history of the Negro in a series of volumes. Said he desired to leave that as his monument. Could do so, he stated, in the next ten years.

My next interrogation was who would write his biography. What a wonderful field for someone with literary bent! I told Miss Revallion she should have kept a diary during her four years here. After Woodson's death it would become invaluable to anyone who desired to write his life. He answered that no one would write his biography because they would have nothing to write about. I discounted that, however. So did he by a sly little laugh. Reminded him that he could not do it as well as someone else who had the facts, for then he could be appraised objectively. We chatted upon one topic or another for over two hours.

He promised to take me to the Congressional Library, secure me a table, and give me leads in certain books down there.

Told me I had heard that he was hard to please, that he was eccentric and did things in fits and starts. I told him that all I needed was to be told what to do. I would do the rest.

I believe I can get along with Woodson. I have worked for men in my youth with whom people had told me that it would be folly to take a position. I refer especially to McQuade and Kneene. The former was a druggist with whom no boy before my time could stay for more than a month. The other was the master-mechanic of a machine shop, and possessor of the undesirable name of a hard taskmaster. Yet, I remained with both of these men for years, and only left the former because there was more money to be made working under the latter. I left Kneene's employ to go to college, and every summer, upon my return home, he gave me employment, if there was any employment to be had. I shall get along alright with Woodson. He is rough, plain-spoken, it is true, but withal scholarly, witty, and even considerate. Told me to take a ten-day vacation.

After office hours went up to Thelma's with Dorothy.

Did not go out.

Woodson asked me to correct some proofs for him. They were for a book of African folklore which he is writing. Promised to do so tomorrow. Spent day correcting extra copies of Baltimore Report, which Miss Revallion had just completed typing. Woodson showed me a manual on style. Said he would order one for me from the University of Chicago.

Thursday June 28 1928

Went over to see Mrs. Hood. She was out. Mr. and Mrs. Adkins were in. She read some of my poems; liked them very much.

Al Smith was nominated today on the first ballot. Polled over 1,000 votes out of a total of 1,100. Quite a difference in harmony from the tragic convention of 1924.

Spent the day reading the galley proof for Woodson's book on *African Myths*. Some fine stories there. One can catch a glimpse of the early African mind in its functioning, and will find that it did not differ one bit from the folklore of Greece, Germany, Ireland, England, and France. Except as environment influenced them.

Friday June 29 1928

It has been simplified for children. On the whole this has been done very well, but there are some stories that I thought a little advanced, especially the crocodile story, "Ngangurane."

However, I learned much today about technical marks for proof reading in order to designate words left "out," etc., besides the knowledge of African folklore.

Was going to New York today. Could not go to the bank, however.

Called Mrs. Burbridge in New York. Not home. Called Bertha.

Went to movies. All indications point to Senator Robinson as Smith's running mate.

Saturday June 30 1928

Woodson asked me to look over another galley proof this a.m. It was the proof of an abridged and simplified edition of his *Negro in Our History*. It is suitable for children in the grades. Interesting, but he finds it difficult at times to bring his diction down to the level of the child's comprehension. That is natural. I checked a number of phrases, words, and even sentences which, by virtue of their containing words either unfamiliar to children or because of their complexity, would minimize the value of the book for a person in the grades.

Today took place the annual meeting of the Board of the Association. The girls confidently expected to be given the balance of the afternoon off after the meeting. They were doomed to disappointment, however. Miss [Hazel] Powell changed from her office to street attire in the expectancy of the half-holiday that never came.

O, yes, Dorothy [Revallion] kissed me today, then looked up as if she had seen a ghost. Leaning back in my chair, I followed her eyes. Soon I heard footsteps and, finally, I saw a man. *It was Woodson.* He looked straight ahead. But he said nothing. I only hope that he saw nothing.

[Wesley] told me that he had enjoyed his stay at Hampton. His address had thrilled his audience. He spoke upon the "Negro Church and Public Opinion."

He imparted to me that his trip to Hampton had proved the panacea for his worries and cares of the past few days. He did appear a little more rested.

I told him of the favorable impression which our work had made upon the Institute. It pleased him greatly. Indeed, he was surprised to know that such favorable comment was forth-coming from them after the debacle of last Monday.

When I informed him that Woodson had written the In-stitute recommending that they set up the Study again, inde-pendently this time, with him (Wesley) as director, Wesley believed it almost inconceivable. "And yet he acted the way he did," he said, ruefully. I did not tell him that as alternatives Woodson had proposed the names of George Edmund Haynes and [B. Gordon] Hancock of Virginia Union.

Wesley informed me that he would write a history of the Negro church. He considers Woodson's unsatisfactory, which it no doubt is.

After the regular office hours, Woodson placed an envelope before me. It was in respect to my engagement by the Associa-tion. The letter read:

Dear Sir:
I have the authority to offer you employment as an investigator at the salary of $166.66 a month, beginning the first day of July, 1928, and continuing as long as your services are satisfactory.
It is understood that you will work under the Director of the Association on the prosecution of certain studies of the Negro.

Respectfully yours,
C. G. Woodson
Director

Within a short while, he returned to the room and stated that I was being employed by the month, which was the cus-tomary rule of the Association. In response, I replied, then, that arrangement was mutual: he to be able to discharge me upon the moment; I, likewise, to be free to accept any other position which might attract me within that time. "O, but you see," he said, "the type of work which you will do will not allow you to break off as abruptly as that, for if you do, it means that just so much money is wasted, because no one could read your notes."

We argued back and forth for a while, he adducing proof to show that he had only fired one person since he had been there; I to show him, that it mattered not whether I was hired by the day or month, since I had a personal interest in the work. I should prosecute it for its own sake. Promised to give him due notice, if I should desire to accept another position.

He told me that, unless I was the most "abject misfit and numbskull," he was quite sure that I could do the work.

Asked me to write a letter of acceptance. Promised to do so.

Upon arriving home, I found that I had left my diary at the office. Returned for it about eight o'clock. To my surprise, I found [John J.] McKinley there in conference with Woodson. McKinley is the young man who sent in such a fine report, saving a few misrepresentations, about Suffolk, Va. He is the Community Background man. Is a graduate of the University of Chicago. Does not look strong. I fear that he is here to resign. Woodson intimated such last week.

Senator Robinson of Arkansas has been nominated for Vice President on the Democratic ticket. A capable and fearless man. A farm product.

Sunday
July 1
1928

Was awakened this a.m. by a heated argument between my aunt and one of the roomers—a female preacher. It seemed that the Reverend lady had inadvertently shaken her dust mop out of her window on the second floor, and the dust had entered into my aunt's room directly below through an open window. Words, words, words! My aunt blurted out, "I have no more to say," then talked more than ever. The preacher— and how could one expect a preacher to be silent, and a woman, too—snapped she was through, but kept up an incessant chatter from her room to the bathroom and back again. The storm blew over after fifteen minutes, only due to the fact that the minister ceased to talk and started singing a hymn in a voice that sounded as if it needed oiling.

Arrived at church just in time to be confronted with their collections. Contributed my usual dime. Also gave a nickel to the poor box.

After church went to the baseball park, where the Boston American League team, Red Sox, won two games from the [Washington] Senators. It was terribly hot at the park. Came home after the games, only to find that I could not get in. My aunt had gone out, locked the door, and carried the key with

her. Had to go out to dinner. From there went to the Kappa
Frat House. Met some of the boys whom I had not seen in
years. [Herman Austin] Warner—Dr. Warner, now—was
there. He is from Hartford, Connecticut, about 50 miles from
my home. Told me he was in my home town last Thursday
looking for me. Said he was driving a large Packard automobile. The "Brothers" invited me to an R.O.T.C. dance
tomorrow evening. It takes place at Camp Meade, Maryland.

Went to the movies with Dorothy and Thelma.

Al Smith, Democratic nominee for the Presidency, was
feted and eulogized in an all-day celebration by his well
wishers yesterday at Albany, the state capital. Smith would
win over any other Republican candidate save Hoover, of
course, excepting "Cautious Cal" [Calvin Coolidge].

Spent the entire day reading proof of Woodson's abridged and | Monday
simplified *Negro in Our History* for children in the grades. It is, | July 2
I fear, more competently abridged than simplified. Some of | 1928
the words and constructions used would puzzle many a college student. I fear that Dr. Woodson had several lapses, during which he lost sight of the fact that his task was partly to
convert his History into a text for children between the third
and eighth grades.

Dr. Wesley called to inquire about our checks. They have
not yet arrived. Dr. Woodson believes that the Institute is
awaiting a final statement of expenditures, etc. before sending
the final checks. That may be true.

Dr. Woodson also apprised me that employees of the Association receive their checks monthly. And on the 1st of the
month, at that! Awkward arrangement, to say the least. However, I shall make the best of it, only I shall have to send my
folks money monthly instead of bi-monthly.

Terribly hot today. My first summer in Washington.

The body of Ronald [Roald] Amundsen, celebrated Arctic
explorer, was unofficially reported found floating in the
frozen waters of the polar regions that he knew and loved so
well. He had been missing since June 16, when he, with two
companions, set out in a French plane to help search for Gen.

[Umberto] Nobile, who had been lost in the Arctic wastes since May 25. The latter, an Italian, and also the co-partner with Amundsen two years ago in a flight over the North Pole, set out in the dirigible *Italia*, to fly over the North Pole. He accomplished the feat and also dropped a cross on the pole, but returning, was wrecked on an ice flow almost one hundred miles from the nearest habitable spot. The immense ship struck an iceberg which tore away the cabin. Then the great bag rose again, carrying with it fourteen members of the crew, who, to date, have not been heard from. Nobile, himself, with a fractured ankle, with the rest of the crew, was left on the ice. Five of the crew attempted to secure help by walking over the ice to the mainland. They, too, have disappeared. After a month of anxious waiting, during which nation after nation—Russia, Norway, Sweden, Iceland, France, Italy, and England—joined in the search for the missing Nobile and his crew, they were finally located last week by an Italian flier. Later a Swedish flier effected a remarkable landing on the ice floe, picked up the disabled Nobile, and brought him to the Italian base ship, *Gelta del Milan*.

Amundsen had been gone only four days when all traces of him vanished. He lent his supreme knowledge of the North to the task of finding Nobile. Greater than that, his utter unselfishness and largeness of heart must be extolled, for he risked and possibly sacrificed his life in an endeavor to rescue Nobile, the man who had once been his partner in a memorable flight, but who later had broken with him.

Aviation, though in its embryonic stage, is already replete with glorious sacrifices on the part of daring and courageous fliers who have risked, yea, even have given, their lives in attempts to succor their fellow men. Witness the case of Floyd Bennett, who contracted and died of pneumonia last April in a gallant but futile endeavor to rescue [Hermann] Koehl, [James E.] Fitzmaurice, and others from their icy prison in the barren wilds of Labrador after they had achieved the honor of being the first to span the Atlantic, east to west, by air.

A report concerning the finding of Amundsen's body is unconfirmed.

Spent the entire day at the office correcting "galleys" for
Woodson's abridged and simplified *Negro in Our History*. It is
abridged somewhat, but not very simplified. The last chapter
on "Art" would be absolutely unintelligible to elementary
school students, especially Negro grade school pupils in the
South, whose level of intelligence is so much lower than that
of Negro children in the mixed schools of the North.

Tonight I am to go to Camp Meade to a dance. It is so hot,
however, that one can hardly keep cool when idle, much less
when he is dancing.

Dorothy had cashed checks for me. Went to get money
from her.

Went to the movies.

Report of Amundsen's body having been found, proves
false.

Started speech for Gladys [McDonald].

Rose at a quarter of seven. Started on Opening Speech for
Intercollegiate Conference. Gladys wants it. Such a good pal,
could not refuse her. But what a subject! "Negro Youth in a
World of Facts." What senseless, intangible, impractical dis-
cussions students can think of! Never come down to earth.
Wrote a few pages on the opportunities awaiting Negro
Youth in such fields as social science, business, art, religion,
and the professions.

While just finishing, Dorothy called. Told me the folks
were waiting for me to go on the picnic.

Rushed to Mrs. Chambers'. Thelma was there, looking
charming in an organdy dress.

It was very hot. The papers had forecast showers for today.
We hoped, though, that the rain, if it did come, would not take
place till night.

The girls had prepared an elaborate lunch. We also took
punch along.

Just as we had found a desirable spot to spread our lunch in
Rock Creek Park, vicious black clouds appeared out of the
west, the wind rose, and soon everyone was gathering cloths,

lunches, and other effects, preparatory to beating a hasty re-
treat before the impending storm.

The girls were particularly disappointed, for the walk in the
hot sun had sorely tired them. Dorothy looked as if she were
about to fall from sheer exhaustion.

The rain proved to be only a ten minute shower. The girls
took refuge in a stone house which covers a well, while Mr.
Chambers and I, coatless, sat under the protecting shade of the
trees.

We had to take our lunch back to the home of Mrs. Chambers, where we ate, then played "500."

Later during the evening we went to the movies. Everyone
was fatigued. In fact, Thelma was so tired she could scarcely
enjoy the picture.

Thursday   I spent the entire day reading over the "galleys" for the *Journal*
July 5   *of Negro History*, July number.
1928   It contained a very interesting piece of research upon the
               "Liverpool Slave Trade," by Jean Trapp of Wellesley; "Negro
               Slavery in the Northwest," by Professor [W. Sherman] Sav-
               age, a Negro; "The First Pan-American Conference," by Pro-
               fessor [N. Andrew N.] Cleven of the University of Pitts-
               burgh; and the "Royal African Documents upon the Negro
               Slave Trade," collected by Miss Ruth A. Fisher, from the
               British Museum Library in London.
                  Two Italians flew from Rome to Brazil.

Friday   When I arrived this a.m., I noticed a strange brief case in the
July 6   office, also a coat hanging on the back of a chair. Miss Re-
1928   vallion told me they belonged to Charles [S.] Johnson, editor
               of *Opportunity*. He is one of the few brilliant Negroes in this
               country, and quite a young fellow. He has recently accepted a
               position to teach economics at Fisk University. Glad to know I
               was working with Woodson. Earlier he, Dr. [E. P.] Roberts,
               and E. Kinckle Jones, Executive Secretary of the National
               Urban League, had tried to persuade me to accept a fellowship
               to the New York School of Social Work. But I was too far
               advanced along the work for the doctorate in history to se-

riously consider changing. They also wanted me to join the Alpha Phi Alpha Fraternity. But my chief friends were Kappa men.

Woodson asked me to read a chapter on "Migration" in his book *A Century of Negro Migration*. Also parts of Taylor's *Reconstruction of Virginia*, and *The Negro in South Carolina During the Reconstruction*. Spent the day on them. My contribution in the *History of Occupations*, he tells me, will be from 1890 to the present.

Paid [Charles S.] Johnson $2.00 I owed him for a copy of *Ebony and Topaz*.

Played cards at T's. Lost a quart of ice cream.

Spent an enjoyable time today going over Woodson's abridged and simplified version of *The Negro in Our History*. He remarked that I had cut into it something terrifically, yet he was glad of it. I think it is too far above the heads of the 4th, 5th, 6th, and 7th grade Negro pupils, especially in the South. The chapter upon Art I found impossible. We had a lot of arguing about the plausibility of a punctuation mark here and there, or of using simple synonyms for unfamiliar words. Miss D [Dorothy Revallion] got many a smile from our little verbal jousts.

Spent practically the entire day upon Taylor's *Reconstruction of Virginia*.

Saturday July 7 1928

Woodson was in a talkative mood. Railed against the Negroes' lack of business enterprise. Called situation in New York pitiable.

Started upon *The Negro in South Carolina During the Reconstruction*. The style is wretched. It bears out Woodson's remarks that it was written in a hurry.

Caught a dreadful head cold. Stayed in to attend to it.

Rose about 9:30. Did not go to Church. Wrote to Harry [Hipp], begging him to go back to school to secure his Master's Degree in History in order that we might collaborate in the production of some worthwhile work. "Rabbit" (Bacote) is doing well as an M.D. I, at least, am starting. How wonder-

Sunday July 8 1928

ful it would be if the other members of the gang would do
likewise. Implored Hipp to go back to school, even though he
finds it unfeasible to postpone his marriage until next summer.
If he but secures his Master's Degree, there will be openings
for him.

Wrote Helen [Notis]. Have not written to her in five weeks.
Also wrote Tynes.

Went to Thelma's. Took enjoyable walk to Potomac Park.

Thelma told me of her *affaire de coeur*, which happily ended
as soon and harmlessly as it did. She met a man last summer in
New York, while pursuing summer courses at Columbia
University. It happened during her last two weeks there. A
handsome man of apparently forty years of age. Guess it was a
case of spider and fly, with Thelma as the fly, entranced by the
wiles of this elderly (comparatively) suitor, who spent money
lavishly in an endeavor to win her affections. She was attractive, new; he was schooled and skilled in the ways of wom-
ankind. He overwhelmed her with attention, rode her for
hours at a time in taxis, took her to shows, cabarets, and
seashore resorts and showered gifts upon her. She—alone, a
stranger in New York—was impressed by his constant attention, his lavish expenditure, and his humor, as well as his
handsomeness.

She left New York, feeling perhaps that at last she had found
her soul-mate. Throughout the fall, while teaching in North
Carolina, she received letters from him weekly, each apparently asserting and reasserting undying affection for her.
Thelma so impressed her mother with the virtues of the gentleman that she invited him to her home for Christmas. He
brought her a beautiful overnight case, completely fitted. She
gave him her "picture." Thelma spent New Year's Day in
New York, ostensibly to visit him.

Throughout the rest of the winter and spring, the letters
traveled to and fro. Gifts of records and candy were received
by the lady. He invited her to spend a week in New York
during the summer. Her mother gave her consent. But
Thelma had also planned to go to her home in Colorado with
her mother. Realizing the heavy expense which she must bear

for new clothes, carfare, etc. if she went to New York, in addition to the heavy cost of the trip to and from Colorado, Thelma decided to cancel the New York trip. She wrote the New York gentleman apprising him of the same and setting forth her reasons. The gentleman maintained discreet silence, did not answer the letter. Two weeks later, feeling that either he had not received the letter or that he might be ill, Thelma again wrote. No answer. Naturally, she felt badly over it. Her mother consoled her by reminding her that it perhaps happened for the best.

Thelma asked my opinion. I told her that by ignoring her letters, the man had but let drop the mask and revealed himself in his true colors. I could not believe his intentions to have been honorable from the first. In my opinion, he deliberately attempted to dazzle her with gifts and his attentions, and also his protestations of love—he even proposed to her on New Year's Day—merely to draw her into his toils, to enmesh and exploit her for his own vicious advantage. I rejoice that it ended that way. It would otherwise have been the same old story, unless Thelma had been strong enough to save herself.

She would have me believe that what she felt towards him was more fascination than love. I agreed, adding, however, that gratitude had also played its part. I told her that I believed she had mistaken her feeling of gratitude, translating it as love for this man.

She confided to me that though she did not love the man, at times she could not prevent her thoughts from dwelling upon him. I hope that she does not imagine her affection to be deeper than what it really is.

I told her in return about some of my own "troubles."

Spent a very enjoyable evening with her. A charming girl.

Spent today on Taylor's *The Negro in South Carolina During the Reconstruction*. Apologist for reconstruction in South Carolina, especially of the Negro and Carpet Bag Government. South Carolina, like Virginia, tried to free the Negro in letter only, as was emphasized by their Constitution of 1865. Put the old slave codes into the Constitution in modified form. South

Monday
July 9
1928

thought Negroes would not work. Taylor disproves that
myth. Negroes in Senate and Legislature until 1896 in South
Carolina. Had some very able men in [Francis L.] Cardozo,
Secretary of State, [Richard H.] Cain, [William J.] Whipper,
and others. Democrats of a more liberal stripe under Wade
Hampton overthrew the "Carpet Bag" regime in 1888, although [Daniel H.] Chamberlain, the last Republican governor, had made an endeavor to crush the corruptionists in the
government. The Hamptonites, who had swept into power
on the heels of intimidation, fraudulent voting, killings, and
whippings, were subsequently overthrown by the poor
whites, under the leadership of Ben Tillman. His regime had
secured the reins of government, under the slogan of "This is a
white man's country and must remain such." With the advent
of the poor whites into political ascendency in South Carolina,
the Negroes' demise as a political factor was inevitable.
Negroes were disfranchised by circumvention of the Constitution, that is, by providing in the state constitution that any
person seeking to vote must first be able to read and interpret
any section of the Constitution to the satisfaction of the exam-
iner. By tacit agreement, the whites were excluded from this
test, since the person seeking to vote must interpret it to the
satisfaction of the registrar.

Brought the book home with me to complete its perusal.

Went to the tailor to return a pair of trousers. Had the suit
cleaned, but the trousers shrunk as to both length and width.
The tailor assured me that they could be stretched.

The three men of the ill-fated *Italia* disaster, who started to
walk to the mainland when the ship was wrecked on June 26,
were sighted today by a Russian aviator. Unable to find a
landing place, he returned to the Russian ice breaker, *Krassin*,
which is painfully but slowly crushing its way through the ice
in a dogged and persistent endeavor to reach the unfortunate men.

Tuesday   Read Charles [Harris] Wesley's *Negro Labor in the United
July 10   States*. A fine piece of work. Very thorough down to 1890. It is
1928   a history of Negro occupations up to that date. Through the

mirror that Wesley holds, we see the Negro at work and also feel the many forces which act upon him as he works. We see him in slavery, in the upheaval during the war, in the turmoil of reconstruction when as a child, economically speaking, he rapidly adapted himself to his status as a free laborer. A fine piece of work, although the author is inclined to sermonize a little.

Went to F's [Thelma Duncan's] tonight to play five hundred.

Today Woodson and I were to go to the Congressional Library, where I was to begin work on the "Negro in Occupations." I had provided myself with all the necessary equipment.

When Dr. Woodson returned from breakfast, I asked him about going to the Library. "Yes, we will go there," he replied. "There is something that I want you to do." He took Wesley's book on *Negro Labor* and in the appendix showed me a table of Negro Occupations from 1890 to 1910. He wished me to fill in the Occupations for 1920, a decrease in numbers for each occupation, then the rate of increase or decrease. Started to work with Wesley's figures. Found them grossly inaccurate. Finally told Woodson I had best secure my own tables. He agreed. It would take an age trying to verify all the figures which Wesley had there and only he knows how he arrived at some of them.

A marvelous suggestion of Woodson's. There is the skeleton for my contribution to Negro Occupations. After I find the increase or decrease, the next question is why? That is my task.

Woodson told me about the work entitled *The Tappan Papers*, which was edited by Professor [Frank J.] Klingberg of the University of California.[1] He called Woodson while I was there. Woodson styles the book one of the greatest research documents ever gotten together. Rates his [Woodson's] *Free*

1. The book is Annie Heloise Abel and Frank J. Klingberg (eds.), *A Side-Light on Anglo-American Relations, 1839–1858, Furnished by the Correspondence of Lewis Tappan and Others with the British and Foreign Anti-Slavery Society* (Washington, D.C., 1927).

Negro Heads of Families as the first. Took three years to collect
the information, had to verify names written in script, etc.
Says that the Negroes who were doing things in 1860 were
descendants of those free blacks. The names were collected for
1790. Will be a gold mine later on.

Went to "movies" with Thelma.

Thursday
July 12
1928

Spent the entire day on the Census Reports. Am bringing
some order out of chaos. The Negro, I find, is engaged largely
in three pursuits: agriculture, which claims over $\frac{1}{4}$ of all the
Negroes over 10 years of age; domestic and personal service,
which accounts for about $\frac{1}{6}$ over that age; and manufacturing,
which claims about $\frac{1}{8}$.

Helped Woodson go over the proofs for an article on the
First Pan-American Congress, by Professor Cleven of the
University of Pennsylvania. He also makes mistakes. It is an
education to be in this office and especially with Woodson.

Ruth T——— called me tonight.

Later went to the theatre. Saw "The Road to Ruin." Just
another effort through picturization to portray the madcap age
of youth, which is depicted as an endless round of gin, petting
parties, wrecked lives, and an all-too-tardy realization of peni-
tence. A sermon, which is common enough these days, when
pessimists view all youth as rushing madly to destruction!
Good, moral picture of immorality. Alright theoretically, but
youth only learns by experience—at least in such matters.

Friday
July 13
1928

Figures! Figures! Figures! Figures in front of me! Figures all
around me! I have read, studied, added, and subtracted figures
until my eyes feel as if they were full of sand!

From what little I have done on the work, however, it ought
to prove extremely interesting.

It is a little difficult to secure the comparison of each occupation throughout the censuses from 1890 to 1920, due to the fact
that all occupations were classified generally, rather than specifically, until the Census of 1910. Each has its advantages and
disadvantages. In the case of the former, the total number of
employees in each group of occupations was given—that is, in

building trades for masons, plasterers, hod carriers, etc. It was a compact method of securing the number engaged in any one branch of occupation at a moment's notice. On the other hand, the specific method, while detailed and showing what each laborer does, is nevertheless confusing and liable to be repeated. For instance, instead of styling all blacksmiths as such under one heading, they are scattered hither and yon as they appear in the different trades, industries, transportation, or what not.

Woodson goes to Alabama Sunday. Asked me to look out for things while he is absent. Also requested that I fill the water bottle for the cooler.

I was caught in a drenching rain on the way home. It ruined my panama hat.

The girls had their first half holiday today. I remained, however, until 6:30. Brought Woodson's copy of [James Ford] Rhodes' *History of the United States from Hayes to McKinley* home with me. Promised Woodson I would come to the office tomorrow morning at 10:00 a.m. Presume he wishes to leave me final instructions during his absence from the office.

Went to movies *solo*.

Saturday July 14 1928

Met Woodson at 9th and Q streets N.W., just about 10:00 a.m. He was hurrying to breakfast. Was late. Had just an hour to eat and make his train at eleven. Asked me to purchase for him two bottles of Bellan's Tablets. He suffers from indigestion. Gave me the key to the office. Told me to await his return.

Woodson returned with Mr. Baker, cashier of the Prudential Bank, about 10:35. He was in a tremendous hurry. Had to get out some mail. I wrote a letter which he dictated. His haste caused him to make the error of putting one letter in the wrong envelope, which he fortunately detected before sending it.

Finally left at 10:52. On the way, Woodson told me about the gas, electric, and telephone bills, which were overdue. I told him I would pay them tomorrow. Asked if I had sufficient money. I was glad to respond that I had. Gave me a key to the

Sunday July 15 1928

office. Impressed upon me the necessity of seeing that all the doors and windows were locked and barred before leaving. Gave me $10 to be used in case of emergency.

We barely reached the station in time, just two minutes before the train's departure. It is and has been insufferably hot here. I hope that it will not be so in Alabama, for Woodson does not endure the heat well.

From the station, having bought a paper, I went to Bertha's, where I sat in her swing, reading, for nearly half an hour before anyone knew of my presence. She persuaded me to remain for dinner.

In the evening, I went to the movies with "Fifi" [Thelma Duncan].

Monday
July 16
1928

Miss Revallion wanted to go downtown this a.m. to shop. I replied that I had no authority to grant her permission. Told me she would go notwithstanding. I responded that I could not restrain her forcibly, that if she did go, it would be embarrassing to me. I was positive that Miss Powell would follow her example. Miss Revallion then asked for a half hour at noontime. I refused that also.

Went downtown and paid the gas, electric, and telephone bills, withdrawing $25.00 from my account to do so.

Miss Revallion took ten minutes at noon, but she was back in the office by one o'clock.

I remained at the office till 5:20. My lunch consisted of peaches and milk. Bought three pretty ties today and 2 pairs B.V.D.s.

Tuesday
July 17
1928

Spent another hot day with the Census Reports on "Negro Occupations." Played 500 at Thelma's tonight. Won one game and lost one.

[Alvaro] Obregon, President-Elect of Mexico, was assassinated today by a half insane religio-politico fanatic, a young fellow named José, who was nearly torn to pieces by Obregon's enraged admirers. [The assassin's name was León Toral.] Obregon undoubtedly was the strongest political factor in Mexico. He gave Mexico its first peaceful administration, from 1920 to 1924, at which time he was succeeded by his protégé, [Plutarco Elias] Calles, a strong character who has defied both the *United States* and the Pope. It is not altogether impossible that Obregon's death may have been inspired by the church's antagonism, religious apologists seeing in the coming inauguration of Obregon no cessation or mitigation of the firm policy maintained by Calles against the institution. Calles had deftly maneuvered for the election of Obregon, who was his friend, in order, some say, to alternate the Presidency between them by intermittent successions, since Mexico's Constitution of 1917 prohibits a president from succeeding himself.

The assassination of Obregon is regrettable in that it lets loose again in the country all the pent up passions of revolution and anarchy which have remained semi-passive, because of the efficient and stern regimes of Obregon and his successor, Calles. Too bad, especially when Mexico had recently given to the world the appearance of having embarked upon a prolonged era of internal pacification and progress.

Received a letter from Hipp today. Ignored, tactfully, the cardinal point in my letter to him of last Sunday, concerning securing his M.A. I am sorry that he evaded the issue.

    The thermometer registered 92 degrees in the office today.

    Went to Bertha's in the evening. Warm, but a slight breeze cooled the atmosphere a little. Astounded her by recounting my experience with E——— [Ellen Adams?].

    Calles seems to have the situation well in hand in Mexico. He, no doubt, will succeed himself.

*Wednesday
July 18
1928*

Dorothy called off the boat ride last night. Thelma was quite disappointed.

    Went to the office about noon.

    At night went with Thelma, Dorothy, and Bertha to Potomac Park. Sat with Thelma watching a brilliantly lighted launch glide along the placid waters of the Tidal Basin.

*Thursday
July 19
1928*

Friday
July 20
1928

This was the hottest day of the year. The thermometer stood at 92 degrees at nine o'clock in the morning. By noon it was 96 degrees. Outside the mercury reached the high-water mark of the summer of 104 degrees F. Many people have succumbed, numerous have been prostrated, and many more have received first aid treatment and been sent home from the hospitals. One man fell off a deck into the Potomac and drowned without a struggle. Miss Revallion looked worn, dazed, and lifeless. About 3 o'clock, I myself felt as if I would collapse, and only persisted in order that I might set an example for the girls, who likewise were suffering. I do believe if Woodson had been here he would have sent the girls home. Why didn't I do so? Am I becoming a "little Woodson"? Even the government offices closed.

Went to Thelma's at night. Mr. Jeter took us for an automobile ride. Stopped at the reservoir.

A heavy storm came up about 10 o'clock. Momentarily, it brought relief, but immediately after its cessation, the humidity became so great that the cooling effect of the rain was nullified.

Thelma is going to Colorado tomorrow. Bought her a box of Velati's Caramels, of which she is very fond.

Received a card from Bacote. He is at Niagara Falls. Suspicious?

Saturday
July 21
1928

Went downtown to pay electric bill of $11.15.

Returning, worked on Census Reports.

Woodson returned unexpectedly at 12:45. What a "bête noire" the *great man* is! Dorothy was eating a sandwich at the time. Although it was lunch time, she became so excited she threw a peach which she was about to eat in the waste basket. Then about five minutes later, after a vain search of her office, she found the peach where she had thrown it—in the waste basket.

Woodson inquired how things had transpired during his absence. I answered, truthfully, very well. Informed him of the terrific heat of last week. Told me that he slept under blankets each night in Alabama.

Refunded me a check for $30.93 which I had expended. I
returned him the $10 given me for emergencies and which I
had not had occasion to use.

Felt very tired and sleepy this p.m. Had to leave the office at
4 p.m. Rested upon reaching home.

Read parts of Rhodes later.

My aunt made an old-fashioned apple pie for me this a.m. I
could detect its odor before rising. My favorite pie and she is a
marvelous cook.

Spent the greater part of the day reading and writing.

Helen [Grinage] called me about 3:30. We talked for an
hour. Of all the girls that I have met, Helen approaches nearest
earthly perfection. Yet, as she suggested, I wait, because of
personal ambition. I fear yet I shall lose the jewel only to secure
the dross in the future. And as she said, the fault will be mine
alone. Yes, the fault and the loss will be mine, for I already fear
that she is promised to another. And it serves me right.

Helen told me that she received a card from Vic (Miss Victoria Snowden), Bacote's fiancée, from Niagara Falls. Are
they married? I'll wager they are. Looks mighty suspicious.
Wonder why Ernest did not inform me. Just like him to keep
me in ignorance of the event in order, as he perhaps thinks, to
avoid placing upon me the onus of a gift or of the payment of
the gang's marital obligations. We (he, Hipp, and I) some
years back had sworn that in the event of marriage on the part
of any member of the triumvirate, the other two pledged
themselves to forfeit a hundred dollars. Where would I secure
such a sum now?

Called upon Miss Helen Massey about 8 p.m. tonight. She
is a school teacher from South Carolina to whom Thelma
introduced me. Since she and her sister both had engagements,
I went to the movies.

Sunday
July 22
1928

Spent the morning preparing tables on Negro Occupations for
Sections and States for 1890. I also made note of the gainfully
employed in each occupation, by sex. I found that the Negro
in New England, New Jersey, New York, and Pennsylvania

Monday
July 23
1928

is, or was, in 1890, confined chiefly to domestic and personal service jobs. In the South agricultural pursuits formed his largest single occupation, with domestic service next. The large number of female farm hands among the Negro population of the South bulks significant. It was not surprising to find that the gainfully employed among Negro females above ten years of age is much higher relatively than that for any other female group in the American population. The reason? The low earning potential of the Negro male, his difficulty finding a job, and loss of hope on the job. On my way to lunch Miss Massey called to me from her window. I stopped and chatted with her for a few minutes. She apologized for her engagement of last night. She accepted my invitation to go to the movies Thursday evening.

Young fellow, a graduate from the Columbia Library School, came into the office this afternoon to see Woodson about Negro history books. He has just been engaged as Librarian at Fisk University, and desires to secure Woodson's recommendation upon books pertinent to the Negro. Woodson explained the worthlessness of the great bulk of the literature upon the Negro, which is mostly of a controversial nature and hence highly subjective. The young man with all the fervid exuberance of youth, proposed the founding of a library of Negro history at Fisk, which would deal with only one phase of the Negro. Woodson ridiculed the suggestion as highly impracticable, because of the scarcity of worthwhile books of any description touching upon the Negro. I went out to lunch, leaving Woodson demonstrating to the young librarian a few books of meritorious value, like *A Tropical Dependency*, by Lady Lugard, the *Tarik es Sudan*, by Abderrahman Essadi, and others.

Tuesday
July 24
1928

Spent the entire day tabulating figures for Negro Occupations for 1900 by Sections and States. Statistics show that the Negroes in that year were almost totally engaged in Agriculture and domestic service. However, the number engaged in industrial and professional pursuits, as well as in trade and transportation, showed an encouraging increase over the previous decade.

Received a letter from Ruth [Beverly] today. She is at Hampton. Strange for her. To think that she would come to D.C. and not call me before going to Hampton. But then perhaps she has realized the futility of persisting in her affections for me. I am sorry, for she is a splendid girl.

Compiled statistics today of the Negro for 1920, for all occupations. Found that the number engaged in Agriculture and skilled labor showed a decrease over 1910. On the other hand, there was a large increase in manufacturing pursuits, and trade and transportation. However, the increment in the industrial field was much larger numerically in the decade from 1900 to 1910. The exigencies of the World War, coupled with the cutting off of the foreign labor supply, can be pointed to as the chief causes for this increase during both decades.

Called upon Helen tonight. She believes, and perhaps rightly, that I am too interested in making a name for myself to give time to marrying. Told me for the first time of some of her struggles to secure an education. To my statement that on many an occasion I had washed a collar in the morning, placed it on a tin plate in the oven to insure its drying quickly, ironed it, and worn it to school, she countered by confessing that having but one dress, she had been forced to go to bed while it dried, having washed it in order to have it clean for the next day. Few girls would have made that confession of sacrifice for an education. A girl like her cannot know failure.

Woodson went to Charleston, West Virginia, tonight. Left me in charge of the office.

Wednesday July 25 1928

Worked hard in an effort to compile percentages of Negro males and females engaged in gainful occupations, by sections and states. These percentages will cover each general occupation. Such work necessitates a great manipulation of figures, for which I never cherished a fondness.

Called upon Miss Massey tonight to take her to the movies.

Thursday July 26 1928

She begged to be excused because her brother desired to take them to listen in on the Tunney-Heeny [Gene Tunney and Tom Heeney of New Zealand] heavyweight championship bout. She asked if I could go tomorrow evening. I replied affirmatively, though inwardly I felt a little bitter, having been forced to dress on such a hot evening, only to be disappointed. Would have refused to go tomorrow night, but she is Thelma's friend.

The fight was a one-sided affair. Stood on the corner of 14th and U streets N.W. and heard the radio announcer broadcast the fight blow by blow. Cut to pieces by the merciless, deliberate attack of Tunney, Heeney was unable to continue and the fight was stopped in the eleventh round to save the latter unnecessary punishment. $100,000 for thirty-three minutes of fighting, although suffering a black eye, is not half bad. Americans certainly put a premium upon brute strength. Charles Elliot, for years President of Harvard University, never earned much more than that during his lifetime there, I'll wager.

Friday
July 27
1928

A day of figures. Got into trouble with the percentages for the South Atlantic States. The percentages totalled 104%, which was positive proof that something was wrong. Finally found and corrected the error by means of the adding machine. Shows how prone to err is the human mind.

Took Miss Massey to the movies tonight. A slight and frail creature, but endowed with that infectiously sunny disposition and charm which seems to be characteristic of Southern girls. Enjoyed my evening with her immensely.

Saturday
July 28
1928

The ghosts of the past have risen to mock me in the guise of figures.

General Nobile, Fascist commander of the ill fated dirigible *Italia*, and his luckless companions were hissed in Sweden as they took a train for Italy. Their arrival at Oslo, Norway, was conspicuous by the absence of official dignitaries and by the chill reception given them by the onlookers. Evidently the people feel keenly the death of Dr. [Finn] Malmgren [Swedish meteorologist], who perished quite mysteriously in the Arctic while trying to walk to the mainland to bring aid to these same survivors of the wrecked dirigible.

Remained in until eight in the evening. Read portions of [Ulysses S.] Grant's *Memoirs.* Wrote letters. Finally took a walk and ended up at the movies. Felt out of sorts today. Did not wish to see anyone.

Sunday
July 29
1928

China still wages relentless warfare against the Reds. Executed seventeen yesterday.

Detected and corrected errors which had impeded my progress on Friday and Saturday in tabulating the statistics for Negroes in Occupations for 1890.

Monday
July 30
1928

Woodson commented upon various Negro organizations, such as the N.A.A.C.P., the Urban League, and the Inter-Racial Conference, stigmatizing them as wholly lacking in a definite program. "The N.A.A.C.P., which is Du Bois, is a propagandizing machine which thrives upon agitation. But the vital race need is not solely agitation but a remedy for its defects. Although it is necessary to keep before a group its oppression in order that they might not become immune to it and thereby become resigned to their evil lot, both prudence and practicality demand that some cogent and systematic plan be devised whereby the oppressed cannot only clamor for redress but himself aid in the acquiring of his right." I agreed. "The Urban League," he added, "is trying to care for all of the social needs of the race; in consequence, it is caring for none." Woodson suggested that the League adopt one specific program—say acquiring of homes for Negroes. "The Inter-Racial movement" Woodson denounced as a farce, "like unto the Colonization Scheme which was hatched in 1816. It means one thing in Alabama, another in New England. Had to in order to enlist the diverse elements for its support. Just so is the Inter-Church movement or the Inter-Racial movement of which George Haynes is the head."

Woodson modestly admitted that the Association for the Study of Negro Life and History was doing something specific. I had to agree with him. "But," he added, "the full import of the work being done by the Association will not be appreciated for the next fifty years."

Woodson's comments upon Negro organizations came as the result of my query upon the practical worth of the American Federation of Women's Clubs, which is meeting here in D.C. He answered, "They do nothing except to wrangle over offices and gossip." In my opinion, they are interested more in the social functions connected with these annual sessions than with any constructive program for racial amelioration.

Returned to the office at 8:00 p.m. Remained there until 10. Would have stayed longer, but the poor lights caused my eyes to pain, so that I was compelled to forego further work.

Tuesday Nothing of any consequence happened today.
July 31   Miss Revallion began her vacation today. Left in a huff
1928   because Dr. Woodson gave her two very important letters to get out near 4:30. She had done practically nothing all day and nourished a premonition that at the last moment Woodson would find something of vital import to be done. She told him at 4:30, which is quitting time, that she had to go to the bank. I was so amused. Out she went—returning about fifteen minutes later with a face as long as an ox, eyes half closed, and lips pouting. I smiled as I glimpsed her out of the corner of my eye.

About five minutes of five, Woodson having left, Miss Revallion asked me to scan the letters for errors. I did. When I did not reply promptly to her question whether I found any mistakes, she shouted, "Please say something!" I smiled in good humor, took the letters to her, and pointed out to her two errors. Seeing my irrepressible grin, she, almost on the verge of tears, moaned, "It isn't funny; it's mean. And I want to get a 7:45 train." I reminded her that her vacation began officially on August 1, which was tomorrow. "O, I could bite you," she laughed in spite of herself, as she rushed downstairs. Though late, womanlike, time had to be taken for cosmetics. "I think it was mean, don't you," she asked while daubing her face with powder, "for Woodson to wait till 4:30 before giving me those letters?" "You must remember," I reminded her, "that you are

officially in the employ of the Association until August first,"
at which the lady flung her head upwards and sidewards and
rushed out of doors. She could hardly restrain her tears. But
she blurted out, "I'll make the 7:45 train yet."

During the evening I read about 100 pages in James Ford
Rhodes, *The McKinley and Roosevelt Administrations.*

[10] Practicing the Historian's Craft

Wednesday
August 1
1928

Worked on statistics. Found that the Negro in 1890, except a few working in the manufacturing and transporation indus-tries, was almost wholly engaged in agriculture. In 1900, in the South Atlantic and South Central sections, the Negroes were almost overwhelmingly engaged in field work, with domestic service coming next. The reverse obtained in the North and West, where domestic service claimed the greater number. Though the Negro ranks high as a farmer in the South, he seems to lose his agricultural proclivities or inclina-tions when he migrates North or West.

Met Bishop [John] Hurst today. He is one of the heads of the A.M.E. Church. Came to the office to secure some informa-tion on Negro business for the Mayor of Jacksonville. Hurst is a little man, about my height and color. He rides about in a splendid car with a liveried chauffeur. If the prospective Negro professional would enjoy the luxury of every comfort, plus the adulation of the mob, a full stomach, and good clothes, I advise the ministry. With all the Negro's innate desire for rulership, he approaches nearest this goal in his quasi-imperial status as a minister, especially Baptist.

Thursday
August 2
1928

Completed statistical chart for Negroes in occupations, by sections and states, for 1900.

Contrary to current notions, the greatest gains in all Negro occupations, even in manufacturing, took place between 1900 and 1910, rather than the following decade, 1910–1920, as is commonly believed. The numerical, as well as the percentage, increase was larger for these occupations in 1910.

Woodson interrupted me this p.m. to ask my opinion about inserting a picture of Wade Hampton (Confederate cavalry leader under General [Robert E.] Lee) in his simplified version of *The Negro in Our History*, which is to be used as a textbook. Hampton was a liberal South Carolina Democrat, who succeeded Chamberlain, the last Republican governor of South Carolina, in 1886. Unlike Ben Tillman—poor-white Democrat who seized the power after Hampton and whose premise was that South Carolina should be a white man's state— Hampton believed that the Negro could best protect his interests by allying himself with the Southern white Democrats and cutting loose from the Northern Carpetbaggers and the Southern Scalawag Republicans, who "used" the former slaves for their own selfish purposes.

Despite the liberality of Hampton's views, Woodson feared lest a clamor rise on the part of certain Negroes upon beholding the picture of an ex-Confederate general in a Negro history book written by a Negro. Of course, the picture of Grant, Sherman, or Sheridan would be perfectly admissible. I told him I believed that scientific, impersonal history dictated that the picture be inserted. Of course, the portrait might become a *coup de grace* to white Southerners on the Boards of Education, whose sanction might be needed for endorsing the use of the book in the schools.

Woodson, looking for a precedent, perused [Edward] Channing's *Students' History of the United States*. The latter, although one of the leading American historians of the day, is biased against both the South and the Negro. His history did not even have a picture of General Lee. [A. C.] McLaughlin, of the University of Chicago, is more liberal. His history contained pictures of Lee, Jefferson Davis, and other Confederate leaders, both military and civilian. Woodson remained undecided. "But," he asked, "how can we study the history of a war without knowing something of the adversary?" We finally decided to include the picture of General Hampton as well as General Robert E. Lee.

Our discussion led from one racial topic to another. I had long contemplated the failure of the Negro to strike one solitary blow for his own freedom during the War of the Rebellion, when he might easily, by an uprising, have plunged the South into chaotic impotency, thereby compelling the return of Southern soldiers to defend their hearthstones. Many Northerners desired just such an event. But the Southern Negro not only did not rise in vindictiveness but even toiled in the field, worked in factories and mines, and built fortifications for his masters. Some free blacks in Memphis and New Orleans even offered their services as soldiers. However, they were politely refused by the Confederates until it was too late. In other words, the Negro forged and repaired the chains for his own bondage when he should have, by revolting, ignited a monster conflagration in the rear of the Confederacy, which would have consumed it much earlier than it was.

When I inquired of Woodson whether he could point to such an anomaly in history, either ancient or modern, he asked whether history recounts a civil strife in a nation, one part of which held in bondage an alien race, and that struggle aiming to free those bondsmen. I replied, "No, but history does show that whenever slaves had an opportunity to rise up against their masters by joining an invading army, they invariably eagerly grasped it." I mentioned the Helots of Sparta and other nations held captive. But Woodson countered by saying, "True, but the average intelligence of the Helots was not inferior to that of the Spartan, whereas the Negro not only was inferior intellectually but 200 years of servitude here had almost crushed the desire of freedom in the breast of the Negro slaves."

Woodson then recounted how difficult it was to bring a white to justice in the South. Narrated an incident which took place in his home in Virginia. A young Negro girl between 15 and 16 was insulted and approached immorally by a white druggist. The girl was accompanied by Woodson's niece, a little thing of 11 or 12 years of age. Woodson had just returned

from Europe. Apprised of the matter by his mother, he became so angry that his first thought was to do the fellow some
violence. Persuaded by his mother, however, he approached a
policeman, recited the incident, and asked what should be
done. The officer retorted, "Have him locked up." This was
done.

But the case was lost because the druggist insisted, and the
girl admitted, that she had returned to the store, accepted
goods from his hand, and grinned as he talked to her. Woodson was rightly provoked. It seemed as if the girl counted the
fellow's advances as a favor. The court did put him on six
months' probation, however. But if the situation had been
reversed, a colored man insulting a white woman, a lynching
would have resulted. (Shameful to relate, it seems that some
colored women encourage the attention of white men. And
some colored men feel that the lowest excrescence of female
society, so long as she be white, is more desirable than the
most virtuous colored woman. This impression was forced
upon me in Chicago last year, where a certain class of Negroes
have a "white woman" craze. Sociologically, it is natural
enough, I suppose. It is but natural for man to yearn for forbidden fruits. The thing "tabooed" invariably assumes a superior attraction because of the prohibition which embellishes it.
Such applies not only to the colored male's inclinations for
white women but, equally as potently, to the white woman's
predilection for colored men. Both groups are restrained in
part only by the selfish masculinity of the white man, in the
form of laws barring miscegenation. The early colonial laws
against miscegenation passed in all the original thirteen colonies, and as early as 1660 in Maryland, testify eloquently to
the universality of this condition.)

[Captain Frank T.] Courtney, the English aviator, together
with his two companions, were saved from the fate of other
intrepid east-to-west-bound Atlantic flyers (an unmarked
grave in that vast, watery expanse of silence) today, when the
steamship *Minnewaska* picked them up in mid ocean.
[Courtney left the Azores on August 1 accompanied by three
companions: E. B. Hosmer, the backer of the flight; Sergeant

Frank Pierce, mechanic; and E. W. Gilmour, radio operator.]
Their seaplane had been forced down after leaving the Azores,
and the men had drifted for almost eight hours before being
rescued. Another triumph for the radio.

Went to the A.M.E. Church on M Street between 15th and
16th (Metropolitan) to attend a meeting of the Federation of
Negro Women. From all over the country their delegates have
met in session here since Sunday last. I was doomed to disappointment, for the meeting at *this* church is scheduled for
tomorrow.

Friday
August 3
1928

Statistics again. Making my own tabulations by interpolating
the Census Reports. Today has been one of the very hottest
days of the year. At 9 a.m. the temperature was 90 degrees in
the office.

Worked diligently throughout the day, taking an hour off
between one and two o'clock.

During that time, called upon Miss [Victoria] Snowden, the
fiancée of my pal, Dr. [Ernest] Bacote. She insisted that they
were not yet married. Finally admitted that the date was set for
Christmas or thereabouts. I had to accept her statement,
though I confessed to her my belief that they perhaps had
stolen a march upon me. She and Bacote have had their little
differences, as she admitted, but I assured her "that the course
of true love never runs smoothly," to cite a very hackneyed
epigram. She agreed. Ought to make an excellent match in my
opinion, if Bacote can control his tendency to be jealous of the
attentions paid her by other men. She did not discourage them
previous to the engagement; neither do I think she should have
done so. Bacote had felt otherwise, with the result that for
approximately two years they were at logger-heads. My belief
is that both are madly in love, the one with the other. That
they will shortly marry is now a foregone conclusion, unless it
has already taken place. I shall be happy, for it was humble I
who introduced them four years ago.

There is, however, one element which threatens to cloud, in
some respects, the intimate relations which for eight years
have obtained between members of our gang—Bacote, Hipp,

and I. Because of the unfortunate outcome of the *affaire de coeur* between Harry and Bea Shorter, where all the members of the gang, both male and female, expected a marital consummation, grave doubts are entertained by me as to the continuance of our close relationships in the event of Bacote's marriage to Miss Snowden. The incident of the Hipp and Shorter case is this: Harry kept company with her during his five years at Howard. When he went to Columbia University to work toward his M.A. degree, it was with the tacit, or shall I say implied, understanding on the part of all the gang, boys and girls, that Harry and she would marry. But fate is no respecter of persons or plans. Harry met Miss Daniel, a New York lady, fell madly in love with her, proposed, and was accepted. Just before the latter, however, he wrote Miss Shorter confessing his love for the New York lady. It nearly killed Miss Shorter, who lived only because of her love for Harry. Being a member of the "gang" and because of the girls, as well as fellows, Harry feels that the girls have changed toward him because of his defection in respect to Miss Shorter. Especially does he consider this to be the case where Miss Snowden is concerned. Bacote has not become reconciled to the change, and Hipp feels that the friendly relations that have always characterized our association will be impossible after Bacote's marriage. Therefore, Harry has decided that he will not visit Bacote. It grieved me to hear him say this, for over the years we three have meant so much to one another. When together, we have formed a little world of our own, much to the admiration and wonder of our other friends.

In all fairness to Bacote, however, although I believe that he favored Miss Shorter over Miss Daniel, he would be the last man to hold a score against Hipp because of his choice in the selection of his life's mate. No man, regardless of his closeness, or connection, can decide that question for another. One can scarcely do it for himself. From my point of view, the heaviest grievance which Bacote has against Hipp is his failure to pursue his academic duties with that seriousness which he demonstrates in other affairs. There is nothing of vindictiveness in Bacote's attitude; rather it represents the acme of altruism and unselfishness, that he should exhort Harry to complete his academic studies.

Bacote's own future is assured. He is brilliant, utterly unselfish, a true friend. He has the happy faculty of reasoning out matters. Sentiment rarely sways his judgment. As I have always reminded Hipp, Bacote is so damned matter of fact, he could have made a success of nothing else than being a physician or mathematician. Evincing a dislike for languages and literature, that field was barred to him; diffident and shy about public speaking, the legal as well as the ministerial fields held no attractions to him. I jokingly told him once that if ever I was apprised of his preaching, I should advise that the Church with all its occupants be boarded up, saturated with gasoline, and set afire, with an armed cordon about the building to shoot down anyone who was fortunate enough to escape the flames. These precautions would prevent anyone from escaping to pollute the neighborhood.

Of course, the above was said jokingly, for Bacote is the most upright fellow among us. He is a man of his word, absolutely dependable, prompt in discharging obligations, punctual in keeping engagements, and devoted to his profession. Truly, I predict a brilliant future for him. We rarely agree, but that part does not obscure his many virtues. We often laugh over an event that occurred during our college days in Washington. We were returning from a party in Fairmont Heights, a Washington suburb, when an argument arose between us concerning some trivial matter. Said Bacote three years later, "I never wanted to beat you so much as I did that night." Often we were like bears growling and snapping one moment, and like playful kittens the next. I have digressed from my main theme concerning Harry, but I am hopeful that Bacote will undergo a change of opinion as memory of the Shorter incident recedes farther into the background. Especially since the lady has already preceded Hipp in marrying.

Woodson was in a reminiscent mood today. Told me of his experiences at Harvard University, where for the first time in his college days he lived like a gentleman and devoted his entire time to either serious study or recreation.

He drew a hearty laugh from me by stating that a monument should be erected to those "poor devils" who have eaten the food at Negro Colleges for four years and survived in spite of it. I could not speak for the Negro boarding student, but I do know that some recognition should be given to that army of Negro students who have sacrificed their health because of insufficient food and overwork in their efforts to obtain a college education. Many a poor fellow has been graduated in his chosen profession, only to die within a month or year thereafter, due to the inordinate demands made upon his constitution during the years of preparation. An eminent Negro physician, Dr. [E. P.] Roberts of New York, told me that his brother died within a year after his graduation from medical school, broken in health, in consequence of his struggles for an education. It brought back memories. As an undergraduate I have lived upon 50 cents a week and have seen the time that a piece of meat was a luxury. Bacote, too, has experienced the same. For nearly four years, our fare consisted alternately of beans, bread, cabbage, and macaroni—and that only once a day. This food we cooked with a piece of salt pork (10 cents' worth). After having cooked one dish with it, we would wash off and preserve the pork, then use it for cooking macaroni, at which time we would eat it. Woodson could not repress a sigh when I told him the above.

Woodson, like other folk who acquire or seem about to acquire something, invariably are much sought after by relatives. Told me he supports his sister and two children, she having had two worthless husbands. I daresay no one at the office would ascribe such a piece of generosity to him.

He spoke to me concerning morality and religion. "There is justice," he asserted, "retributive justice, and no man can sin with impunity, without reaping the reward of his folly. Every man," he continued, "ought to so live that he will be at peace with his own conscience. That is all the religion one needs." To my surprise, he agreed with me that religion is inherent not in words but in the guidance of one's life by lofty principles— unselfishness, utter lack of vindictiveness, and service rendered to one's fellow men. "Never," he counselled, "and this

Lorenzo Greene in 1930. *From the author's collection.*

Carter G. Woodson in 1928. *Courtesy Moorland-Springarn Research Center, Howard University.*

Charles H. Wesley, *ca.* 1932. *Courtesy Moorland-Springarn Research Center, Howard University.*

Harcourt A. Tynes, *ca.* 1940. *Courtesy of Helen Tynes.*

Ernest Bacote with a friend in 1924. *From the author's collection.*

Florence "Cap" Bacote in the 1920s. *From the author's collection.*

Bertha Baylor in the 1940s. *From the author's collection.*

Helen A. Notis in the 1920s. *From the author's collection.*

Greene with Nannie Hagans, 1926. *From the author's collection.*

Greene with Ruth Beverly, 1924. *From the author's collection.*

Rose Alleyne in 1923. *From the author's collection.*

C. M. "Sweet Daddy" Grace in the 1940s. *Courtesy Moorland-Springarn Research Center, Howard University.*

Greene's eldest brother James, Greene's wife Thomasina, his sister Careatha Anderson, and his niece Naomi Ridgeway in 1977. *From the author's collection.*

Greene's brother Charles with his two sons in the 1930s.
From the author's collection.

William M. Brewer in the 1950s.
Copyright 1959 by the Associated Publishers, Inc.

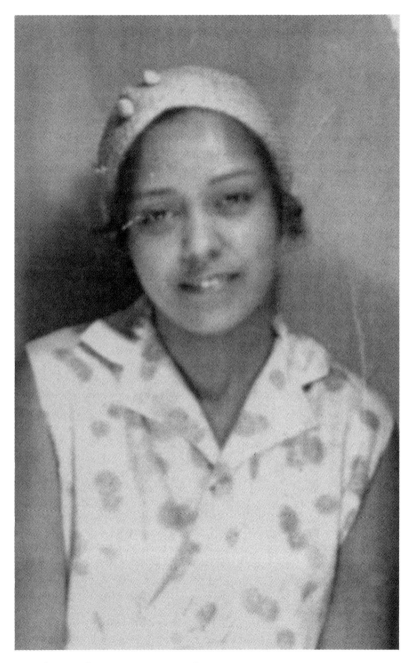

Dorothy Revallion, *ca.* 1929. *From the author's collection.*

John R. Hawkins, *ca.* 1930. *Courtesy Moorland-Springarn Research Center, Howard University.*

John R. Lynch, *ca.* 1925. *Courtesy Moorland-Springarn Research Center, Howard University.*

Oscar DePriest, *ca.* 1930. *Courtesy Moorland-Springarn Research Center, Howard University*

Thomasina Greene, *ca.* 1940. *From the author's collection.*

should be taken seriously by you—do anything that you would not have someone else do to you." I responded that to do to another as I would have him do to me is my religious creed. Sounds silly to some, but I try to live up to it.

As an instance of his lack of vindictiveness, Woodson told me of his brother Robert, who, together with him, bought a home for their parents. They put it in their mother's name, to insure against its seizure for any liabilities that either one of them, or their father, might sustain. The brother donated three-quarters of the purchase price, Woodson the remainder. Yet, contrary to the agreement made between the two, the brother sold the house during the absence of Woodson and built a new house in his own name, although he placed his mother therein. When Woodson learned of it, he said nothing. I marvelled at his forbearance.

Later, he told me that when his mother died in 1916, the brother, fearful lest a claim be made to apportion the value of the house among the children (pursuant to the agreement that the property belonged to their now deceased parent), hastened to sell the house to a stranger. As a result his sister and her children were turned out of doors. Yet, Woodson added, during all these years he has yet to discuss the sale of the house. To me, the failure on Woodson's part to mention the matter, much less to take an aggressive action against his brother, is truly remarkable. His belief in retributive justice was illustrated later he said, for his brother has lost everything he formerly possessed.

Woodson has a fine sense of humor. He told me of a telegram from this same brother imploring monetary aid as follows: "Am in financial trouble. Please save me." Woodson thereupon wired back: "Sorry, cannot save you. I am already lost."

Asked me if I had attended any of the sessions of the Federation of Negro Women. Responded I had not, but was planning to go tonight. Told me he was surprised at the fine work they were doing, also at the orderliness of their meetings.

He was taking one of the delegates to dinner. Brought me home by taxi, going out of his way to do so.

I attended the last session of Federation's meeting tonight, and the impressions given to me by Dr. Woodson were abundantly corroborated. I arrived early, when the large auditorium was about one-third filled. Towards eight-thirty the church was practically full. All of a sudden a burst of applause caused me to turn to ascertain the cause, and I beheld a well-formed, charming black woman walking up the aisle smiling and bowing. That smile was like sunshine. Her very presence was positively illuminating. I whispered to a lady beside me, "Is that Mrs. Bethune?" "Yes," she replied. I thought Mary McLeod Bethune, whom Hipp apotheosizes and whom everyone loves and admires, was beautiful. She is the President of Bethune-Cookman College for Girls in Daytona, Florida, and a nationally known educator.[1] For President of the Federation, no happier choice could have been made.

Before the meeting started, President Bethune, noting Kelly Miller, "the Black Prince," to use Harry's phrase, called him to the platform. A former leader of the Negro, Miller's place has now been usurped by younger men, or older men with more advanced ideas concerning the solution of the race problems.

A professor, whose name I did not get, rendered two organ solos. One was the almost dirge-like song of hopeless love, sung by Wolfram from *Tannhäuser*, and the other the "Pilgrim's Chorus," from the same opera. Both were well done. It brought back memories of the Metropolitan in New York City. Mr. Wormly then rendered the "Two Grenadiers," which he did satisfactorily. This was a vocal solo. Next a Miss Mason played a piano solo which smacked suspiciously of one of Bach's "Fugues."

Kelly Miller then was introduced. He said a few words in

---

1. At this time, Bethune-Cookman College was a two-year coeducational college under the auspices of the Methodist Episcopal Church. In 1904, Mrs. Bethune founded the Daytona Normal and Industrial Institute for Negro Girls, which she merged in 1923 with Cookman Institute, a Methodist-supported school for boys in Jacksonville, to form Bethune-Cookman College. James P. Brawley, *Two Centuries of Methodist Concern: Bondage, Freedom and Education of Black People* (New York, 1974), 184–91.

praise of both the outgoing and incoming presidents and sat down. Thank Heavens!

It was uncomfortably hot and very humid in the church. Everyone was fanning, and feeling more unrelieved by doing so. Emmett J. Scott, Secretary-Treasurer of Howard University and former Secretary to Booker T. Washington at Tuskeegee, took his seat on the platform, steaming, perspiring, and fanning assiduously. He bowed profusely as he recognized the ladies sitting about him.

Charming President Mary Bethune then rose to introduce Emmett Scott. She called him one of the outstanding Negroes of the country. Cited his career at Tuskeegee and Howard in support of her statement. She made, or painted, Scott as the greatest Negro in the world today, which evidently was a burdensome load for even Emmett J. to carry on this hot August night. But Mrs. Bethune, in my opinion, overstepped the bounds of diplomacy in her eulogy of Scott when she said: "Whenever we think of Howard University, we think of Emmett Scott." On the contrary, most people usually think of Kelly Miller. I wondered how the remark fell upon that exalted personage, who sat directly behind Scott. Miller partly hid his face behind his fan, grinned momentarily, then fanned more assiduously than ever.

Scott's address was devoid of anything which would attract interest on this hot night. First he read from a manuscript, secondly, his articulation was poor and his voice did not even carry to the door of the church. Thirdly, his subject, the achievement of women, dealt with efforts of women in general to secure legislation affecting domestic or marital relationships in the various states. It did not directly touch the Negro women at all. They listened because it was "Emmett J." and it was too warm to do anything else.

The *pièce de résistance* of the program, however, was the vocal solo rendered by a Mrs. Viola Hill of Philadelphia. With a rich, full soprano voice, and singing apparently without effort, she filled the hall with her clear, resonant notes, thrilling the vast audience; and when she negotiated and held high "c" in the *finale*, a storm of applause broke and continued unbroken until she sang an encore. Her remarkable effort was a song in Italian, and once again I pictured myself sitting at the feet of the divas of the Metropolitan Opera House. That one selection more than compensated for my coming here tonight.

The Negro male certainly has every reason to envy this organization composed of members of the so-called weaker sex. 150,000 strong, embracing every state in the Union, they have an organization larger than any Negro male group. What pleased me so was the forward-moving program which they are espousing and carrying out. Women seem to inject a greater amount of personal enthusiasm into special projects than men. Sometimes they are prone to indiscretion because of their inexperience, but that may be ascribed to their over-whelming zealousness in carrying on the work, rather than to lack of effort.

According to a Mrs. Smith of Tennessee, the Federation was organized in 1895. She is a member of the Nashville branch and helped to entertain the National Convention at its sessions there.

By the way, the only Negro fraternal order which has ac-complished anything worthy of note had its representation here tonight. The Order to which I refer is the Elks, and its President, J. Finley Wilson, a brown man, below average height, with short neck, and of a portly stature. Fanning and perspiring fitfully, the latter so much that his collar had com-pletely collapsed, Wilson spoke (between desperate efforts to keep cool) upon "Citizenship." His message developed into an unconnected diatribe upon whites. He then went on to say that he was proud of his citizenship (all Negroes ought to be), and they should fight, to the last drop of blood, every effort to despoil them of any of the rights, privileges, and immunities appertaining thereto. He also informed the Federation that the Elks were building a million dollar apartment house in New York on 137th Street, which will have the largest and most beautiful auditorium ever owned by Negroes in this country.

Hurray for the Elks! Condemned solely as a "good time" organization by people in general, the organization has launched an educational campaign which is the admiration of serious and thoughtful Negroes the country over, and is proof of what concerted effort can accomplish. The Elks not only aid needy students by granting scholarships, etc., but have pledged themselves to lend their moral support to stamping out illiteracy among our people.

To return to the Federation. The program to which they have dedicated themselves may be gleaned from their resolutions, which touched upon religion, politics, social ethics, industry, the press, and youth. The organization also has raised an amount of money—some $27,000—which they have distributed evenly in the three colored banks: The Prudential Bank of Washington, D.C.; the True Reformers Bank of Richmond, Virginia; and the Binga State Bank of Chicago.

In their work, which includes the fostering of education among Negroes, the inducement for self-betterment, the encouragement of ideals for home life, recreation, and religious training, plus aid rendered to embryonic race businesses, the Federation of Negro Women's Clubs is doing some much-needed work, worthy of emulation by Negro individuals and societies as well. And let us not forget the Elks! A very profitable evening.

Saturday
August 4
1928

Spent the entire morning and afternoon till 2 p.m. on statistics. Woodson, in speaking about books, mentioned Mrs. Lugard's *Tropical Dependency*. It was intended by the author, he added, to be a history of her husband's administration of Nigeria, but resulted in a history of the Sudan, and a startling exposition of the high Negro civilization in that country, which was destroyed in the 17th century. The closing of North Africa by Christendom, and the inaccessibility of the country from the rocky coast of the west, sealed the fate of the greatest Negro empires in history—empires whose culture was equal to and in some respects farther advanced than that of Western Europe at the time.

Woodson then picked up a book by Félix Dubois, a Frenchman who wrote like Mrs. Lugard, from travel, oral communication, and original Sudanese documents. Dubois uses much of the same material that Mrs. Lugard later had access to. He believes, however, that the Sudanese civilization came from Egypt, in contradiction to Mrs. Lugard, who holds that civilization moved from the Sudan, Libya, or Mossï into Egypt. The Sudan is the cradle of civilization, to paraphrase Mrs. Lugard. It can readily be seen that her statement traverses that of Dubois. The latter went into rhapsodies over Jenné, a port on the Niger, in truth an inland port on the Niger. He extolls its markets, its prosperous merchants, its fine houses, and the social courtesies of its inhabitants. Going into Timbuctoo, he was disappointed at its appearance. Jenné far surpassed it. The houses were tumbled down, the inhabitants poorly and untidily dressed, and the markets in marked inferiority to those of Jenné. However, he found that this appearance was the result of attacks by pillaging bands of nomadic Tuaregs, who plundered the country, despoiling merchants of their wares and houses of their furniture; and even the people of Timbuctoo, he said, had become mysterious. Hence the title of his book, *Timbuctoo, the Mysterious.*

Dubois dilates upon the high scholarship which formerly obtained in the Sudan, the love of politics, literature, astronomy, and other arts and sciences. He met men who could recall the glories of Timbuctoo.

On the whole, he is eminently fair, although he feels his superiority over the blacks. He attempts to detract from the Negro's ability to found a great empire by his studied effort to prove that the Songhays, though black, are not Negroes. The Songhays, be it remembered, were masters of that formidable empire that endured from the fourteenth century under three distinct lines of sovereigns. He recounts celebrated Negro teachers, clerics, and historians. Of the latter, Ahmed Baba, the great Songhay scientist, and Abderrahman Essadi, author of the *Tarik es Sudan,* or *A History of the Sudan,* are worthy of mention. Woodson has a copy of the *Tarik,* a thick paper-back book, written in Arabic. He also owns the French translation.

The book is certainly a good cure for those skeptics who believe that the Negro has never created, nor ever will create, anything of importance in either the political, economic, social, or military realm.

Gloating over the great black civilization of African blacks, I asked Woodson, why not have the French version of the *Tarik* translated into English? He enlightened me by replying that bias, errors, misinterpretations, and omissions, deliberate or otherwise, resulting in translation from a translation is highly undesirable. "I am waiting," he added, "to have a Negro who knows Arabic translate it from the original Arabic."

Remained at office until 7:00 p.m. reading.

Sunday August 5 1928

Remained in all day reading and writing. Finished James Ford Rhodes' *The McKinley and Roosevelt Administrations*. Rhodes' delineation of [Theodore] Roosevelt shows the latter was an indefatigable worker, equally at home in the diplomatic field as in domestic affairs. Without a doubt, Roosevelt was the most dynamic personality to grace the White House since Andrew Jackson, whom he passionately admired. Roosevelt, unlike [William] McKinley the arch protectionist, was essentially a trust buster. He became the *bête noire* of Wall Street, and thereby earned their undying hostility. The Great Northern Securities Case, which was fathered by James J. Hill, who sought to monopolize the railroad business of the Northwest, established him beyond peradventure as the foe of combinations which he deemed at variance with the best interests of the people. Roosevelt did not frown upon Big Business, but merely believed that, like the little fellow, it, too, should be answerable to the law.

It is humorous to read between the lines to realize that Roosevelt still desired the nomination for a third term, even though he announced that never again would he become a candidate for election. In his autobiography, he reasoned both *pro* and *con* as to whether he should again become a candidate for the presidency. However, when he finally stated that his public career had ended with the termination of his second term in 1908, he could not foresee 1912, when he was to become the Judas of his party. By splitting the Republican ranks, he prevented a continuous rule of Republicanism from 1896 onward. But due to his formation of the Progressive Party, composed of those secessionists who followed him from the ranks of the Republican Party at Chicago in 1912, Roosevelt made it possible for Woodrow Wilson, a Democrat, to be swept into the Presidency.

No historian (American) that I have read seems to exhibit the fairness which Rhodes employs in his delineating of history. His style is marvelously simple, lacking the elegance of a [George] Bancroft or a [W. H.] Prescott, but easy, entertaining, and so interesting that I always regret to lay aside the book. Rhodes combines scientific delineation of history, based upon prodigious inquiry in primary sources, with a distinct genius for organization and interpretation of the material so collected. In addition, his style is so charming that one is almost minded of the incomparable writing of John Fiske, who, while not a scientific historian, popularized American History by making it read like a novel.

Wrote until 5:30. Rode out to the National Training School in Deanwood. Went to movies later.

Received an agreeable surprise this morning in the person of my dear friend Glenn Carrington. He had just come from New York. Carter Woodson had sent for him. Glenn Carrington was a classmate of mine at Howard; rather he was a member of the class behind me. An excellent fellow, although both Bacote and I experienced quite a struggle before we could take him to our bosoms. After his graduation from Howard, he went to the New York School of Social Work, having won a fellowship there. He became somewhat radical, both as to political theory and religion, on account of his association with intellectual radicals. He travelled through Europe during the summer of 1926, visiting England, Germany, France, Russia, and other countries. A wonderful experience for him.

In 1927 he began social work in North Carolina, under the direction of one Mr. Oxley, who had received a grant from a foundation to make a study of the Negroes in that state. Glenn remained with Mr. Oxley until November, at which time, the latter having run out of funds, he was forced to look elsewhere for employment. He found it in a little Negro school in Texas, about 250 miles from Houston. There he remained until the

Monday
August 6
1928

close of the term. They were elated with his work and expected him back next year. The school is denominational and the "profs" are required to attend church with regularity and to comport themselves likewise from a religious point of view. Glenn said that only by a prodigious effort did he persuade himself, now and then, to attend church.

His business in D.C. was chiefly because Charles Johnson, former editor of *Opportunity*, a Negro magazine, the official organ of the Urban League, recommended Carrington to Woodson for the position of business manager. This was unknown to Carrington. He, having received a letter from Johnson to get in touch with Woodson, did so, with the result that the conference of today was arranged. He asked me what Woodson might desire him to do. I could think of nothing other than the work that McKinley, our advance agent, had been pursuing. I told him so. I should have stated that Woodson was out when Carrington arrived, and we had over an hour to chat and discuss old times and friends. Woodson was surprised that Glenn and I were acquainted. I told him that we had "starved" together in New York, while attending graduate schools.

Glenn accepted my invitation to dinner. We dined with Dr. Woodson. Later, on the way home, Glenn told me that the business with Woodson had been in respect to his assuming a business role, to travel from place to place, interviewing the heads of schools, organizations, churches, etc. in order to create a demand for the publications of the Association. Glenn declined, he added, because he felt that he lacked business capacity and intuition. However, he told Woodson that he was interested in Anthropology and would like to engage in graduate work in that field. Woodson acquiesced, directing him to have a transcript of his record forwarded to him.

I think that Glenn chose unwisely when he designated Anthropology as his field for research. He lacks the foundation courses, has had no biology and no languages. He should have chosen, in my opinion, some branch of social service. But, if Glenn had the *temerity*—I should say *audacity*—to teach Biology, not having had a course in that subject, what a trifling affair it must appear to him to do graduate work in Anthropology, not having had a course therein, nor the prerequisites therefor. Glenn, in my opinion, lacks any sure foundation upon which to engage seriously in any field except social work.

Through Glenn, I had the pleasure of meeting one of our most widely heralded Negro Poets. I speak of Georgia Douglas Johnson, widow of Henry Lincoln Johnson of legal fame. She is, I should judge, about forty-five, fair, of medium height, and may have been fairly pretty in her youth. Now, however, she is subject to nervous prostration—which is the privilege of talented folk—and her pulchritude has suffered accordingly. I found her quite entertaining and charming, although Glenn assured me that she was not herself tonight. A fit commentary upon her power of writing and holding one's interest is eloquently attested to by the fact that, where we went but to exchange formal greetings, we remained over three hours.

A word about Mrs. Douglas Johnson. Having lost her husband, she has heroically met the emergency of educating her two sons by participating in various endeavors. By day she is a government employee. In addition, she edits an "Advice to the Lovelorn Column" in the Pittsburgh *Courier*, a Negro newspaper published in that city. Then, of course, being a poet, she must of necessity at unspecified intervals woo that elusive Muse. She also has a corner in the Pittsburgh *Courier* devoted to witty sayings, under the caption of "Homely Philosophy." She is quite frank concerning the herculean efforts which she is putting forth for the purpose of granting an opportunity for higher education to her sons. Her health is not the best, so much so that, in an interview with a reporter of the Pittsburgh *Courier*, she doubted very much whether she would live to see her fondest wish fulfilled—namely the education of her sons.

Mrs. Johnson's "Advice to the Lovelorn Column" shows how weak, after all, is human nature, or better, how natural, how fundamental is human kind. Although either prohibited expressly in most states, or frowned upon generally in others, legal miscegenation still takes place among the races. Where the actual consummation is forbidden by the statutes, the desire to choose a mate outside the bounds of one's own race still remains. And *mirabile dictu*, according to Mrs. Johnson, they come from both races, white especially. She told of a white girl of Bridgeport, Connecticut, a stenographer, who wished to marry a colored man, and who requested Mrs. Johnson to introduce her to some nice young man. She states that the girl comes from a very good family, is a high school graduate, and desired the young man to be at least as well educated as she.

But the most touching affair of this kind came from a white girl from Big Stone Gap, Virginia. An only girl, she writes that she is in love with a Negro man. Her brothers and parents, of course, were shocked, irritated, and finally told her that her reception of the young man's attention must cease. The girl confesses her love for the colored boy. In exasperation, her family threatens to kill the youth unless she renounces him. Her retort is that if anything happens to him, she will kill *herself.* She wrote Mrs. Johnson asking for advice, offering her a nice present if she can only suggest some solution. Her letter ends, "I just loves him and I loves his old black mammy too." Asked if she realized that she would be the mother of black children, she responded "yes" and she would love them even as she loved the father.

The outcome of the affair would have been interesting to know. But, beyond a doubt, it proves that the natural instinct is for one to choose his mate, regardless of race, color, or creed; and any barrier which renders such impossible or confines one's choice in even the smallest measure is an infringement upon man's most inalienable and fundamental right. I am not an advocate of the admixture of races *per se*, but I do believe where two persons become seriously attached to one another, no artificial barrier in the form of a decree, statute, or consideration of racial purity should stand in the way of such a consummation.

We discussed poetry, plays, politics, etc., and Mrs. Johnson seemed to be well informed upon them all. She remarked, however, that she has a feeling of weakness whenever she appears before an audience. I remarked that many a time I have experienced that very same sensation. A sort of chill. But, with me, it appears upon my beginning to speak.

Glenn told her that I wrote poetry, whereupon I made haste to explain that I but "dabbled." She asked me to bring some of my work over sometime that she might glance over it. I told her that it could not be called *poetry*. "Oh," she remarked, encouragingly, "I, too, thought likewise at one time." I think I shall let her look over one or two of mine.

We left about nine thirty. A very charming woman, well read, refined, yet with a pleasing frankness. She is unsparing in delineating herself. I gathered that until recently she lived in better circumstances, for she spoke of driving her "Scripps Booth." And that is a car the average person cannot own. Though not reduced to penury by any means, she had to hold several jobs in order to obviate straitened circumstances.

My throat is troubling me; I called at Dr. M——— this morning before going to the office, only to find that he is out of town. Disappointed, for I consider him a competent physician. There are so few Negro doctors who are efficient. Not that they do not receive adequate training, but that they usually regard their commencement as the final end of all study.

Tuesday
August 7
1928

Went to the Bureau of the Census. Woodson had given me a letter of introduction to take to Dr. [William Chamberlin] Hunt, the Assistant Director. He is a wizened little man with hair growing over his face. He looked like a pet monkey. A fine man. Courteous, affable, obliging, he gave me what aid he could by presenting me with a bound volume (IV) of the 1910 Census, covering all available data on Occupations for 1910. To my query whether any information could be secured covering Negro Occupations since 1920, he told me that nothing would be available until 1934. That meant my work, if I am able to complete it, will be out of date in 1934, or within five years after publication.

A Mrs. Miller called to see Dr. Woodson this afternoon. She is white, a descendant of an old Quaker family whose ancestral home is in Maryland, not far from the District. Woodson said the family has always been opposed to slavery. Also added that she is a staunch supporter of the Association. She has often, he says, invited him to her home to spend weekends, but he has never accepted. Why? Her visit is just an illustration of the support which both whites and Negroes are now giving the institution.

It rained heavily all during the evening. Miss [Helen] Massey called and asked me to postpone our movie engagement, for she feared the lightning which was playing quite vividly and sharply.

Read the *Nation* and *Current History*. Terribly hot today.

Wednesday Had my troubles today with the "Occupation" statistics. Over
August 8   400 listed singly for males and females for the different states,
1928   and no totals given. Without the aid of the adding machine I
           would be lost.

Took Miss S [Pauline Stewart?] to the movies. Still hot.

Thursday   Statistics. Statistics. I am immersed in them. And I hate fig-
August 9   ures. But then, these figures are to tell a story. They are the
1928   skeleton. I have only to clothe them in a literary medium and
           my task will be complete.

Picked up *Mongrel Virginians* by [Arthur H.] Estabrook and [I. E.] McDougle. These two men have made a superficial study of race intermixtures. They deal with a small group of "numbskulls" at the base of the Blue Ridge Mountains in Virginia, called by them the Winn Family, in whose veins flow the blood of whites, Indians, and Negroes. These biased "scholars" have arrived at the monstrous conclusion that so feeble is the black strain that when racial admixture occurs, black characteristics are wholly obliterated. Therefore, it follows that the white strain is the strongest, the Indian next, and the Negro the weakest. Yet, paradoxically enough, after admitting that the Negro strain is the weakest because the Winn group exhibits little of those characteristics usually associated with Negroes, such as geniality, love of music, etc., they then declare that the lack of progress, sexual perverseness, and the other vices inherent in the present group is traceable to Negro blood. Thereby they refute their original assumption that the white blood is the stronger, by admitting that the Negro characteristics of indolence, mendacity, etc. are strong enough to overthrow such cardinal traits as thrift and truthfulness in the white strain. Like all consciously intended white supremacy arguments fathered by race-amalgamation-frightened-Nordics, their well-intended and carefully prepared reasoning becomes a boomerang to explode their own fallacies. I believe the book was written to lend moral strength and influence to the statutes passed by Virginia last year prohibiting intermarriage.

To show to what extremes men may go when writing about the Negro, I contrast *Mongrel Virginians* by Estabrook and McDougle with E. Raymond Turner's *The Negro in Pennsylvania*. The latter is a masterpiece of research. It was the prize essay of the American Historical Association for 1908. Delving into the sources, perusing diaries, letters, newspapers, pamphlets, state and municipal documents, and other records, Mr. Turner has developed a work of the highest type. His fairness is equalled only by his scholarship and research. He treats slavery from its early inception in the state, notes the first efforts to curb it, its final abolition, then the treatment of the freed Negro. He brings the study down to the Civil War. I could not but note the likeness to slavery in Pennsylvania of that institution in New England. As in New England, the slaves in Pennsylvania were relatively kindly treated. Their status at first was that of servants; then laws were codified regulating their movements and status, as in New England. When they were finally released from physical bondage, they were still enslaved politically, hated by the whites because of their color and their competition in the labor market. Riots were very common in Pennsylvania, although I have found no instances of them in New England.

The very first written protest against slavery in America came from Pennsylvania in the person of Daniel Pastorius of the Germantown settlers in 1688. These Germans, self reliant, religious, and actuated by the highest moral sentiments, uttered lofty protests against slavery when all the world looked upon the traffic in human souls with as little aversion as they did the vending of vegetables or beef.

The Quakers, led by Anthony Benezet, John Woolman, and others, came in for their share of praise in the eighteenth century.

Turner notes the economic status of the "Free Negro" in Pennsylvania. Many of them, he states, lived as well as any of the whites; some were wealthy. One, James Forten, a sail maker, was worth $100,000 before the Civil War. They had churches where orderly services were conducted. Another group lived in moderate circumstances, but a great many, says Turner, lived in the alleys, which became dens of vice, crime, and disease. But in fairness to the Negroes in Pennsylvania, Turner notes that this condition was brought about largely by prejudice against the influx of Negroes from the border states of Virginia, Maryland, and Delaware. Pennsylvania freed her slaves by gradual emancipation in 1780.

Pennsylvania, like the New England states, exhibited the anomalous picture of a state and section which refused to hold the Negro permanently in bondage within their borders, yet which refused to accord him those rights and privileges to which he was entitled as a free man. In other words, these states feared and hated the Negro after they had freed him. In extenuation for their attitude, however, as the historian must recognize, these states were looked upon as a haven by escaping and freed Negroes in the slave states, and the harsh laws levelled against the Negroes after abolition in these states were quasi-protectionary. They aimed to prevent the states from being overrun by fugitive slaves who, if remaining within the state, were apt to become idlers or, if unable to secure employment, would become public charges.

Two other things in the book arrested my attention. One was the novel construction which Turner placed upon the terms abolition and anti-slavery. Disagreeing with A. B. Hart, who he considers an authority on slavery, Turner takes issue with his definition, or, better, his interpretation of the words *abolition* and *anti-slavery*. *Abolition*, says Turner, preceded *anti-slaveryism*. By the former, an attempt was made to get rid of slavery by peaceful and legal means, and it extended only to the limits of the state in question. But anti-slavery, he adds, comprehended the entire *Union*; it assailed slavery unequivocally. It advocated immediate manumission at whatever cost. It would free the slaves, even if the government must be overthrown and the Union dissolved. Hart interprets the two terms in the opposite manner. So do I. Even Woodson said, "for once I must agree with Hart." Both he and Wesley believe Hart to be a "joke" as a historian.

The second incident was the Christiana Riot. It took place in Christiana, Pennsylvania, in 1851. A man, one Gorsuch from Maryland, came to the above town to recover his runaway slaves. On his arrival at the house where the Negroes were said to be secreted, a mob composed of Negroes armed with guns, knives, sticks, and stones attacked Gorsuch and his companion, and beat the former to death with sticks and stones. And the marvel of it, not a man was found guilty. It is a replica of what the Negro suffers in the South today and of the familiar verdict that no one in the mob was recognized. In my small acquaintance with history, the Christiana Riot stands out supremely and lordly as an instance where a white was done to death by a black mob, and a white judge and a white jury acquitted the black perpetrators.

An excellent piece of work is Turner's *Negro in Pennsylvania*.

[11] Deeper Involvement with the Association

Friday
August 10
1928
Statistics again today. Received a letter from Thelma [Duncan], who is vacationing in Colorado. Speaks about the natural glories of New Mexico, Arizona, Colorado. Wish I could have gone there with her.

Woodson told me in reply to my comment upon Turner's *Negro in Pennsylvania* that it is one of the best books ever written on the Negro. He said he tried to get Turner to contribute to the *Journal of Negro History*. But Turner replied he was not interested in Negro History. If he could write such a book, the subject having had no appeal for him, what would he do in some field in which he had such an attraction?

Begin to rain tonight.

[General Umberto] Nobile wishes to return to aid in the search for the missing airmen.

Saturday
August 11
1928
It rained all day. Remained at the office until 5:30. On the way home we discussed the attitude shown by most of the northern states toward the Negro after they had emancipated them as slaves. Took home Woodson's galleys for book of *African Myths*, which I shall read tomorrow. Woodson desires to have it on the way to the publishers by tomorrow night.

Rain fell in torrents throughout the night. I made no attempt to keep the appointment with Miss [Helen] Massey.

Remained in all day, reading the galleys for African Myths.
Could not have gone out even if I wished. I have never beheld
such a downpour of water. A perfect deluge: And surprisingly
enough, it has not lessened since last evening. A storm of
tropical proportions—the tail end of a hurricane which had its
source in the West Indies and which, for the past few days, has
swept over Florida and Georgia, leaving a path of ruin and
desolation in its wake. We escaped the wind but received a vast
quantity of water.

Bertha called at noon. Asked if I had a book here. Wanted
something romantic. "Joshed" her over the phone. She
laughs, but deep down inside of her heart, there is a scar left by
me. I have hurt her cruelly, though God knows not inten-
tionally. All pretenses of human affection fade beside her love.
She has given me an entirely new conception of the term. Her
love has been a holy thing—exalted, unselfish, whole-souled,
sublime. Love at its finest and best. In her, love has approached its closest to the divine source from which it sprang.

Went to Woodson's with the galley proof sheets at six in a
driving tempest. He was in. He started comparing galleys. I
had found numerous typographical and a few grammatical
errors in them. Also I had checked several sentences for sim-
plification and for style. Woodson had eliminated some of the
cuts and also reduced the entire number of sheets. Therefore,
we had to rearrange the *entire* book in order to make them
conform. Some of the pages we filled out with proverbs (African) or with an occasional cut from the *Negro in Our History*.

An amusing incident was our attempt to insert the cut of a
man walking. It was a good cut of a native with his walking
stick. We decided to insert it at the end of the story of the
"Three Rival Brothers." All of them with good reason
claimed the daughter of the King. Neither King, judge, nor
people were able to declare to whom the princess should be
allotted, so even were the claims put forth by each of the
brothers. Our perplexity was increased by whether the man
should represent one of the brothers departing in desperation,
the King departing in perlexity, or the judge leaving at his

wit's end. We could not give any of the brothers undue prominence; the King was not sufficiently important in the story to
merit such distinction; therefore, we finally decided to call him
the judge going home in a quandary after his inability to settle
the case. We later had a spirited argument over the correct use
of a conjunction. I believed that "as" should be substituted by
"because" in a certain sense. Woodson took issue, then
brought forward a grammar published in 1865 to prove his
point. He did. I yielded, since either could be used in a casual
sense. What an experience I am gaining in book making.

Later Woodson asked that I contribute something to the
Journal. It came about by his speaking of his inability to acquire
a literary style. Said that was one of his objects in taking the
doctor's degree. He believed it would give him *per se* the
power to write. I told him that such was my fear that I shall
never be able to write anything of value because I am totally
lacking in anything that suggests literary talent. I picked up
my essay on the "Decline of Negro Slavery in New England"
to prove my point. He asked that I allow him to look it over,
that it might be worked up into an article for the October issue
of the *Journal of Negro History*. I was delighted but afraid that
after he perused it he would not feel like allowing me to go on
with the "Study of Negro Occupations."

Left him at 11:30 p.m.

Hoover finally accepted the nomination yesterday in California.

Monday
August 13
1928

Worked on statistics and finished the "Occupations of
Negroes" by sections and states for 1890. Woodson went to
the Congressional Library. Failed to find African Proverbs for
his volume on *Myths*. We had inserted some white proverbs,
but did not care to mix the sayings of Caucasians in a purely
African book.

Remained at the office until six o'clock reading a book on
anthropology, by an author whose name escapes me.

Called Bertha. Wished to take her to the movies. She had an
engagement. So had Miss Stewart[?]. Miss Massey[?] was ill,

so I went alone. (Last year this time we were having a glorious time at Hampton, while selling magazines.)

Felt very ill at the office this morning. I became so weak I thought I should surely faint. Later I was convinced that it was due to indigestion.

Remained at the office until 3:45. Went to the Library of Congress. On the way I stopped by the doctor's office. Saw Bertha. Later took dinner with her.

Looked over a list of books in a second hand shop on G Street. Liked a set of 24 volumes of the World's Best Literature. Would like to purchase it. Price is $10.00, though I did hear it can be had for less.

Spent the evening with Bertha. Quite enjoyable. I think a great deal of her, more perhaps than she imagines. I am inclined to believe that she is on the verge of falling in love with Yarborough. He has offered marriage, but she refused him. This she confided in me. I wonder whether her old love for me impelled her answer. Yarborough is madly in love with her. But she hesitates to marry on the possibility of learning to love afterwards. She has refused excellent offers before. At times, I feel quite grieved that I am the cause of her refusal to marry. Simply because she had loved me with a love almost divine, and which I am powerless to return because of the lure of scholarship and the responsibility of caring for my parents. But even I fully realize that such a love as hers will never again be known to me. Still, I am inclined to believe that she is succeeding in an endeavor to suppress her affection for me and will in all probability yield to the importunings of Yarborough, and finally give herself to him in marriage. What will be my reaction, I know not.

(Glorious ride on the bay at Hampton this night last year.)

Woodson shocked me this morning by telling me that he would like to publish part of my essay on "Negro Slavery in New England," which I had done as a seminar paper last year for Professor Dixon Ryan Fox. Woodson suggested that I expand certain parts, especially my statement concerning the raising of slaves for the market. He proposed a change in title to "Slavery and Awakening in New England." I agreed.

Went to the Library in the afternoon. Had previously gone to the bank, where I secured a five dollar gold piece for Bertha. It is her birthday. A man is usually at a loss as regards the choosing of an appropriate gift for a lady, and I was no exception. I pasted the gold piece on the inside of a birthday booklet by means of a seal. Stopped at her home enroute from the Library. Told her that I was presenting her a birthday card, but did not feel that she was worthy of my spending two cents for a stamp. Therefore, I brought it to her personally. She laughed, laid it on the table, and embraced me, remarking that I shall always be comical.

Went to the movies in the evening.

Thursday August 16 1928

Went to the Library to secure some information upon the "Conversion of Slaves in New England." Woodson referred me to a tract by Jernegan entitled "Slavery and Conversion in the American Colonies."[1] An excellent account of the Christianization of the Negroes, but not quite full enough concerning New England, though I found it helpful. It is shocking to think that such a small privilege as Christianity would be denied the slaves, but then the masters had to live among these malcontents. Economic values also entered, since the prevailing notion was that if slaves were baptized they straightaway were entitled to manumission, which would have entailed considerable property loss. Read portions of Cotton Mather's *Diary*. He apparently treated his slaves as if they were members of his own family.

Found [Mary S.] Locke's *Anti-Slavery in America* very helpful, though I had practically all of her information on New England and in much greater detail. Looked also into the *American Statistical Review*; [John Stetson] Barry's *Historical Sketch of [the Town of] Hanover, Mass.,* and other works.

1. Marcus W. Jernigan, "Slavery and Conversion in the American Colonies," *American Historical Review*, XXI (1916), 504–27.

After dinner tonight went over to Bertha's. She was to go out with me but felt a little indisposed. Thanked me for her present. I had refused to see her on her birthday, feeling that Yarborough would not look with equanimity on my intrusion. To this she objected strenuously, but I prevailed. Discussed my loneliness with her. She reminded me that she had warned me that ambition, though laudable, was not the ultimate good in life. Suggested that I make preparation for my social as well as intellectual future. Could not but feel that she was in a large measure correct.

This day, a year ago, still stands as an unforgettable one in my memory. 'Twas the night of the reception for the tennis players at Hampton. What a wonderful round of enjoyment we magazine-selling students had, capped by the delightful ball over the beautiful bay. 'Twas there I met charming Marguerite Skeeter. Then, too, the arrival of Campbell and his team, like serpents gliding into the garden. Then the cantaloupe eating episode later in the Wigwam—the incomparable Nathaniel Dett—his fall while descending the stairs— Campbell's humiliation at my hands, all rise up before me as I contemplate this day.[2]

Friday
August 17
1928

Desiring more data for the New England slavery article, I again visited the Congressional Library at 11 o'clock. Becoming engrossed in the research, I remained there until 8 p.m.

2. The year before, 1927, Greene and two other students—Sidney Wells, a music student at New York University, and a student from the University of Pennsylvania by the name of Martin—were at Hampton Institute in Virginia selling magazines for the Union Circulation Company of New York City. Hosea Campbell, who had convinced the company to use black students, led a team and was in charge of all of the teams of black student salesmen. The company limited the black students to soliciting subscriptions from black customers.

On the evening Greene was reminiscing about, the young men attended a dance, which was also attended by the famed musician and Hampton faculty member Nathaniel Dett. They returned with Dett to the Hampton dormitory where they were staying—known as the Wigwam—and the residents served them cantaloupe. During the evening, Dett slipped and fell downstairs but was not injured.

Campbell, whom Greene seemed to dislike, brought his team to Hampton. While there, he attempted to reorganize the teams by exchanging a member of his team for Sidney Wells, a member of Greene's team. Greene believed he had come out ahead of Campbell in the confrontation because, despite threats from Campbell, he refused to accede to his demand.

What a marvelous repository of knowledge this library is, and how widely used! Although it is the vacation season, the reading room is well filled. Most of the readers are mature men and women who are seriously interested in research. Occasionally one sees a Negro. I have a card of admission to the files, but it avails me naught at present because an inventory is being taken. This may last for the remainder of the summer.

Ate dinner at 9 p.m. I know that such is unwise, but there is a fascination about historical research that grips and holds me. Took a long walk. Returned home about 11:30.

Saturday
August 18
1928

Went directly to the Library. Worked assiduously to collect sufficient information that I might complete the article over Sunday. The Library closed at 1 p.m. Therefore I brought several books away with me, including Locke's *Anti-Slavery in America*, to which I alluded some time ago; and George H[enry] Moore's *Notes on the History of Slavery in Massachusetts*, which is the best account of slavery in that state that I have seen, although the author's feelings creep in. *Historical Notes on the Employment of Negroes in the [American Army of the] Revolution,* by the same author, is a series of notes on the employment of Negroes and the arguments *pro* and *con* before it was actually decided to use them. Valuable because it is practially the kernel of the sources. *Colored Patriots of the Revolution,* written by William C. Nell, a free Negro of Massachusetts in 1855, aims to tell of the significant achievements of the Negro down to 1860. The title is a misnomer.

Returned to the office at 1:30. Tried to revise the section on "The Slave and Christianity," but to no avail. Finally left it and corrected other sections of the manuscript.

Office is topsy-turvy. Painters, plasterers, and paperhangers are here to renovate the place. Woodson was removing books, tables, chairs, etc. when I arrived. Refused to allow me to assist.

Asked me to read over the galleys for his book "Negro Makers of History." Wished me to do so tomorrow. I told him of my plans to finish the manuscript. He decided the latter had better be done first.

Mr. [William M.] Brewer came in, bringing a manuscript for the *Journal*. It was an appreciation of John Russwurm, editor of the first Negro newspaper in America, *Freedom's Journal*, published in 1817. He also enjoyed the distinction of being the first Negro graduate of an American college (Bowdoin in Maine). He was also an orator and a colonizer.

Mr. Brewer has just returned from Harvard University, where he pursued a seminar under Professor [C. H.] Van Tyne in Political Theory. How I envy him!

(Both Campbell and Steele were humiliated at Hampton a year ago today.)

Spent all day on the slavery manuscript. Rising at 7:30, I took just enough time for breakfast and dinner between that hour and 7:30 p.m. I decided that it would not be wise to submit but one part: First, because it is almost an entity within itself. The year 1775, the actual outbreak of hostilities between England and the colonies, is a logical place to stop. And secondly, because of the lack of time to secure sufficient information on slavery and State Constitutions, which was the gist of the second part. I shall be ashamed for any student of history who is at all familiar with Negro Slavery in New England to peruse part one, for he will perceive at a glance that I have just scratched the surface. And badly at that!

Worn out. A bath refreshed me. Took a walk. Stopped at the "frat" house. Met an interesting character in one McHeathcock, a teacher of physical culture and former business man of North Carolina. We walked and chatted until 11 o'clock.

Sunday August 19 1928

Spent the entire morning on the manuscript. It was with many a sigh in consciousness of its insufficiency that I finally turned it over to Miss Harvey. Poor girl, she has my sympathy. I wish, however, Miss Revallion were here to type it. She understands such work; then too, she has read my wretched scribbling before.

Read over Mr. Brewer's article on John Russwurm. The style is indifferent. The organization leaves much to be de-

Monday August 20 1928

sired, and the author makes his dissertation an outlet for his emotions rather than the reflection of impersonal, scientific history. Then, too, obviously necessary details in any biographical sketch are omitted. Both the birthplace and the date of the subject's nativity are left to the tender imagination of the reader. Woodson reminded me that that is the way history should not be written. I beheld where he had tried to give it coherence, unity, and style. I felt pretty anxious, however, for my manuscript may receive the same sort of criticism. Dr. Woodson informed me that Mr. Brewer has been unfortunate in his education. He is a graduate of Paine College, then went to Harvard, where he worked intermittently for the M.A. degree.

Next I read "The Mohammedan Slave Trade" by an unnamed author. It contains some good secondary material, but as to organization and style, Lord help me, it surpasses Brewer's in its imbecility. It does, however, give some very interesting facts concerning slavery in the Middle Ages. I never dreamed that the Mohammedans carried on in such a wholesale manner, a slavery that reached from the Steppes of Asia to the Atlantic and from Northern Europe to the Sudan. Russians, Mongolians, Slavs, Bulgars, Greeks, Italians, Germans, French, Spanish, English, all fell under the Mohammedans' auction hammer. Then, too, the extent to which Christians sold Christians was shocking. Fathers even sold their children. Then the Jews—who became the greatest of all traders in human flesh, although they were later prohibited from vending Christians. The efforts of the Church to stop the traffic also elicited no little attention from us because of its inability to do so. Those who in the smugness of their ignorance believe that the Negro has been the only race to cringe under the lash of bondage, will suffer a rude shock when they read this essay.

At lunch time I met a very charming and exceedingly pretty girl at the "Y." It made my lunch hour pass very pleasurably.

Started reading the galleys for Woodson's book this morning about 4 a.m.

Believe me, I shall know a little about the inside of book making when I leave here.

Met Miss [Victoria] Snowden—Bacote's fiancée—and mother on the way home.

Went to the movies. Surprised to see Woodson come in with a stunning young lady.

Dreamed that he was married, that his wife had obligingly presented him with triplets and when I arrived at the office I found that he had discarded his books for babies. 'Twas all a fantasy, however.

Woodson ate two pounds of grapes for lunch. I marvel at him. Despite his position, he is not too proud to work manually. He removed all the books from the stock room, and refused to allow me to assist him.

Spent the entire day on the galleys. There is hardly a place left for me to work now. The paper hangers and painters are upstairs and downstairs. Masons are in the yard and cellar, and Woodson and I are in the kitchen, which is mostly occupied by books. *Tuesday August 21 1928*

Enjoyed talking to Miss Stewart at luncheon.

Miss Harvey is having her troubles with the manuscript. Yet, she is doing splendidly.

I called upon Miss Boyd this evening. Was a member of our gang. First time I had seen her in three years. She was going out, however.

Called upon Mrs. Hood. Was out. Mrs. Adkins and her husband were home, however. Kept them laughing as usual.

Finished reading the galleys at 3:30. Miss Harvey has been quite fortunate in that only twice has she had to bother me about the manuscript. She types it slowly but efficiently. *Wednesday August 22 1928*

About 4:20 I picked up a book called *Nojoque,* pronounced "No Joke," I suppose. Its author is Hinton Rowan Helper. His having written such an estimable book as *Impending Crisis* makes it exceedingly marvelous that he could sink to such a low depth in ten years as to write the nonsensical trash welling up from deep-seated rancor against the Negro. I have never read such abomination in the name of literature. Hate—hate—hate! Powerful propaganda, denying any virtue in the Negro, labelling him as a foul excrescense, bereft of all the capabilities of the whites, and advocating extermination of all races which are not blessed with a white skin. To please this one son of South Carolina, over two-thirds of the entire population of the world must be smitten with a plague, cast into the hottest fire of hell, or swallowed up in the maw of the ocean, so that on this beautiful earth whiteness might not be marred by any face other than that of the "milk-white" Caucasian. For, to him, black is evil, is night, is darkness, is a hideousness that must be far, far removed from the delicate countenance of the whites. Such epithets as Helper hurls at the poor Negro would make a person who believed such trash smart with a feeling of impotency and inferiority. Helper quotes from biologists, naturalists, ethnologists, physiologists, psychologists, and poets to show that the Negro is inferior mentally and physically to the white man, that he *is* and *always has been* a fit instrument for slavery. Moreover, he adds, "God wills that the whites hate the Negro. The two races cannot live together. What then is the remedy? Extermination!" An assuring doctrine to be sure. But we pity him! Such a book is a curiosity, a pointed example of the degree to which hatred can lead its victims.

Bertha called about 9:15, just as I was about to go out for a walk. Asked me to walk in her direction as she had something to tell me.

Bertha informed me that her friend, a Mrs. Bennett, feels she has made a mistake in her choice of husband. Bertha could not understand why she married him in the first place. Said she had counselled her against it. But then only the one who is concerned can see the virtue in the person she loves. I am sorry for Mrs. Bennett, for she is certainly deserving of happiness, if anyone is.

Thursday
August 23
1928

Today I spent upon statistics, for the first time since last Tuesday. Worked out the participation of Negroes in occupations by sex and age groups. Found that a far greater percentage of Negroes between the ages of 20 and 24 and 65 and over were at work in 1890 than any other group in the American population.

Miss Harvey is experiencing great travail with the manuscript. Has gotten through 27 pages in 3-1/2 days. The fault is chiefly mine although abetted by her inexperience with such things. Miss Revallion is a past-master at such. Too bad she is vacationing.

Order is rapidly being brought out of confusion here. Most of the papering has been completed. Woodson will be doing the painting.

I helped to suggest questions for his *Negro Makers of History*.

Woodson told me that a girl whom he had discharged and her mother threatened to sue him in consequence of it. Woodson threatened a countersuit. Finally they begged him not to do so. Said they needed money in order to get home. What Woodson finally did, I don't know.

Told Woodson about Helper's *Nojoque*, that monstrosity of venom and hatred. Said he never considered Helper a friend of the Negro merely because he advocated the extinction of slavery. Neither did I for that matter; he was more interested in the "emancipation" of the "poor whites."

Wrote Florence [Bacote], [Sidney] Wells, and Ernest [Bacote].

Returning from the Post Office, I met Mrs. Powell and daughter, Hazel. Asked Hazel why she had not been at her desk at the office lately; she told me that she had been discharged. I was shocked. Her mother informed me that she was at the office last night when I left. What she said about Woodson "hurt" my ears. I don't like her.

Today I spent on statistical tabulations. The office is a regular hive of industry. Between paper hangers, clerical work, and research work, there is little time for idle rumination. Dr. Woodson has been cudgeling his brain all day to append questions at the close of each chapter of his *Negro Makers of History*. He read some of them for my criticism.

Friday
August 24
1928

We discussed the future prospects of the Negro. He believes that the South is the best place for the Negro. He follows Booker T. Washington here. Woodson says the Southern Negro unconsciously is buying land, for he is working the farms, and whoever owns the land always has a source of wealth. He (Dr. Woodson) discoursed upon the moral degeneracy of the Negroes in Cincinnati, where vice, prostitution, and crime flourish. It surprised me, for I had visualized a very respectable and prosperous group resident there.

I did not tell Dr. Woodson that I had already met Mrs. Powell and her daughter and of the aspersions which they had cast upon his unprotected head.

Lest I forget, yesterday Woodson showed me a letter from Professor [Edward A.] Hooten, Head of the Department of Anthropology at Harvard University, offering Glenn Carrington a fellowship there. Of course, it came through Woodson's influence. It seems that he can get pretty much what he desires in that line. Is so highly respected by social scientists. Glenn is fortunate. It is up to him to make good. Maybe difficult for him, since he has had practically no biology and no foreign languages. I wish him success, though, as well as envying his good fortune.

Went to movies. Saw a powerful anti-Bolshevist picture, "Orphans of the Storm." A warning to the people that the overthrow of government is at best a risky business. To exchange the tyranny of kings, czars, and nobles for that of the masses is no guarantee of a better life for the latter. The picture, of course, dealt with the French Revolution and with the following reign of terror. It showed only the brutal and excessive side of the movement, portraying none of the inestimable benefits that humanity derived from that most terrific social upheaval of modern times.

Saturday
August 25
1928

Dr. Woodson shocked me this a.m. with the news that Carrington had refused the scholarship on the grounds that his financial assistance was necessary to aid in sending his sisters and younger brother to school. A $1,200.00 fellowship and refused! Woodson is more or less disgusted. "Frankly," he said, "most Negroes are not worth a damn." He complained that to secure money for the education of a Negro is a small matter compared with the difficulty of finding one who will do the work. Scholarships at Harvard are so highly prized, he added, that many persons would pay for the privilege of studying there on those terms. Woodson was so exasperated that he wrote Carrington, telling him that if he refused this fellowship, "he ought to go to an analyst and have his head examined." I must agree with him. Yet, it is an extremely praiseworthy sacrifice on Glenn's part.

Miss Harvey finally finished the manuscript on "Negro Slavery in New England." I spent the afternoon correcting, deleting, revising, and adding to it. She did careful, neat work, although she confused several reference notes. But considering the degree of unintelligibility of my calligraphy she did most excellently. So striking is my inability to write with even a fair degree of legibility that Dr. Woodson asked me to address an envelope for him, then, upon reflection, added, "No, if you do, the letter will never be received." I did address it, however, but must add that I took scrupulous pains to make it readable. And I blush to say it was barely so.

What a many-sided person is Dr. Woodson! This morning he was attired in pyjamas like a coolie and was cleaning like an ordinary charwoman. Later he painted, touching up several of the windows. After that he oiled the floors. Then at 6:30, having worked right up to the time of his departure, he left for the session of the Social Science Research Council meeting at Dartmouth College, Hanover, New Hampshire.

I suppose, coeval with his intellectual capacity, some compensatory qualities should appear in him. Woodson is very absent-minded. It is common to see one of the girls looking for his glasses when he has misplaced them. Today he made ready to go, only to discover his wallet could not be located. We searched the entire office. He finally found it upstairs, where he no doubt had unconsciously placed it. But Woodson is a fine man to be in contact with. I hope that I shall imitate the sponge rather than the spoon, and soak up all the knowledge that flows from his marvelous intellect. He knows the Negro as no other man knows him.

Just before Woodson departed, a heavy storm arose. The streets were flooded, and it rained as I had only seen it rain two weeks ago. I had to take a taxi home.

Read *Batualo*, a prize novel of 1923 by René Moran. [René Maran's novel, *Batualo or Batouala*, was published in France in 1921; an English translation by A. S. Seltzer was published in New York in 1922.] Stark naked description of African customs and Africans' attitude toward the whites. Deals with the native black in his native environment. Moran himself is a black. He castigates France in his introduction for her exploitation of the blacks.

Read also W. E. B. Du Bois' *The Negro*. A pretty fair work, although he let his personality creep in from time to time. Traces the Negro from Ancient Africa to about 1915. Much of the material on Africa is found in Lady Lugard's *Tropical Dependency* and Félix Dubois' *Timbuctoo, the Mysterious* and Leo Frobenius' *Voice of Africa*. A fine book, however, for one who desires to secure an uninterrupted conspectus of the Negro from antiquity to the present.

Sunday August 26 1928	Took poetry to Miss P———. Went to see Bertha. Had dinner with her. Took a walk with her in the evening. She looked glamorous in white, with her hair parted in the center and done in a Psyche knot behind. Her oval face, embellished with a pair of pearl earrings that dangled from her ears, aided in beautifying an already lovely creature. Though rain threatened, we walked out to the park at P and B Streets, S.W.
Monday August 27 1928	Nothing of importance at the office today. The news today is of international scope and prominence, the signing of the Kellogg-Briand Multilateral Anti-War Treaty. (Don't put too much faith in it.)
Tuesday August 28 1928	Read over 100 pages in [George B.] Davis' *Elements of International Law*. According to him, International Law, as we now comprehend it, had its inception with [Hugo] Grotius. Was

fascinating reading. Also read several chapters in [Edwin R. A.] Seligman's *Principles of Economics*.

After dinner went out to Anacostia, where I called upon the Beverlys and from there upon Leona (Mrs. Turner). Returned in time to go to the movies. An extremely hot day.

Another scorching day. Went to movies in the evening in order to overcome my loneliness.

Wednesday August 29 1928

After a day spent upon figures, I went to Bertha's to get Woodson's umbrella, which I had left there Sunday. Left after spending a delightful evening. Rain came to cool an extremely torrid day.

Thursday August 30 1928

Woodson came in unexpectedly this a.m. He had been attending a conference at Dartmouth. And his umbrella was at my aunt's. I realized that he would soon have need for it, since he had informed me that he had not eaten since noon of yesterday. And it seemed as if rain would descend in a downpour at any moment.

Friday August 31 1928

In order to save both of us embarrassment, I went home at 1 o'clock to get his umbrella. Just my luck! It began to rain even as I started. When I returned, Woodson had gone out. I left the umbrella and went to lunch. Returned, I said to him, "I took your umbrella home last night." He interrupted by saying, "And you forgot it." "Yes, I am sorry." Woodson: "And I had to go out in the rain. But never mind, it is alright." No doubt, he felt a little irked. My reaction was a resolve never to borrow it again.

Woodson kept quite busy for the remainder of the day. Yet he found time to tell me of Carrington's acceptance of the fellowship in Anthropology at Harvard University after all and also of the subject matter discussed at the Social Research Council at Dartmouth. He asked me to read a manuscript by a Mr. [Rayford W.] Logan on "The Mandate System in Africa."[3]

3. Rayford W. Logan, "The Operation of the Mandate System in Africa," *Journal of Negro History*, XIII (1928), 423–77.

A very clear and well constructed account drawn chiefly from Dr. [Raymond Leslie] Buell's late researches in the above field and Moon's *Imperialism and World Politics*. I doubt whether anything new has been introduced. Yet it contains matters of which the average layman knew virtually nothing.

In the evening I took [Helen Grinage?] to the movies.

Saturday
September
1
1928

Woodson is going away this a.m. Was a little irked at the absence of Miss Revallion, whose vacation ended yesterday. 3000 letters all to be sent out by the tenth. Asked me to have the girls work on nothing else but them. Requested that I verify the work done daily by a young man who is coming in on Monday to address envelopes.

I went to the ball game in the afternoon. Saw New York beat Washington 8 to 3 in a listless game.

Later bought some paint. Stopped in a second hand shop. Purchased 27 books: History, Philosophy, Sociology, novels, etc. Cost $2.70, or at the rate of 10 cents per copy.

Sunday
September
2
1928

Went to church in Georgetown. Failed to find my mother's cousins there. Went to their home in Rosslyn. No one home. Disappointed, for this was my first visit there since May. I am ashamed of myself, and I know they are exasperated with me. Left a note.

Called Bertha. She seemed to derive quite a bit of pleasure over my failure to find my cousins at home. Invited me to her home.

Teased me about getting there habitually at meal time. Told her I only ate to "please" her. Spent an exceedingly agreeable afternoon. Left at 7:00.

Later I went to see "Fi" [Thelma Duncan], who had just returned from Colorado. Took her to the movies.

Monday
September
3
1928

Labor Day and a holiday. I availed myself of it by calling unexpectedly for "Fi" at 2:00 to take her out to my cousin's, in Hall's Hill, Virginia.

Stopped en route in Rosslyn to see cousins whom I have not visited since May. They had gone out. However, returning to the bus line, we met Mr. Alleyne, cousin Rose's husband, who told us that they had probably gone to pay a few calls but would return within an hour. Invited us to wait at home for them. Declined to go back to the house with him, but promised to return at 6 p.m.

Quite a bumpy and roundabout ride to Hall's Hill. We did get a view of the Potomac River just before entering the bus, which would have delighted the eye and heart of an artist. The river, glistening in the sunlight, stretched lazily before us, its banks lined by a verdant cluster of trees which rise so perfectly in serried ranks, the one behind the other, as to give the impression that a gigantic hand had painted an undying masterpiece upon a mammoth canvas. How peaceful and quiet are those hills that bend their green-clad slopes over this placid stream. I went into ecstacies over it. So did "Fi."

When we arrived at Hall's Hill, my cousin, who, womanlike, stood talking with a neighbor, fled precipitately upon spying us. I called out that it was no use running now.

What a pleasant home they have. A lovely little bungalow surrounded by flowers, grass, and shrubbery.

Both Almira and her mother, Cousin Jane, fell in love with "Fi," and no wonder, for her disposition is positively charming. She is the babyish type of female. A spoiled and only child. I intended to stay no longer than an hour, but first we must go to a baseball game, where we saw an old-fashioned contest between married and single men, with a football score as a result.

To my dismay, when I proposed that we leave in order to honor my appointment in Rosslyn, "Fi" felt disinclined to do so because of her attachment to my cousins. Therefore, poor impotent man! What chance had I against three women? I yielded, perforce.

After dinner, Cousin Jane and I had plenty of fun at the expense of "Fi" and Almira. We played "500." That is, "Fi" and I acted as instructors to my cousin and one of her nephews.

There was also a little outdoor dance being held. I found that I had only $2.00 with me and therefore felt disinclined to go, not knowing what the price would be; felt quite relieved when

I found out it was but a quarter. We had an enjoyable time—I
especially interested myself in the people. Country folk all: the
girls were dressed nicely, on the whole, the young men, some
well groomed, some coatless, or collarless. The girls outnum-
bered the men, much to my interest. Then to make matters all
the more embarrassing for the ladies, only a small percentage
of the men danced. Why? I asked a lady. Most of them do not
know how, was her retort. Hall's Hill, because of its proximity to Washington, suffers from a dearth of young men, like
most other rural districts, for they invariably forsake the country for the city. However, all of us enjoyed ourselves.

We left there about 11:30, with my cousin entreating "Fi" to
remain overnight and inviting her to spend her weekends
there. "Fi" seemed to have enjoyed herself, and reminded me
several times that I have been selfish to have denied her the
privilege of meeting my cousin earlier. Said she, laughingly,
"You must have been ashamed of me." Returned I, still laughingly, "Yes, I was." However, "Fi" knows how to construe
such sallies.

A very pleasant day.

Tuesday   When I arrived at the office at 9:45, Miss Revallion, along with
September   the other girls, stood waiting to get in. Dr. Woodson had
4   remarked on Saturday that he did not know whether she
1928   would return. Miss Plater's brother also began working here.
Started them all on the 3000 letters which must be gotten out
by the 10th.

About 3:30 Miss Harvey, the bookkeeper, came to me ex-
citedly and informed me that some men had broken into the
building and opened the back gate in order to place a tank in
the yard. It seems that the engineer had come to install an oil
burner and, to Miss Harvey's surprise, told her that his men
had brought the tank there this morning, and that it even now
lay in the yard. She told me that Mr. Plater, about 8:30, had
seen two men issuing from the basement while he was waiting
to be admitted. I repaired forthwith to the cellar, the agitated
Miss Harvey behind me, and found that the latch had been

broken, the door forced, and ingress effected by that means. I confess I saw red, and immediately called the heating company, telling them what had happened and ordering them peremptorily to remove the tank from the yard. I also reminded them of the seriousness of such action—the forcible entry into private premises. Then, too, the potential damage was the problem. What might not have been stolen or destroyed? Of course, the manager was profuse with his apologies, calling later and offering to send a Mr. West, who would make good any injury suffered.

I felt especially chagrined that this should have happened during Woodson's absence, and especially while I was in charge. I know he would be wild, and with reason.

I nailed up the cellar door and also the fence.

Met Bertha after 5:30 at 14th and G Street, N.W. She wanted to borrow $10.00, which I willingly gave her.

Surprised me by telling me that she, a lone woman, had paid almost $600 for a piano within less than three years, on a salary of $10.00 per week and with a 10 year old son to care for. I must admire her. I fear she will get precious little aid from her son, who seems utterly unappreciative and unmindful of the many things she does for him. He may change, however. I hope so, for he certainly has a rare mother.

Today was uneventful, with an exception of the afterglow from the forcible entry of our premises of yesterday. I awaited the arrival of Mr. West all day, but he did not put in an appearance. It rained all day.

In the evening I played cards at Fi's.

Wednesday
September
5
1928

Received a letter from Woodson, who is now at Atlantic City. Instructed me to have some course announcement cards and bulletins for the Home Study Department printed at once. The *Bulletin* was to be reproduced *in toto*.

The changes to be made were confined solely to the Course Announcement Card. These alterations struck with a peculiar significance. They convinced me, as nothing else could have

Thursday
September
6
1928

done, that the rift between Woodson and Wesley cannot be bridged. At least for the present. The courses which were taught by Wesley were disposed of as follows: "Selected Topics in Negro Economic History" was deleted altogether; the other, "Economic History of the Negro," will be given by Dr. George E. Haynes, of the Social Science Research Council. Too bad, for I certainly hoped that Wesley would succeed Woodson in this estimable work when the latter was forced to step aside by either old age or death. It was with a heavy heart that I pencilled those courses.

It rained exceedingly hard all day.

Oh, yes, I found a note this a.m. telling me that Mr. West had called in reference to the damage done by his men, but had been unable to find me. Dr. Woodson later requested that I arrange for Mr. Logan to meet him at the office tomorrow evening at 8 p.m. He desired the cards and announcements to be printed immediately so that they might be enclosed in the letters, dated September 10th. The printer promised to give them to me on Saturday about 3 p.m.

Friday
September
7
1928

Mr. West called me this morning. Told him I had referred the matter to Dr. Woodson, who would take it up with him tomorrow at 10 a.m.

Mr. Goins called me about 5:30. He told me I might secure the proof of the "Course Announcement Card," which he wished to verify before the final printing. I assured him that he would have the proof early in the morning. Left a note for Woodson to that effect.

By a stroke of good fortune, Mr. Logan called and thereby saved me the pain of attempting to locate him.

Went to A———'s with "Fi" tonight. Returning from there, went to a party at her friend's, a sweet little girl named C———. Later I said farewell to "Fi," who is leaving for Richmond Square, North Carolina, where she teaches. Wanted me to give her two records. Told her I could not even buy food. A sweet girl. "Babyish" to an extreme.

Miss Harvey had informed Dr. Woodson about the trouble with the Automatic Heater Company. He took it with greater calm than I had anticipated.

Mr. West called about 10 o'clock. He is the aide of the construction manager. Agreed it was a shame that such had happened. His company deprecated such, and would make every effort to locate and punish the offenders. I asked did he not know whom he had sent with the tank? He pretended, much to my exasperation, that he did not. Woodson took it all stoically. He and Woodson finally settled the matter.

Miss Harvey seems so nervous this morning! She is a plugger but a bit clumsy.

Woodson reminded me that he would give me a week to go over and verify my findings so far.

Rushed home, buying a tie en route. Met Dr. Lorenzo Turner, one of my former English teachers at Howard. He and Professor Peters, recently dropped from Howard, have started a newspaper, *The Washington Sun*. Strikes a new note in Negro journalism, I believe. Yet, I doubt its chances of success, because it appeals only to the "higher-brow" set, to use vulgar parlance, and the average Negro has not yet reached the stage where he can appreciate news for news' sake, presented in literary form. What does the man on the street, black or white, care about a column on Art, Drama, Music, etc.? Sensationalism in journalism is what they demand, and must be given, if the newspaper (Negro in particular) does not intend to become simply a charitable institution.

Seems the entire country is baseball mad. Philadelphia (Athletics) has, after three years, finally dislodged the New York Yankees from first place in the American League and now perches upon the uppermost berth, a half game in front of its once doughty rivals. The teams meet in New York in a doubleheader tomorrow. About 100,000 are expected to attend. All reserve seats are sold. I shall try to be one of the lucky ones to see this titanic struggle.

Left for New York on an excursion at midnight. Crowded cars. Everyone was talking baseball, even the women. Odds are on Philadelphia. I dozed most of the way. Lost my "frat" pin. May have been stolen.

New York!

What a Glorious Day! Arrived uptown, bought "Capt." [Florence Bacote] a book and a box of candy. How glad she was to see me! In almost one breath she told me of the wonderful time she had had during the summer, playing tennis, bathing, dancing, etc. She showed me her bathing suit and knickers, tennis racket, etc. She is barely eighteen and, youthlike, rejoices in the glory of feeling that she is in love. The "unfortunate" person seems to be a classmate of hers.

Mrs. Burbridge and husband seem to be hopelessly estranged. She refused to live with him and has taken another house where she now lives, having given up the old one to Mr. Burbridge and her stepson, Harry. Did not think she had the nerve to do it. The usual result of a man's marrying a younger woman. She is twenty years his junior. She tolerated him and his eccentricities while her daughter lived. But now, well, it is a different story.

Harry Burbridge seems to have a grudge against Harry [Hipp], my pal. Threatened to do latter bodily harm. Accuses Harry of being the cause of the separation of his father and Mrs. Burbridge. Swears he will kill Harry. I am not alarmed, for Harry B was ever a boaster.

Poor [Clarence Tinney], Mrs. Burbridge's son-in-law. He looks very woebegone and dejected. With three children, no job, he is a man without manhood. He is ever going to do something, but never does. Beatrice's death robbed him of all his initiative.

Called on Nannie [Hagans]. Was glad to see her. She professed the same. Had been thinking of me, dreaming of me, and only a few days ago had called her fiancé by my name. We might have been sweethearts, but that is an old story. Perhaps we both cared for one another. I had been told that she was married, but she denied it. Asked me to write her.

Met Harry [Hipp] at Mrs. B's. Glad to see the latter. Harry and I embraced. Is my dearest pal. Needless to say, we rejoiced to see one another. Astonished me by telling me that he would be married next Sunday, and that I was to be his "best man." Forced me to gasp, for although I knew he would marry this fall, I had no idea that it would take place so suddenly. Harry certainly looks well. He probably is pursuing the wisest course, since he feels that he can no longer lead a bachelor's life. However fundamental marriage bulks in the life of one, I cannot but regret that he did not complete his graduate work before assuming the responsibilities of a husband. That was Bacote's criticism of his impending union. Then, too, the lady is propertied, an only child, etc. He is not; therefore, in my opinion, he should have brought something else to counterbalance the lady's financial advantage. Then, too, there is the "in-law." I hope for the best, however.

Harry is a prince of a fellow. No one could be more considerate, no one could be a stauncher friend. He is sympathetic to an extreme. I have seen him weep on occasions less provocative of tears than a funeral. He is mindful of the other fellow's point of view, yet has the courage of his convictions, as both Bacote and I will attest.

The lady! She is the type who is at her best as mistress of her home—which quality she rightly inherits. She is efficient; perhaps that best sums up her qualities. I believe that she also would prove a true friend and faithful wife, and should be an admirable companion for a person of Harry's calibre. I wish them "oodles" of luck.

Harry, "Capt.," and I called on Gladys [McDonald]. She was just rising. Her wonderful mother was as glad to see me as I her. Gladys, the incomparable, came in, smiling as usual. There is a subtle tie between us, although our bond is the result of platonic friendship only. At least, on my part. Gladys is too tall for me, else I know not what might have resulted. I spent ten very delectable minutes with her, then rushed over to Mrs. Daniel, Harry's prospective mother-in-law.

Muriel, Harry's fiancée, met us at the door. She looks well, though a trifle thin, I thought. I am no company there, nor care to be, therefore was escorted without ceremony to the most desirable room in the house, the kitchen. There Mrs.

Daniel sat preparing dinner. She, although not as plump as when I last saw her, nevertheless appears to be in better health. She has heart trouble, I understand. Thought she would not last through the winter of '27. She thought I looked well, yet I know that I am several pounds lighter than in April, when they last saw me. Invited us to dinner, but we refused on account of the ball game. Bade them adieu. Muriel reminded me of next Saturday.

Called upon [Harcourt] Tynes. Found him eating breakfast. Both he and Helen, his wife, were amazed at seeing me. Caught in the enthusiasm over the ball game that fairly exuded from me, Tynes left his breakfast after gaining his wife's permission, and hastily dressed. Mrs. Tynes playfully allotted him $1.50 for divertissement.

To the ball game! That had been the impulse which had brought me to New York. Everyone was talking baseball. Everyone was hastening to the place—Yankee Stadium! By subway, surface car, bus, elevated, automobile, and foot they came, wending their way by the thousands to the game. Never have I known such baseball interest. Never has New York been engulfed in such a paroxysm of baseball fever. We could not get to the park fast enough. Long before we arrived there, we saw thousands of automobiles parked. Over a quarter of a mile from the park, we saw frantic thousands milling about the stadium, while over 200 mounted policemen and patrolmen sought to keep them moving. Our hearts sank, for even at that hour (one and a half hours before the start of the game), we realized the futility of winning our way inside that coveted ball park. We could not even get near the ticket offices. Even if we had, there would have been nothing to buy. Every seat and every inch of standing room had been taken, even before 9:30, I found out later. Even World Series frenzy had not attracted such crowds. We were prevented by the police, who kept everyone moving, from even remaining in proximity of the park. Disappointed, we went back to Tynes' home, taking some pictures on the way.

Tynes is collecting a fine library. Asked him to choose a book for me each time he secures one for himself.

By the way, Harry called Mrs. Daniel, telling her that, after all, we would accept her invitation to dinner. There we went, where I told her that of the two attractions, the ball game and her dinner, we, of course, chose the latter. In truth, as even she was aware, we were but salvaging something from the wreckage. And it certainly was welcome, for, in my enthusiasm over meeting my friends and over the ball game, I had not eaten.

Left after dinner, with a thousand professions of gratitute for such a fine exhibition of hospitality on their part, and with the importunity of Harry that I be present next Saturday.

Called on the Skeeters. Found no one but Leslie home, however. The other girls, including Marguerite, had gone riding. There are five of them there now, including Ira and Dora. Leslie was so surprised at seeing me she could scarcely talk.

Stopped at Mr. Grinage's on 143rd Street. Have not been there in almost two years. Mrs. Grinage nearly fainted when she saw me. Her nieces kept me roaring with laughter concerning the gossipings of the good females of Littleton, North Carolina. In truth, the spirit of bigotry and intolerance of the older generations of Negroes, and their utter lack of sympathy with the aims, problems, and pleasures of their children, is one of the outstanding causes for the rapid egress of Negro youth from country to city. "There," said one of the nieces, even in the presence of the mother, "we must go to church all day Sunday, must not be caught talking to a young man, must participate in no diversions such as dancing or card playing in pain of social ostracism." She declared that she was in New York to stay, that under no consideration could she be brought to live in Littleton, North Carolina, again. Her aunt corroborated her statements. The mother argued that "to praise God, eat, and sleep was sufficient pleasure for any person." However, it will not be enough for these young people. There were some half dozen present—all girls—and each one declared flatly that she could never live South again. And I could not blame them.

On the way home, to my intense satisfaction, I found that

the Yankees, N.Y., had won the first game from Philadelphia 5–0. A great moral as well as physical victory. I did not think that this wobbling team could put itself together sufficiently to beat the onrushing Philadelphians.

Left for D.C. at 6:10. Held up in the subway. Just barely caught the ferry at Liberty Street at 7:00 p.m. Uneventful ride to D.C. I arrived home at 11:30. Very pleasant trip.

[12] The Many-Sided Woodson

Spent the day with agricultural statistics. Told Woodson I had some tables, etc., for Miss Revallion to copy. Assented, telling me that he would take a week with me to go over the figures, then a week at the Congressional Library.

Monday September 10 1928

I think that Woodson bemoans the fact that Wesley and he are at odds. In one of our discussions that came up today, he reiterated his belief in Wesley's ability to do exceptional research work, but felt that his fondness for money-making overshadowed the possibility of his ever duplicating such a study as his *Negro Labor in the United States*. Too bad! Woodson has been painting the office all day.

After leaving the office, I took dinner at the YMCA, and went out to Anacostia. Called upon Ruth. She has a cold.

Woodson and I began discussing school, etc. Told him of my parents' hopes that I become a doctor, also of my high school principal who would have made me a lawyer. I told him of my debating against Silverstein, my Jewish friend, who was recognized as the high school's best. Also, of the first time I doubted whether I had passed an examination in history. (Dr. Evarts B. Greene's course in United States History, at Columbia University.) Woodson told me of certain subjects which he had pursued at Harvard and in which he had made excep-

Tuesday September 11 1928

tionally good grades, so much so that he became sort of a cynosure for the eyes of other students on the campus.

I told him I heard that his protégé, [Hosea] Campbell, was to teach at Wilberforce beginning this fall. He said he had withdrawn support from him "because of his inability to comprehend serious History."

Woodson mentioned my friend [Harcourt] Tynes. Told me the latter had been recommended to him, but that his record was not at all impressive. Best mark was in "Public Speaking," which did not particularly commend itself to him as a requisite for a research investigator in history. I was surprised, for I did not know that Woodson had had any connections at all with Tynes, who is one of my dear pals. Tynes is a very conscientious student. Is handicapped only by lack of faith in himself. He flatters me by reminding me of my ability to do historical research, when, without any affectation of modesty, I know precious little history. I am afraid to open my mouth upon any historical subject before Woodson, or anyone else who comprehends it.

Woodson amused me by narrating several experiences in the South. For example, someone asked him whether he was acquainted with "Professor" [Leo] Hansberry. The latter is an instructor in History at Howard University, brought there by Emmett Scott. He dabbles in African History, though he has none of the qualifications for serious study, possessing only a B.S. degree, and that a War Diploma. Without biology, which is fundamental, lacking familiarity with French, German, Portuguese, and Arabic, in which languages everything worthwhile on Africa has been written, he is like a man who goes fishing with a bare hook. At any rate, to return to Woodson, it seems that Hansberry has done some "stunt" speaking in the South, with a view to popularizing his own "peculiar" knowledge of African History. He undoubtedly caught the imagination of the people, for someone said to Woodson, after a speech, "You were almost as good as Hansberry." And at another place, "Do you know that great professor of African History, Leo Hansberry?" "Yes," answered Woodson. "Have you finished any courses under him?" "No," answered Woodson, "but I have read his 'works.'" I laughed. Woodson said that it would not have done to have unmasked Hansberry's imperfections, historically speaking. Woodson thinks he ought to go off to school and study. "Scott (Emmett), Secretary-Treasurer, had brought Hansberry to Howard, then later, wishing to get rid of him," said Woodson, "asked Wesley, Head of the History Department, to recommend his dismissal." Despite Woodson's suggestion, Wesley took no action in the matter, since Hansberry had been brought there without anyone's consulting him.

We talked as Woodson painted. I admire him. No sort of work is too menial for him to perform. He likes to paint; it's a hobby of his. Says it is like a vacation. It was now after seven and he had not eaten since noon, and then only two pounds of grapes, a can of sardines, and a few crackers.

I left, doing so only because my body cried out for sustenance.

Received a very pleasant surprise today. Woodson informed me that he desired me to either make a speech or read a paper at the Annual Meeting of the Association in St. Louis, in October. I confess I feel both honored and befuddled, for I doubt whether I can justify his confidence. I had just previously told him how nervous I am before I speak. Well can I recall Suffolk, where, in a cold auditorium, I shook like a leaf while speaking. However, I shall do my best. *Wednesday September 12 1928*

Woodson told me of the failure of A. A. Taylor before the students of Union University. Taylor had been invited by him to say a few words upon *The Negro in South Carolina During the Reconstruction*, which book he had written. After 15 minutes of speaking, said Woodson, Taylor became so confused and excited that he precipitately quit the platform, adducing illness as the cause. Woodson said he was afraid Taylor would "wet his pants." Woodson said that he was compelled to finish Taylor's speech. I doubt whether I would do that, however, if I knew my topic, for once on my feet I can speak indefinitely, as proved from high school on.

Harry's [Hipp] letter, received today, contained a note of

anxiety over his mother's impending marriage. I believe he allows his filial affection and his eagerness to be the sole recipient of his mother's love to becloud his consideration for her happiness. Since he refuses to live South, and his mother does not care to live North, I cannot understand his objection to her marriage, since he visits her so infrequently as to leave her practically alone. Then, too, his mother is young, comparatively speaking. Harry is marrying now. Why shouldn't she? He fears that her husband might not be as kind to her as he (Harry) would desire. However, his mother, no doubt, has carefully weighed the gentleman's virtues and found the proper ones predominating. In short, since Harry feels the need for companionship and is answering the call to such, he must take into consideration that his mother is swayed much the same way, for human beings are by nature gregarious.

Just as I was about to leave, a Mr. Ferguson entered. He is an elderly man, handsome, straight, tall. At first I thought him white, but it turned out that he was colored. He told me that he was the son of a Confederate Captain and a Negro woman (his mother), who was sold from Richmond by her father, a Captain Ferguson. The latter belonged to the "blue-blooded" southern aristocracy. The father, he added, fulfilled none of the paternal obligations toward his child. His mother, then living in Alabama, sent him here (Washington, D.C.) to study, but he wasted his time there. Later, having approached the age of 35, he became an indefatigable reader. Taking a government examination in the eighties, he rose until finally he became the confidant of Marcus Hanna and held several political offices of trust, serving on the Commission which investigated the Brownsville shooting affair in 1903 [1906].[1] Contended that the investigation proved the Negro soldiers blameless, that their guns, upon inspection, showed that they

---

1. Marcus Alonzo Hanna (1837–1904) was a Cleveland, Ohio, businessman and politician. He earned a fortune from his various business ventures in areas including the iron and steel trade, banking, newspaper publishing, and Cleveland's street railway system. He became a powerful figure in local, state, and national politics. In 1896, Hanna conducted William McKinley's successful campaign for the presidency. The following year, Hanna was elected to the United States Senate. He was an intimate adviser to Presidents McKinley and Theodore Roosevelt.

had *not* been fired. Holds [Theodore] Roosevelt sacrificed them upon the altar of Southern hatred and prejudice.[2]

Said he met his father one day in New York. Was introduced to him by Mark Hanna (Senator). Captain Ferguson remarked about the phenomenon of their names being identical. Asked him where he was from. Ferguson retorted "Alabama." "They tell me," he said, "that my father is Captain Ferguson, an ex-Confederate, etc." Captain Ferguson turned red, then asked his son to come see him at his home. Ferguson told Mark Hanna about it. Hanna advised against his going. They have not met since. I do not know whether or not the Captain still lives. The case is not unique at all, for thousands of such instances could be cited, as a heritage of the plantation era when the slave—whether comely or not—belonged body and soul to the master and every comely female slave was an object of sexual desire in the eyes of either the master, his son, the overseer, or any white man.

Mr. Ferguson is devoted to his mother. She sought to educate him, but he cared more for gambling and horse races and women than for books. It was not until he was over thirty that

2. When, in July, 1906, the 1st Battalion of the all-black 25th Infantry Regiment was sent from Nebraska to Fort Brown, near Brownsville, Texas, the white citizens of Brownsville showed their displeasure by abusive behavior toward the soldiers. On August 3, 1906, there was an altercation between a member of the battalion and a white Brownsville merchant. As a result, the town was placed off limits to men from the black unit. On the same day, a rumor spread that one of the black soldiers had attempted to rape a white woman. That night, a group of armed men moved through the streets of Brownsville, wildly firing their weapons. One white man was killed; and two others, including the chief of police, were wounded.

Local officials accused the men of the 1st Battalion of assaulting the town. Although an inspection the morning after the incident showed the battalion rifles to be clean and all ammunition accounted for, military investigators assumed the black soldiers to be guilty. Since all of the enlisted men denied having any knowledge of the incident, it was charged that there was a "conspiracy of silence."

In November, 1906, President Roosevelt instructed Secretary of War William Howard Taft to dismiss from the service, without honor, all of the enlisted men of three companies and to declare them ineligible for future military or civil service. Protests from black leaders and from black and interracial organizations led to further investigations.

It was not until 1972, however, that the Army changed the discharges of the 167 soldiers from dishonorable to honorable and cleared the military records of these soldiers. Mary Frances Berry and John W. Blassingame, *Long Memory: The Black Experience in America* (New York, 1982), 310–12; George E. Mowry, *The Era of Theodore Roosevelt, 1900–1912* (New York, 1958), 212–14.

he formed an attachment for reading for which he now has an insatiable appetite.

Mr. Ferguson admonished me to remember those who have befriended me. Never forget your relatives, he counselled. They are the ones who will stand by you in emergencies. I must confess that there is something interesting about Mr. Ferguson. He has a wealth of information, gleaned not only from books but from personal contact and experience. He has rubbed shoulders with all the most influential men in the country during the last thirty-five years. Marvelous experiences, and I must sit at his feet and drink in some of them.

Hurricane in the West Indies. Struck Puerto Rico and the Virgin Islands especially hard. Reports say that 1,000,000, or half the total population of Puerto Rico, are homeless.

Friday
September
14
1928

Today passed uneventfully.

Went to the movies in the evening. So lonesome I had to do something. Picture was good, I thought. Story of a brother who, through self-sacrifice, resurrected a once famous family.

Rose at 6:30, painted aunt's home until 8:00. Reached office at 9:00.

Saturday
September
15
1928

Another uneventful day. Yet Harry's wedding day. I sent him a telegram at noon. I am alone now of all the "gang." Both Ernest and Harry are married. I feel isolated, yet wish them both happiness. Sorry I could not attend the wedding. Seems so hard to lose Harry. How I would like to have him here with me engaged in this work. But, then, I should not be selfish. I must bring myself to realize that, after all, the mating instinct of man, like all other animals', is fundamental; and because I do not feel that I could, with any stability, take unto myself one object of affection and swear to cherish and love her for the rest of my days, is no good reason why he should not, if he feels so inclined. I wish him all the happiness in the world, and hope that time will prove that I have gained a *sister*, rather than lost a *brother*.

Surprised this a.m. to receive a call from Bacote, who "phoned" me from his wife's home on Westminster Street. He had just driven down with his bride from Lawnside, New Jersey, where he is practicing medicine. He told me he was coming over to see my aunt and me. Told him for God's sake not to bring anyone with him. The house was being painted and everything was a mess. Nevertheless, he came over within two hours, accompanied by his blushing bride and the couple with whom he lives in Jersey. We had barely time to exchange greetings. He was off, requesting that I call him at 4 p.m. Did so, but he had left a little earlier in order to evade an impending shower.

Went outside to read. Locked myself out by leaving my key in my coat pocket, which latter article reposed indoors in my bedroom. Had to sit for two hours under a broiling sun in my shirtsleeves until Mr. Taylor, who lives next door, returned from church. Through his kindness, I gained access to my aunt's back yard by jumping over his fence. Once over, entrance to the house was gained by going into the cellar from the yard, thence up the stairs into the kitchen, the door of which, fortunately, was unlocked.

Later went to Rosslyn. My cousins were as delighted to see me as I them. First time I had seen them since May. I told them my troubles concerning living "quarters."

Hurricane sweeping Florida.

Sunday
September
16
1928

Uneventful day here at the office. Dr. Woodson has stained the floors. A versatile, hard working man, he enjoys painting. The office looks like a new place altogether.

Called up P——— and talked for a few moments.

Received letter from Harry assuring me that even though he is married, even his wife understands the bond between us. My "frat" pin has come, he told me.

The wedding passed very quietly. Just the bride, groom, the bride's mother, her friend, and the best man. It took place at the church at 2 p.m. Saturday. A variety of presents have already been received from friends. (One of the most gratify-

Monday
September
17
1928

ing symptoms, from my point of view, was his recounting the fact that Mrs. Daniel had shown her affection for him by a motherly kiss on both cheeks.) May all happiness be theirs!

Palm Beach, Florida, reported destroyed by hurricane. Damage estimated at $100,000,000; loss of life reported at 2,000.

Tuesday
September
18
1928

Nothing to note of interest today. I received a letter from Mr. Davidson, Bursar at Columbia University, acknowledging a payment of $20.00 from me, but designating it as the August installment, which I had paid on August 1. This latter remittance was sent last week. I must call the Bursar's attention to this fact.

Woodson had interested himself to the extent of finding a position for a very worthy young lady who was informed, quite unexpectedly, that her services as a school teacher would no longer be required in Arlington, Virginia. She is an orphan, and Woodson has taken a sympathetic interest in her. She manifested her gratitude by telling Woodson that she loves him, much to the good historian's embarrassment. Said he last week, "I shall introduce her to you." "Why?" thought I. Did not have time to respond, for the entrance of Mr. Ferguson interrupted my doing so.

Woodson went to see Mr. [S. W.] Rutherford, President of the National Benefit Life Insurance Company, with respect to securing a position for her there. Remarkable coincidence! Mr. Rutherford had already employed her Saturday, much to Woodson's elation.

I informed Woodson that I shall be ready for him to verify my figures tomorrow. It will be a task!

Looked in Tappan's *Sidelights on Anglo American Relations*.[3] Found that Irish immigrants entertained hostile sentiments toward free Negroes in the pre–Civil War era. Reason may be ascribed to economic competition.

---

3. This is a reference to Annie Heloise Abel and Frank J. Klingberg (eds.), *A Side-Light on Anglo-American Relations, 1839–1858, Furnished by the Correspondence of Lewis Tappan and Others with the British and Foreign Anti-Slavery Society* (Washington, D.C., 1927).

Came home and painted the outside door.

We received the tail end of the hurricane tonight. It did no damage, however.

Received a letter from Helen Notis this a.m. Also an invitation from Harry for his reception, October 13. Shall try to be present.

Woodson waxed enthusiastic over the upcoming Annual Meeting of the Association for the Study of Negro Life and History in St. Louis. Will certainly be an ordeal for me.

A Mr. Adams from St. Thomas, Virgin Islands, called upon Woodson this a.m. He is the supervisor of music in the schools there. Promised to recommend several publications of the Association, especially the *Negro in Our History* by Woodson and *African Myths*, for use in the public schools there. He also gave us some first-hand information on the terrible social conditions in St. Lucia.

Wednesday September 19 1928

Disappointed today that my figures for Agriculture for 1920 were found to be inaccurate when Woodson essayed to verify them. However, there was an extenuating factor, for in the endeavor to make the 1920 Census Occupations classifications conform to those of 1900 and 1890, certain combinations had to be effected which depended mainly upon the point of view of the compiler. That is why Woodson and I disagreed. He suggested that I let Mr. [William Chamberlin] Hunt, one of the Directors of the Census, straighten out the mooted points—namely, whether overseers included all those engaged in any agricultural pursuit or merely pertained to foremen on farms and plantations. I held the former view; Woodson the latter.

Was shocked to find that Mr. [Joseph Adna] Hill, [Assistant Director, Bureau of the Census] could throw no more light upon this perplexity than to admonish me of the impossibility of attempting to boil down some 500 specific occupations into approximately some 300 more general classes. Mr. Hill took me to see Dr. [Alba M.] Edwards, who he assured me was the best informed man upon this subject. Dr. Edwards, a slight

Thursday September 20 1928

middle-aged man, encouraged me by informing me that he had made an unsuccessful attempt to revise the 1920 Census classifications in order to harmonize them with those of the preceding censuses for purposes of comparison. This task, he informed me, had taken him three months, with a staff of workers. He believed that it was almost impossible to make such a classification. He allowed me to copy his revision of the 1920 "Census for Occupations" in conformity with that of 1900, but refused to permit me access to the entire scheme for fear of being quoted.

Woodson's comment on the United States Census Bureau is that it is the most inefficient branch of a woefully inefficient government.

Friday
September
21
1928

Woodson and I spent the day together. I fear it did not redound much to my credit, for he discovered numerous mistakes with my figures. My old weakness—inability to figure—became, and remained, painfully patent as we progressed. Finally we got through "Trade and Transportation." Believe I had fallen in Woodson's estimation when it was over. But then mathematics was always my bugaboo.

Bertha called me. Went to see her. Told her of my intention to leave my aunt's. Both she and Cousin Winnie acquiesced. Said they could not comprehend my living there. I wanted to remodel my aunt's house, but she vetoes it. Cousin Winnie promises to talk to her tomorrow.

Saturday
September
22
1928

What a time on figures! True, Woodson has reason to be disappointed in me. Many of my figures were wrong because I had to make arbitrary combinations. But then I made inexcusable errors. Once Woodson told me sarcastically that I had best relearn my principles of arithmetic. Indeed, I thought he looked quite contemptuously at me when I made a palpable error. But I am tired. No vacation, and after seven years struggling through school, it is a wonder my brain functions at all. Finally, finished at 5:30. What a relief!

A Mr. Ralph Bunche, a clean-cut, intelligent young fellow called upon Dr. Woodson this afternoon, bearing a letter of introduction from Professor Munro, head of the department of Government at Harvard University. Mr. Bunche is a graduate of the University of Southern California, and took the degree of Master of Arts in Government from Harvard. He begins duties as instructor of that subject at Howard University this fall. I asked him whether he was acquainted with Hosea Campbell, who has been seeking a doctoral degree from Harvard for the past four years. Woodson interposed disdainfully that he (Campbell) had received his Ph.D. after leaving Harvard. I was shocked when they told me that his name had appeared in Negro periodicals as a Doctor of Philosophy from Harvard. Brass, to say the least! Bunche remarked that Professor Edward Channing, Head of the History Department at Harvard, has declared that when Campbell receives his Ph.D. from Harvard, the University will close its doors.

Cousin Winnie, pursuant to her promise of last night, has persuaded my aunt to have the house remodelled. I rejoice. Shall start work upon it immediately. Of course I shall pay for it.

On my way to the theatre, stopped at a second hand store and looked over some books. Found some very excellent works on philosophy, history, and literature. Bought 18 for $3.00.

Went to Bertha's. Dined with her. Remained until 5:40, when I left for the Congressional Library to keep a six o'clock appointment with Woodson. Bertha assumed that I would not leave her, but I was forced to make her realize the import of meeting Woodson.

Sunday September 23 1928

Woodson was late. So was I, for that matter, but I preceded him by some twenty minutes, which time I spent jotting down references for the "Occupation" study from *Poole's Periodical Index*. When Woodson arrived, he followed the same procedure, beginning with the volume from 1800 to 1816. We noted all references to the Negro under the captions of "Freedmen," "Labor," "Negro Occupations," and "Industry."

Woodson has one outstanding fault, if I may make bold to

say so. That is that he measures the ability of everyone else by his own, which though native is fortified by over twenty years of experience. He is not the man to instill confidence in the inexperienced student of history, but rather to destroy whatever little faith in himself the latter might have possessed before coming in contact with him. In this respect, he is Wesley's counterpart. Wesley is a teacher, considerate, kind, and hence a fount of inspiration.

Woodson and I looked over the *Periodical Index from 1819 to 1923*, taking all references to the Negro in "Occupations," "Industry," "Freedmen," "Manufacturing," etc. Left the Library at 10 p.m. I am to start there in the morning.

Monday
September
24
1928

Went to the library at 9:30. In Desk 12 I found periodicals. Found very little else today, although I looked through the volumes of the *Nation, New Republic, Eclectic Magazine, Review of Reviews, Catholic World,* and others.

Returning home, I could not get in. Aunt had gone out. I went to Bertha's, where I remained until 11 p.m.

Tuesday
September
25
1928

Found information on Negro puddlers, core makers, foundrymen, etc. in Pittsburgh. Latter hired to replace stubborn Irishmen. Also reports on Negro efficiency in manufacturing and other employments.

Stopped by the office. Woodson seemed gratified with the work I am doing.

[Greene did not make entries from September 26 through October 6.]

Sunday
October 7
1928

Went to Lawnside, New Jersey, today to spend the day with Ernest and Harry. Harry, though a newly-wed, has left his wife on his first Sunday in New York, to spend it with the "gang." The boys met me at the Philadelphia station. Can't express my delight over seeing them. Felt quite strange in the presence of my married brothers. I am the only bachelor now. Bacote took us on a pleasant ride to Lawnside. Is a little town, tenanted wholly by Negroes. Colored mayor etc. I was favorably impressed with it.

Spent the day looking over the *Colored American Magazine* and the *Nation*. Found information concerning Negro manufacturers, caterers, and professionals. Found almost nothing in the *Nation*.

Left library at 5:30. Painted bathroom in the evening. Bertha called. Oh, yes, whites on Houston and Texas Railway asked owner to discharge Negroes. Company refused to do so. Shows what a little courage can do, plus the main fact that Negro labor is cheaper than white labor.

Perused the volumes of the *Nation* for the decade of 1890–1900. Found some material on colored miners acting as strike breakers in Arkansas and Illinois. In the former case, where the whites struck, white miners secured an injunction to restrain the company from importing black laborers. But the decision by the judge of the Federal Court dissolved the injunction. The court held the Fourteenth Amendment makes it possible for any person to move from one state to another in search of employment, so long as he is not a member of an interdicted class, namely "lifers," convicts, or persons afflicted with contagious diseases. Commendable, to say the least. Is one means of the Negro getting into industry. In Illinois, during the late nineties, a strike took place at Pana. Negro coal miners, brought in from Alabama, were at once made the object of attacks by white miners. The Governor sent troops to the scene, and declared that he would mow down with Gatling guns any such laborers (Negro strikebreakers) brought into Illinois. The captain of the militia then so instructed his men as to nullify their efforts in protecting the Negroes. Result: at a little town in Christian County, in the southern part of the state, five Negro miners were killed by a mob of white strikers.

Negro tenants of South Carolina, it was reported, are driving whites from the best lands in that state, due to their ability, it is said, to pay a higher rent, since their standard of living is lower than the whites'. Paradoxical, but it seems that economic competition is the crux of the Negro question in the South.

Negro manufacturers found today included a boat builder of Pittsburgh, Pennsylvania, who builds boats and sells them to coal companies. He is an engineer.

Wednesday
October 10
1928

Perused the volumes of the *Colored American Magazine* again today. Found information concerning skilled mechanics in Oklahoma and Indian territory. Noted founding of Afro-American Realty Corporation of New York, capitalized at $500,000, of which Phillip Peyton, Jr., was President, and Emmett Scott one of the trustees, and also the Mercantile Realty Company of New Jersey. Found Negro inventors of bread machines; and one Lee of Boston, of ice cream moulds.

Also dug up information on singers, brickmaker's unions, upholsterers; razor strap, coat, jacket, sweater, and apron manufacturers. All in the decade of 1900–1910!

Stopped at the office. Woodson said he came to the library yesterday to see me, but I was out "refreshing" myself. Wanted to see me relative to the references brought for Miss Revallion to copy. Felt some were irrelevant. Perhaps so, but I told him I thought them quite pertinent. "Invited" me to prove it to him tomorrow morning.

I stained floors at home in evening.

Thursday
October 11
1928

Woodson and I engaged in a little verbal duel this morning. He thinks details unnecessary. My system of notetaking is to pre-empt everything which falls under my purview. We argued especially about the relevancy of Negro wages, which showed a large discrepancy as between North and South. He desired to know what bearing that would have on increase of Negro mechanics. I told him it would not have so much influence upon increasing the number of these artisans as on changing their *locus operandi*. He held that a skilled laborer in the South, say a carpenter, receiving $2.00 "per diem," might go to Pittsburgh and make $4.00 per day as a common laborer, which would have the effect of diminishing the number of skilled workers in the field. I agreed it might, but also asked, would it not tend to draw off poorly paid Negro farm hands in the South to these industries in the North, thus transforming them from agricultural laborers to industrial workers, thereby increasing the Negroes employed in the latter class at the expense of the former?

We reached no agreement here. Woodson felt that sketches of Negroes engaged in business, etc. was unnecessary. Also believed that the study should be so general that it not discuss sections. I failed to agree because of the fact that the Negro is preeminently a denizen of the South, therefore is chiefly employed there. Then, too, in the North and West, divergent industrial conditions change the complexion of his chief occupation. While it is farming in the South, it is chiefly domestic and personal service in the North and West. However, I shall persist in my determination to take notes in my own way, gathering in all the data which appear to throw any light upon my problem, then critically appraising them later. Obviously, we take notes differently. He also told me that much of the material which I had gathered from magazines can be found in books of the author, Woodson. How was I to know that? Then, too, when one is engaged in research, he gathers all the pertinent information he happens to find.

Left there about noon for the library. Woodson wrote a letter to Mr. [Herbert] Putman, the head librarian, in reference to the table for me, which has been many times promised but, to date, not delivered.

A bottle of ink turned over in my brief case. Luckily, it injured nothing but the New York *Times.* My diary fortunately escaped.

Spent the afternoon on *Colored American Magazine.* Nothing of importance found.

Went to see Bertha. Returning home, I found to my surprise and joy that Henry had arrived. Opportune, for he can aid me in finishing the painting.

Went to the office to return two books to Woodson. Two letters and a telegram awaiting me. Telegram advised my coming to New York immediately for my books and trunks. I had left them at Mrs. Burbridge's on Edgecombe Avenue, where I lodged while attending Columbia University. Told Woodson I would leave for New York tomorrow. Asked me when I would return. Responded Sunday night.

Woodson had asked me to prepare a paper to read at the Annual Meeting of the Association for the Study of Negro Life and History in St. Louis. I had intended to write upon the "Economic Status of the Negro" from 1890 to the present. But another disappointment stares me in the face. It develops now that I must take charge of the office during Woodson's absence, thus losing a fine opportunity for contact and publicity by my failure to go there. Woodson had intended that a Mr. Plater should take charge during our absence. Evidently, the latter changed his mind. Oh, well, better luck next time!

I showed him a table which, in my opinion, contains the essence of the study. It demonstrates that Negroes since 1890 have tended to decline in agricultural and domestic and personal service employments and to gravitate toward industrial occupations: trade and transportation, manufacturing, and mechanical pursuits. This tendency is seen in the census figures. In 1890, about 51 percent of the Negroes gainfully employed were engaged in agriculture, with about 32 percent in domestic service. In other words, more than four-fifths of all Negroes gainfully employed engaged in these two lowest classes of occupations. On the other hand, those working in manufacturing and mechanical industries composed only 6% of all the Negroes gainfully employed.

The decade 1900–1910 properly marks the high point of industrialization for Negroes. During this period the percentage engaged in manufacturing and industrial pursuits increased roughly 100% (6.2 to 12.3%).

In 1920 the number of Negro workers in agriculture and in domestic and personal service stood at about 45% for the former and approximately 23% for the latter. This was a de-

crease of approximately 12 percentage points for those engaged in agriculture and 9 percentage points for those occupied in the field of domestic and personal service, as against
an increase of 12 percentage points for those engaged in manufacturing and mechanical pursuits. However, the above tell
only a half truth, for, on second sight, it is easily discernible
that the numbers of Negroes in domestic and personal service
and agriculture decreased about 9 percentage points (or approximately 28%) of the original percentage in 1890 for domestic and personal service, whereas the decrease of 12 percentage points engaged in agriculture marks a decline of only
21% of the original percentage of 45% in 1890. Contrasted to
the relative decrease in these two fields, the increase in
Negroes engaged in manufacturing and mechanical pursuits is
all the more significant. Due to the large influx of Southern
Negroes to Northern cities to fill the industrial gap caused by
the stoppage of foreign immigration during World War I, the
percentage of Negroes in manufacturing and mechanical pursuits showed an alarming rise, almost treble the figure (6.2%)
in 1890 to more than 18% in 1920.

I went to the Library. Sent a telegram to Ernest [Bacote] of
Lawnside, New Jersey, to meet me at the Broad Street Station
in Philadelphia at 10:45 p.m. I remained at the Library until 5
p.m. Found nothing of consequence. Secured long-promised
table today.

Returned home, buying gallon and a half of paint. Mixed
the color desired and left it, hoping that Henry would do some
painting during my absence.

Left for Philadelphia at 7:45. Ernest met me at the West
Philadelphia Station. A young woman was with him. I am
afraid that she will be very embarrassing to him if he is not extremely careful. She is young, beautiful, and has a fine figure.

The Graf Zeppelin, a lighter than air airship, with Dr.
[Hugo] Eckener, a crew of forty, and twenty passengers, are
crossing the Atlantic from Germany to New Jersey. An
epoch-making flight! Tonight they had passed the Madeira
Islands.

Saturday   This is Harry's day—his wedding reception.
October 13
1928

[No entries were made for October 14 and October 15.]

Tuesday   I perused volumes of the *Nation* to 1903. Found Negroes
October 16   forced out of even menial pursuits in the North by violence. In
1928   Indiana, Negro waiters were driven out and the employers
             were forced to promise not to hire any more.
                 Went to the office at 3:30. Spent over three hours trying to
             reconcile two sets of figures in an effort to reduce to literary
             form the essence of the study, showing the tendency of Negro
             workers to advance from menial occupations—agriculture
             and domestic and personal service—to industry, trade, trans-
             portation, and the professions.
                 Woodson informed me today that a man must be at the
             office during his absence as his excuse for not taking me to St.
             Louis. Afraid the office and all included will go to "hell,"
             although, frankly, Miss Revallion could run the place as well
             as I. She has done it before. Wonder if he feels I am not
             qualified to fill the bill as speaker. Yet, I have the temerity to
             believe I could, even to the extent of opening the economic
             discussion. Surely no one is better armed with facts as far as
             figures are concerned, and I do believe I could interpret them
             so that they would show significant trends in Negro employ-
             ment over the period of the last 30 years. The contact I surely
             need, for, as Woodson already had observed, I know very few
             outstanding men among Negroes.

Wednesday   Spent the morning with Dr. Edwards of the Census Bureau in
October 17   an effort to make Table A conform to the totals for the main
1928   classes of Negro occupations for 1910 and 1890. Dr. Edwards,
             though able to make agriculture totals conform, with a diver-
             gence of only 4% in over two million, felt that the figures for
             trade and transportation and manufacturing and mechanical
             pursuits would present an almost hopeless task.
                 Went back to the Library. Searched the files of the *Nation*.

Most important development: some Negroes entering industries as strikebreakers retain their jobs after the stike is over.
Case of teamsters in New York, also building trades in
Chicago (1900) and stockyard strikes there in 1904. In some
cases, Negroes have changed the entire complexion of jobs,
converting what was once regarded by owners to be strictly
white men's job into Negro employment. Case of boners'
strike in Chicago illustrates this. Negro boners supplanted
whites in such numbers that white workers took them into the
Union.

I painted until almost midnight.

Have perused the *Nation* to 1916. Most important data were Thursday
whites striking in Key West, Florida, and Mobile, Alabama, in October 18
order to help secure demands of colored workers. In Key 1928
West, all the white carpenters struck because two Negro carpenters had been laid off. In Mobile, 2,000 Negro longshore-
men struck for more pay; whites struck sympathetically. They
could hardly have done less, since all belonged to the same
Unions. Yet, it is a step forward in the achievement of
workers' solidarity when such action takes place.

Negro government officials suffered a set back, however,
by the election of Wilson in 1912. Senators [James K.] Varda-
man, [Cole L.] Blease, [John Sharp] Williams, and other
Southerners, either by influencing Wilson or by bringing pres-
sure to bear upon Negro appointees, have caused a significant
decrease in black appointees. Of course, the sanction is the
"integrity of the Anglo-Saxon race which can be best achieved
by keeping the Negro in his place." Mr. [Adam E.] Patterson,
a Negro of Oklahoma, offered the position of Registrar of the
Treasury, declined because of the hostility of Southerners.
When a railway mail clerk on the Norfolk and Southern Railway was identified as a Negro, the Congressman from the
district ([John Humphrey] Small of North Carolina) immediately took up with the Civil Service Commission in Washington the heinous offense of Negro mail clerks with white
subordinates. The Commission dutifully acted in the defense
of racial supremacy and notified the Negro clerk that his status

had been changed to that of "helper." Whereupon Congress-man Small and the good people of North Carolina heaved a deep sigh of relief and warmly congratulated the Commission with "Well done our good and faithful servant."

Painted till 10:30.

Sent cards to Ernest to be enclosed in gifts for Harry and Nannie. I am highly pleased with Harry's gift [of silverware] though sorry we did not include bouillon and orange spoons for him, which would have made sixty-one pieces. But later perhaps.

Nothing of much importance from the *Nation* files today. National Convention of the American Federation of Labor at Atlantic City voted to take Negroes into the Union, especially throughout the South. It means little, however, for the local unions not only are autonomous but are so prejudiced against the admittance of black workers that they will seek to render every effort of the national Federation void. Then, too, the locals have the sole right to direct their own affairs, i.e., decide who they shall admit or reject. Negro labor in industry was stimulated by the Immigration Law of 1924, which limited the number of incoming foreigners to 150,000 a year. These open-ings the Negro will partially fill. It is to his advantage that the Immigration Laws not be altered if he would maintain his gains. Also full employment is a "must," for white workers will not look with equanimity upon Negroes working while they are jobless. The East St. Louis riot [1917] and other dis-turbances in 1919 are good examples of outbreaks caused by racial competition for jobs. Jobless whites blamed their pre-dicament upon the influx of Negroes in industry.

Did no painting tonight. Too tired. Stopped at the office about 8 p.m.

Woodson manifested his literary versatility by reading to me a letter of congratulations to the salesmen of an insurance company (National Benefit, a Negro concern). The agents had sold a million dollars or more worth of insurance in a month, in honor of the birthday of its President, Mr. [S. W.] Rutherford. The latter had invited Woodson to draw up the letter of congratulation and appreciation, and the latter certainly "put it over" with his characteristic vigor. He seemed even to enjoy it. Amid a florid display of elegance and rhetorical flourishes, he interspersed such business sagacity and common sense philosophy as: "Though it is good to strike the iron while it is hot, it is still better to strike the iron until it becomes hot" (that is, create opportunities). Again, "achievement is the ultimate criterion of ability," and "great is he who can govern the storm, but greater still is he who can cause the storm and then direct that which he has incited."

Intellectually, Woodson certainly commands my admiration and respect. But on the other hand, I cannot say as much for his personality. He is dogmatic, conceited, sarcastic, and less than sagacious in dealing with people—particularly his subordinates. I often wonder what would happen if he manifested a little more humility and understanding and less arrogance toward the potentially gifted, but inexperienced, young people who work under his direction. To do so, I believe would infuse in such persons a burning desire to emulate him by searching out, uncovering, and recording the untold and perverted history of the Negro both here and abroad. Such budding scholars would be Woodson's crowning achievement. He could rejoice in the knowledge that he had implanted the seed of Negro history in them, nurtured it carefully, and watched it blossom forth in scientifically trained Negro historians. He could then retire from his labors with the assurance that he had passed on the torch to younger hands. This should be his greatest source of gratification: that he had left behind him an array of well-trained, competent, dedicated scholars who would carry on the work which owed so much to his initiation, courage, diligence, and personal sacrifice. But sometimes I wonder???

Woodson is going to St. Louis tomorrow, where he will direct the Annual Meeting of the Association. Asks me to stop at the office at 12 p.m.

Called on Bertha. Surprised to find Yarborough there. My bet is he has fallen completely under her charms. And who could blame him, for she is a rare jewel. I promised to paint her bathroom on Sunday. She had already painted the window. Told her she had placed the cart before the horse, that it would be almost impossible for her not to damage the window during the washing and painting of the ceiling and walls. Her reply was that she could do so without dropping a speck of anything upon the freshly painted window. To her rejoinder, I maintained a discreet silence.

Another would-be Atlantic flyer lost.

Smith and Hoover still slinging mud in their campaign for the Presidency.

[13] Woodson, My Research, and the Election of 1928

Called at the office at noon. Became flunky general or what you will. Specifically, I folded letters and envelopes, stamped them, and placed them in mailsacks. At least, I helped. Over 3,000 letters. It is an experience. Woodson left for St. Louis at 1 p.m. Requested me to help. Always glad to assist in anything that will further this work. Dr. Woodson sets a wonderful example. There is nothing that is too menial for him to perform. Otherwise, the Association would long ago have perished with his fastidiousness. I am happy to cooperate in whatever manner possible.

Woodson advised me to send him no telegrams. Might open them. Also, that I visit the office in the a.m. and p.m. in order that the girls might realize that someone is near in a supervisory capacity.

Left the office. Bought paint for Bertha's bathroom. Promised her I would paint it tomorrow. Came home. Felt first symptoms of a head cold.

Did nothing tonight.

Painted shutters at home until 11:30 a.m. Ate and went to Bertha's, where I found her washing kalsomine on the walls. I stood and joshed her about the ludicrous picture she presented upon the stepladder. In return, she threatened to "smite" me with the wet rag with which she was washing the walls.

Still more mud slinging in the Presidential Campaign. Governor [Theodore G.] Bilbo of Mississippi, arch-defender of the purity and integrity of Southern womanhood, openly accuses The Honorable Herbert Hoover, former engineer, Food Administrator, economist extraordinary, and Republican candidate for the Presidency, "most ordinary," of having actually called upon a colored woman in Mound Bayou, Mississippi, and "horrors of horrors" even danced with her. Now, this most "unpardonable sin" absolutely disqualifies "Sir" Herbert Hoover as President of the United States. Why, Sir, first thing you know, in case he is elected, Hoover might stage a celebration in honor of his victory in Jackson, Mississippi, and invite all the Negroes in the city. Then what would hinder his dancing with all the colored women there if he cared to, and worst of all, what would prevent him, if after having sipped the sparkling punch, he should gather all the guests about him and drink a toast to social equality for both blacks and whites, to the intensive horror of all loyal "nigger-hating Southerners." This, Governor Bilbo and his stalwart defenders of Southern chivalry and of female chastity (white, of course, Negroes having none) and racial purity can never countenance and will always condemn. Thus must Hoover, regardless of his other qualifications, be sacrificed upon the altar of Southern bigotry, race hatred, and bogus white superiority.

How we worked! I tried to wash off the ugly brown kalsomine that still remained on the wall. Scraped it with glass, etc. Finally, after I had nearly cut my hand, Bertha persuaded me to paint over it.

Surprised to find that the paint was a dark gray instead of white. Had to take a taxi home and get a gallon of paint I had mixed for the woodwork there. Finally painted the place with a thin undercoat, Bertha aiding; then after dinner put on a finishing coat. Bertha lauded me, declaring that the job looked fine. Could not concur with her. The paint was not well rubbed out. As I told her, the best looking feature of the bathroom was the window which she had painted.

Turpentine made both of us a little giddy. Finished at 10 p.m. A hard day's work for both of us. And the Sabbath, too. But "the ox was in the mire." I certainly admire Bertha. As good as she is beautiful. And she loves me, or did love me.

Spent the day at the office. Received a telegram from Wood-son asking me to send proof of his "Annual Report of the Association" and "Full Financial Statement" lying on the desk in the consultation room. Found such after a prolonged search. Sent it air mail. Monday October 22 1928

Went to Bertha's to get paint in order to exchange it for white. Helped her to put up curtains in the bathroom. White curtains half-way, with rose draperies on each side, with a panel across the top. Looked very lovely and attractive. She had made them while at her office during the day. Remarkable how a woman's touch beautifies the commonplace. Desires me to paint her room. Will put pink curtains in it. A remark that fell from my lips manifested the hidden love she bears for me. "Bertha," I said, "your brother told me 'your prepara-tions would lead one to believe you were getting ready to marry.'" "And it looks even more so," I said, "since you are planning to renovate your room." "Yes," she said, softly, while her arms encircled me, "I wish I were fixing it for you and me." Something within prompted me to say "I wish so, too," but I remained silent.

Spent the day at the office on occupation chart. Nothing of importance happened. England disclosed the naval accord be-tween her and France. Britain acquiesced to France's insistence upon a large army. France reciprocated by removing all lim-itations upon Britain's cruiser and submarine building pro-gram up to a certain tonnage. And what more only the next upheaval will bring to light. Tuesday October 23 1928

Henry came in last night. Despite my cold, I painted along with him, knowing full well that if I stopped, he would do absolutely nothing.

Wednesday October 24 1928

Completed occupation diagram. Started on actual writing of synopsis of the study for Woodson's perusal. On way home called on Almira, a second cousin, graduate of Cornell. She has a piano studio in her home on Vermont Avenue. Glad to see each other after interval of four months.

Harry wrote thanking Ernest and me for his wedding present. Was elated with it. Has inaugurated a precedent, says he. Suggests china for Ernest. I prefer silver. More lasting. Will better perpetuate our friendship, for no one can tell when one of us, especially I, may fall by the way. Wrote Harry stressing the improbability of my attending the Kappa affair in New York on November 8. Painted tonight till after midnight, although feeling quite indisposed with a cold.

Thursday October 25 1928

Started to reduce to literary form the figures developed yesterday. My purpose is to show the tendency of the Negro in occupations since 1890. I find that Negroes tend to forsake the field of agriculture and domestic service, where and whenever possible, and to enter the higher types of occupations: trade and transportation, manufacturing, mechanical industries, and professional pursuits.

Industries which had been closed to Negroes prior to 1910 were opened to them; the attitude of trade unions altered in their favor, in some industries. Then the quality of Negro labor—its dependability, efficiency, and skill—increased. The undesirability of farm labor, the lure of the cities, openings in mining and lumbering also were factors. Finally, the speed-up of industry, together with a shortage of foreign labor caused by the War and immigration laws, worked toward the same end.

Painted tonight till 12:30.

Friday October 26 1928

Nothing of importance. Miss Revallion typed the outline of the study for Dr. Woodson's perusal. Hope it will half-way meet his approval. No details were given—none were intended.

Went to see "King of Kings." Excellent portrayal of Christ. Tribute to the educational value of the movies. I wonder what will be the ultimate future of moving pictures. Woodson believes it will tend to concentrate knowledge among a few, for one has but to attend the theatre and see the whole world virtually moving before his eyes. And, *mirabile dictu*, he can even hear it. I myself have heard, as well as seen, the cheering throngs in Berlin greeting [Paul von] Hindenburg. Among other things, the shouts of the crowds, the playing of bands, even the tramp of marching feet were plainly audible.

Played cards at "Fi's" [Thelma Duncan]. First time there in almost two months.

Dropped in at the office after 4:30. Woodson had returned from the Conference. Too busy to see me about the Study. Declared Annual Meeting in St. Louis a success. Would go over my paper Monday.

Although not feeling well, painted kitchen tonight. Henry did not come in.

Saturday
October 27
1928

Painted all day—that is, till 5 o'clock. After dinner went to frat house. Then to see Bertha, who was ill.

Graf Zeppelin, after its remarkable flight of four and a half days from Friedrickshafen [Germany] to Lakehurst, New Jersey, . . . took off perfectly this a.m. for Germany. Aboard were twenty passengers, a crew of forty, and a stowaway. *Fröhlich Reise.* Too much praise cannot be allotted Dr. Hugo Eckener, designer and pilot of the craft, and his valiant crew. They have demonstrated the feasibility of the dirigible as the safest means yet devised for trans-Atlantic air travel, both commercially and for regular passenger service. Airship carried a bale of cotton.

Sunday
October 28
1928

Going over the files of the *Outlook*. Finding nothing of great value.

Arrived at office 5 p.m. Found Woodson had already left for dinner. Left a note informing him that I could come at 9 a.m. tomorrow.

Dorothy [Revallion] called. Wants me to go to a Halloween

Monday
October 29
1928

party and dress as a woman. She offers to furnish the costumes.

Put another coat of paint on kitchen ceiling and walls. Henry came in and did nothing, as usual. Promised to come in early tomorrow evening. He is uninterested in this work. Perhaps due to changed status existing between him and *ma tante*.

Tuesday
October 30
1928

After perusing the *Outlook* till about 2:30 was interrupted by the advent of Dr. [Lorenzo D.] Turner, who, upon espying me, came over to my table to chat. Was formerly my English teacher at Howard. Received his Ph.D. degree about two years ago from the University of Chicago. Had been dropped from position as Head of English Department at Howard University last June due to charge of improprieties with female students. I shall not comment upon either the veracity or falseness of the accusation. He is now engaged in publishing a newspaper, *The Washington Sun*, in conjunction with his brother and Professor Peters. The latter was also an ex-English Professor of mine, and is now famous, or infamous, as one of the professors dismissed from Howard.

Dr. Turner asserts that the paper is gaining in circulation to a degree which is highly encouraging. And the paper merits it. In my opinion, it ranks as the highest-toned Negro newspaper published. It deserves support. Dr. Turner is interested in research. I assured him that with his English training, plus his scientific capacity, he should be able to synchronize both to produce works of an exceptionally high character. He expects to interview Woodson concerning the publishing of his Ph.D. thesis.

From the library arrived at the office at 4:30. Woodson was out. Came in about 4:30. We took up the manuscript respecting the study of the "Negro in Occupations" about 5 p.m. He was pleased with the gist of the thing, and the tendencies which I emphasized, although he warned me not to stress professional service. That is just what I did not do; thus his idea must have been gained by some mis-interpretation. The figures he could not accept without verification. I conceded that. He advised that we send out letters to various industrial schools respecting the part they have played to increase the number of Negro artisans.

Woodson thought the *Nation* was not worth consideration after the accession of [Donald Garrison] Villard to the Editorship. Saw little benefit in going over the files of the *Review of Reviews* or the *Outlook*, although he suggested that the *Independent* be exhausted.

Painted tonight.

Zeppelin arrived in Friedrickshafen, Germany, tonight.

Did not feel like going to library today; therefore, I stayed home and painted.

Wednesday October 31 1928

Sometimes my aunt drives me to desperation, but I suppose one must take into consideration her nerves.

Later I went to party at Ada's. Bought a haired mask *à la Lon Chaney* as the "Hunchback of Notre Dame." "Fifi" was dressed as a boy. Met Mrs. Terrell and Miss Wilson. The latter is a charming girl from Seattle, Washington, but too tall for me. She had lots of fun with me in the role of buffoon. Yet, I cannot say I really enjoyed myself. Too tired.

Zeppelin landed at Friedrickshafen this a.m. Had a stowaway, a young American.

Today, I have been made to suffer pangs I have never experienced hitherto. After all the labor and expense in trying to renovate my aunt's home and render it a habitable place to live in, she eternally complains about the house being upset, that this did not happen when Henry painted years ago, but now, as a result, she is handicapped in her laundry work. She also tried to make me believe, and has done so for over two weeks, that I have caused her nothing but inconvenience. And yet, I am taking invaluable time from my own work to give to painting the house.

Thursday November 1 1928

Tonight was the most exasperating of all. Bertha came up to help me. She washed two floors, then helped me paint and varnish. And all my aunt did was fuss: "She would never have any painting done again. Would be so glad when it was finished." (Who wouldn't?) I could contain myself no longer;

therefore, I told her how ungrateful and selfish she has been, despite the fact that she utilizes every moment to harp upon religion. I told her that if her religion could not bestow tolerance and patience and respect for the other fellow's feelings, it ought to be discarded. Told her that I would leave. And I shall. I'll finish the painting *in toto* and turn over to her a respectable looking place. She will be far better to visit than to live with. I became so outdone by her continual complaining and criticisms that I determined to finish painting as soon as possible, for my work was not appreciated. Therefore the baseboard, which I intended to paint to match the door, I varnished.

Her fault-finding would not be unbearable if she had cooperated, but during the entire six weeks of work upon the house, the labor has been *mine*; the suggestions, always adverse, *hers*. Had she cooperated as Bertha did that one evening, the house long ago would have been ready for the reception of visitors. As it is, nothing is finished. I am thoroughly disgusted. Told Aunt Fannie, Bertha, and Cousin Winnie so. They are aghast that Aunt Fannie has made no move to help me. Told them I would do nothing more even for my grandmother.

[Herbert] Hoover appears to be leading in the Presidental race.

Friday November 2 1928	Went over to Rosslyn. Saw my cousins, Rose and Grace. All of us aired our views upon the House of Prayer of which my aunt is a member. Is a throwback to the old plantation religion. Yelling, dancing, rolling, epileptic fits, etc. Half of them who go there do so with every other purpose than to serve God. Disciples of a scoundrel and hypocritical skin-flint, a self-styled "Bishop Grace." While he rides around in a luxurious Packard automobile, with hired liveried chauffeur, his adherents—mostly women—are, like my aunt, working their finger tips off to maintain him in such style. He is their healer, both of body and spirit. And horrible to relate, his followers believe it. One of the most pathetic instances of this belief was portrayed by my own cousin, who refused to call a doctor for

her only son. She allowed the boy to die, depending upon a healing magazine which she had bought from the "Bishop" for five cents to restore him to health. I believe she should have been arrested and the Bishop sentenced for murder. But the strong will ever prey upon the weak, will suck their pitiful substance by either force or fraud. And religion offers the most profitable means of painlessly extracting the hard-earned pennies from the poverty stricken Negroes. Of course, it is only the old-time and ignorant Negroes who swallow such a doctrine.

Finished perusal of the *Outlook Magazine*. Over 100 volumes. Found some important material. Dealt mostly with attempts of Negroes to enter industry, and efforts of whites to exclude them.

Saturday
November
3
1928

Stopped at office. Woodson had written several biographical sketches of Negroes for the *Encyclopaedia Britannica*: "Richard T. Greener" and "Peonage" were two of them, the latter historical. Greener, born in 1844, died in 1922. A graduate of Harvard College, he taught philosophy and logic at the University of South Carolina during Reconstruction. Also served as counsel to Bombay and other places. Average person does not know that; I didn't.

The article on "Peonage" was a tribute to Woodson's genius as an historian. Though his race has suffered incalculably from the horror of peonage in the South, Woodson discussed the subject generally, and so objectively that the reader could not tell whether the author was white or black.

Woodson lamented the fact that Wesley would not give further time to Negro History. So did I, stating that it was an irreparable loss, since only he and Wesley were qualified for such work. Then he astonished me by saying, "you can do it also." I did not believe he had that much faith in me.

Wrote Florence [Bacote] a long letter reprimanding her for late hours and not giving sufficient time to school work and rest.

Sunday
November
4
1928

Painted all day at home, then went to Bertha's and painted a floor for her. I was tired. She also.

Again, my aunt showed her religious intolerance. It seems that every unorthodox sect, perhaps to direct criticism from itself, assumes a "Holier than thou" attitude, constitutes itself a self-righteous and self-appointed tribunal to inquire into other people's beliefs, and gloats in assuring them that they are doomed to sulphurous and tormenting flames, unless they believe as they.

Now my aunt. An old lady, kindly, obliging, loving, had been staying there, but my aunt's fanaticism literally drove her away. Sunday she came again. My aunt condemned the entire world except those few *holy* and *sanctified* persons of which she, of course, is one. I demurred. The old lady supported me. I told my aunt religion—Christianity—is best and most easily discerned by the acts and lives of its believers. Words signify nothing. He who goes to church most frequently, prays and shouts the loudest, is usually the basest villain and hypocrite. I decried the necessity of church attendance each night in order to be a Christian or to live uprightly. Christianity is naught but love, is best exemplified in the attitude toward one's fellows. The church's four walls are symbolic of nothing. One carries his temple within himself. His conscience is sufficient guide.

The lady supported me. My aunt turned upon her so bitterly that the old lady withdrew from the fray. After her departure, my aunt castigated her as an evil person who ought to be in church instead of supporting and condoning evil. I remonstrated with her, told her the old lady was as religious as she, and as good, if not better.

Again, coming in from church in the evening and having mislaid her keys, my aunt accused the old lady of having come in and stolen them. I sighed not for the lady but for my aunt. It showed me the hollowness of her religious ranting.

Wrote Helen [Notis]. Sent her tickets to Kappa prom.

On way home I learned Hoover, according to the *Washington Post*, is far ahead of [Alfred E.] Smith, with about 270 votes, and only 266 needed to win.

Began on *Literary Digest*. Best source of information so far, because of its excerpts from newspapers. Went over 18 volumes.

[Captain C. B. D.] Collyer and [Harry J.] Tucker, two fliers who had lowered the cross country, non-stop record from east to west last week, were killed near Prescott, Arizona, last night during blinding storm of wind, snow, rain, and sleet. Their plane, the *Yankee Doodle*, crashed into a mountain. However, the steadily mounting toll of deaths diminished not one whit the enthusiasm of countless other fliers who, in this pioneering age of aerial transportation, risk and give their lives to make the world as safe for flying as land travel for future generations. They are martyrs to science and are rendering a service as great as or greater than that of those who fall on the field of battle.

The election is tomorrow. Hoover, the Republican candidate, is virtually conceded the winner. Already 273 electoral votes are given as certain for him. A victory for Smith would be little more than a miracle. A record vote of 43,000,000 is forecast.

Election Day. Beautiful weather and every natural facility favorable for the biggest outpouring of voters in history. To-day, 43,000,000 American men and women will go to the polls to register their choice for President and Vice President of the United States for the next four years. There, unfortunately, is little to choose between the two men. Both are capable: Hoover, with an impressive war record as Food Dictator, feeder of starving Europeans, and a post-war record embellished by his work in the Mississippi floods of 1927; the liberal Democratic candidate, Smith, on the other hand, blessed with an infectious personality, has carved an envious record for himself as Governor of New York State. His gubernatorial efficiency alone would be sufficient recommendation for his election. But, unhappily, in *this* presidential campaign, there is only one burning issue—all others are merely subterfuges, a camouflage to hide the real question—namely, shall a Catholic

President sit in the White House for the first time in the Nation's 153 years of existence?

Today will tell the tale. Ere another sun has risen, the world will know whether it is still possible in this twentieth century to crucify a man politically because of his religion; whether the United States, the arch-defender of religious tolerance, is at heart as bigoted as 16th century England. I do not believe Smith will win. Religion will prevent that. Were it not for his Catholic faith, I believe he would defeat Hoover handily. Even that cradle of conservatism, the South, shows ominous signs of disruption, a radical about-face to the Republican party to offset the "horrible" menace of a Catholic president.

Negroes, too, have been voting against the G.O.P. in large numbers. 'Tis well! A change is always refreshing. But what do they expect of the Democrats? No political plums if Smith is elected, for he dare not offend the South by lavish black appointments in return for Negro votes. Not from the Republicans, if victorious, for they dare not weaken their chances of entering a wedge in the Solid South by Negro appointments. Therefore, both candidates have, with consummate tact, avoided any outspoken discussion of the Negro. The Negro, by his shift of allegiance, may cause his vote to be sought after by both parties. This is desirable. If he can achieve that, his desertion of the G.O.P. will redound to his advantage.

Stopped at Bertha's en route from library. Went to office. Secured mail. C——— has already made arrangements for the Kappa affair, therefore cannot be Bacote's guest. Helen Notis informs me she knew nothing of Harry's reception. Thought it strange she was not invited.

Helped Bertha till 11:30. Painted floors and helped her put up curtains. She made the draperies shorter than the panel, and since the windows reached the floor and the draperies stopped about a yard therefrom, I likened it to a picture of a colonial dame holding her dress to avoid a muddy spot, and disclosing, inadvertently, her pantelettes. Then, in order to remedy it, Bertha shortened the panel to match in length the draperies, which simulated the appearance of a six-foot man wearing an overcoat calculated to fit a man five feet tall. She laughed and finally decided to add more material to the draperies. They looked beautiful. Pale green over white. Bertha is a wonderful worker, a sweet and charming, as well as beautiful, woman. Would make an ideal wife. However, we get along like two "strange cats" apparently. Are always "fighting." She suggested cold cream for cleaning paint from my nails. I scoffed at such, holding that a nail brush and soap, after rubbing off surplus paint with turpentine, was far more efficacious. She was obdurate and, to prove her point, despite the lateness of the hour, cleaned my nails with cold cream, applied with cotton on an orange stick.

The morning papers state that Herbert Hoover has been elected by an overwhelming majority, which bids fair to attain avalanche proportions. It seems that he has carried the entire East, with the exception of Massachusetts and Rhode Island (which are in doubt this morning); swept the entire North from New York to California; and broken the Solid South, with Texas and Virginia and Florida already in his column, and North Carolina doubtful. He even carried Smith's own Congressional District.

Wednesday November 7 1928

What caused this monumental "Republican landslide"? Simply this: 43,000,000 Americans were challenged as to the advisability of placing a Catholic President in the highest office of the United States. And approximately 35,000,000 marched to the polls with a solemn vow that never, so long as the power of the ballot was theirs, would such an "unspeakable crime" be perpetrated; never would the annals of American History be sullied by the fact that, when the United States was threatened by all the imagined horrors of "popery," enough strong-sinewed, one-hundred-percent Protestants could not be found to stay so foul an intention. And so they voted down the *Catholic* Smith, voted in the *Protestant* Hoover, and made the United States safe for *Protestantism, Ku Kluxism,* and *white supremacy.*

Smith is facing one of the worst defeats ever sustained by any presidential candidate. Despite all efforts to contrary, he was defeated the moment he announced his candidacy—sacrificed upon the altar of religious sectarianism and bigotry. Even the South forsook him. Texas, Virginia, Florida, and Tennessee, Democratic strongholds, went Republican for the first time since Reconstruction.

Religion and race were the main factors in Smith's defeat. Significance, however, is attached to the fact that, although New York voted for Hoover, she elected a Democratic Governor, Franklin D. Roosevelt, a cousin to "Teddy." The import of his election to the Governorship is the obvious certainty that he is being groomed to lead the Democratic ticket for 1932. But, in my opinion, unless something unforeseen happens, he will have to wait till 1936 to head the Democratic ticket with any possibility of success.

Thursday
November
8
1928

Hoover has received the greatest electoral vote ever given a candidate for the Presidency—444 out of a possible 566. Smith received but 87. Yet Smith gained a greater popular vote than any previously elected president received and also the largest for any defeated candidate. While successful in the large cities, the rural communities upset him. Such was the case in New York.

Rhode Island and Massachusetts in the East, together with South Carolina, Georgia, Alabama, Mississippi, Louisiana, and Arkansas in the South, were all that Smith had to show for his strenuous campaign. Eight states. The French Canandian and Irish vote of Massachusetts helped materially to win him that state.

But the Hoover landslide carried everything before it. Even North Carolina and Virginia and all the border states went over to his banner. Yet the New Orleans *Times Picayune* does not believe that sectarianism in any way influenced the result. But the Jacksonville *Florida Times* believes that religious loyalty was the decisive factor in Smith's defeat. I concur. When one recalls the fanatical speeches of Mrs. [Mabel Walker] Willebrandt, the influence of the Protestant Press, the Klan and other agencies in creating an impossible picture of "papal tyranny" in the minds of the common people should Smith be elected, what else could be expected?

What of the Negroes? The significance for them is that their tenure of office-holding in the South is terminated. Must be, if the Republicans would hold their recently won gains. However, the Negroes have demonstrated that they are capable of at least a change in political allegiance, if nothing more. Oscar DePriest, a Democrat of Chicago, has been elected to the House.[1] He is the first Negro to win a seat in Congress since Reconstruction. That is one gain for the Negro, but insignificant. A St. Louis lawyer, Joseph L. McLemore, running on the Democratic platform, failed in his bid for a Congressional seat in the same year.

Received a mortifying as well as discouraging blow today. After struggling for almost two months to get the house painted and made habitable, I was notified by my aunt, upon my returning from the library, that she would put no new furniture in the living room. She had promised some time ago that both she and I would cooperate in buying a new dining room and a parlor suite. By degrees, she allowed the promise of the dining room suite to be dissipated. I said nothing concerning that, for we could make out without a new one. But the living room is absolutely *hors de combat* without a new suite. 'Twould have entailed no expense upon her.

Her reasons would have done credit to an inmate of an insane asylum: She could not serve the Lord so well, if she had new furniture, because she would have to devote so much time to keeping it clean that it would interfere with her church going. Then, too, persons seeing that she has a new living room suite would bore her by visiting. Again, so much furniture might exhibit the appearance of wealth, which she heartily desired to avoid. She did not care for a nice home. Just

*Friday
November
9
1928*

1. Oscar DePriest was the first black person elected to Congress from the North. DePriest, like the twenty-two blacks from the South who served in Congress between 1869 and 1901, was a Republican. He was reelected in 1930 and in 1932; but in 1934, Arthur W. Mitchell, a black Democrat, defeated him.

wanted to "serve the Lord and be saved" when she died. O, religion of fools! What fiat has the Almighty decreed by which one is to spend his allotted time here preparing to die? As if death were not assured. To be saved? What is the possibility of being lost? I am tolerant of everyone's religion with the exception of the bigot's. His is more pretense than sincerity. Imagine the Divine Spirit counseling my aunt not to buy, or allow me to purchase, a parlor suite and her harkening thereunto.

Told her I would have to leave. Could not remain unless furniture was secured as promised. She refused to allow me to buy it. I could have wept, for I came here purposely to help her fix up her home. And she refuses. And the time I have spent working day and night when I could have employed it to so much greater profit upon my own research or in making social contacts I have denied myself during my six months here, because of the unwholesome appearance of this house.

She offered to pay me for labor and money which I had expended. Was an insult, for I did what I did freely, willingly. Lastly, Ernest, Hipp, and I had vowed that the first one of us to get a job in Washington would fix up the house so that we might hold reunions there, besides showing our gratitude to my aunt for her kindness to us during our student days here. And moreover, even though I shall leave, I shall finish the painting completely. Told her I would accept nothing from her when she offered to compensate me, that mine was a labor of love.

Went to Bertha's. Told her about decision. I had intended to work tonight upon the second installment of "Negro Slavery in New England," but could not. No one can comfort like a woman. Although she berated me for having remained there as long as I had against her counsel, she finally—womanlike—cheered me, spoke soothingly to me, laid my head on her bosom, caressed and kissed me, advised me to forget, and seek other living quarters. I shall.

Saturday
November
10
1928

On the way to the library, I left a dollar with my aunt for a boy to wash windows. At the library secured information regarding Negro slavery in Connecticut from [William Chaunery?] Fowler's *Historical Status and New Haven Society Papers*. Returning from library, stopped at the office. Dr. Woodson was to have gone to New York, but cancelled trip. Told him I had decided to join Association. Promised to take life membership. Also desired six copies of the *Journal* [*of Negro History*] containing my article on "Slave-holding New England and Its Awakening" [XIII (1928), 492–533] to send to friends. He gave them to me or at least said he would see that they were sent out.

Stopped at Bertha's to get paint brush. She came in before I left. Had bought a new black coat. Looked quite *chic* in it.

Promised to see her tomorrow.

Both my aunt and I remained in all day. Strange she did not go to church during the afternoon as is her wont. When I went out, she was in bed. And Bertha waited for me to call her. The telephone, however, was in my aunt's room. Since I did not call her, Bertha "phoned" me about seven o'clock. I explained aunt was here. She replied that she had wondered what happened to me.

Later, we went to movies.

Sunday November 11 1928

Nothing extraordinary at the Library. The ship *Vestris,* bound from New York to South America, sank off Virginia Coast. Over 300 persons in peril. Eleven ships rushing to aid.

Painted floor of dining room tonight.

Monday November 12 1928

Vestris' passengers picked up by U.S.S. *Wyoming, American Skipper,* and other vessels. Storm signals reported disregarded. Over 108 people unaccounted for. Harrowing stories told by survivors. Some afloat 18 hours on pieces of wreckage. Captain Carey, skipper, perished.[2]

I stopped at the office. Gave Woodson $3.00 for one year membership in Association. Could not spare $25.00.

Tuesday November 13 1928

2. The liner *Vestris*, which left New York on Saturday, November 10, 1928, headed for Barbados and South America, sank on November 12 about 240 miles off the Virginia Capes. Rescue vessels brought in 205 survivors of the 328 persons aboard. Most of the women and all of the children were among the missing. Captain William Carey went down with his ship.

Went to meeting of Historical Society at the Y.W.C.A. on Rhode Island Avenue. Promised Mr. [William M.] Brewer yesterday I would attend. No one there. Called on Bertha. She was tidying up dining room. Had just bought beautiful new suite.

Wednesday
November
14
1928

Captain Carey blamed for loss of *Vestris* by passengers. Sent S.O.S. too late. Should have been sent Sunday.[3]

Al Smith stopped in D.C. today, en route to Florida. Noisily greeted. In a radio speech last night, he accepted defeat philosophically, lauded the victor, and thanked those who voted for him.

I bought a pair of shoes for $5.45. Gave the poor salesman more than an hour's trouble. Said he, "$5.45 for the shoes and $5.00 for my trouble." He deserved it, but I did reward him with the price of a 25 cent cigar.

Sunday
November
18
1928

Have been so busy I've had no time to make any notation in diary since Wednesday. Fortunately, nothing of great importance has occurred during the *interim*.

Monday
November
19
1928

Spent the day at the library gathering information for second installment of "Negro Slavery in New England."

3. According to reports in the New York *Times*, survivors charged that Captain Carey took an unseaworthy vessel to sea and that he failed to maintain discipline among his interracial crew. They also claimed that the lifeboats containing women and children were not in good repair and broke up and sank. Crew members were accused of beating off passengers in the water who tried to board lifeboats containing crew members.

[14] The Study and Personal, National, and International Jottings

Stopped at the office tonight. Had a long chat with Woodson over the possible treatment of the subject of the "Negro in Occupations." I had planned to develop it from *decade to decade*, in order to get a cross-section of the Negro at work during each period. Woodson suggested that the Negro in each occupation be treated *topically*, the result being a continuous thread in each occupation from 1890 to 1928. I agreed that for continuity and unification such would be desirable, but it would lack what the survey set out directly to portray, a cross-section development of the Negro at work from decade to decade. I believed also that much repetition would result, but Woodson stressed that far more repetition would be inevitable in the method espoused by me. Advised that I start writing. Later invited me to dinner at the "Wage Earners" tomorrow night, given in honor of the Presidents of the Land Grant Colleges.

Tuesday
November
20
1928

When I arrived at the dinner I was aghast to find that my host was habited in business attire, as were the other men. I alone wore a dinner jacket. Woodson introduced me to several of the men who were present, most of them from Mississippi, Louisiana, and Georgia. Felt relieved when Dr. [Edward P.] Davis, Head of the Department of German at Howard University, entered attired in a tuxedo. He was formerly my German

Wednesday
November
21
1928

teacher at Howard. Is quite proficient in German. He believed
I had gone into medicine.

While chatting with him, in came Dr. Alain Locke, petite,
nervous as usual, and exuding his superfine culture. I can
never feel comfortable or at ease in his presence. Perhaps I am a
boor and he a Rhodes Scholar and a Harvard Ph.D. He taught
me philosophy and aesthetics at Howard University. Now he
believes I am connected with Kittrell College, a school in
North Carolina. Why he presumed so is a mystery to me. Was
quite surprised, however, to find that I was in the city, associated with Dr. Woodson. Dr. Locke is disappointing from
my point of view. For all his superior education—and I doubt
whether any Negro in America has had the benefit of better
training—he has produced nothing original. True, he has edited a couple of compilations of Negro plays and other literature, but from the point of view of original production, he has
yet to be heard from. He lacks the practicality of Woodson.

Mr. John W. Davis, President of West Virginia Collegiate
Institute and one of the leading educators of the country, came
in; also Mr. [Garnet C.] Wilkinson, Assistant Superintendent
of public schools in Washington, D.C. Recognized me immediately, although he had not seen me since May, 1919, when I
took a post graduate course at Dunbar High School.

The dinner was a huge success, especially the after-dinner
speaking. I contributed a grave *faux pas* when I started to eat
my oyster cocktail with a spoon. Lack of contact. And gra-
mercy! Locke, that apotheosis of culture, sitting beside me.

What an admirable host Woodson makes. With poignant
remarks interspersed with irrepressible humor, he introduced
some of the men. There were now over fifty from as far north
as New Jersey and as far west as Oklahoma. The chief burden
of the presidents seemed to be the need of educating the Negro
in that field which would fit him for the greatest service in his
community. All these schools are mechanical and normal institutions, with one or two, like West Virginia Collegiate and
Virginia State, giving college courses in the Arts and Sciences.
All the presidents concurred in regard to the changing sentiment among White Southerners favorable to Negro colleges

[as shown] by the State legislatures. Such a view was pointedly emphasized by Mr. [Benjamin F.] Hubert of Georgia State, whose school was formerly given but $10,000 a year, but now is receiving several times that amount. The same experience was detailed by other presidents.

[The author made entries for the period of November 22 through December 31, but this part of the diary was misplaced.]

Helen Notis presented me with this diary (I am writing in it) as a Christmas gift this morning. A delightful surprise from one of the most charming girls I have ever known.

New Year's Day. Rained hard. Helen was to come over at 12 noon. Jim (my brother, with whom I was staying) did not go to work. Harry Hipp called. . . . Had him call Helen. She phoned me later. Apprised her of change in plans. She came over at two. We decided not to attend Alpha vs. Omega basketball game. Jim loath to allow us a moment together. Fear Helen has been cheated.

Attended tea with Helen at Miss Payne's at 8 p.m. Harry and his wife, Muriel, were there; also Florence Bacote. I read several poems, including "Wine," "Passion," "Love." Were well received, I thought.

Went back to Jim's. Left later for Newark to take Helen home. A loveable creature, if ever there was one. . . I sometimes wonder whether she loves me a little. And I am so unworthy.

Tuesday
January 1
1929
New York
City

Returned from Newark at 5:45 a.m. Tired. . . . Jim shook his head sympathetically. Dozed till 9:05. Started to dress. Harry called. Faithful friend that he is, had been waiting at the Pennsylvania station for me since 8:45. Saw him at the station. Took 11:15 train to D.C. in order to chat with him. Discussed Marguerite (Skeeter) and her sisters. Harry waxed eloquent on Jim's lack of propriety and good taste in reference to Helen. Harry was more provoked than I. But then he has a case.

Dead tired on way to D.C. Tried vainly to sleep. Met Emile

Wednesday
January 2
1929

Holley, "frat" brother and Howard University professor. Talked. Made engagement with him for dinner tomorrow at 4 p.m.

Arrived D.C. at 4:30. Saw Woodson at 5 p.m. Wants me to give him the manuscript by March 1. Has another proposition for me: collecting old manuscripts relating to Negroes. I am to collect them. He will do so until I finish the occupation study. Is job for next year.

Thursday
January 3
1929

Despite the fact that I retired at 9:30 last night, awoke tired this a.m. Reached library at 11. Remained till 4:20. Met Holley at Thurston's Cafe at 4:50. We decided to take an apartment. I was slated to live with the Davidsons, 1333 R St., N.W., but of course, I prefer the apartment. One likes to feel that he is lord of his domain, however tiny. Inquired at real estate office on U St., N.W. Agent promised to secure apartment for us tomorrow.

We walked to Girard and Georgia Avenue. Saw new apartment building ready for occupancy. Surprised to find Roselle Molleson (nee Gilbert), former Howard classmate, as resident manager. Beautiful apartments. Expensive, however: single room and kitchenette, with bath, $27.50 a month; 2 rooms, kitchenette, and bath, $50. A great venture for me. Is the price I pay for attempting to render my aunt's dwelling habitable. This need not have happened. However, I like the apartment. Has frigidaire and self-service elevator. Two school teachers, Miss Twitty and Mildred ————, offered to help us fix up the apartment.

Friday
January 4
1929

Went to barber shop this morning. Left my razor in New York or would have shaved myself. Needed haircut, however.

Went to the library. Started to write first chapter of book on "Negro Occupation." Difficult to start. Finally completed a page.

"Question Mark," army aeroplane, trying to set record for continuous hours in the air, is on its fourth day. Is being refuelled by auxillary planes.

King George is improving.

Went to Thelma's (Duncan) tonight. Have not seen her since November. Has been ill. Took her box of candy. Played "500" and whist.

For once, I sympathize with the poor housewife. I have had my shopping Gethsemane today. First we signed a contract for the apartment. Then, I rushed to pay an electric deposit for lights. Then furniture. Mildred and Miss Twitty took us to Sloan's Auction Room. Holley bought a day bed for $12, a revolving book case for $2.50, a leather pillow for $2.50, and an end table for $2. I got a chair which I believed Mildred was bidding on for me. Later told me she desired it for herself. I had to be chivalrous, of course, and let her have it.

Now a trek for a bed. Salesman at a furniture store asked $32 for a bed like Holley's. I told him I did not want to buy his entire stock. Went then to a second hand store. After one and a half hours of fruitless searching in the rain, finally saw one desirable. "Jewed" down the owner from over $20 to $18. Bought chair for $1.50. Have spent nearly $75. All I see is a bed.

Went to see Bertha. Told her of renting apartment. Told me I should have done so long ago. Will help to get my room in shape.

"Question Mark" has broken all records, save that of "Dixmude."

King George is better. Hoover returns from trip. Slept here tonight for first time.

Saturday January 5 1929

Helen called this morning before I had time to dress. Would not be home tonight. Wishes to inspect apartment. Could not speak freely with her. Will call her Wednesday morning.

Went to library. Did very little writing. Took additional notes until 4 p.m. Stopped at office. Saw Woodson's secretary, Dorothy Revallion. Kissed me as long as she could. (Woodson was out, thank heaven). Secured mail. Woodson finally came in. Asked him if books could be drawn from Library (of Congress). Said "no," because of a book that was

Monday January 7 1929

lost: Small and [George E.] Vincent, *Introduction to [the Study of]* Society. Asked me to find out cost etc. and phone him tomorrow.

Went to meet Bertha. Did not see her at her office. She was to help me buy bed linens, etc. for the apartment. Walked to the Palais Royal (Department store). Met her there. Bought blanket, sheets, pillow cases, bath rug, and towels. Told Bertha anyone seeing me now with her would swear I was married to her.

Ate dinner with her. Paid for what she bought. Poor girl. She is a wonderful pal. Promised to help me Saturday. . . . Bought silverware and dishes today at the five and ten cent store. Mrs. Moss, a lady whose apartment on the first floor faces the elevator, and whom we heard served meals, was unable to accommodate us. She gave me a table.

Tuesday
January 8
1929

Ate my first meal at Mrs. Davidson's today. Was satisfactory. 60 cents per meal or $15 per month for dinner. Is cheaper to pay by the month, but, then, some meals I may take elsewhere, thus paying for what I do not get.

Received touching letter from Helen Notis today. Why is it that some parents make distinctions between their children? And why, especially, to the disparagement of the most helpful one? Poor Helen! Despite all she does at home, she is made to feel that she is tolerated, nothing more. And her sister, one who has two children and no husband and who has given the family all the trouble, is the "pet of the family." Poor Helen gives to, and does for, all the family, yet is always reminded that she can get out if she doesn't like things at home. Fact is, Helen is different, is a higher intellectual and cultural type than her sisters. O, if I had a sister like her! Would it not be a joy to exhibit her? And she has told me all her troubles. Someone might take her away from all that. I should advise that she herself make a change.

Wednesday
January 9
1929

Holley and I went down to Sloan's Auction Room again this morning at 9:30. What bargains: graphophones $3; a Harding piano $15; a roomful of roller coaster wagons, kiddy cars, etc., for a quarter apiece. Enough springs for 75 beds, for 50 cents apiece, plus a dresser, etc. I bought a parlor chair, kitchen chair, and taboret. Emile bought a good rocker for $4.00. I paid $1.50 for the parlor chair, 60 cents for the kitchen chair, and 30 cents for the taboret. Also secured two file cabinets for 80 cents. Bought a chiffonier for $5.00.

But what bargains! A magnificent mahogany bedroom suite went for $40; a fine wicker suite for $15. There is a great amount of exhilaration in the bidding. . . .

Worked on manuscript at library until dinner, then worked until 11 p.m.

Up at 7:30. Ate a cold breakfast of frozen grapefruit, two eggs, and pint of milk. . . . Thursday
January 10
1929

After a long day at the office, or rather at the library, went to dinner. From there to the movies, where I saw "Uncle Tom's Cabin."

Met Mrs. Moss and Roselle on the way to the apartment. Chatted with her for a while. Mrs. Moss is a charming woman. Must be well off. Has the most elaborately furnished home of anyone in the building.

Called Bertha. She was to help on Saturday. Wanted it changed to Sunday.

Remained all day. Succeeded in completing the "Negro in Occupations in New England." Took me a long time to write it. Not as easy a task as I had imagined. Friday
January 11
1929

After completing the first section of the chapter, called upon Roselle. Mrs. Moss again was there. Invited me to her apartment and showed me her floors, which had just been polished.

Emile brought me a copy of Ulrich B. Phillips, *American Negro Slavery,* from the Howard University library. I could not find it at the Library of Congress.

Dr. J. Franklin Jameson lectured on "Manuscripts in European Libraries." Dealt chiefly with the Mediaeval Period. Better arranged, he said, than in American libraries. Was stimulating. Dr. [E. C.] Burnett will follow with a lecture on

"Papers of the Continental Congress" next week. Hope to hear him.

Spent a hectic day at the library. Don't believe I accomplished much.

Went to the office after dinner to see Woodson. Helped him to stamp packages. Was careful not to mention manuscript of first chapter. Felt relieved when he did not either. Told him of Dr. Jameson's lecture on "Mediaeval Manuscripts." He was pleased.

Met Randolph on the way home. Fine fellow. Bertha is virtually engaged to him. Wouldn't that shock Harry and others who know that she loves me. I also know that she loves me, but then, I cannot afford to stand in the way of ameliorating her condition. I have advised her to marry him. Love will come afterwards . . .

Today, or at least until 1:30 p.m., was spent in cleaning, scrubbing, and polishing. Emile cleaned the bathroom while I polished the floors. Quite a task. For once, I'd rather not be a bachelor.

Bertha was supposed to come up this afternoon. Did not call her.

A fool is born every day. Proof: I spent 60 cents in taxi fare to save a 50 cent dinner.

Called Bertha after dinner. She was indignant because I had not called earlier. . . .

Went to the office. Remained until one o'clock. Accomplished nothing. Went to the Library of Congress. Somehow my brain would not function.

After dinner, returned home and worked until 11 o'clock.

O, yes, Mrs. Moss told me she went downtown today and that she would have sent me up something (for the apartment) but nothing was on sale. Also told me she was going to Woodward and Lothrop (department store) tomorrow. A sale is in progress there. Told me she would get me a lamp.

[The author did not make entries for the period January 15 through March 31, 1929. He did not choose to publish the entries for April 1 through April 3.]

My work is not progressing as well as I would have it. I seem to be suffering from mental fatigue. Perhaps the struggle for an education, after seven and a half years of denial and privation, is about to claim me as one of its victims, as it has so many others. My strength, bodily resistance, is at low ebb. Then, too, I have been laboring, perhaps too strenuously, in this work. Have not secured proper rest or recreation. Woodson's personality does not help. In addition, my diet has been none too varied or wholesome. It would be a shame to disappoint Dr. Woodson and so many well-wishers. But should I fail in this study, it will be because of my health, rather than mental inability to complete it.

Thursday
April 4
1929

Began work about 9 a.m. Before that had trouble with Mrs. Molleson, with whom Emile and I take breakfast. For the past three or four days, we have been getting next to nothing for breakfast. Either there is no butter, no cereal, no eggs, no milk, or no fruit. For two mornings, we brought down our own fruit and were so exasperated that we said nothing. Another morning oranges given us were over ripe. We left those untouched without comment. But this a.m. breakfast consisted of grapefruit, cereal, cocoa, two pieces of bacon, and two slices of fried apple, over done. We could stand it no longer. Mrs. Reuther [an employee of Mrs. Molleson] was sick or feigned illness. At least, she remained in bed and left Cleo, the little thirteen-year-old awkward country girl, to face the music.

Friday
April 5
1929

We complained and loudly. Mrs. Molleson could hear clearly. We told her we were at the end of our patience, that no longer would we pay her for food, then furnish the same or part of it. There was no butter on the table. Emile got up to look for some. Cleo saw him, informed Mrs. Molleson, and that dignitary, ensconced among the pillows in her bed, hailed us before her dread tribunal. Yes, she admitted, for the past few mornings breakfasts have not been up to par. But whose fault was that, we countered. She had run out of change. Again, that was not our concern. We had paid in advance, all too unwisely, it developed.

Mrs. Molleson reprimanded Emile because he helped himself to butter Tuesday morning. Then we "got her told." Informed her that by giving us a little fruit, cereal, eggs, and cocoa in the morning, she could board both of us for the price she charged one. The other would pay for her and Cleo's breakfasts. No, she averred, she makes nothing off the breakfasts. Just took us for accommodation.

But the reason we can get no food is because she is assisting in the boarding and clothing of a friend who is more than able to care for himself. She informed us at parting that she expected to be either ill or in New York Saturday and Sunday, hence could not prepare our breakfasts. Would make up for them next week, after which there would be no more breakfasts served. Little does she realize that we know her dismissal is to occur within fifteen days.

Stopped work long enough to call Bertha. She will come up tonight to assist me in map making.

Had altercation with Mrs. Molleson about 3 o'clock. She talked very uncivilly over the phone to me. I took umbrage. She later apologized, pleading that she had previously been angered by two white men who refused to remove their hats in her home. Told her I saw no good reason why she should vent her spleen on me.

Had much fun with Ophelia Davidson, a cute librarian [at Howard University], at dinner. She has a sore throat.

[The author chose not to publish part of the entry for April 5 and the entries for April 6 through 14.]

Monday
April 15
1929

A terrible day, cold, dreary, and the rain falls in torrents, driven by a northeasterly wind. . . .

Finished "Domestic and Personal Service." Began "Trade and Transportation."

The only description that I can give of today is that it exceeded yesterday in tempestuousness. A cold wind drove the rain, which came in a steady downpour all day. Made critical progress on the chapter today. Alice Holley [Emile's wife] cooked dinner. Baseball opening game washed out.

Tuesday
April 16
1929

Today fine but cool. Finished "Trade and Transportation." Have not seen Woodson in over a week.

Called Bertha. Told her to come up tomorrow or Friday.

Wednesday
April 17
1929

Worked all morning on "Manufacturing and Mechanical Pursuits."

Thursday
April 18
1929

Went to dinner at Davidsons'. Was welcomed by Ophelia, Mrs. Davidson, and others, as if I were a prodigal son. Good thing I did go to Davidsons' because they had threatened to visit me tonight.

Emile persuaded me to attend a dance at Howard tonight. Second one since I have been here. Enjoyed myself. . . .

Friday
April 19
1929

Still working on "Manufacturing and Mechanical Pursuits."

Went to the Kappa Alpha Psi Alumni (dinner) meeting. Everyone appeared in formal clothes, much to my liking. Is mandatory. Otherwise a fine is imposed. First experience with the famous "blackball" procedure. Member desired to bring in a friend. Had submitted name at previous meeting. Was well received by members. Empowered (him) to solicit candidate. Did so, brought in name. But candidate rejected by one blackball. Caused a storm. Member who had brought in name was mortified, humiliated, and angered. With flushed face, swore he would never offer another candidate's name. Others took the same vow. Then came retaliatory threats. One member pledged himself to blackball every name presented thereafter.

Bad procedure, I thought. Would make fraternity closed corporation, which would encompass its stagnation and decay. Too much power wielded by one man.

Saturday
April 20
1929

I met Armand Scott, noted lawyer; Judge [Edward W.] Henry of Philadelphia; and others.

Banquet was served at 1:30 a.m. and poor Emile had not eaten his dinner. Furthermore, he had tried to persuade me not to do so. So hungry was Emile that when dinner was finally served, Emile, seeing a brother opposite him who had just been served carving his chicken, was so wrought up that he picked up his knife and fork and began carving the thin air. The most remarkable case of autosuggestion I have ever witnessed.

Returned home about 3 o'clock and cleaned up.

O yes, told Ophelia I would bring Mr. Holley to dinner tomorrow. Also Mr. [Harry] Hipp. Both, I persuaded, were deeply enamoured of her.

Sunday
April 21
1929

Harry and his wife came today. 'Twas a pleasure to see my "brother." Brought his famous fever blister along. Harry looked well. Seemed happy with Muriel. Suppose I'm missing the big things of life.

[The pages of the original diary containing entries for the period April 22 through May 8 were misplaced. They were lost after the entry for April 29 was transcribed.]

Monday
April 29
1929

Worked at home all day. Did not feel well. Went to dinner. From there called upon Dr. Albert Stuart of Connecticut Avenue. He is a white physician. He will do what the majority of Negro doctors feel is a useless expenditure, i.e., give me a complete examination. His diagnosis: bad nasal passages, a tired condition. Tonsils once supposed to have been removed, but now found to be only scooped out. Sides and roots were still there, giving me trouble. Nerves weak, and muscles of the heart weak, due to bad tonsils and teeth presumably. Prescription: Nerve tonic and mixed glands for nerves. Also nasal wash. Price $25.00. One more visit included, however. Lungs perfect, said he, also kidneys. Expectoration due to congestion falling from nasal passages into throat.

From the doctor's went to see Dr. Woodson. He seemed a

trifle exasperated at not having received a chapter on the "Wage Earner." Told him of my illness. He asked sarcastically if I desired him to remove my tonsils. The man is positively unbearable at times. I see him as little as possible in order to keep myself under control. Told him I would give him the chapter this week.

[The author chose not to publish the entries for May 9 through 12.]

Worked on "Negro Farmers." Finished them. Went to the movies tonight. Saw a picturization of one of Alexandre Dumas' novels, "The Man in the Iron Mask," taken from *The Three Musketeers* and the *Adventures of D'Artagnan*. I did not know that Louis XIII had twins. It was my opinion that Louis XIV was his only male heir, or at least the only one who had a legitimate claim to the throne. What might France have lost if the other twin had been king?

Monday
May 13
1929

Finished "Domestic and Personal Service" today. Took them to the office.

Have two more chapters to write. Went to the library tonight.

See Bertha Thursday.

Tuesday
May 14
1929

Appalling catastrophe in Cleveland. Clinic destroyed by explosion of X-ray films. Bromide gas and nitrous oxide released. Snuffed out lives of over 100 persons. Fire added to destruction and death. Was one of the famous hospitals in the United States. Internationally-known doctor (George W. Crile) at the head. Many acts of heroism. Outstanding, that of a Negro, named [Robert] Chares, who, noticing the gases and smoke pouring from the doomed building and seeing panic-stricken persons at the windows crying frantically for help, left his car-washing, and, seizing a ladder, hurried to the building. Finding the ladder too short to reach the windows, he, nothing undaunted, placed it upon his shoulders and held it while ten people climbed down to safety. Then, dropping the

Wednesday
May 15
1929

ladder, rushed inside and saved the lives of fourteen more persons. I was gratified to note that Chares, while cast in his heroic role, was described as a "giant" rather than a "burly" Negro. I suppose it all depends upon the act performed.

Thursday
May 16
1929

Bought a suit at Saks. Needed it. Have only two decent suits. . . .

Friday
May 17
1929

Nothing of import today insofar as work is concerned.

The "Graf Zeppelin," the giant German transatlantic dirigible, with two of its motors dead, was forced to turn back on its trip to America after having reached the point of the Balearic Islands off the Spanish Coast. After having been buffeted by violent storms and strong winds, and almost swept into the Mediterranean, the Zeppelin, due chiefly to the expert handling of Eckener, its commander, was finally moored to a mast at Coeur, France, with the aid of a large body of troops. Just what caused the engine trouble is unknown. The Zeppelin carried eighteen passengers and a crew of forty-one. Had made the round trip from Germany to America last October.

[The author chose not to publish the entries for May 18, 19, and 30; June 1 through 5 and June 7; and July 3, 5, 7, 11, and 14. No entries were made for the other missing dates from May 18 through August 30.]

Tuesday
July 9
1929

Gave Dr. Woodson two chapters: one on "Agriculture" and the other on "Domestic and Personal Service." His comment: "not enough data illustrative of agriculture. 'Domestic and Personal Service' reads much smoother." By the way, I met Mr. [Morris] Lewis, Congressman DePriest's secretary, at dinner. A very likable fellow.

Saturday
August 31
1929

Received a letter from Harcourt Tynes this morning telling me he would arrive here from New York City on the five o'clock train. Did not want him to come. I am ill, cannot eat, and may be more a bore than a host for him. Yet, Harcourt is a very dear friend of mine. Moreover, Helen [Notis] was to come to D.C. for a two weeks' vacation.

The agent came and took the radio, for I decided I could not keep it while I am spending money on this all-important stomach. It has already cost me about $150.00.

Went to see Irene [a pseudonym] for a few minutes. Is as sympathetic and lovable as ever. Left her about 12 o'clock. Went to Rosslyn. Bertha is ill there. I met Mr. Rollins (friend of my cousins). Hearing that I was ill, he not only sympathized with me but went out and bought me a spring chicken and some sweet potatoes. He left the latter with my cousins. They dressed the chicken for me. Dr. Taylor came in to see Bertha. She is much better, but the doctor stated she has to remain in bed for at least another week. I left to get Tynes.

He called from the station at 6 o'clock. I was glad to see him. It was mutual. I took him downstairs to dinner. Could not dine with him. We discussed history, then took a walk around the reservoir before retiring at 10 o'clock.

A beautiful day. Helen [Notis] called me from the station at 3:30. Gave me her address. She is staying with friends (Mac-Williams) in Northeast Washington. She promised to see me today. Tynes and I took another walk around the reservoir before breakfast. I had some peaches with cream, some cream of wheat, and a soft-boiled egg. I could not take milk. Tynes ate much more robustly, and I was glad of it. Later we lay about, dozed, and talked of our New York experiences.

Sunday
September
1
1929

There was a knock at the door. Opened it, and Mr. and Mrs. [Thomas and Sadie] Georges entered. He is a good friend of mine. He runs a cafeteria. Tynes was also happy to meet him. Georges said he had been trying to reach me for some time. Took us for a ride out to Northeast Washington in order to have Helen cook for us. Could not find the house, however. Returned home. She had already called, I found out later.

We cooked the chicken. Had some of it at dinnertime. Helen and Mrs. MacWilliams arrived at 5 p.m. Helen looked charming in a tan dress. Later on we took a ride to Falls Church.

Labor Day—beautiful but hot. Mrs. [Lillian] Mickey from upstairs rang my bell. Told me that she had prepared and brought me a good dinner yesterday, but was disappointed to find that I was out. Laughingly berated me for leaving a note on the door telling Helen I would be back later. Told me her sisters were in town. Went to the store. Bought corn on the cob, carrots, cream of wheat, fruit, lamb chops, etc. Had a good breakfast. Had plenty of cream, which Tynes enjoyed. The refrigerator had been full of four or five kinds of fruit and more than a pint of cream when Tynes arrived. I bought another half pint of cream each morning. According to the doctor, it is good for my stomach.

Georges finally arrived about 1 o'clock. I was late, as usual, in dressing. Finally got Helen and started to Rosslyn. Georges had neither gas nor money. He said he had expected to go to the bank. Fortunately, I had money.

Stopped at my cousins' in Rosslyn. They were eating dinner when we arrived. We had just eaten before leaving, but my cousins insisted, and in view of the great dish of nicely-browned fried chicken and other appetizing dishes on the table, my good friends could not resist. They said they were not hungry, but, oh my! Georges and Tynes vied with each other in eating. Although I did not dare eat, I enjoyed watching them, and it was plenty of fun, for both Georges and Tynes were interesting and humorous. So was Bertha, and then I was there. Later Bertha called me upstairs to talk with me. She was feeling better. Will go home tomorrow.

Went to Aunt Margaret's in Falls Church, Virginia. It is a beautiful place, but the roads were terribly dusty on account of detours. The main road is being widened. Remained there until 6 o'clock.

Returned, for Emile was to come here at six. He arrived later. We played cards until almost twelve. Georges took Helen home. By the way, she prepared some creamed chicken on toast for me since I had not eaten in Rosslyn. Under such gentle care and attention, it is a pleasure to be ill.

Tynes and I decided to walk around the reservoir first. We discussed European history and some other highlights during our walk. It was a lovely morning. Later on we decided to go to the Congressional Library. However, we could not get out of the house until almost two o'clock. We first went to the office, where I showed Tynes around, pointed out my manuscript as it stood, and finally introduced him to Dr. Woodson. Woodson treated him affably. Tynes was understandably nervous in the presence of Dr. Woodson. I could not blame him, either, for the latter so over-shadows one, especially us in the field of history, that it is difficult for a lesser person to maintain his composure in his presence. During the conversation Woodson asked Tynes whether he thought I was going to die of TB (meaning tuberculosis). Tynes answered that when he arrived, he thought that I had about given up hope (which was true).

Tuesday September 3 1929

We discussed the possibility of separate schools in Philadelphia. If so, Woodson believed it would be due to the selfish desires of a few Negro teachers to obtain teaching positions, even though it meant sacrificing the great principle of mixed schools there. It now seems inevitable that Philadelphia is doomed to segregated schools. According to Woodson those misguided teachers and their supporters are "selling their souls for a mess of pottage." No such thing is contemplated in New York City, fortunately. The latter city is saved, so far, only by its cosmopolitanism.

I should add that although I took several cathartics last evening and more again this morning, they have not yet acted, with the result that my stomach is terribly swollen and I feel miserable. It was not until while chatting with Tynes in the office that I secured some relief, after which I felt better and became more cheerful. I know I must have been depressing to Tynes. However, he never showed it; in fact, his coming probably saved my life. I really had given up.

After leaving Woodson's office, I took Tynes to Thurston's Restaurant. Later, I came home to pick up what I could here. I could not eat the restaurant fare. We walked again around the beautiful, moonlit reservoir tonight. The walk was enlivened by discussion of fraternities. Tynes told me the inside story, why my friend, Harry, and I had difficulty (unknown to me) in being taken into the fraternity. The sharp debate within the group was simply because he (Tynes) had sponsored us. [Ernest] Hemby, our sponsor, he added, finally turned against him and decided to withdraw our candidacies. Tynes fought so implacably for us, however, that the members were forced to yield to him. A decided rift occurred, thereafter, in his relationship with Hemby, partly as a matter of policy and partly on our account. Both of us agreed that fraternities are not worth the loss of good friends.

About 2 a.m. we were awakened by the ringing of my doorbell. Went downstairs and there stood my old friend [Oliver W.] Crump, a former pal, classmate, and fourth member of our "gang." We fell on each other's necks, so glad were we to see each other. Out in the car sat [John] Harmon, a little fellow from Texas, who also was a Howard classmate of mine and later received his master's degree in business from Columbia University. More recently, Harmon had assisted Woodson and [Arnett] Lindsay in a survey of Negro business which our Association had published. The title was *The Negro as a Businessman*. Another chap, Bozeman, a squat black fellow, was asleep in the rear of the car. Bozeman woke up and accompanied us to the apartment. He teaches at Paul Quinn College in Waco, Texas. Crump teaches at Wiley College in the same state. Both have master's degrees from the University of Kansas. We walked them upstairs. Tynes was delighted to meet both of them. Kidded Crump uproariously about his knickers. The upshot of the matter was that Crump was to stay with us. Bozeman and Harmon were to take the car to Flagler Place, where they would spend the night.

Crump told me that they had been on a tour, which had brought them from the Middle West to New York City. They have a new Ford sedan. Had seen and just left Hipp in New York. Crump, too, is disturbed that Harry does not teach or do something academic. Got very little sleep. I only had one bed, a day bed, which would sleep two comfortably, but not three. So we did as we generally did when we were students at Howard—flipped coins. The odd man would sleep in the middle. Crump was the unfortunate. I slept on the end near the wall. Was squeezed so tightly against the wall that my very nose was pressed against it. In that awkward position I lay until time to rise gave me some relief.

We had breakfast there. Crump set the table while I cooked. Tynes prepared the fruit. Division of labor, if you please. Later we went to find Harmon and Bozeman. By 11:30 we were ready to go and sallied forth to the United States Senate, which is convening today. We got in, despite the fact that Tynes feared we would be too late. I called Helen in order that I might take her there. Unfortunately, could not get in touch with her.

Wednesday September 4 1929

Disappointed in the Senate—no decorum. Lacked the dignity of such a body, I believe, when such giants of state craft as [Henry] Clay, [Daniel] Webster, [John] Calhoun, and others held forth. It was opening day, and nothing of importance was discussed. Did see the demagogue, or at least one of them [Senator Cole Blease], a great, shaggy-haired, crusading, racist-type of man from South Carolina, dressed in a white linen suit. Also heard a few words from the Progressive Senator, Robert La Follette of Wisconsin, and Senator [George W.] Norris, a liberal of Nebraska. A very dignified person, Vice President [Charles] Curtis, presided. What little discussion there was concerned the seating of Senator [William Scott] Vare of Pennsylvania, who, since 1928, has been denied a seat because of alleged election fraud in securing his election.

Left the Senate. Went to Manassas for the first time since 1922. Saw some friends. Went seven miles on the outskirts of town to a farm. On the way back, bought three dozen eggs (one dozen for Mrs. Mickey). Her sister had cooked a fine meal for us the day before.

Today shall always be remembered as the beginning of another episode in our lives. First of all, my company left. After a fitful nap of three hours, which, by the way, is not conducive to the recovery of a sick man, I was awakened by Tynes to prepare breakfast for Crump and Bozeman. By my allocating certain functions to each individual, breakfast, consisting of peaches and cream, oatmeal, cream of wheat, puffed rice, bacon, eggs, and cocoa, was fully prepared and eaten by 7:30. The honor of "massaging" the dishes was confined to the tender care of Bozeman, who confessed his inability to do anything else.

Crump and Bozeman, with Harmon, left about 10 o'clock. Was sorry to see them leave. We had had so much fun. Then to make matters worse, Tynes left at 1 o'clock, after we had made an unsuccessful attempt to see Dr. Wesley.

Leaving the station, I intended to go to the doctor, but decided to call Helen first. Mr. and Mrs. MacWilliams, with whom she was staying, invited me to dinner. I felt as if I were imposing, since it required extra work to cook for a patient on a diet. However, I did go.

I was dead tired, having had very little sleep the past two nights. Then, too, my apartment was topsy-turvy—unwashed dishes, dirty towels strewn here and there where the boys had bathed and left them, and the washbowl and bathtub just as men generally leave them. I wanted to go home, clean up, and hopefully secure a little rest before attending the card party with Helen tonight at the MacWilliams'. She offered to go along and help me clean up. I hesitated, realizing that it would be an imposition on her. Finally yielded, however.

Reached home about 6 o'clock. Within a short time Helen had the house in order. It is remarkable how quickly she does things.

We left for the whist party about eight o'clock. I played, but was so tired and sleepy that I felt as if I should faint. Played the first two games on sheer nerves alone. The party was dull, the room stuffy, and it seemed that Helen's presence alone made the people bearable. I finally left, after making profuse excuses, about midnight. Was so tired I did not even feel like undressing. The strain of the last three days seems to have taken its toll.

Although I had an engagement with Helen at 2:30, the fact that I lay down for a nap after breakfast, along with the stopping of my watch, caused me to miss the engagement with my doctor, as well as to arrive at Helen's at 5:05. By the way, I stopped en route at Holley's. He had been expecting me at 1 o'clock, yet it was almost 4 when I arrived.

Friday
September
6
1929

Arriving at Helen's, I found that she had been dressed since 2:30 sharp. Looked exceedingly charming in a green dress. Had scolded me before my arrival, but once I was here, she was all sweetness, as usual.

I persuaded her to come home with me. We were to go to McMillan Park around the reservoir. Instead she came here and cooked a very nice dinner for me: lamb chops, corn, carrots, rice, salad, cocoa, and ice cream for dessert. We ate at a little table. She chided me because I did not have sufficient china or silver. Georges came in with his wife. Promised to call for us later to take us for a drive. We were to walk around the reservoir; therefore, I gave Georges the key in order that he might be able to get in providing we had not returned upon his arrival. . . .

Georges has a fine sense of humor, which he shows to advantage. Is excellent company. A fine fellow, although lacking in polish. Is one of nature's jewels, true and tried metal beneath a rough exterior.

I invited Georges and his wife to breakfast tomorrow morning along with Helen. Sounds interesting with one plate, two forks, two teaspoons, no tablespoons, two cups and saucers, etc. Helen promises to come. Breakfast is to be at 8:30. On the way back, the Georges begged to be excused on the grounds of business and the fact that Mrs. Georges must leave tomorrow for Pittsburgh. Forced to acquiesce although I am not loath to have Helen here as the sole guest.

It is about 1 o'clock when I retire. Terrible hours for a sick man.

Lest I forget, Bertha is to have Helen and me to dinner

Sunday. Wanted me to come down to help her make arrangements tonight. Had to cancel it, however.

[The author chose not to publish the entry for September 7.]

Sunday
September
8
1929

Eat breakfast alone this morning. Bouyed up with the thought
I will see Helen later.

Arrived at Bertha's about 10:30. Helped her to prepare
things till 12:30. Poor thing, she is not well but could not let
Helen come here without having her to dinner. I certainly
appreciate her spirit, although I assured her that neither I nor
Helen expected such of her knowing her indisposition.

It is so late when I leave Bertha's that I phone for Helen to
meet me here. She does so. Is resplendent in a beautiful tan
dress with hat and slippers to match. We are late for dinner.
Bertha playfully chides me. Weinberg [Boyd] is there, looking
as amorously at Bertha as usual. [Weinberg has replaced Yarborough as Bertha's suitor.]

Very nice dinner. I helped Bertha to "massage" the dishes
afterwards. Then, we finally left, Weinberg taking us for a
drive in his car. Went to Potomac Park and for a drive around
the reservoir. Started to rain. Came home. Georges and a lady
came in later. Girls looked at him askance, because of what to
them appeared to be infidelity to his wife, who had left for
Pittsburgh only yesterday. Georges kept us roaring with
laughter over his many varied and unique experiences. Is a
widely travelled fellow, possessing a fine sense of humor.

Bertha and Weinberg leave about 10:30. Georges takes the
lady home. Calls for me and Helen at 12:00.

He promises to take us to Annapolis tomorrow. Attempts
to persuade Helen to cook breakfast for us tomorrow. She
declines to do so, saying that she has other things to attend to
but will cook lunch.

Monday
September
9
1929

What a day was today. I was up early, ate breakfast, and picked
up two weeks' laundry from the washerwoman before Helen
arrived at 11:30; Georges a few moments later. On now to
Annapolis! Georges' car gave trouble all the way. About seven

miles from Annapolis, the car reminded me of a steam engine. We stopped for water. After filling the radiator, we could not get the car started. It had to be towed. I tipped the driver 50 cents. Finally arrived at Helen's brother's in Annapolis. He resembles my brother, Jim. Is an upholsterer. He and wife are very likeable; made us feel right at home.

We left, after a brief stop in Mayo, a town about ten miles away, to bring a little girl to D.C., who is to work in Georges' cafeteria and, meanwhile, attend school. She is a pitiful spectacle of an ignorant child, reared by a still-more-ignorant mother. She was about sixteen, short, dark, and very well developed for a girl her age. Her hair looked as if it had not been combed in some time. She wore a plain, cheap black dress which seemed to constitute all the clothing she had on, with the exception of a pair of men's oxfords. The stockings, obviously dirty, were rolled down to the top of her shoes. An old-fashioned black staw hat was pulled down over each ear. In her hand were a tattered suitcase of soiled clothing and a live chicken. There were also a few dollars which she held clenched in her hand. These constituted, it seemed, all of her worldy possessions. My heart went out to her, as did also Helen's and Georges', as without any show of maternal or filial affection, except a casual goodbye, the girl came forward to take a seat in the car beside Helen. The mother seemed to think her duty was done when she gave the girl a live chicken and a couple of dollars. It reminded me of the tale of the prodigal son, only in this case the girl was the actor and her patrimony a chicken, instead of the more romantic gold.

Meantime, the car was losing so much water that we had to carry a five-gallon can full with us. Every three or four minutes the car needed water. Meanwhile, the radiator steamed and spouted like a "puffing billy." Added to that was the stench of burning oil, mingled with smoke. Steam poured from the engine in clouds. Finally, I made the discovery that the steam, water, and oil were issuing from the exhaust with each stroke of the pistons. That convinced both Georges and me that the cylinder head was broken. This opinion was further substantiated by a one-armed white man who appeared to know something about the mechanism of a car, of which I am frankly ignorant.

Nothing to do now but to try to find the nearest garage. We pushed the car to the top of a grade—the one-armed white man kindly assisting. It coasted down, leaving me, a sick man, almost a quarter of a mile in its wake. Finally, we engaged another white man to tow us to the nearest garage, about a mile and a half away. I must say that white persons were far more obliging than Negroes in this particular instance, for every Negro we approached had some excuse: either he was afraid that he would damage his car or he did not have time; yet all they were doing was just idling around.

The mechanic at the garage diagnosed the trouble as a broken cylinder head and told us we could not get the car until tomorrow noon. How disconcerting! Georges had business in D.C., Helen was expected back home, and there was Margaret [the child], eager to see Washington. As for me, here it was 6:30 p.m. and I, officially a sick man on a diet, with regular meals imperative, am stranded, with no food in sight! Then, too, we had fish, tomatoes, spoons, knives, forks, plates, dishes, etc., for Helen was going to cook a fine dinner with cornbread, etc. The upshot of the matter was a trek back to Annapolis for Helen, Margaret, and me, where Georges took a train to Washington. Happily, the mechanic took us to the car line.

Helen's brother laughed to see us again. His wife started preparing dinner immediately—cooked our fish, broiling mine. So wonderful of her. Helen and I went to the store, where we got crackers, since I could not eat white bread. Helen was so solicitous for me. Arrangements were made for Margaret to stay in Annapolis over night and Georges would get her in the morning. Helen and I would return to Washington by train. Her brother drove us to the station. Helen called the MacWilliams from Annapolis, telling them of our accident. They promised to meet her at the station. They did, taking me home first, and then taking Helen home.

Dr. Woodson called. Told me he was going to Cleveland Saturday. Asked if I could come in. Assured him I could. He just wanted me to be in the office during his absence. Promised him I would be there. . . .

I had promised Helen that I would take her to Arlington Cemetery and also would give her an opportunity, en route, to see some of Washington, D.C. We started out for Arlington, but I had to stop at a drug store and purchase some citrate of magnesia, drinking it there. We went from there to Rosslyn, where I wanted Helen to say goodbye to my cousins. They wanted us to remain for dinner, but we could not spare the time.

Helen was very favorably impressed with Arlington National Cemetery. We went through Lee's Mansion, saw the slave quarters, the Arch of Fame, and imposing monuments erected in this silent city to the heroes of the nation. Then I pointed out the mast and anchor of the battleship *Maine*, blown up in Havana harbor in April, 1898, which gave us the excuse to wage war with Spain, by which we acquired Puerto Rico, the Philippines, and a protectorate over Cuba. I also showed her the Confederate Monument, taking pictures of all these. Then for the most imposing and inspiring spectacle of the entire Cemetery—the amphitheater, a beautiful and spacious building, patterned after the old Roman *circus maximus*. It has no roof, but along its corridors three-thousand persons can be accommodated. There are no seats in the pit, but marble benches such as one would have encountered if he had visited the Rome of the Caesars. We took several pictures of this pretentious building, including one of me on the colonnade and one of Helen on the steps.

We were both hungry and tired. Therefore, we set our steps toward home. Helen again obliged by cooking a fine meal.

I hated to see her go, but it was late, almost 10:30, and so, reluctantly, we took a taxi, and back to the MacWilliams she went.

Friday   Just as I finished breakfast, Georges came in. He brought with
September   him a young man named Pittman, the grandson of Booker T.
13   Washington.[1] He appears to be a rather dissolute young fel-
1929   low. Is a junior at Howard University. We played whist until 5
              o'clock. Georges called his wife in Pittsburgh. Very hu-
              morous in his conversation.

              I invited Georges to dinner. He agreed. We went out to
              Thurston's Restaurant. Georges kept me in stitches by his
              marvelous sense of humor. 'Twas well because I could not
              eat. . . .

Saturday   Arrived at the office about 1:50. Woodson left for Cleveland at
September   3:15. Before going he gave me certain instructions, namely: to
14   see that the office was securely locked, and that the windows,
1929   etc. were carefully barred. He also asked me to take care of his
              mail, opening that addressed to the Associated Publishers; to
              see that whatever orders contained therein were filled; and,
              lastly, to be there each morning at eight o'clock in order that
              the girls might be able to get in. He also advised my getting in
              touch with one Alonzo Brown in case I should not be able to
              come to the office.

              Mr. and Mrs. Mickey [Bushrod and Lillian] took Helen and
              me to the Howard Theater. I went, not because I desired to,
              but because it was in keeping with the desires of Mrs. Mickey.
              Personally I detest the place. It caters to a lower class of
              Negroes. The show was the poorest excuse for a play that I
              have ever seen. Entitled "Hit the Deck." In my opinion, that is
              what should have been done to the players. The cast lacked
              everything—histrionic ability, verve, personality, and even
              beauty. Only one girl exhibited anything akin to personality

---

1. This was William Sidney Pittman, Jr. (1908–1967), the son of Booker T.
Washington's daughter, Portia Washington Pittman. William Sidney, Jr., entered
Howard University in 1927 with hopes of becoming an architect, like his father. He
earned an A.B. from Howard in 1931, in the depth of the Depression, and was
fortunate to find employment in the Washington, D.C., Post Office. Portia's biogra-
pher, Ruth Ann Stewart, characterized him as being, among Portia's three children,
"the solid, steady one, just like his father." Ruth Ann Stewart, *Portia: The Life of Portia
Washington Pittman, the Daughter of Booker T. Washington* (Garden City, N.Y., 1977).

and beauty, and she was placed in the rear, where she could not be shown to advantage. The male actors were horrible. We have much to learn. I was glad to get home. . . .

[The author chose not to publish the entry for September 15. No entries were made from September 16 through October 3.]

Friday
October 4
1929

A significant day upon which to resume my diary. A most distinguished guest arrived in D.C. today. He is no less a person than Ramsay MacDonald, the Prime Minister of England. He is a Laborite. Mr. MacDonald was accompanied by his daughter, Ishbel, who is about 26 years of age.

The purpose of MacDonald's visit here is to confer with President Hoover and Secretary of State [Henry L.] Stimson, in order to ascertain whether a concordat between the two great English-speaking nations, England and the United States, respecting naval strength, is possible. To date, several conferences have been held since the Washington Disarmament fiasco in 1922. At that convocation of the powers, we were made the goat, scrapping millions of dollars' worth of first-class battleships and uncompleted vessels to scale down to the agreed on 5–5–3 ratio. In return, England, always the master diplomatist, proceeded to demolish a couple of unseaworthy and obsolete ships, then, with the utmost *sangfroid*, constructed the most powerful naval base in the world at Singapore. We were hoodwinked then.

Several conferences at Geneva during the Coolidge Administration to bring about some restriction in naval armaments, while assuring us parity with the strongest naval power, England, consistently failed. England strictly maintained that she must have ample ships to guard her far-flung commerce. And we as strongly maintained—after having had our fingers singed in 1922–that whatever the size of England's navy, ours must be on parity. Thus failed the conference of 1927. Also the conference of 1929. Both were held at Geneva.

Last year it seems that we became sort of peeved and told

England, frankly, that if she did not heed our claim to parity we would simply build the most powerful navy in the world. And even the mistress of the seas could not deny us the ability to do so. We had the money. England did not.

Neither the Liberal nor the Conservative government of England could be depended upon to consider any naval reduction which would insure equal naval strength to the United States. MacDonald's efforts at least seem to have behind them some aspect of sincerity. If the Scottish premier cannot arrange an agreement acceptable to both nations, it will be doubtful whether any British statesman will be able to consummate the same in the near future.

Of course, I am ready to agree with MacDonald that, were it a question solely between the United States and England, naval reduction could be decided within five minutes. But John Bull must always be wary of a possible coalition of its potential enemies: France, Japan, Italy, and Germany. In order to maintain her insular integrity, and at the same time to protect adequately the vast sea lanes which bring to her the vital necessities of life, in order to ensure these commodities in case of war, England feels that her navy must be equal to the combined strength of at least the three above-mentioned powers.

There exists little likelihood of a struggle between the United States and England, unless something very extraordinary should happen. An accord with us, if the other nations could be left out of the equation, would not be difficult of accomplishing.

This is virtually the first chance a Labor Government has had in England. That is, if we exclude the brief tenure of the party in 1924. At that time a coalition, which put the Laborites in office, was not able to sustain it [office] on a vote of confidence. Now the party seems to be more strongly entrenched; and [Philip] Snowden's coup at the Reparations Conference last month, where he obstinately and successfully held out for England's share of the indemnity from Germany under the Dawes Plan instead of according to the Young Settlement, served to bring the party even closer into the esteem of the British people as a whole. Not only that, but it exerted the desired effect of aligning Conservatives and Liberals as well-wishers of the new government.

Mr. MacDonald arrived here at 4 o'clock, having come from New York by special train. Is tall, with a very pleasing and amiable appearance. Miss MacDonald is somewhat shorter, a little plump, but presenting a picture of clean, vigorous, strong-limbed womanhood. She does not use either paint or powder. Her fondest wish is to see a baseball game. That desire will be gratified, for the Mayor of Philadelphia has invited both the Premier and his daughter to see the World Series, part of which will be played in that city.

Naturally, all the papers are featuring the MacDonalds both in the headlines and in pictures.

A more sinister bit of news has been the rioting in the State Prison at Canon City, Colorado. Here 150 prisoners mutinied and set fire to many of the buildings. They captured the arsenal, took several guards prisoner, and barricaded themselves in one of the buildings. Here, for a day and a half they defied over 500 officers and national guardsmen. From their stronghold, they dispatched communications to the warden, threatening to kill the guards unless he permitted them free access to quit the prison. The warden refusing, the convicts murdered seven guards in cold blood. Another lost his reason as a result of fear. Finding all resistance futile after 36 hours of fighting, the ringleaders of the outbreak committed suicide.

The prison situation has certainly become acute. Outbreaks are occurring with startling frequency. Everyone remembers the desperate mutiny of the prisoners at Dannemora and Auburn prisons in New York State and at the Federal Prison at Leavenworth, Kansas. Overcrowding was the cause in those instances. The fact remains, however, that our prison population is becoming a problem. However, so long as crimes are still being committed, due chiefly to "Volsteadism" [prohibition], our prisons will likely be well-tenanted and troubles will continue to occur.

Arrangements are being made for the funeral of Herr [Gustav] Stresemann, Germany's Foreign Minister, a great post-war statesman of that country. Died suddenly Tuesdsay.

My work is progressing slowly. In fact, I should not be working at all. Hope to complete the survey by October 31st. I know Woodson is quite impatient. But I have given my all on this work, especially up to the last of June, when I collapsed in the office. I should have taken a rest in April.

By the way, Woodson has a scathing sense of humor. I met him on U Street last night on my way home from dinner. The weather had turned sharply cold and, espying me without a topcoat, he remarked, "You'd better get your overcoat, Mr. Greene," adding sardonically, "if you have one!"

Saturday
October 5
1929

MacDonald goes to President Hoover's camp tomorrow for a chat. It is quite possible that these two matter-of-fact men will talk things over while indulging in Hoover's favorite sport of angling, or while resting in the secluded fastnesses of his estates.

America has taken Miss MacDonald for its own.

Received a letter from Harry [Hipp] today. Relieved my mind upon a very tender subject.

Sunday
October 6
1929

Beautiful day. MacDonald is President Hoover's guest at the latter's lodge outside of Madison, Virginia, on the historic waters of the Rapidan River, reminiscent of one of the Civil War's bloodiest encounters. According to today's *Washington Post* they discussed the possibilities of world peace before the burning logs of an open fireplace.

It has developed that the American Federation of Labor does not look with favor upon any formal meeting with Mac-Donald, although the latter is a Laborite. According to Mr. [William] Green, President of the American Federation of Labor, he will not be present at the dinner given in honor of MacDonald in New York on Friday, October 11, nor will he designate a committee to represent him. The reason is because of the inclusion of Socialists, against which party the A.F. of L. is irreconcilably opposed.

Whiskey still floods the country, even the capital. Our dry amendment is a laughing stock. A new dry squad has just been named to stem the flow of *"spirits frumenti."*

Marcus Garvey, leader of the Negro Improvement Society [Association] and chief protagonist of the Back-to-Africa movement, with a vast array of hollow titles, has been jailed in Jamaica on a contempt of court charge. Garvey is dangerous to England because of his potentiality for sowing seeds of dissension among the black and other colored races of England's heterogeneous empire. He would be even more dangerous than Ghandi, did the Negroes have such thoroughness of organization as characterized the Indian's followers.

Garvey started his Negro Improvement Association in 1920. [Garvey founded the Universal Negro Improvement Association (UNIA) in Jamaica in 1914 and brought his movement to the United States in 1916.] His object was to free Negroes throughout the world from social, economic, and political oppression and send them back to Africa; and in the heart of that country (God only knows from where, how, or from whom he would secure the land) would rear a magnificent black empire, which, in time, would restore the glories of the ancient Songhay Empire and would hold its own with the great white states of today. Although this project was a realization only within the area of a fertile and imaginative brain, Garvey had already clothed himself with the high-sounding title of Emperor, and rumor has it he had even created certain nobles for his court. At any rate, judged by the splendor of his uniforms alone, he would be deemed by the casual observer as mighty as the former Czar of all the Russians. Garvey was jailed in the United States in 1920, allegedly for using the mails to defraud, then was deported.[2]

I am heartily in favor of one aspect of his plan, namely, to render the Negro as *economically self sufficient* as any group might hope to be in this age of social and economic interdependence. But the back-to-Africa movement is at best

---

2. Charges of using the mail to defraud in connection with selling stock in his Black Star shipping line were brought against Garvey in 1922. In 1923, he was convicted and sentenced to five years in the federal penitentiary, but he remained free while his appeals were being heard. Garvey's appeal was disallowed in February, 1925, and he began serving his sentence. In December, 1927, President Calvin Coolidge commuted his sentence, but Garvey was deported to Jamaica as a convicted alien felon. He died in England in 1940.

chimerical. What could not be done between 1820 and 1860, under the goad of slavery, certainly offers little probability of success in freedom, despite the political, social, and economic disabilities under which the Negro lives.

So many schools of nursing bar Negroes that it seems of interest to note that two young Negro women, Misses Frances Harris and Letitia Campfield, of Roxbury and Cambridge, Massachusetts, respectively, have been admitted to the nurses' class at Boston City Hospital. According to the Washington *Post*, "The action of the trustees establishes a precedent in the qualifying of Negro students. The entrance of the young women to the hospital nursing classes marks the first time in the history of the Institution, according to officials, that young women of the Negro race have been admitted."

It is indeed a refreshing bit of information, which I hope will be followed by other Northern hospitals and nurses' training schools, for Negro nurses with sound training are badly needed, especially in parts of the South where black physicians are few and white doctors often refuse to treat Negro patients.

Went to see Emile after dinner. Surprised to find him ill—an attack of the grippe. Mr. Shean, a young man who has recently been appointed Professor of Romance Languages at Howard University, came in. Informed me of Hosea Campbell's eccentricities at Wilberforce University in Ohio. The latter was compelled to leave there after three months' service. Is now head of the Lincoln Scholarship Agency. I really don't know how he does it!

Monday
October 7
1929

MacDonald and Hoover have reached a rapprochement upon the naval problem. To quote the British Premier: "We have met together and we have said 'What is all this bother about parity?' Parity? Take it without reserve, heaped up and flowing over. That was the only condition under which competitive armaments could be stopped and we could be stopped, and we could create a public psychology, which could pursue the fruitful and successful avenues of peaceful cooperation."

Today the Prime Minister spoke to the Senate. He hoped,

among other things, that his visit will remove misunderstanding. To judge by a cartoon in the *Washington Star*, that has already been consummated. Tonight John Bull and Uncle Sam were depicted pipe in hand and slapping one another playfully on the shoulder, their faces wreathed in a broad grin.

It is to be hoped that war will be outlawed, but not with the present cosmic *status quo*—with the colored races of the world submerged by the Caucasians. War, unfortunately, is apparently the only medium through which the darker races can rise to their own proper sphere. Had such a covenant as the Kellogg Multilateral Peace Treaty been in force in 1775, in all likelihood there would have been no United States today.

Faint echoes of the past were heard again today when a jury of eight men and four women was chosen to try ex-Secretary of the Interior, Albert B. Fall. The latter has been under indictment for bribery, growing out of his alleged acceptance of one hundred thousand dollars in the leasing of naval oil lands to Edward L. Doheny, oil magnate. This case has dragged along since Harding's administration. It is the sequel to the famous Teapot Dome Scandal, when Senators, the alien property custodian, and cabinet offices were involved. Truly one of our great national scandals.

Invitations will be sent this week to the great powers—United States, France, Italy, and Japan—for a naval conference to be held in London sometime in January. England is preparing for an exchange of ambassadors with Russia, after a long suspension of diplomatic relations.

The loss of Stresemann, late Foreign Minister of Germany, may cause a storm, not only in Germany, but in Europe as a whole. He favored the Young Plan of reparations settlement, as well as a French-German rapprochement. He also lent his support to [Aristide] Briand's plan for a United States of Europe. He objected, however, to any combination of European powers aimed against the United States. Dr. Julius Curtius, German Minister of Economic Affairs and one of Germany's representatives at the Peace Conference, has been assigned Stresemann's portfolio, *ad interim*.

In the Far East, the death of Baron [Giichi] Tanaka of Japan left the Conservative Party, of which he was a leader, in disarray.

Sputterings of war and revolution still are audible in Manchuria, and clashes are reported to have occurred between Russian and Japanese troops.

Concerning the Negro: Columbia University is backing Negro education in the South. One thousand dollars has been given by that master friend of the Negroes, Julius Rosenwald, to bring Negro speakers to Teachers College, that great incubator of Negro teachers, to discuss the needs of the Southern Negro regarding education. Miss Mabel Carney of Teachers College announced that educational opportunity for Negro children in the United States is only one-fifth what it is for white children. Teachers of both races will study the educational problems. It was found that states like Mississippi, Alabama, Georgia, and South Carolina have only about six thousand dollars in taxable property behind the education of each child, whereas Nevada, Iowa, and Oregon have between thirty-four and twenty-eight thousand dollars. No wonder Southern Negroes are victimized educationally!

In this connection, Count [Hermann] Keyserling, the German social philosopher, opines that the white man may yet lose control of America. Says he, the only distinctive contribution of America has been the Negro's: namely, his songs and his dancing. Feels the Negro has undergone a metamorphosis since his transfer from Africa.

Dr. Woodson is busy arranging for the Annual Meeting of the Association. I am glad to see that Dr. Wesley is scheduled to speak. It probably means that the two have buried the hatchet. At least I hope so. They are the two outstanding men in the field of Negro History, with Wesley as Woodson's logical successor. It is a pity they cannot get along professionally.

Negroes are still scoring successes on the stage abroad, especially in England and France. The Prince of Wales personally congratulated Nora Holt Ray, a Negro singer, after she had carried the London Theatre by storm through her rendition of *West End Blues*.

It is definitely known that bids for the naval reduction conference to be held in London in January, 1930, have been received
by the various nations. Japan was the first nation to make this
evident to the world, publishing her invitation today.

The invitation, consisting of about a thousand words, states that agreement had been reached on the following:

1. The Kellogg-Briand Pact is the starting point of the agreement. (This anti-war pact is a tribute to ex-Secretary of State Frank B. Kellogg and was ratified last year.)
2. Anglo-American parity in all naval categories shall be reached by the end of 1936. *Our* demand is granted here.
3. Desirability to reconsider battleship replacement programs of the Washington Conference of 1922 with a view toward diminishing the amount of replacement construction therein implied.
4. Total abolition of submarines, subject to conference with other naval powers.

Although official Washington is at variance as to the wisdom and ultimate success of the forthcoming conference, one must admit, at least, that it is a step in the direction of peace, a step forced more by the awful destructive potentialities of war and the diminishing exchequers of foreign powers than by anything else. Then, too, there is an anti-war psychology existent among most nations today.

Am still busy at the office. Woodson is making plans for the Annual Meeting.

World Series started today. Philadelphia Athletics beat Chicago Cubs: 3–1.

Ex-Secretary Fall, on trial for conspiracy in the leasing of government oil lands, was stricken in the courtroom here today. It is feared the trial may be delayed. Fall's doctor holds continuation of the trial will result in the patient's death. Fall is afflicted with bronchial troubles.

Bertha came by tonight to wash her hair.

Wednesday
October 9
1929

It is generally believed here in Washington official circles that the accord on naval policies will end the suspicion of powers on disarmament. Old Aristide Briand has already laid the British invitation to the Disarmament Conference before the French Naval Conference, asking them to study it in detail. Prime Minister MacDonald apparently finds his stay here quite profitable so far.

The second horrible murder here within a month has shocked this city. This morning a girl was found strangled to death at the fashionable Roosevelt Hotel on Sixteenth St. N.W., with her paramour kneeling beside her death-bed, where he had kept vigil for 24 hours. A few weeks ago, the strangling of a pretty nurse caused upheaval in the police department, due to alleged attempts of officials to cover up evidence. Only the persistence of policeman Robert Allen forced an inquiry into the murder by the Grand Jury. It resulted in the suspension of two high officials, the exoneration of Allen, who had been suspended, and the incarceration of [Robert] McPherson, the husband, on a charge of murder.

Went to movies tonight alone.

The Athletics beat the Cubs again, 9–3.

Thursday
October 10
1929

Ramsay MacDonald quits Washington, D.C., today for New York, where he will spend four days. Apparently, he is satisfied with the outcome of his mission to the United States.

It seems that despite all the hullabaloo engendered over mixed marriages, events still prove that human nature is far stronger than man-made restrictions. The latest advent into mixed matrimony is Phil Edwards, sensational runner, Olympic star, track luminary of New York University, and team captain, who will be wedded to Miss Edith Oedelshoff, daughter of a former German offical, next Thursday. They have the consent of their parents. The bride-elect is 19; Edwards, 27.

That "great race orator," DePriest, who probably has busied himself dispensing more "nothing" from the platform (or rostrum, as you will) than any other Negro since his election as Representative, now threatens to introduce a bill in Congress to compel all unnaturalized foreigners, including black West Indians, to pay a residence tax. Impractical as it is absurd, but it is like all of DePriest's rantings. He injures his cause by his excessive loquacity, and the Negro newspapers cause more detriment than good to the race by playing up his every utterance and gesture. Some of his speeches are quite crude. But then, they are as refined as [J. Thomas] Heflin's, the Southern demagogue.

The race prejudice bugaboo again! Last week a Boston hospital shattered precedent by admitting two Negro girls as student nurses. This week Miss Ellen C. Daley, who has been superintendent of the Institution for 10 years, resigned, giving no reason. Circumstances point to her resignation, however, as a silent protest against the admission of the Negro students. It will be interesting to see what further developments follow in this, the cradle city of American liberty.

Marcus Garvey, who intimated that several of His Majesty's Justices are notorious tiplers, is now lodged and boarded as a "guest" of the British government in a cell in Jamaica. He asserts, however, that "only death can cease my activities in a cause I believe righteous. I can promise my enemies that I shall be an everlasting flea in their collars." Thus Marcus Garvey! Pity the wearer of the collars!

Although Negro Federal appointees have not yet materialized, several are holding desirable positions under the various state governments. Last week Governor [Louis L.] Emmerson of Illinois appointed Charles Rice, Negro of Mound City, Illinois, Assistant Commerce Commissioner on the Illinois Commerce Commission. This post, formerly held by DePriest, carries an annual stipend of five thousand dollars.

[15] My First Annual Meeting

Friday
October 11
1929 New York has taken Prime Minister [J. Ramsay] MacDonald unto its heart today. The Britisher shows signs of fatigue. Italy has accepted the arms invitation.

The preparations for the Annual Meeting of the Association for the Study of Negro Life and History go on apace here. The office is a veritable beehive. Dr. Woodson works incessantly.

Today a white salesman called on Woodson. He told Woodson he could make him rich on his books. Woodson listened, then told him he had no interest in getting rich. Personally I thought Woodson made a mistake not to accept his offer. Did not tell him so.

Woodson expects to write "The Negro in Africa" during the winter; it will be the first volume of the Negro History Series. I should like to see the series divided as follows: Volume I, *The Negro in Africa Until the Beginning of the American Slave Trade*; Volume II, *Negro Slavery in the North*; Volume III, *Negro Slavery in the South*; Volume IV, *The Negro in Reconstruction*; Volume V, *The Negro Since 1890*. I think that would make a fairly respresentative covering of the topic. I should certainly like to write the volume on the Northern Negro.

My work is progressing slowly, but surely. Woodson is going to Norfolk tomorrow in search of manuscripts.

There seems to persist here a rumor that an alliance has been consummated between America and Britain. However, Secretary of State [Henry L.] Stimson today declared such statements unfounded. The two countries will use "moral influence" to preserve the peace.

Secretary [Albert B.] Fall, whose trial was halted because of his precarious health condition, entered court today in a wheel chair. His counsel successfully opposed the government's motion for a mistrial.

Woodson went to Norfolk, Virginia, at 6 o'clock. By the way, he is doing part of the work that I am being paid for. I hope that by November I shall be able to take the field myself. Wonder what he thinks of me? That I am a damned bad investment, as so many others, in his opinion, were? Probably more so. But my fault is bad health. My interest in the field is as large as that of anyone whom he might employ. I have my ambitions also in the field of history. However, abnormally ill health can cause the partial wrecking of these hopes. Left office about 6:30.

Took Bertha to the movies tonight.

What a world this! While in America we make merry with wholesale murders, lynchings, stranglings, etc., old Ireland goes us one better. Yesterday fourteen masked men held up a truck containing eleven girls who were on their way to a dance at a British fortress near Londonderry, Ireland. The girls were forced to disrobe and stand shivering in the cold wind while their dresses, shoes, stockings, lingerie, and other wearing apparel were piled in a heap and burned before their eyes. They were then ordered to line up and prepare for death by shooting. Only the fact that two of the girls made their escape (which fact, being noted by the robbers, caused them all to decamp) saved the girls from death. I doubt whether the men would have made good their threat. It was believed that the men were jealous suitors, whose ire was aroused by the girls going to the dance at the fort manned by British soldiers.

What an uncertain pastime is baseball! Today the Chicago Cubs went into the 7th inning, leading 8–0. When the inning

was over, the Philadelphia Athletics were ahead by the score of
10–8, which, incidentally, was the way the game ended.

Today dawned bright and warm. One of those beautiful fall
days which makes one feel happy to be living. Rose an hour
later than usual this morning. Up late last night. After breakfast, went to the office, where I worked on manuscripts until 1
o'clock. Did not do much. Don't seem to be able to make
much progress lately. Mentally fatigued, no doubt. My physician has ordered rest, but I am hard headed.

Planned to go to Rosslyn, but by the time I had shaved and
secured a haircut it was 3:30. Fearful that my cousins had gone
out, I returned home.

Went to the park. Read several instructive as well as enter-
taining articles in the August issue of *Plain Talk*. One article,
"Do Defects Cause Genius?", by Ellen Lemond, I considered
quite plausible. The author's thesis is that for our physical
defects, we have compensatory attributes. Her thesis is that
many of the world's geniuses were consumptives, like Francis
Thompson, Percy Bysshe Shelley, Robert Browning,
[Thomas] DeQuincey, Edgar Allan Poe, John Locke, and Sir
Walter Scott. Of contemporary luminaries, Havelock Ellis,
Eugene O'Neill, Anton Chekov; deformed persons like the
great Samuel Johnson and Lord Byron of poetic fame; victims
of insanity like the Lambs [Charles and Mary], Dante, [Dante
Gabriel] Rossetti, [Samuel Taylor] Coleridge, [Arthur]
Schopenhauer, and [Friedrich Wilhelm] Nietzsche. Napoleon
was undersized; therefore his genius, she says, found expression in an insatiable longing to accomplish *big* things and to
formulate within his mind the mad scheme of dominating all
Europe. This is vicarious compensation. History will attest to
how closely Napoleon came to achieving his end. All in all, I
think her theory quite applicable to such persons. Even *I* may
aspire to something big, being undersized, ugly, etc. It certainly comforts me.

Also, there was contained therein a delightful article upon
that French master of prose, [Gustav] Flaubert, by Rose Du-
rant, the philosopher, and an unmasking of Martin Luther,

founder of Protestantism, which showed, by documentary evidence, that even Luther was fond of wine, beer, and women and did not scruple to dissimulate, if he thought the personage was of rank sufficient to warrant it. Very enjoyable reading.

Went to the office at 10 o'clock. Everything was okay.

Made some custard this morning before leaving for the office. Arrived there at 8 o'clock sharp, despite the fact that so much time was spent in preparing breakfast.

Monday
October 14
1929

I had just started the stenographer on the manuscript when a telegram came from Woodson telling me to start the girls folding letters. Obeyed his instructions.

An odd thing happened yesterday, according to the New York *Times*. A regiment of Canadian troops helped to celebrate the 150th anniversary of the birth of [Count Casimir] Pulaski, the gallant Polish general, who gave his life for American Independence in 1779, while leading a charge against the British troops at Savannah, Georgia. Could old George III have witnessed such a thing, he would probably have risen from his grave in a supreme gesture of protest.

The poor Negro worker is fast seeing the doors of occupation swinging shut against him, even in the South. According to a Houston, Texas, paper, the City Council of Jacksonville, Florida, several weeks ago, passed an ordinance restraining Negro mechanics from pursuing their trade in predominantly white districts. The same ordinance applies to white mechanics in black neighborhoods. Though on its face the law seems fair, the loss is all on the side of the Negro, for his own people cannot give the Negro artisan sufficient employment to make a living. Thus, little by little, that great army of Negro mechanics, who held sway in the Southland before the Civil War, is gradually being reduced, until soon the black artisan will find himself in the same relative position in the South as his Northern co-worker.

The Athletics put on another 9th inning rally and this time sent the dejected Cubs to final defeat in the last game of the

World Series. The Cubs have been overwhelmingly out-classed.

Irene [a pseudonym] was waiting for me. Came in. Talked with me for almost an hour and left. Is quite charming. Did not believe I had made the custard.

Expected a letter from Helen [Notis] today. Disappointed at not receiving it.

President Hoover and wife attended the ball game in Philadelphia today, while Ramsay MacDonald picked apples at Saugatuck, Connecticut.

Tuesday
October 15
1929

Rainy today. Woodson had returned when I reached the office. From the room adjoining my office floated the delicious aroma of bacon, from which I deduced he was preparing his breakfast. A wonderful man! Combined with his marvelous capacity for scholarly work, he cooks, sweeps, scrubs, washes dishes, and does every other sort of labor. This, of course, is due to the weak financial condition of the Association, which prevents him from employing much-needed help. Told me he had fair success in obtaining manuscripts.

[Charles] Lindbergh and his wife have returned from a nine-thousand mile journey in the interest of archeology. Their itinerary took them through Mexico, the West Indies, and Central America. In Yucatan, they sighted remains of the old Mayan civilization—gleaming white marble columns in the midst of the jungles. The greatest flier of all times and the least assuming! He has made a name for himself worthy of Columbus. Today, he is and has been the idol of the world since his epic-making solo flight of May, 1927.

The migration of the Negro to the North since the war has enhanced his political power. It was demonstrated by Oscar DePriest's election to Congress. Nor did it escape notice when a young Negro lawyer, Joseph L. McLemore, in St. Louis was defeated for a similar office. Now a Negro named [Hubert T.] Delaney, a former Washington school teacher and relative of Emmett J. Scott, is running for Congress from Harlem, New York, and according to the Washington *Star* and the New York *Times*, his victory is conceded. Delaney's bid was made possible by the marshaling of the Negro's political strength in Harlem, aided by the efforts of James Weldon Johnson, De-Priest, and others. His victory would be easy if the Negroes would manifest sufficient interest in politics to pay their poll tax and vote. But it is human nature, I suppose, to agitate for a privilege until it is granted, then ignore it after having received it. One likes to know that he is not prohibited from what is generally engaged in by other people. Therefore, the nearly two-hundred thousand Negroes of Harlem, the largest Negro city in the world, have been impotent politically until now. May this spell an awakening! Of course, the Negro in Harlem is handicapped, not only by the lack of interest in politics (strange, since the Negro has more freedom in New York City than elsewhere in the United States), but also because of the large West Indian element who have not become natural-ized. [Delaney won in the Republican primary by a 5 to 1 vote, but he lost the election to his white Democratic opponent, Joseph A. Gavagan.]

Negroes, too, the nation over are agitating for political plums. It was said by the Washington *Post* this morning that several Negroes are anxious for appointments as Registrar of the Treasury and Ambassador to Haiti, posts that were gener-ally held by Negroes up to the Wilson regime. Hoover's reac-tion, so far, has been a dignified silence.

After reaching home I had much fun with Irene.

Japan has wired her acceptance of Britain's invitation to attend a Naval Reduction Conference in London in January, 1931 [1930]. Acceptance, couched in about 800 words, expressed pleasure that the Kellogg[-Briand] Peace Pact had opened the way to the Conference, and that all would be the basis of agreement to restudy the Washington Treaty schedules of ship replacement with a view toward their reduction.

Wednesday October 16 1929

France, however, seems to be holding out. She does not favor the outlawing of submarines. Neither does Italy. France feels that submarines are her best security against England's overwhelming cruiser and capital ship strength. Italy, quite aggressive under [Benito] Mussolini, does not seem at all peace-inclined, for he continually prates about the coming greatness of Italy, its need for dependencies, etc. I don't want to seem ultra-pessimistic, but I would not be over-surprised to see this Conference end like the last one in Geneva—in failure.

Two distinguished personages arrived late yesterday. One was Madame [Marie] Curie, the discoverer of radium, now old, feeble, and in ill health. She comes to join in the [Thomas A.] Edison celebration, which commemorates the fiftieth anniversary of the invention of the electric light. The other distinguished person was Charles Dawes, Ambassador to Great Britain, together with his underslung pipe. Dawes won the hearts of the British people by refusing to attend court in conventional knee breeches.

Henry Ford is still trying to re-create, in Menlo Park, the original Edison City, embracing all the apparatus used by the famous scientist and the inventor when he discovered the electric light. Ford, with his vast resources, has even moved parts of the shed and whatever scraps he can find of other relics of Edison's invention, to his Edison City in Detroit. He has even had the General Electric Company re-create two dynamos which Edison used in inventing the electric light, which were subsequently lost.

Between a lobby investigation, the inquiry into the police force, plans for enforcing the liquor laws here, and the trial of Secretary Fall, reading Washingtonians have plenty on which to focus their thoughts.

Expect to finish the chapter on "Manufacturing" by tomorrow. Hope to give this study to Woodson within the next ten or so weeks.

Met Dr. [Alain] Locke yesterday. He had just returned from France two weeks ago. Is somewhat disappointing to me. With all his unusual education and contact, in my opinion, he has achieved comparatively little. I would prefer to be Carter Woodson. By the way, the latter still works indefatigably upon the Association's forthcoming Annual Meeting during October 27–30, inclusive.

[No entries were made for October 17 and 18.]

Woodson told me today why I have no place on the program of the Annual Meeting of the Association for the Study of Negro Life and History. To my surprise, he feared that I may, like A. A. Taylor, one of his former associates, and author of several studies under him, be suddenly afflicted with stage fright and be unable to deliver my paper. Evidently, he little knows how I can "gab." Dr. Vernon Johns, against whom I debated in New York, New Jersey, and Connecticut, I am sure, could disabuse his mind of that fallacy. (If that was the *real* cause?) In the case of Taylor, Woodson said (as already noted) that while speaking to the students of Union University in Richmond, Virginia, Taylor nearly collapsed from fright on the platform. Added, he feared Taylor would "wet his pants." No wonder! Woodson, himself, was there. I reminded Woodson that it was but natural that the pupil would manifest symptoms of nervousness while on trial before the "master." He retorted that Taylor was no *pupil* but an *employee* then. Granting that, with the scoffing attitude which Woodson assumes towards his subordinates, it is virtually impossible for a person to perform at his best in his presence. He is too unsympathetic, has not the faculty to put one of his colleagues at ease or for inspiring one to rise to the heights. It is a wonder how anyone can reach his full potential under Woodson.

He asked me to help him and Mr. [William M.] Brewer distribute posters tonight. I could not do so, for Mr. Brewer was at the library, and we were dependent upon the use of his car. Therefore, we postponed the distribution until Monday.

What a blessing that I was late coming home tonight. It enabled me to escape a most embarrassing situation. . . .

After setting my apartment in order, went to Rosslyn. Took my cousins a box of chocolates as a peace offering, since I had not been over to see them in more than a month. All of them had colds.

They took me to see Cousin Margaret in Falls Church. Then we visited a friend of the latter's who lives about five miles from her home. It was an inspiration. A small, but exceedingly well-kept, farm of 20 acres, with all sorts of fruit.

The house was splendidly appointed, with electric lights and furnace, and now water is being installed; bathroom fixtures are already in. The entire farm is enclosed by a wire fence, and is kept in excellent condition. Within a part of this enclosure are 400 leghorn hens.

Monday
October 21
1929

Today is the 50th anniversary of the invention of the incandescent electric lamp by Thomas Edison. In his honor, the entire world today acknowledged the debt of gratitude to this great man through the celebration of the golden jubilee.

President Hoover has gone to Michigan to speak. A radio hookup, which, in the last analysis, was made possible by Edison, enabled the aged inventor to hear the voice of [Albert] Einstein, the wizard of relativity, speaking from Germany. Truly a marvelous world in which we live, but which to our posterity will be as slow, plodding, and backward as the old horse-car of a generation back.

Woodson asked me to help distribute posters today. Unfortunately, Mr. Grant Lucas, who was to take me around, could not do so until tomorrow. I stopped by his home on my way to dinner, where he informed me of his inability to do anything tonight.

Started back to the office to distribute some of the posters myself, but met [Ned] Poe coming in. He is a serious student and fraternity brother. I showed him the apartment downstairs, upon which I have lost $26.75. He became enthusiastic over it. Wanted to rent it for the fraternity.

While going downstairs I met Irene. She looked exceedingly attractive. Said nothing more than a mere greeting. She looked at me, however, as if she desired to say something more, but the moment was far too inopportune.

Incidentally, Plant, a friend of mine, had come by at noontime. He had decided not to move in with me after telling me he would take the apartment. What a pretty predicament I should have been in! I told him that his attitude convinced me of his lack of faith in the matter. He admitted it but ascribed it to some financial trouble he had experienced. Meanwhile,

I am paying for an apartment and a half, with the use of only one.

A cold, blustery day. Rained in torrents, driven by a stiff east wind. It cleared in the afternoon.

Edison has been honored by the entire world. President Hoover, in his speech at the celebration in Dearborn, Michigan, referred to the aged electrical wizard, who sat at his side, in the most glowing terms. The president stated that every American—he might with greater truth have said everybody, or the entire world—owed this genius not only a debt for the great benefactions he has brought to mankind but also a debt for the honor he has bestowed upon our country. Edison also demonstrated before an enthralled audience how the first electric lamp was conceived fifty years ago. And, to make the exposition all the more realistic, his twenty-year-old assistant at the time, now a white-haired man of seventy, performed the actual demonstration. His name is Francis Jehl.

Diplomatically, Senators [David A.] Reed of Pennsylvania and [Joseph T.] Robinson of Arkansas have been appointed to serve on the American delegation to the London Conference, which meets in January. It makes no difference whom America names in such a capacity. We would do well to keep prepared, for we are virtually tyros in diplomacy.

The stock market experienced a wild day yesterday when feverish selling saw $2,500,000,000 wiped out. That is, on paper. It was the most tremendous trading ever experienced in the market since March 26, when 8,246,740 shares were turned over, establishing a record. Today's trading stopped at about 6,000,000 shares.

Distributed placards today. Mr. Brewer drove me about. Had him come in to look at my apartment. Offered him a glass of wine, which he graciously accepted. He is a Harvard man, teaches history in the school system here. A very fine fellow. Brewer was approached for a position as teacher of history at Howard University, but turned it down. Says he will accept a professorship at the new Teachers College here.

Woodson is still busy on the convention preparations. Works indefatigably. Tells me my name appears on the program as a member of the housing committee. Modestly, he informed me that he did not desire his name to be employed too frequently. I shall function when he is not there. Told me that both Professor [E. A.] Hooten and Young are young fellows. Hooten is the Harvard Professor of Anthropology. Donald Young teaches at the University of Pennsylvania. I shall gladly cooperate, wherever, and whenever, I can.

Went to Howard University, where I had a delightful chat with Dean [Dwight Oliver Wendell] Holmes. The latter told of his playing baseball in what is now Times Square, New York, and riding on the horse cars here. He was offered a position to teach at Howard University in 1903 for $400 a year. That was considered big money then. He refused and went to St. Louis, where he received $1,040 a year. Later, in 1919, he came to Howard University. He was one of my teachers there during my student days.

Wednesday
October 23
1929

Woodson told me he wanted me to place the delegates in homes here. That was to be my work. Negroes are not accepted in the hotels. I left the office at noon. Called on Ellen Adams on my way to the library. A charming and interesting person. She told fascinating stories of her experience while serving on the grand jury. Also spoke of the timidity of Negroes in court, even when testifying as witnesses against each other. She gave various examples. Told me they were exceedingly timid when testifying against whites. She also informed me of the rank discrimination in cases where the defendant is white, the plaintiff black, or *vice versa*. The poor Negro usually is given less justice and a heavier sentence for similar crimes. She gave various illustrations, which escape me at the moment of writing.

Returned to the office about 5:30. Woodson wrapped bundles until 6:30. He works hard on the Annual Meeting.

Thursday
October 24
1929

I went to the library in the morning. Remained there until 5 o'clock digging out material.

Was late for dinner. Came home. Went back to the office.

Remained until 8:45. Went to see Bertha. She told me of a discussion she had had with a Mrs. Summers. Bertha's son, Wilcie, spent the summer in camp. Mrs. Summers contends Bertha owes her for a week's lodging and board for Wilcie. Bertha contends she paid her in advance. . . .

Met Mr. Logan, Principal of the Shaw Junior High School, today.

Friday
October 25
1929

Woodson and I had an interesting discussion on the Negro as a business man. Woodson scornfully described the Negro business man, comparatively speaking, as a *nonentity*. I spoke of the flagrant cases of exploitation in Washington and New York City. Particularly did I refer to the situation where, under the very shadow of Howard University, a Jewish store-keeper reaps a silver harvest from the students who crowd his store at lunchtime. It is as true now as it was during my student days. Woodson agreed, adding that when Jews have a holiday, the entire community is embarrassed, sometimes even unable to purchase certain needed commodities. On the other hand, he continued, when Negroes have a holiday, one would never know it, unless a number of them are arrested for disturbing the peace.

Had dinner very late this p.m. That same dull ache in the small of my back and gas on the stomach.

Found a place on Westminster Street, N.W., to house two delegates.

Saturday
October 26
1929

Called the office of the real estate man who rents the apartments in my building. Did so before he sends me a writ of dispossession. I would have paid the rent long ago, but expected to move. Had paid a half month's rent on the apartment below me, only to lose $26.75 because the person expected to share the apartment with me could not pay his share. And at this time of the year, too!

Dean [William Benyon] West of Howard called upon me at noon. Offered to rent me an apartment on the top floor of his home. Is a fraternity brother. Told me of his struggles to get an education and his subsequent coming to Howard as a teacher, his marriage, and his effort for a marginal existence. Is married and has two children. I told him I would consider his offer.

Took Bertha to see Mrs. Summers after dinner. Was amazed at the latter's attitude. Was absolutely mean. Only through the good sense of Mr. Summers was his wife made to see that Bertha, having paid her a week in advance, owed her nothing at the end of that period. Bertha was upset; Mrs. Summers, though silenced, we left in even worse humor, vowing that she would never accept another child.

Sunday October 27 1929	Did not feel well. Recurrence of stomach ailment. Suffered from headache. Ate breakfast much later than usual. Dr. Woodson called me at 2:15 p.m. I had just begun to dress, preparatory to going to the office. Woodson asked me to come down immediately. "Would he permit me to shave?" I inquired. He consented. Arrived at the office at 2:50. Found Woodson visibly perturbed. Said he could not locate the pastor of the church at which the meeting was to be held. Neither could the sexton be found. Asked me to go to the church, find either the minister (Dr. [R. W.] Brooks) or the sexton, and see that the church was opened. The meeting was scheduled to begin at 3:30 and, so far, he did not know whether any arrangements had been made for the reception of the people. Told me to look out for Miss Nannie Burroughs and Miss Jane Hunter of Cleveland. Miss Burroughs is a nationally-known person, head of the National Training School for Negro Girls in Washington, D.C. Miss Hunter is almost equally prominent for her splendid work in Cleveland, Ohio, where, through her untiring efforts and unflagging zeal, she built the Phillis Wheatley Community Center of which she is the head.

Upon arriving at the church, was gratified to find that it was not only open, but that a number of people were already present. Miss Burroughs and Miss Hunter entered a few minutes later. Miss Burroughs is a woman of medium height and build, dark complexion, and not at all good looking. However, she possesses a marked comprehension of human nature, is a very pleasant converser, and impresses one as belonging to that group of persons who do things. I believe her age varies somewhere between 40 and 50. Miss Hunter resembles Miss Burroughs as to height and build. She, however, is a mulatto and is possessed of one of the most charming personalities that it has ever been my privilege to detect in a person at first meeting. She speaks softly and her words are accompanied by a smile that issues forth like soft and delightful music.

Dr. Woodson arrived about two minutes later. I told him that I had already shown Miss Burroughs and Miss Hunter to seats in the front of the church. Woodson introduced me to them. Miss Hunter told me of her work in Cleveland. She intended at first to incorporate with the general YWCA, but then decided that she would be subject to their dictates, which would have thwarted the plans which she had in mind. Instead, she broke away, secured aid from prominent white persons, won the confidence not only of them but of her own people, and finally outgrew place after place, until today the Phillis Wheatley Community Center is housed in a magnificent, new, nine-story building. The Center now (1929) stands as the greatest factor for social good in the lives of Cleveland Negroes.

My position today was something in the nature of a *factotum*; that is, Woodson asked me to distribute programs. But, to tell the truth, already I have begun to feel the quickening impulse which this convention was to have upon me. To help, regardless of the capacity in which I served, took hold of and fired me. One could not but feel that way, bearing in mind the sacrifices of its great founder, to whom no work is too lowly.

The meeting began promptly on time. Miss Hunter presided. She told of the work of the Association in that intimate, charming fashion of hers.

Mrs. H. R. Butler, an elderly woman of Atlanta, Georgia, was next. She spoke on "Acquainting the Negro Child with his Forebears." Mrs. Butler is president of the National Congress of Colored Parents and Teachers. According to her, this

Congress, which meets regularly with the white Congress, is doing much to bring about better relations between the races in the South. A very interesting talk and well received!

Mrs. Charlotte Hawkins Brown of Palmer Memorial Institute, Sedalia, North Carolina, then spoke upon the value of the written record. She demonstrated that in the written accounts of the past, such as diaries, letters, wills, deeds, etc., are contained those indispensable materials for the impartial delineation of history. Stated also that much history has been perverted, because the historians, or some of them, failed to go to the sources. Appealed to the Negro to save all records of this sort. Well delivered, but not scholarly. She is not an historian.

Following Mrs. Brown came Dr. Mordecai Johnson, President of Howard University, and one of the leading orators of today. Gifted with a full, deep, resonant voice, fluent of speech, and blessed with the faculty of a marvelous choice of diction, this impressive speaker lauded the work of the Association. Not only did the Association, in his opinion, provide scientific works upon the Negro, setting forth, without passion, his past; it also served as a lamp, a guide to the feet of our youth in the exploration of their past, and an inspiration to achievement in the future. In addition to these things, the Association was not only educating Negro youth, but it, at the same time, bred a greater feeling of respect for the Negro in the minds of white persons. Finally, it helped to bring both races together in a bond of common brotherhood. In conclusion, President Johnson paid such a glowing tribute to Dr. Woodson that, as I listened to his words and felt the impression which they created in the minds of the throng that filled the church, had I been asked my choice between becoming either President Hoover or Carter G. Woodson, at that moment, I would have answered unhesitatingly—*Carter G. Woodson.*

No collection was lifted, although Dr. Woodson did tell the audience that anyone who desired to join might give me his subscription upon leaving the church. Several persons did so.

Met Mr. Cooley from Cleveland. He teaches in the Phillis

Wheatley Community Center and came to the conference with Miss Hunter. A very likeable fellow. Is a fraternity brother. Miss Hunter charged me to bring him to the tea, given later for the delegates and their friends at Mrs. Shippens, 1901 Nineteenth Street, N.W. [The account of the meeting published in the *Journal of Negro History* stated that the tea was at the home of Mr. Zeph Moore.]

I took the remainder of the programs back to the office. Cooley went with me. I showed him around. He was gratified to know we had such a place.

Cooley is stopping at Mr. and Mrs. Davidson's, where I formerly boarded. He went there while I came home for dinner. Could not bring him here because, since I am dieting, I knew that my food would be utterly tasteless to him.

Ate in a great hurry. Took program to Irene. She gave me some custard.

Was late in calling for Cooley. Promised to do so about 6:30; arrived about 7. Off we went to the tea.

It was an elaborate tea in a very beautiful and spacious home. The College Club was the host. Beautiful Mrs. [Louise] Wesley poured tea. We were introduced to a long line of hostesses, including Miss Milton, a French teacher. She is a cousin of Mrs. Thomas Anderson of Shelton, Connecticut, a friend of our family. I also met Mr. [S. W.] Rutherford, head of the National Benefit Life Insurance Company, the largest Negro business establishment in the world. Invited me to the office on Tuesday. Mrs. Rutherford was also quite charming. Some years ago [1898], she said, her husband started his business in an attic and sold insurance from a bicycle. Today he employs over 200 persons and his business is valued at $6,000,000. It is housed in a five-story building. Mrs. Lena Trent Gordon of Philadelphia was also there. Did not like her. Appeared too haughty. Then, too, I was so short. Had a very fine chat with Mrs. H. R. Butler of Atlantic City. Became very fond of her. Mr. [John Anderson] Lankford, one of the two Negro architects in Washington, D.C., was also present. A man of commanding presence. He deplored the fact that the Negro had lost his once-high position in the trades here. I only wish that this tea, with its beautifully-gowned women, its refined and cultured gentlemen, the large, finely-furnished and decorated home in which it was held, and the assemblage of men and women, high in every walk of life, might be viewed by some of the other group, who hold that refinement, culture, and high attainment are foreign to people of Negro blood.

Left the tea in a rhapsody of joy that I was connected with such an institution. Took Cooley to the theater. Leaving, my head was aching terribly. Stopped en route home and had the druggist prepare a dose of castor oil for me.

Monday
October 28
1929

Felt somewhat better this morning but far from well. After a day at the office, left for the dinner at the Whitelaw Hotel in honor of the members of the Association and the visting delegates. Accompanied Dr. Woodson. Took programs and membership cards along. Saw my good friend, Mrs. Butler, just before dinner. Chatted with her. The dinner itself was attended by a hundred or more persons. I sat at the table opposite Dr. Donald Young of the University of Pennsylvania, to whom I was introduced by Mr. Brewer, who sat opposite me beside his charming wife. Dr. [Alain] Locke sat at a table just above me. Glad he was not beside me. He always makes me feel a little uncomfortable, yet I know he is an outstanding man.

I should mention that my life is virtually being taken in my own hands to eat this food, fried chicken, etc., when, for over two months, I have been dieting. But then, I could not very well absent myself. We kept up a spirited conversation at our table. I found Dr. Young a likeable chap. Is a young fellow, also. By the way, he is one of the chief speakers on the program for tomorrow. I should mention, also, that Mrs. Harris, Dr. Woodson's personal secretary, was also present. Poor thing! She felt woefully out of place and requested me to remain near her. She told me afterwards that she had eaten virtually nothing. As well as she liked fried chicken, she confessed that she feared to cut it, lest it jump out of the plate and embarrass her. She had my sympathy.

Oh yes, the customary speeches! Dr. Woodson introduced Dr. J. Hayden Johnson, a physician, who was to act as toastmaster. The guests were welcomed in an address by Dr. D. Price Hurst. It consisted chiefly in an adulatory reference to Dr. Woodson, which was certainly merited.

After the response, a Mr. Hodges, a member of the Kansas City Branch of the Association rose. He was introduced by Dr. Woodson. He told a humorous story which Dr. Woodson had related upon seeing him in the corridor of the hotel. The former's version was as follows: Reverend Bacote of Kansas City had asked him (Woodson) to speak at a certain function in that city. The reverend gentleman had taken special precautions to impress upon Dr. Woodson that his appearance at the meeting was imperative. Therefore, when he met Dr. Woodson at the station, his greeting was, "Well, nigger, you did keep your word, didn't you?" Dr. Woodson had told Mr. Hodges that seeing him there reminded him of the words of Reverend Bacote. Now Mr. Hodges told the story, much to the delectation of the guests.

Incidentally, Mr. Hodges suffered gross inconvenience in attending the conference. He left Kansas City Saturday and arrived only a few hours ago. He made the trip by bus and found, to his dismay, that practically every convenience was lacking for the colored passenger. He could secure nothing to eat, even at the regular bus stops and depots, despite the fact that he was above the Mason-Dixon Line. As a result, he arrived tired, bedraggled, hungry, and nursing a well-developed animosity against the bus company concerned. According to him, he has experienced his last ride of any considerable distance by bus, and he holds that no Negro has any business riding on such conveyances. One pays heavily in this country for the "privilege" of being black, or possessing any recognizable iota of such "despised" blood.

From the dinner we now repaired to the Armstrong [Manual Training] High School Auditorium where a pageant, "When Truth Gets a Hearing," is to be staged by students of the National Training School for [Negro] Girls, of which Miss Nannie Burroughs is principal. First, however, Dr. Woodson and I took Mrs. Harris home. He is very considerate of her, asked whether she had a car to get home. Meanwhile, I secured her wraps from the checkroom, together with those of Mrs. Georgia Douglas Johnson, the Negro poetess. On the way home, Mrs. Harris remarked she was hungry. Said she would eat dinner before going to bed. I was shocked.

The Armstrong Auditorium proved a revelation to me. This was my first visit here. It is commodious, beautiful, with a large stage. The play was an allegory: A court of justice with Justice presiding. *Ill Will, Opposition,* and *Prejudice* open their case against the Negro: He must be kept down, must have a place and be kept there. And, furthermore, he cannot rise because he has not done so in the past and, surely, his future will be no more glorious. The Negro, assured by *Justice* that all who come before her court will be dealt with impartially, presents his case. With the aid of *History, Goodwill, Fair Play, Love, Mercy* et al., he cites overwhelming proof of his progress and also the impediments placed in his way by *Oppostion, Ill Will,* and *Prejudice,* such as *Segregation, Jim Crowism,* the defilement of Negro women, and the denial of equal opportunity for the Negro to share in the blessings of the land he has helped to create. Of course, *Justice* renders a decision in favor of the Negro.

The play is the most powerful piece of propaganda I have yet seen on behalf of the Negro. It ought to be seen by white persons as well as black. It is a little too long (it consumed two and a half hours), it contains a little too much religion, and some of the songs are not appropriate to the characters. But it also possesses a wealth of feeling and, in its utter simplicity, renders itself easily understandable even to those of meager intelligence. Moreover, there is nothing in it to give offense to the white group even if shown them. I thought highly of it. The acting was commendable, especially that of *Opposition* and *Justice.* Dr. Woodson felt similarly concerning it. He will publish it. We both congratulated Miss Burroughs.

Somehow I feel uplifted, something akin to the person at a revival meeting, who is full of the spirit, and can't tell the people about it. Was introduced to Mrs. Shadd [probably Miss

Marion P. Shadd, Assistant Superintendent of Schools], Mrs. Dumas [probably the wife of Mitchell O. Dumas, a dentist], and Mrs. McAdoo. The former is a member of Washington's old Negro aristocracy; the second, the wife of one of the city's foremost physicians; and the latter, the director of the YWCA. I acted as their escort, taking them home. They proved good company. Finally arrived home about 11:30. Tired, but stimulated.

Arrived at the office just in time to leave with Dr. Woodson for Garnett-Patterson Junior High School, where the first session takes place at 11 o'clock. Registration, however, was scheduled to begin at 10. The auditorium here is even more spacious than Armstrong's, with a projector, large stage, etc. I should mention that the school embodies the latest designs and advancements in school buildings, and is the newest and best-equipped junior high school in the city for white or black. It has a splendid cafeteria, moving picture machine, radio, automatic ventilation; in fact, everything that the ultra-modern school demands. I had an opportunity of speaking at Shaw Junior High School in place of Dr. Woodson. This is another fine school, situated at Seventh Street and Rhode Island Avenue N.W. It was formerly McKinley High School, for white students only. This illustrates the intra-urban movement of Washington Negroes in the Northwest section pushing toward Howard University as white residents migrate to the suburbs.

Tuesday October 29 1929

The first session this morning was taken up with a round-table discussion on Negro History. It seemed to be unanimously agreed, from Bishop [R. A.] Carter, who presided, to the lowliest person there, that the Negro was suffering from an inferiority complex, and that the best means of combating such was to inoculate him with a virus of the achievements of his own race, mainly through Negro history, such as Dr. Woodson is sponsoring.

[No entries were made for October 30 through November 10.]

Monday   Felt a recurrence of my stomach ailment today. After dinner
November   went to movies. Taxied home in the hope that I might arrive in
11   time to hear part of the opera *Aida*, broadcast from the
1929   Chicago Civic Opera Company. Disappointed. Spent 50
cents extra for the ride home, missed the exercise the walk
home would have given me, only to find that the opera would
not be broadcast until 11:00 p.m. And when that hour arrived,
everyone who had a radio, much to my dismay, was tuning in
on jazz. My love of good music will yet prompt me to purchase a radio. Must apprise Dr. Woodson of my plan for a
book of African folk hero tales tomorrow.

[16]   Woodson, the Study, and Fund Raising

On my way home from the office tonight met Helen Massey. Looked both charming and pretty. Although I was hastening, because of my intention to return to the office, I could not resist accompanying her to a drug store at the corner of Seventh and Florida Avenue, N.W., where she purchased some soda mint tablets. She is suffering from indigestion. Took her to the movies. Told her of my apartment. She wanted to come up and see it a moment. Waxed enthusiastic over it. I went out to get some ice cream. Returning, found her ensconced among the pillows on the sofa. Looked like a little doll under the soft red light. We ate, laughed, and joked. She became drowsy. Finally took her home.

Rose about 9:00 a.m. Helen dropped by. Helped me prepare breakfast. Became reminiscent. Told me that she had been married. Her husband was a graduate of Hampton, a plumber by trade. Married and lived in Summit, South Carolina, for a year or more. Was supremely happy for a while. Worshipped her husband, and thought he loved her. No doubt he did. They had a little child about seventeen months of age, and were buying their home, which was very nicely furnished. All the plumbing work had been installed by her husband. She taught school and, out of her savings, bought a new piano,

upon which she gave lessons to the children of the neighborhood. Again, she repeated that, so far, her married life had
been a replica of heaven.

But a serpent in the guise of religious fanaticism was to
destroy the happiness of these young people, even as it has
blasted the joys of many a home in the past. Her husband
suddenly became seized with the inspiration that he was God-
ordained to preach. Along with it, he straightaway forsook his
trade. She, willing to encourage him in every way, advised
that he continue his vocation, while seeking holy orders, so
that during the transition, the family would not suffer. To this
he paid no heed, his every thought being so concentrated upon
religion that it warped and dwarfed every other feeling, sentiment, or rational element within him. While he discoursed
upon the preparation for eternal rest, she had to carry on the
expenses of the home by teaching school and giving piano
lessons.

Finally, she said, his fanaticism grew to such an extent that
he threatened to kill her. For a long while she feared to go to
bed. One night, while asleep, she was wakened by his leaving
the room. Feigning sleep, she listened while he crept downstairs. She could hear him plundering through the drawers of
the kitchen cabinet. Finally, she said, he returned, stole into
the room, and approached the bed. As he neared it, she suddenly sat bolt upright, stifling a scream, for in his hand he
carried a long, naked bread knife. Gathering presence of mind,
she shouted, "If you come near me, I'll kill you." Though
unarmed, her words had the effect of cowering him, and he
slunk away from the bed and sat down in a rocker. Throughout the remainder of the night, she feared to close her eyes.
Neither did he come to bed, but sat there staring at her with
the knife in his hands.

I interrupted to ask whether she had brought charges against
him. Her answer was, "No." He was not only her husband,
but such a disclosure would result in scandal and notoriety
being visited upon a family which had always been respected
in the city. I admired her courage, also her faith, when she
added that she hoped he would soon find himself and put aside

his fanaticism. Unfortunately, I advised her, usually only death relieves us of such bigots.

The climax of the affair came when her little child was taken ill. In despair, she asked him to go to the drug store for some medicine. He refused, saying that he had to go to church. Afraid to leave the infant alone with him, she sent a message to her mother, who lived at the other end of the town. He paid no attention to the little one, in the meantime. Her mother found the child desperately ill. Specialists were called in, but their skill, combined with the ordinary practitioner's, proved futile, and the little child passed away. All the funeral arrangements, payment of bills, etc., fell upon her. To add to her woes, he accused her of having murdered the child, notwithstanding the fact that he had refused to lift one solitary finger to aid it in its illness.

Then came the basest part of the actions of this prospective man of God. After the funeral, her mother wanted them to spend a week at her home in order that they might forget their bereavement. He advised *her* to go, saying that he would join her on the following day. She did so. The next day, however, he did not appear. Another day, and another, elapsed. A week passed. Fearing that something had happened to him, she returned to her home. Upon entering it, she found it empty. Everything had been removed. The house was barren. Overcome, she went next door to his mother's; there she found he had deposited the furniture. Her piano was sold. He himself had vanished. Naturally, she felt as if her world had crumbled and fallen all about and upon her. Her hopes, so bright a few years ago, now absolutely blighted! Crushed, she returned to her mother's, careless of whether she lived or died. During the next few years, only her mother, she confessed, enabled her to live. I interrupted her to ask whether she had him prosecuted. "No," she replied, "if he desired to go, let him." She did recover her furniture, however, but only through the aid of a lawyer. Her piano was never retrieved.

I listened, and my heart went out to this sweet little woman, even as my feelings have leapt in commiseration at the tale of blasted love and happiness recounted to me by others.

She also told me of one Maxwell, the book dealer where she worked for a while. Spoke of his advances, and of his callousness, his desire to make his employees his mistresses, and the subsequent loss of her job as a penalty for refusal. Told me of his seraglio. She seemed relieved after divulging the story of her broken marriage.

After dinner went to the office. Told Dr. Woodson of my plan to prepare a book of African hero tales for Negro youth. In my opinion, as I pointed out to him, in order to get Negro history across to the Negro, in order to inspire racial self-respect, a pride and a consciousness of being black, and to furnish the Negro a means for dispelling his inferiority complex, the medium must be the child, who is at once plastic and receptive. Also to give the child that solid background, that inspiration to achieve, because of the knowledge that his race has risen to dazzling heights in the past.

My plan, as I outlined it to Woodson, was to select eminent Negroes, men who would measure up in their particular field with the great white personalities of their day. In the sphere of great emperors and conquerers, I would mention Gonga Musa of the Mandingo Empire of the fourteenth century; Sonni Ali, one of the greatest kings of the Songhay Empire, and a contemporary of Ferdinand and Isabella of Spain, and Henry VII of England; Askia, the Great, contemporary with Charles V of Spain and Henry VIII of England; and Edris, who was king of Yoruba, when Elizabeth, the Great, of England was parrying with Spain until the time would be ripe for her country to answer affront with affront. Scholars, like Essadi and Ibn Ahmed; poets, like Antar of Arabia and [Aleksandr] Pushkin of Russia; engineers, like the "Negro of Peter the Great," who helped lay out the city of St. Petersburg; novelists, like Alexandre Dumas, *père et fils* (Alexandre Dumas, father and son); inventors, such as [Jan E.] Matzeliger and Elijah McCoy; businessmen, such as Thomy Lafon and James Forten; and a host of other men and women who were outstanding in their various fields.

Woodson was elated. Told me he had been thinking along similar lines. Had even selected certain stories to be included in such a work. We made a list of those men whom we thought it well to include. I would include no men of modern times, except George Washington Carver and, of course, Dr. Woodson. The latter disagreed. Said he, "To do so would precipitate a storm from all of those persons who consider themselves race leaders and who have their own pet theory as to the best means of solving the race problem." I was forced to agree. "Furthermore," he added, "you will not be able to begin this project until the completion of the present book." Yet, I was sure that the latter work could be finished in a few weeks.

Mr. [William M.] Brewer came in just as I was reading over a release of Dr. Woodson's for an advertisement. He mentioned *The Tragic Era*, a book by Claude Bowers, a Congressman, who delivered the keynote speech before the Democratic Convention at Houston, Texas, last year. The book deals with the Reconstruction Period. Unfortunately, it is biased, although Bowers has consulted several original sources, including newspapers, etc. However, says Brewer, he has employed them to support a pre-conceived thesis. It is not objectively written history. Bowers is biased against Thaddeus Stevens, the friend of the freedmen. He devotes three pages to an exposition of Stevens' relations with his Negro housekeeper.

Brewer also spoke of Professor Leo Hansberry of Howard University, who "professes" to be teaching Negro history. Told of Hansberry's being on the verge of dismissal, and of his subsequent draft of a "document" to the University authorities in which he set forth the dire consequences, academically, that would follow, should he be ousted from the University. It amused me so, that I told Dr. Woodson and Mr. Brewer of the real genius of Hansberry, which lay in his extraordinary ability to attract students to his courses for the sake of an easy passing grade. While Hansberry's classes were filled to overflowing, so that the students virtually enveloped him, those of well-trained and excellent teachers, like Alain Locke and Lorenzo Johnson, were extremely fortunate to contain ten students.

The same Hansberry had invited me to continue my education under him after my graduation in 1924, so that we might be joint authors of a volume on African history on which he was working. Not only did my parents and friends counsel me to continue with my medical training, but, as early as then, I could perceive that Hansberry lacked the fundamental prerequisites for such serious work. He knew very little science and almost no foreign languages. He admitted to me that he had been a victim of Negro education in Mississippi, where those subjects had not been taught in Negro schools. He wanted me largely because of what he considered my above-average background in languages. I had had four years of Latin, three years of German, two years of French, and a year of Spanish in high school. Since I expected to do graduate work in medicine at the University of Heidelberg in Germany, upon finishing the Howard Medical School, I had increased my knowledge of foreign languages as an undergraduate. In addition to what I had studied in high school, I supplemented with scientific German, scientific French, conversational German, and conversational French, later adding a year of Portugese.

I told Mr. Hansberry that I still intended to study medicine, and later registered at the New York School of Medicine. On the way back to my home in Ansonia, Connecticut, I talked with Dr. Payton Anderson of New York City, a specialist in tuberculosis. He is a friend of our family and formerly from Shelton, Connecticut. After I told him about my dilemma, he persuaded me to go into the social sciences, stating that we needed more scholars in that field. On my way home, then, I decided to go into history, and went over to Yale to enter the Graduate School there. However, the Dean told me that my nine quarter hours of history at Howard University would not give me the ranking of a sophomore in that area of Yale. He suggested that I go to Columbia University, enter the extension area there, take 30 hours of history, come back, and Yale would be happy to receive me as a graduate history student. I went to Columbia, thank God, and after three years of study there, I now consider myself better prepared for serious historiography than Professor Hansberry. My remarks concerning Hansberry were quite amusing to both Brewer and Woodson.

The former left about 11:30. Dr. Woodson complained,

after Brewer departed, that the latter always comes in and interrupts his work. And poor Brewer! He is so solicitous, so fearful that he is intruding. Of course, he *is*, but I had to assure him to the contrary. Yet he had succeeded, all unconsciously, in keeping us there until nearly 1 o'clock. And Dr. Woodson is to leave for Dover, Delaware, on the following morning at 8 o'clock. We still had to get out some letters and wrap books. I was dead tired when I left, for I had secured precious little sleep last night.

Put in a good full day. Returned home at 6:30. At 8:30 I was in bed.

Thursday
November
14
1929

Felt quite refreshed today. On my way home, to my great surprise, met my good friend, Dr. Vernon Johns. He is now President of Lynchburg Theological Seminary. Was formerly pastor of the First Baptist Church of Charleston, West Virginia, where he succeeded the famous Reverend Mordecai Johnson, when Johnson left to assume the Presidency of Howard University. Johns subsequently became head of the Baptist Educational Center of New York City. A splendid man, brilliant scholar, and a powerful and convincing speaker! In my opinion, one of the three great Negro ministers boasted by our race: Mordecai Johnson of Howard University and Lloyd Imes of New York City are the others. Johns is a big, hearty fellow, with the mark of rustic Virginia still in him. What times we have had together debating in New York, New Jersey, and Connecticut! He gave me a bear hug that left me gasping, and him laughing.

Friday
November
15
1929

I first met him in Charleston, West Virginia, in 1927 while selling magazines. Later in New York, where we debated for two months, which enabled me to live during February and March, 1927. Congratulated him upon his appointment to the presidency of Lynchburg Theological Seminary. Told him I was convinced that the school would prosper under him.

Johns informed me that he had a bouncing little son. He certainly has a wonderful wife.

Asked him to come to the office. En route, he told me that I would have to protect him from the wrath of Dr. Woodson, who had sued him once.

Arrived at the office, Johns met Woodson, and his infectious personality soon thawed the frozen exterior of the latter, and soon both were talking and joking with gusto.

[No entries were made for November 16 through November 19.]

Wednesday
November
20
1929

Attempted to see Georges today, without success. Asked Dr. Woodson whether Dean [William Benyon] West had replied to his letter requesting the names of students who would like to earn money for Christmas by selling books. He answered that the worthy Dean promised to give it his attention. I told Dr. Woodson I would find boys. Spoke of Georges and his desire to take the whole thing over. Woodson felt, however, that student salesmen under his supervision would get very little done. Told him Georges would arrange that. Also advised Woodson that he try girls as salesmen. People would buy from women through sympathy. Woodson replied, unfortunately, that was not business. My reply was, what of it, as long as the dollars flowed into the office? He laughed.

Irene came by tonight. Had a pleasant time listening to music from the Boston Symphony Orchestra. Wants me to come to New York Sunday in order to return with her. Told her I would have to "pray over it."

Thursday
November
21
1929

Book sales are falling off because of unemployment due to depression. Dr. Woodson had decided to have Paul Miller, son of Kelly Miller, instruct prospective salesmen in the art of selling books. Miller wants $12.00 for six lectures. Woodson thinks that is cheap enough. He even offered to throw in a little more money for good measure, if Miller makes good. The project is to sell three books: *The Negro in Our History*; *African Myths*; and *Negro Makers of History*, a simplified and abridged version of *The Negro in Our History* for children. These books, which ordinarily retail for five dollars and fifty cents, will be sold, especially for Christmas, at five dollars, 40%, or two dollars, going to the salesman. A wonderful chance for a student to make Christmas money! Would like to do it myself but, of course, that is impossible now.

Miller believes girls will do better than boys. Dr. Woodson plans to recruit girls from the YWCA, which is right across the street (Rhode Island Avenue at Ninth Street N.W.). I shall secure the fellows. Woodson, upon the advice of Miller, advertised in the Howard University *Hilltop Magazine*, the Armstrong High School *Torch*, the Washington *Evening Star*, and Washington *Tribune*. I told him of my experience selling magazines in New Jersey and Massachusetts. He seemed impressed.

Heard opera, *Faust*, broadcast tonight from the Chicago Civic Opera Company. I really enjoyed it.

[Georges] Clemenceau, the Tiger of France, is dying. Secretary of War [James William] Good's funeral was held today; the body later sent home to Iowa.

Snowed today. It has been some time since I have seen snow in Washington so early in November. Clemenceau's condition is the same. Worked hard all day on "The Negro Wage Earner." Cold tonight.

Friday
November
22
1929

Another hard day, but not too much accomplished. I am fatigued. Cold and snowy today. No hope for Clemenceau. President Hoover urges governors of 48 states to start any sort of public construction work which will enable the country to recover from the recent panic.

Yale was beaten by Harvard 10–6 in an upset.

Called on Irene for about half an hour. Nothing worth while on radio. Went to movies alone.

Saturday
November
23
1929

Clemenceau, the grand old man of France and great wartime Premier, died this morning soon after midnight. He was 88 years of age. The family, a priest, and a nun stood by as the

Sunday
November
24
1929

aged Premier, without waking, breathed his last. So passed France's greatest son of the past century, the Father of Victory and the outstanding Allied statesman of the Great War. His death had been anticipated for some time.

After dinner called Miss [Ophelia] Davidson, a charming little lady. Spent an hour and a half in animated repartee with her. Met Mr. Wells, engraver and specialist in wood cuts, who came in later.[1] Is a Columbia man.

Stopped at Mrs. Georges' in an effort to see her husband. Latter was out. Left word for him to see me tonight. Georges is the proprietor of the *Negro Business Review*. He said he would be able to secure some salesmen for us.

Called upon Mr. Arnold of the YMCA. Was not at home. Mrs. Arnold told me he is out West. Will not be back until December 1. Told her of our need to have him recommend some students to us for selling books. She promised to give him my message. Also became interested in *African Myths*. Allowed her to borrow my copy.

Georges arrived at my place about 10:00 p.m. Informed him of Woodson's proposition. Also told him that Woodson had engaged Paul Miller, the son of Kelly Miller, eminent sociologist and mathematician, to secure prospective salesmen at the YMCA. In fact, Miller's job would be to train these persons, men and women, in selling books. Told Georges I regretted this work could not have been given him.

He deprecated Miller's ability as a salesman; said he is a printer. Moreover, they are in partnership and, by agreement, Georges thought that this work should have come to him. Believed, also, that he could put the job over better than Miller. Even offered to reimburse the latter for the monies he would receive for his salesmanship lectures, if we would allow him to take over. I told him he would have to see Woodson about it. Personally, I feel Georges is the man for the job. Has ambition, plenty of initiative, and the personality so essential to successful salesmanship. And, best of all, I feel he is honest.

1. This was James Lesesne Wells, a graduate of Teachers' College, Columbia University, who also studied at the National Academy of Design. Wells moved to Washington, D.C., in 1929 to teach art at Howard University.

Arranged for him to see Woodson tomorrow. Georges wanted to take me for an automobile ride, but feeling quite fatigued, I begged him to excuse me in order that I might get some much-needed rest.

Georges met me at home after lunch. I took him to see Dr. Woodson. The latter was busy but spent a half hour with him. I introduced him to Woodson as the young man "who wants to make fifty thousand dollars for you." Woodson looked at Georges quizzically and, without cracking a smile, said, "He is young, you say, but he looks like an old man." Upon which all of us laughed heartily. Georges admitted he was 35. Insofar as the conference was concerned, Woodson, though clearly impressed by Georges, stated that his hands were tied by virtue of his prior agreement with Paul Miller. He informed Georges he was sorry Miller had not advised him of their arrangement, but, of course, that was outside the question as far as Georges was concerned.

Georges then unfolded his plan of buying the books from Woodson, employing white and black salesmen, thus making money for both himself and Woodson. The latter could not subscribe to this proposition, because, he averred, it would break faith with his patrons, since Georges' plan would necessitate an increase in the price of the books, in order to give his men sufficient inducement in the form of commission. Woodson also felt that if an agent received less than 40%, he would not bother with the work. True to his scientific spirit, he advised Georges to go to Baltimore and see what he could do there. If he made good in that city, perhaps, Woodson said, he might be able to talk business with him. After giving him a sample of each of the three books, Woodson bade Georges come back, following three days' work in Baltimore, and talk business with him.

I read over the proof of a pamphlet for Negro History Week, which is celebrated in February. In it, Woodson has virtually written a resume of the Negro in all fields—art, science, invention, literature, war, labor, etc. I asked him why he never referred to America as the Negro's country. Told him I noticed his almost-conscious circumvention of such a connection. It is either the Negro "fought for this country," or he labored in order to establish "the institutions of this country," but never "for his country." He replied that it was an oversight. But with such an oversight, in my opinion, being performed so many times in an unconscious manner, it may almost be taken for granted, I remarked, that the writer does not conceive of America as his country, or, if so, feels that he is not a real part of the American environment. I told him that he might almost be accused of lacking national spirit. He smiled and answered, "Well, you know that many Negroes say that we have no country." "Yes," I retorted, "but if we have no country in America, what group has? For surely no nationality, of all the polyglot nations that comprise our great American people," I continued, "has a more valid claim to the name of *American* than we, unless it would be the *red* man?" I recalled the assertion of the Negroes of New England more than a century ago. In response to the movement to transport them back to the so-called land of their nativity, by the American Colonization Society, they could say, "This is our country, and if we are not Americans, then the descendants of those Englishmen, who came over generations ago, are not Americans. Here we were born and here we shall die." "Yes," said Woodson, "those Negroes took high ground, didn't they?"

I gloried in it, for one of the most pronounced statements concerning the intense national pride in America by Negroes, even when under the yoke of slavery, came from the Negroes of Hartford, Connecticut, my own state. Oh yes, I *glory* in the fact that I am an *American* and a *New Englander* to boot.

Getting back to book selling, I was treated to another instance of Woodson's humor. Sometime ago, he stated, he engaged a man to sell books, paid him $35 a week and expenses. Sent to Baltimore, the man sold $21 worth of books in two weeks. When he continued at that rate, Woodson soon decided he had to drop him. The man then sued Woodson, because the contract called for a month's notice before either side could break it. Woodson was then teaching at Howard University. Called up before the University officials, he told them of the contract between the two, of the losses suffered by him because of the failure of the man to "*work at a profit, except to himself.*" Then he added humorously, "this fellow is now suing me for non-support." Both sides saw the absurdity of the case. It was quashed and Woodson was retained.

Arrived home about 7 o'clock. Helen [Massey] was to come here at what time I did not know. Stretched out on the day bed and relaxed. Was just dozing off when the house phone rang. Answered it. Later door bell rang. It was she—petite, winsome, and charming. . . .

Arrived at the office at 9 this morning. Remained until 10:30. Stopped by Helen's on my way to the library. She is moving. Later I went to Rosslyn. Cousins Rose and Grace were bemoaning the fact that their Washington cousins were still at odds with one another. Although one was seriously ill in the hospital, the other sister refused to visit her, or even to call or inquire concerning her. A terrible state; I do not believe anything could happen to deter me from coming to the aid of my worst enemy, if he were ill and sent for me.

Felt lonesome tonight. Finally went to the University, where I met Miss [Carol] Horne, a dietician at Freedman's Hospital. She told me of a friend of hers who had a radio to sell. Informed her I would look at it. She promised to find out the particulars and call me tomorrow evening. . . .

Tuesday November 26 1929

Went over some proofs before going home. Miss Horne called me about a quarter of nine. She wanted me to meet her within a half hour at the hospital in order to see the person who had the radio. Arriving there, I found that I knew her. She wanted $75 for it. I offered her $25. She could not accept that. Knowing that radios have undergone marked reductions, I held to my offer, although I realized full well the value of the instrument. Finally decided to give her $50 cash. She will call me Saturday.

Went to the movies later. Saw Woodson there alone. Strange, he never seems to take a lady with him.

Georges called just as I was preparing for the bath. Told me

Wednesday November 27 1929

he would have to postpone the trip to Baltimore until next Friday. Hopes to sell $200 or $300 worth of books. Hope he can, but I believe he is over-optimistic. Woodson's interest in selling books stems from the fact that the Depression is drying up the funds of the Association. People are unable to buy books as usual.

Thursday
November
28
1929

President Hoover is taking what in some circles is regarded as commendatóry action to prevent a nationwide period of unemployment during the coming winter. This action has been taken in view of the panicky situation caused by the crash of the New York Stock Market of Tuesday, October 29, when more than 16,000,000 shares were wiped out. The result has been business failures, idle factories, unemployment, poverty, and a drain on state and local governments. To help pull the nation out of its economic chaos, more than two billion dollars' worth of improvements, building, etc. will be undertaken by public utilities, corporations, railroads, state improvements, Shipping Board programs, etc. These building programs have been directly stimulated by the President, who, following the collapse of the stock market during the closing weeks of October and the first few weeks of November, called the nation's business chiefs together for a conference to arrest the panic. First to meet were the railroads, whose heads pledged a building program of a billion dollars. Then the manufacturers also went on record as intending to keep production and wages up to their present high level. Labor chiefs, construction magnates, state governors, and public utilities heads also pledged the same. Following are some of the estimated expenditures to be launched upon building and improvement programs by various agencies for 1930:

Utilities Works	$1,400,000,000
State Improvements	4,460,000
Shipping Board Organizations	175,000,000
Railroad Improvements	1,000,000,000
Other Industries	25,000,000

This is commendable but one wonders how much of this expenditure will seep down to the little man.

By the way, this is Thanksgiving Day. I am taking a much needed day off. Took Carol to Rosslyn, where we had dinner at my cousins'. Carol is a dietician at Freedman's Hospital in Washington. Bertha was there with Weinberg [Boyd], looking as beautiful as ever. I could realize fully her matchless beauty by contrasting her with Carol. Reverend and Mrs. Penn were also guests. The former is pastor of the First Baptist Church of Georgetown and a professor at the Howard University School of Religion. A splendid man.

Evidently he had forgotten the young fellow who used to come to his church periodically, and was usually introduced as "my little cousin." At any rate, he wanted to know what I had done and what I was doing now. That was sufficient. We forthwith started upon Negro history, and before I realized it, the history of the Negro before his transportation to America as a slave was being rapidly unfolded. Reverend Penn doubted whether Essadi, author of the *Tarik es Sudan*, was in reality a black, or whether those African Kingdoms were really Negro states. I cited Madame Lugard, Félix Dubois, Roth [possibly Jean Rauch, *Contribution à la histoire des Songhay*], and Leo Frobenius and modern authorities, then fell back on Ibn Batuta, an Arabian scholar of the fourteenth century, who told of the magnificent civilization of those Negro States; and Abdul Ahmed, contemporary with Essadi, and other Arabians— all of whom agreed that these states were of Negro origin.

In response to Reverend Penn's retort that white authorities styled these states *black*, but not *Negro*, empires, I answered that it has never been to the advantage of white historians to ascribe anything creditable to the Negro unless forced to. Moreover, the fact is that the current idea among white scholars is that the Negro has never created a state, and where Negro administration has been tried, it has proven a colossal failure; that because of his black skin, the Negro not only is inferior to the proud Nordic physically, mentally, etc., but that these inherited characteristics would forever place him on a lower social and intellectual plane than the white group.

This thesis compels them to decry anything black, and also, in order to maintain their consistency, to deny anything of merit as originating from a Negro. And where this cannot be done without trespassing upon ordinary common sense, then the procedure is to ascribe such achievements to the "white" blood in the Negro, even though he be black as midnight. Witness Professor E. R. Reuter of University of Iowa, for instance, calling Professor Kelly Miller, outstanding mathematician, etc., a mulatto; also the poet, Paul Laurence Dunbar. I waxed so enthusiastic, if not eloquent, that Mrs. Penn invited me to speak at the church on December 15. I accepted.

A fine dinner; good cheer. Got into a friendly argument with my cousin's husband, Charles. Told him his lodge ought to invest its savings in business, which would not only give employment to boys and girls of our race but would also create respect for our group on the part of the whites. Added that the best white stores in Washington do not want Negro patronage. Phillipsborne, only a month ago, under a Southern manager, told Negroes that their patronage was not desired. Said he turned away $25,000 worth of Negro trade, but received in return $100,000 worth of white patronage. Cousin Charles reminded me of my youth, my inexperience, and also that his order was benevolent. He talked so effusively, being also warmed by holiday spirits, that I willingly conceded every point, fearful lest the guests be otherwise embarrassed. Later we danced and had lots of fun.

Left about 7 o'clock. Went to Emile's. Played "hearts." I was the "chump." Won both games, when I should have lost.

Friday
November
29
1929

Cold today. The Nationalist Government of China is appealing to Soviet Russia to stop the war on the Manchurian front. The stake at issue: the Chinese Eastern Railway, lately seized by the Chinese. The Manchurian troops crushed by Russia, the government of that province has sued for a separate peace, which the Chinese Nationalist government now repudiates. China now appeals to the League of Nations and threatens to invoke the Kellogg[-Briand] Peace Pact. That would bring the United States into the controversy.

Commander [Richard Evelyn] Byrd and three companions today started upon their 1,600 mile aerial journey to the South Pole from their Antarctic base. Some fears were felt today, since no word has been heard from them, but in all likelihood, the low-pressure atmosphere prevented the sending of wireless messages.

An odd situation now arises as a result of Byrd's Antarctic explorations. England now lays claim to the entire region. It is doubtful, however, whether her claim will be acquiesced in by the United States, which also claims this barren ice pack. Secretary of State [Henry L.] Stimson transmitted a letter to the British Government today concerning this claim. What good is this barren land anyway, except for whales and ice cutting, neither of which is important to civilization today?

Slavery still exists in Africa and Asia; according to a statement in the Baltimore *Afro-American*, there are six million slaves, mostly black, in Liberia, Sierra Leone, Transvaal, India, Nepal, and other nations of the East.

Went to a party at the Lovetts [Edward P. and Lucille], although I had fully intended retiring at 9 o'clock. Enjoyed playing whist. Met several old classmates of mine. By the way, Lovett enjoyed himself to such an extent, dancing with other ladies, that he had to be reminded by his wife that he had danced with her but once, and that merely half a dance. At which Lovett promised to do penance. When I left about 1:45 a.m., his wife possessed him entirely, for she was sitting on his lap, and being a little heavier than Lovett, he perforce had to stay there. A fine couple, however. They have a beautiful apartment, and to see them so happy, at times, fills me with yearning for similar conjugal felicity.

It is quite cold today. Another interesting chapter has been written in American history. Commander Byrd, the first man to fly over the North Pole in a heavier-than-air machine (May 26), has just flown over the South Pole, making the record trip of 1,600 miles in 19 hours. With him were three other intrepid men: Burt Balchen, pilot; Capt. Ashley C. McKinley, aerial surveyor; and Harold I. June, radio man. The plane left its base

Saturday
November
30
1929

at 3:29 p.m. Thursday (10:19 Washington time). A tri-motor Ford plane was used. It was thrilling, perilous, over hazardous fields of barren wastes and mountains of ice. Byrd, however, was not the first man to reach the Pole. Roald Amundsen, the Norwegian, who lost his life last year (1928) trying to reach General Nobile, the Italian flyer, won that honor, reaching the Pole on December 19, 1911. Used a dogsled team. The second was an Englishman, Captain Robert F. Scott, on January 18, 1912. Scott lost his life trying to return to civilization. Byrd was the third. His was also the most pretentious undertaking. To facilitate his journey, he was in constant touch with civilization by wireless. He also had with him 65 men, each a specialist in his own field.

Sunday
December
1
1929

If it has done nothing else, prohibition seems to have stimulated a rash of murders. Today the Washington *Herald* reported its survey of prohibition killings since the enactment of the Volstead Act in 1919. Enforcement, according to it, has exacted 1,360 lives in the last ten years. Not very encouraging for a law supposedly supported by popular sentiment.

Visited Dr. [Roy Underwood] Plummer and his wife this afternoon. Doctor is former classmate of mine. Mrs. [M. H.] Plummer is principal of Francis Junior High School. She invited me to speak at her school during the observation of Negro History Week in February. I consented.

Later on, my cousin, Almira Streets, a Cornell graduate and music teacher, called me. She wants me to speak at the First Baptist Church in Georgetown, which she attends, on Sunday, December 12. I promised to do so.

Georges said he wanted to see me, but failed to come to my apartment tonight.

The Old Guard Republicans refused to seat Senator [William Scott] Vare of Pennsylvania, but don't want the seat taken by a Democrat. Vare was accused of election fraud.

Monday
December
2
1929

. . . Tonight only two or three persons came out for the salesmanship talk at the YMCA.

Irene called me. Was quite excited. Fears her husband is in some sort of trouble.

United States, Great Britain, France, and other powers sent notes to the Soviet government and China, preparatory to invoking the Kellogg[-Briand] Peace Pact to stop the war on the Manchurian Front.

President Hoover, in his Annual Message, asked for the entry of the United States into the World Court. Deplores U.S. Marines' occupation of countries, and says government finances are in sound condition. Added that laws are made by the people. Latter bound to obey them, until repealed. Referred to prohibition. Also, advocated justice for rich and poor alike.

Tuesday
December
3
1929

Soviets refused peace overtures of United States and other powers. Signed separate pact with Manchuria, making for joint use of the Chinese Eastern Railway.

Wednesday
December
4
1929

Called Helen [Massey]. Told her of opportunities for selling books. She promised to come down to the Y.W.C.A. this evening. Miss Adams also promised to attend the class. Coming at 6 o'clock, if she could.

Arrived at lecture about 5:45. Expected to find Miss Adams there. Did not appear.

Miller was late. Tonight he had a large class, reinforced by some girls from the "Y" who occasionally work at the office. One, a [Miss Harris] from Pittsburgh, has plenty of personality. She is quite plump and wears her hair combed out. Also, wears her dresses so short, that when she is sitting, it is quite disconcerting to the eyes of the gentlemen present. No less an authority than Dr. Woodson admitted that.

Miller put the class through some practical salesmanship, after lecturing. In my opinion, lectures mean little. Salesmanship is acquired through experience, although the theory, naturally, is good. The students made such a mess of trying to sell books to one another that I took a book to demonstrate how easy it was to sell, with the young lady from Pittsburgh as my customer. Persuaded her to buy a set. Woodson was very optimistic over the results. Miss Madden, Miss Lomax, and

Miss Murray, a little lady who had sold $8 worth of books, I believe, will make good salespersons.

Rushed home. Georges came in. Told me of a plan to start a radio station. Says he already had two white men interested. One is connected with Radio WRC. Would be affiliated with this station. His station would be located on U Street N.W. in Negro business section. I warned Georges that if such happened, it should not be accepted as a platform for every ambitious, loud-mouthed Negro to preach his particularistic dogma to fan the fires of race hatred. Our Association aims to bring people together. Georges is enthusiastic, swears he will make me his radio announcer. Agreed with my sentiments, but I am afraid my voice prevents my acting as announcer. Georges feels, however, that with a radio he could sell a million dollars' worth of books.

Georges took me to O Street, N.W., where we found Mrs. Porter. I bought a radio from her for fifty dollars. She will send it to my apartment later. Georges had something for us to type, but, man-like, could not find it.

Thursday
December
5
1929

Negro newspapers came out with glaring headlines that President Hoover intends to keep Marines in Haiti. An outbreak is reported to have occurred there, in which five Haitians were killed. Was excuse for us to send Marines there. More dollar imperialism.

Helen came to the office this afternoon to see Woodson about selling books. Talked with me for half an hour. Don't know whether Woodson heard our conversation or not. After her conference with him, she told me she was about to leave, but first decided to ask me, why did I not tell her a deposit was required of a prospective salesman? I told her it was not expedient to put too many obstacles in her path at the beginning. Don't believe she will make a good salesman. She needs money, but I think she is a little too frail for door-to-door selling.

Talked with Irene this evening. Helped her put up a pole in a closet. Started to the library but was too late.

Went to office, then direct to library. After considerable trouble, finally found report of United States Coal Commission.
Secured information from various State Departments of Labor issues. Back to office at 12:45. Home for lunch. Took
Helen three dollars, which was a loan for her to purchase a set
of books for display purposes. It is to be refunded when she
returns the books. She has a nice room, very well furnished.
Lives with a Mrs. White. I left a trifle skeptical. She has too
much company.

Returned to the office at 4:45. Later went to dinner, then
back to the YMCA at 6:15. Was late tonight. Only a few
persons came, however. Fine illustration of the survival of the
fittest. Helen did not come. Was quite disappointing to me.
Her word seems as fragile as thin ice. Miller rambled in his talk
tonight. Got off on some pet theories about Negroes being
traditionally lazy, etc. Assigned territory to three salesmen.
Miss Madden and Miss Lomax gave experiences in selling.
Woodson asked how to sell to a physician who claims to have
no time for such reading. The girls could not answer; neither
did Miller make any attempt to do so. I tried to answer by
saying:

1. He is the leading Negro in the community and has the
   best education.
2. He might be called upon to meet all distinguished visitors who come to town.
3. Many times he plays host to them.
4. He must mingle with all groups.
5. He may be called upon to speak about anything on any
   occasion. He, therefore, must be prepared.
6. The material in books is blocked out in paragraphs. He
   could easily pick out information desired.

Woodson was pleased. Miller seemed satisfied. After the
lecture, Woodson told me Georges had been to the office.
Wanted books but had no money for deposit. Woodson demanded a deposit. A matter of business, he said. Finally gave
Georges books on condition that *I* would become surety. Sur-

prising, because I was not even there at the time. Nevertheless, I agreed to stand surety for Georges. Woodson feels Georges will not make good. I think he will!

Woodson asked me to read proofs of *Negro Plays and Pageants* [possibly Alain Leroy Locke and Gregory M. Locke (eds.), *Plays of Negro Life* (New York, 1927)], which we are publishing next month. About 354 pages. Shall begin tomorrow. Woodson also reminded me he would be happy if I would finish the study of Negro labor as soon as possible.

Arrived home about 9:35. Called Bertha. She has a cold. Found note from radio man in the door.

<table>
<tr><td>Saturday
December
7
1929</td><td>Read proofs of following plays: Sacrifice, by Thelma Duncan: Simple, well done, but style weak. Old theme of sacrifice treated, but simply and well told. Antar of Araby, by Maude Cuney Hare: A classic. Powerful, dignified. Choice of diction good. The Black Horsemen, by Willis Richardson: Too long-drawn out. Not well motivated. House of Shame [by Richardson]: Devoid of dramatic suspense because of author's telling how an emergency will be met in advance. Not skillfully portrayed, too long-drawn out. Riding the Goat, by Mary Miller: Pretty fair. Pageants: The Light of Women. Abominable. No virtue in it. Out of the Dark, by Reverend Cox: Fair. Ethiopia at the Bar of Justice: Powerful, as a whole, yet has situations which must be ironed out. Contains music scores, but interspersed throughout play without appropriateness. Too much religion. Effect, however, is powerful. King's Dilemma. Fair.</td></tr>
</table>

Will finish reading them tonight.

Woodson again descanted on Dr. Du Bois and his lack of program. Don't believe Woodson cares much for Du Bois. The same may be true for Du Bois regarding Woodson. Strange, I have never seen Du Bois at the office since I have been here. Dr. Woodson also stressed the inconsistency of Negro leaders in their adopting a "so-called" Negro National Anthem. "Thereby," he said, "Negroes renounce their allegiance to America, while at the same time contending for full rights of American citizenship." Felt Negroes wrong in agitating for a Negro memorial. I agreed with Woodson, for if, as he stated, we demand a monument to commemorate the deeds of the Negro, then why not one to honor the contributions of the Irish, Scotch-Irish, Germans, Poles, Huguenots, Dutch, Italians, and others?

The Negro is steadfastly endeavoring, says Woodson, to make himself a group apart in America. If he felt his *Americanism*, and demanded his rights by virtue of such a status, and cut out all such "tomfoolery" as agitation for naming monuments and other things that make for differentiation, he would have less to "grumble and whine" about. The trouble is, he continued, we have too many demagogues and not enough real race leaders. Even Mrs. Harris, the stenographer, spoke to me against such agitation today. I agree with Woodson that we should do more, cry less, and be adamant in contending for full citizenship as one hundred per cent Americans. Mrs. Harris promised to come down to the office tomorrow to go over plays with Woodson.

Surprised this morning, about noon, to receive a visit from Mrs. Harris. She brought her little nine-month-old baby with her. I jokingly told her that people might be led to believe that she was bringing me my own child in a most dramatic fashion. On the contrary, she laughingly retorted that people would consider her above suspicion, since she had a little babe in her arms. She remained only a few minutes. I took her to the Lovetts on the same floor. She returned for about five minutes to read some poetry. Has marked inferiority complex.

Sunday
December
8
1929

Went to the office at 2 o'clock. Read plays. Mr. [Willis] Richardson, author of several of the plays, came in about 4:30. Dr. Woodson, in the meantime, was completing the reading of a galley proof that we might compare corrections. Mr. Wells, the engraver, came in at five o'clock. About 5:30, Mr. Richardson, Dr. Woodson, and I started to bring some sort of harmony into the musical scores of *Ethiopia at the Bar of Justice*. The author, with no appreciation of music, had made *Tannhäuser* (that is, "Pilgrim's Chorus" from that opera) represent labor. We substituted "Old Man River." For Business and

Professional Men, his musical score was "Old Black Joe." I suggested that the music be cut out here. No real business music. Does not inspire art. We finally straightened it out by process of elimination. I wanted to make dramatic and literary corrections in the various plays, but was overruled by Dr. Woodson and Mr. Richardson on the grounds that we could not tamper with the author's intentions. Nevertheless, I retorted, there remained obvious errors, both of omission and commission. Palpable, grammatical errors in the mouths of educated persons!

Poor Mr. Wells had an engagement at 6 p.m. I had one at the same hour. When I left, and I had not yet eaten my dinner, it was 7:10, and Wells and Woodson still had to confer. Neither had Dr. Woodson had his dinner.

Called Mrs. Harris. Told her I would call for her about 8:00 o'clock. Within fifteen minutes I had to walk three-quarters of a mile, warm and eat dinner, deliver a book for Dr. Woodson a half mile away, go home, still another half mile, dress, and call for Mrs. Harris, who was still a mile distant. I did it, but was about 10 minutes late.

Went to see "Rio Rita." It is a gorgeous musical spectacle. Mrs. Harris did not feel well but persisted in seeing the picture through. I went home. A wasp was flying about in the house. Had to dispatch it before going to bed.

Monday
December
9
1929

Told Dr. Woodson I intended to call his attention to Richardson's play *The House of Shame*, in which the element of dramatic suspense had been entirely destroyed due to the author's deliberately telling the reader how the play is to end, then dragging him through almost 30 pages of worrisome reading to a conclusion which one already knows. Woodson agreed with me. He suggested we see Richardson about it. Strange that Woodson, who has already seen the play, did not detect this aberration.

Another salesmanship meeting tonight. Only three persons there. Miller seems to have "petered out," insofar as instruction is concerned. Spent all of his time on African myths.

Should devote more effort, I think, to demonstrating ways to sell *The Negro in Our History*. Miss Murray is doing well.

Woodson asked me to find out what has happened to [William Sidney] Pittman [Jr.], Booker T. Washington's nephew [grandson]. Has not attended a class since last Monday, when Miller held him up to ridicule before the group.

I had Pittman come to my apartment tonight. Asked why he had not come to the classes; he said that he had gone with Georges. Secondly, he lacked a person to become surety for the deposit required of him. He asked if he could come to the office today and talk with Woodson. I told him, certainly.

Georges called. Got me out of the bathroom. He seemed overjoyed. Had good reason. His wife had presented him with a little baby girl. Congratulated him. Mrs. Georges is doing fine.

Put in a day of hard work on last chapter of my book. After dinner Irene dropped in. Bertha called. Wanted me to look over certain things which she had. Thought they would be useful for my work. Later the radio man came and took back the machine.

Tuesday December 10 1929

Nothing of import today. Lecture to salesmen by Miller tonight was disappointing. Evidently, he has "shot his bolt." Woodson also agrees. Only one salesman present—Miss Madden. Very discouraging. Although she and two others are doing fairly well, things are not going as well as I think they should.

Wednesday December 11 1929

This morning I spent at the library. Secured information on Negroes in Africa. Read one of Leo Wiener's books (Volume I) on *Africa and the Discovery of America*. Amazing! Wiener proves that cotton, tobacco, and wheat were introduced into America by African Negroes. More important, he says Africans discovered America. Also, from *Diary of Columbus* [*Journal of Christopher Columbus*], shows clear proof the latter fabricated, or else allowed his preconceived notion of Earth to run away with his judgment. I also read *Saga of Eric the Red* and *Adventures in Vinland*. Telegraphed Lillian [Greene], my sister-in-law, to find out whether dad and mother have a radio. Have bought excellent one to send home. Will surprise them.

[17] The Speakaphone

Nothing of import during the day. At night Georges came to see me. Brought a Mr. Alexander and a Mr. Ullman with him. One is a radio engineer with WRC (that is, Ullman); the other is an orchestra leader. They have been interested by Georges in a proposition of putting a radio in Washington, D.C., operated by Negroes. A bold thought and potentially a veritable gold mine. We discussed the possibilities. Mr. Alexander, who stutters very disconcertingly, then announced that he had been to the office of the Federal Radio Commission and they refused, presently, to license any more Washington stations. There is now considerable conflict concerning them. However, he felt that if Congressman [Oscar] DePriest would intercede, such a right might eventually be granted.

Ullman corroborated Alexander's statement. Alexander then spoke of the Speakaphone proposition. Told us it was using the microphone to reproduce human voice on a record, which could be done instantaneously. Singers, speakers, advertisers, mothers, children, he said, all could use it. It is an innovation. Owned by the Speakaphone Corporation of America. A Mr. Hayworth has the rights for all of Maryland, Virginia, and the District of Columbia. If we wanted to go into the business, we would secure the privileges from him. Would cost about $800 to set up, according to Ullman. Machines are leased. I was interested. So was Bright, also

Georges. I should have said that Georges brought his friend Bright to the apartment with him.

Ullman heard us speak of the Masonic Temple as the place ideal for such a studio. We went down to see the ballroom. Impossible to get in. The janitor did not have the keys. We were shown around the Bamboo Inn, a very nice dancing and dining cafe for Negroes, run by Japanese. There Ullman and Alexander, who are white, waxed enthusiastic over the place.

Decided that silence should be observed until we are ready to act. Ullman, in particular, recommended that we not divulge his connection, for it would result in the loss of his job with WRC Radio. I agreed. Served the men ginger ale before they left.

Received telegram from my sister Lillian [Greene] today. Unfortunately, my parents have a radio. They did not tell me. Wanted to surprise *me* at Christmas time. Sorry, because I know they have gone into debt to do so.

Friday
December
13
1929

Miller gave his last talk to the salespeople tonight. About five attended. Miller had so little substantive to give. Miss Harris, a short, attractive, though not pretty girl from Pittsburgh, who wears her skirts at a distressingly short distance from her waist, told him she sold books merely by acting natural and how impossible she finds it to persuade a customer to buy when she becomes a stereotyped salesman. Little Miss Murray says she sells by her emotional appeal, womanly charm, and a smile. After all, I believe that one sells his personality to customers and that they take the goods as a corollary. Both, in my opinion, would make good salesmen. Miller feels that Miss Harris will not, because she does not put his theories into practice. I say, however, if one can sell on a smile, let him do so.

Dr. Woodson expressed satisfaction with Miller's work. Gave him a check. I felt that Miller had done a fair job.

Miss Helen [Massey] called me about 10:35. Told me I was supposed to give a party last week but did not do so. Emile [Holley] and [Emmett] Dorsey, two friends of mine, she said, had expected to come. Told her I was busy reading manuscript at office. Would have it tomorrow. Told her to call me tomorrow.

. . . Late coming home. Started to clean up apartment. Irene came in. While here, Mrs. Harris called. Irene kept fooling with the radio. Devilishly made it louder so I could not hear. Told Helen [Massey] to come and help me get ready. Washed dishes, bathtub, scrubbed kitchen, bathroom, oiled floors, and dusted. Went to borrow punch bowl and card table. Helen made sandwiches and punch. Party disappointing; only three couples came. Helen's friends failed to put in an appearance. Had been invited at last moment. Emile could not come. Had taken castor oil the night before. Professor Edmonds, dramatic instructor at Morgan College, Baltimore, came over. Brought Yolande Cullen, former wife of the poet Countee Cullen, and daughter of Dr. W. E. B. Du Bois, with him. Had lots of fun. Went to bed remembering that I had to speak in Georgetown tomorrow.

Saturday
December
14
1929

Tired today. Remained in until time to speak in Georgetown. Tiresome program. Typical of ill-conceived and directed Baptist Churches. About fifteen persons participating in a B.Y.P.U. Program. Most of them read excerpts either from the B.Y.P.U. Manual or the Bible. After a wait of 50 minutes or more, I was finally called upon to speak. Started out by *shocking* the audience. Told them that of the twelve million Negroes in the United States, there is not one that is not diseased. Audience looked at me in amazement. Explained to them the Negroes of this country suffer from a disease more deadly than cancer or consumption—an inferiority complex. Told them it could not be removed by resorting to the adoption of a Negro National Anthem, which, at best, is illusory. Told them they must become acquainted with their past. Must look upon slavery as merely a passing evolutionary phase in the glamorous span of a race, which incident—slavery—all races and nations have experienced. Recounted glories and contributions of Africans to civilization—iron, sculpture, painting, domestication of animals, iron ships, etc. Also dis-

Sunday
December
15
1929

cussed contributions of Negroes to America. Urged them to learn of their past in order that they might feel themselves men and women, and command the respect which they justly merit, not only of themselves, but of the majority group. How? By buying and reading the books Dr. Woodson and others are researching and publishing! Judging by the applause, I probably did a fair job.

Miss Madden came in this morning. Wanted me to arrange a talk in Anacostia or in Hall's Hill in order to facilitate her selling books. Promised I would do so.

Tonight Irene visited me. Left at 8 o'clock. Messrs. Alexander, Ullman, Georges, and Powell came at 8:30. Took me to the Speakaphone company in the Pass Building, 13th and F Streets, N.W. Met Mr. Hayworth, who holds the Speakaphone franchise for Washington, D.C., Maryland, and Virginia. Is a young man; so are his associates. Did not like the way he addressed us as "boys." We answered in kind. He was friendly. Showed us how the Speakaphone works. One speaks into the microphone, from which runs a wire to a machine, something akin to a graphophone. Instead of playing a record, however, the wire connects with a diamond needle, which, agitated by the sound waves coming from the microphone, records on a disk made of an aluminum alloy. The record is then produced upon an ordinary Victrola, and thus, within two and a half minutes, a person may hear his voice either in song, conversation, speech, or any sound, reproduced on an ordinary Victrola. The price varies from $1.50 to $3.00, depending upon the size of the record. Hayworth apparently was doing a good business, for the waiting room was just being emptied at 10:30. Swore we could make plenty of money with Speakaphone. I confess that I feel we might make *some*, at least for a time. Hayworth's terms were $750 for the machine and $250 for the franchise. Records are to be bought as needed. Cash is demanded. We decided to meet at my apartment on Wednesday to make more definite plans.

Georges was exuberant. Wanted to start immediately. I cautioned him not to be too precipitate. He thought me conservative. Perhaps so, but it does not pay, in my opinion, to rush blindly into such things only to make [oneself] wiser but poorer.

As to Alexander—who stutters horribly—I cannot fathom the role he plays. He would like to participate in the formation of a company. Yet, he is friendly with, and apparently is informed of all the dealings of, Hayworth and others. If he is actuated solely by a desire to make money, as he says he is, all well and good. But if he is merely a go-between, then one had best be careful. Cautioned both Georges and Powell to be careful. The latter is weak. Is a veritable "yes" man. Agrees with everything Hayworth utters. Georges has a mind of his own, thinks independently, but is rash.

Alexander suggested that we meet tomorrow to discuss our plans before meeting with Hayworth and others. We agreed. Also, we agreed to meet at my apartment at 6:30. Georges promises to bring wine.

Put in a busy day. Left for home, arriving at 6:30. Found Georges awaiting me. He could not remain. Had to go back to the hotel, where he is head waiter. Told him I would call him, saying that his wife is ill, in order that he might leave early. By the way, she just left the hospital today. Her little baby girl was born. Told Georges I do not like the too-obsequious type of person. Added that of the two I preferred Bright. Georges replied, "Bright has no money," but he could drop Powell. I suggested we get Dr. Wesley to come into the company. Georges agreed; said, moreover, that he was skeptical of Alexander. Left, after giving me telephone number to call him at 7:30.

Tuesday December 17 1929

Alexander was late arriving. Had not eaten. Told him Georges could not return until 7:30, therefore he had better go to dinner. He did so, after admonishing me to secure the studio. Told him that no definitive step would be taken until the transaction had been closed. Alexander went upon his stuttering way, promising to return at 7:30. By the way, he dines at Georges' hotel.

During the interim, Irene came. Looked lovely. Listened to

organ recital by Lew White. Thrilled to it with me. Counseled me about entering into anything that could cause me financial trouble.

Georges returned at 8:30. Alexander did not arrive until nine. We decided to allow Alexander to manage the studio during the day on commission. Georges would do so at night. We three would form the company. Alexander would invest nothing, for he has nothing, according to him. I doubted whether Alexander would do as well as a Negro in such a position. Told Alexander so. Also stressed the fact that, even as a Negro in a white studio would exert a depressing effect upon white patronage, just so would the presence of a white man in a Negro studio react similarly. He was forced to admit it, while strongly protesting his lack of racial bias, although he is a Virginian. Alexander promises that he can secure a piano and Victrola for us. We decided to wait until tomorrow.

Wednesday
December
18
1929

. . . Georges came in about 8:30. I had already apprised Mr. [Bushrod] Mickey an important meeting was to be held. Hayworth and Rose Hayworth came in later. They are not related, however. Alexander came with them.

Hayworth's proposition was: exclusive rights for Washington, D.C., $1,000, including machine for the first year; second year, $550; third year, $350; and $200 for every year thereafter. Terms: cash.

I objected on several grounds. First, that no business proposition of today is consummated on a strictly cash basis, that it is provocative of suspicion when cash is demanded upon a novel proposition, the success of which is problematical; secondly, the franchise is a little too steep, taking into consideration the smaller earning power of Negroes compared with that of white persons, which would automatically make for a smaller spending power, especially for luxuries. For example, I reminded him that the average white person makes $20–$30 per week, while the average Negro makes $8–$15 per week.

I would only consent to undertake the proposition at a reduced figure with a definite downpayment in cash, the balance to be discounted in notes over a stipulated period of time.

Hayworth saw that we were not to be drawn into this project with our eyes closed. Powell, as usual, either played the role of the acquiescer or else remained silent.

Georges finally suggested that Hayworth put the machine in our studio for a trial. If satisfactory, his terms would be met within a month. During that time, all proceeds would be untouched and would be turned over to him, that is, Hayworth, if we failed to accept the offer. Hayworth could not agree to Georges' proposal. But, instead, offered to take ⅓ of the stock of the company, make no charge for the machine, and our only expense would be the $250 per year for the franchise. I vetoed that because if the scheme should succeed, Hayworth would secure many times the original $1,000 in dividends, etc. Alexander agreed with me. Georges finally fell in with us, although reluctantly.

It was finally decided that we would accept the proposition for $1,000, $250 cash, and $250 again at the end of the first month, the balance to be discounted in notes over a certain period of time. Georges promised to form a company; would incorporate it for $10,000. He and I would hold 51% of the stock.

After Alexander and Hayworth had gone, Georges told me that I erred when I opposed his proposition. We could have made money, he asserted, without the necessity of expending any money at all. As I saw it, the proposition may have lacked popular appeal, or, if not, may have retained it only for a limited time. I became even more dubious, musing that, after all, perhaps it would not be so bad, especially when the rapid displacement of phonographs by radios would curtail the making of Speakaphone records.

Alexander came to my office about 11 o'clock. Remained nearly an hour and a half. Had important news. Told me another Speakaphone studio, an independent concern, had been set up on F Street, N.W. A different machine was being used, but was a better make than Hayworth's. However, he used Speakaphone records but, according to Alexander, he would soon make his own. I asked whether Hayworth knew

Thursday
December
19
1929

this. Alexander replied affirmatively. Then it dawned upon me that because of the independent concern, Hayworth had tried to stampede us into closing the deal and for cash. Our franchise would not have been worth a picayune. And Hayworth knew this.

Despite this knowledge, Alexander was anxious to clinch the deal. This man would let us have a machine for $500. Franchise money would not be needed. Cash was desired. That is what frightens me, for I believe something is crooked whenever anything must be consummated on a cash basis. Told Alexander we would do nothing until Georges had been advised.

Showed Alexander *Negro Makers of History* and *African Myths*. He waxed enthusiastic over them. I asked him what would be the possibilities of reducing these stories to a Speakaphone record? He felt the prospects admirable. Suggested, however, that we hold them until it was determined whether or not we could secure a radio station. Told him I would introduce him to Dr. Woodson. He was delighted with the prospect. Alexander took me to dinner. Promised to call at 4:30 to see Woodson.

During the afternoon, I told Dr. Woodson about the Speakaphone and radio propositions. He was delighted with them. Told me, however, that Howard University was attempting to secure a radio station. I hope not, for President [Mordecai] Johnson might make it a vehicle for social propaganda, whereas a radio is designed to be primarily a form of information and entertainment. Informed him that Alexander was coming back. He said he would meet with him.

Alexander returned at 4:30. Woodson was busy helping to get out Christmas cards. Finally, he came in. Was in jovial humor. Alexander explained to him that the Speakaphone could advertise the Association's publications. The stories, transferred to the Speakaphone record, then played before the microphone over a station like WOL would be sensational. Ideal for children. Something new. Would take like wildfire. Woodson manifested interest. Wanted to know the cost of the machine. "Seven hundred and fifty dollars," said Alexander.

Said we could get a machine, and advised us to do so immediately. Woodson added, however, it would be better to let
the matter rest for ten days until he returned from Pittsburgh.

Alexander asked me to engage a studio in the Masonic
Building on U Street, N.W. I advised that it would not be
timely, since we had not yet closed the deal with either Hayworth or the Independent Speakaphone Company.

Tonight Irene dropped by. She brought me a fine shirt for a
Christmas gift. I did not want to accept it, for I had asked her
not to get me a present.

Called Georges. He was in a hurry but came up to see me.
Was too busy to talk here, he said. Therefore, he drove me
down to the Lincoln Theater, where he had to wait for Mr.
Jones, a newspaper man. Told him of Alexander's chicanery.
Georges was very lukewarm over the proposition. Said he was
sure plan as outlined to him was best. I am now inclined to see
it the same way. Like me, he refused to give Hayworth $1,000
or to pay cash for a machine from either party.

On the way home took a dose of castor oil, for my stomach
was again bothering me.

About Alexander's discovery, how much was real and how
much was theatrics? This man may be an underling of Hayworth's. Who knows? And Alexander's informing us may
have been for the purpose of speeding us up in order that we
might have priority in opening up such a studio. On the other
hand, Alexander may have been actuated by our own interest
in securing this information. He told me he had taken the rest
of the week off to secure all the information possible.
Howbeit, my interest, like that of Georges, is waning.

Pretty busy day. The girls had petitioned Woodson that they
be paid before Christmas. He at first told them that to do so
would only mean that they would be broke on New Year's
Day. They felt that he was heartless, but he is very human
beneath his rough exterior. Today he paid them through their
January 1 salaries. Even paid me, although I dislike such and
told him so. I gave the check to Bertha to keep for me until I

Friday
December
20
1929

called for it, knowing only too well that if it were put in the bank, I would be tempted to buy too many Christmas gifts.

Returned to the office at 1:20. Woodson said he had intended to call me before leaving for Pittsburgh. Gave me instructions as follows: first, the manuscript must be finished, then letters filed, and 3,000 letters made ready to be sent out on the 3rd of January. Gave me the keys to the cash register, his desk, etc. Mr. [William M.] Brewer came in. We went out and nailed a couple of boards on the fence in the rear. Afterwards, I stamped several letters. Dr. Woodson gave me $30 in checks to be cashed, should additional funds be needed, and instructed that if too much money accumulated, to deposit it. He left at 11:30. Going to Pittsburgh for a rest. He needs it, for he works, on an average, sixteen hours a day. He looks quite fatigued. Told me I could reach him, if necessary, at 2325 Mahan Street, or at the YMCA.

Saturday December 21 1929

Put Miss Meyers on the manuscript this morning. Mrs. Harris did not come in. I deposited $110 at the Metropolitan Bank in the name of the Associated Publishers this morning. Quite a few checks came in the mail. I opened all except Dr. Woodson's personal mail, which included a large number of Christmas greetings.

A fire a few doors from the office brought me outdoors to ascertain whether flying sparks might set fire to boxes of paper in the yard. I have often intended to speak to Dr. Woodson about this menace. The paper should be either baled or placed in metal containers. Nothing happened as a result of the fire, much to my relief.

Had Miss Dunlap send a copy of *The Negro in Our History* to Harry and Ernest, and a copy of *African Myths* to Tynes and Gladys McDonald. These books I asked the bookkeeper to charge to my account.

Remained at the office with Miss Dunlap until 6 o'clock, helping her to send out packages. Rushed to dinner in a taxi. Driver waited while I ate. Came immediately home. Expected Helen. Did not come. Listened to *Aida* by the Metropolitan Opera. Its excellence was diminished by too much verbal explanation, which almost transformed it into dramatic story-telling. Called on Helen later. Could not get out. Her word is not to be depended upon. Returned to office about 10 o'clock. Went up to see the Mickeys [Bushrod and Lillian]. She had bought two bags for me to be given as Christmas gifts. Were beautiful. Wrapped and prepared one to send to Helen Grinage; the other was for Helen Notis. This one was grey. I did not like it as well as the other. She told me that I could exchange it.

Alexander called me this morning. Told me we ought to decide what to do about the Speakaphone proposition. Later he came up to my apartment. I told him flatly we would not give Hayworth a thousand dollars now. Neither could we accept even the machine on his terms. Asked him why should we pay $750 for Hayworth to leave a $750 machine with us for a year, then $300 the second year, etc.? In fact, the more I dwelt upon it, the more irritated I became. Did he take us for fools? Whoever heard of anyone paying 100% of the cost of a commodity to lease it for a year? It is preposterous to think that a person leasing a $50,000 building for a year would pay the entire cost of that in advance. Only a madman would consider asking for such a thing. Told him we would have to see Georges.

On the way to Georges took Emile's blanket. Spent twenty minutes there. Georges was out when we arrived at his home. Alexander promised to bring Georges to the office in the evening. I went to the office in the afternoon for three hours. Left for dinner late. Wrapped parcels to send home to the family for Christmas.

Snow and sleet this morning. When I got to the office I started to clean the snow. The girls arrived. I put both Mrs. Harris and Miss Meyers on the manuscript.

Mrs. Mickey brought a beautiful bag for Helen Notis. Leather underarm bag. The texture of the leather is beautiful. She and her husband joshed me about buying such a beautiful gift. Swore that she must be the future Mrs. Greene. I could only smile. Mr. Mickey wrapped it beautifully for me. They

Sunday December 22 1929

Monday December 23 1929

are certainly hospitable and kind to me. Returned to the office. It was a terrible night—rain, snow, and sleet. Mr. [Willis] Richardson had been there. By the way, I had called him in reference to the title page for _Plays and Pageants_, which the publishers—the Van Reese Press—had called for. He made out a title page and left it in the letterdrop. I later sent it to Dr. Woodson for his approval, asking him to forward it, if satisfactory, to the Van Reese Press. Wrote twenty-one cards. Sent them from the office, carefully noting the number of stamps used, for which I shall pay Miss Dunlap in the morning. Noticed, moreover, that very few stamps of the 500 which she had purchased the other day are still there.

Tuesday
December
24
1929

Went to the bank at 2 o'clock this afternoon to deposit money for the Associated Publishers. On the way back, stopped at several stores in an attempt to get something for my cousins in Rosslyn. Found nothing satisfactory. Gave Miss Dunlap money this morning to get handkerchiefs for the other three girls. She, herself, is so greatly in need of aid—she cares for herself, mother, and sister (and is herself threatened with tuberculosis) on $75 a month—that I gave her $5.00 Saturday as a Christmas token. The other girls all thanked me before leaving.

Went to the office but returned to listen to the Capital Cathedral Capital Chimes. Mr. Mickey called me about 11:30. Invited me to breakfast tomorrow at 9:30. Accepted with pleasure.

Christmas
Day
December
25
1929

A very quiet Christmas for me. Enjoyed breakfast with Mr. and Mrs. Mickey. They gave me a beautiful tie. I had expected nothing. They make me feel so much at home. Listened to radio programs from Holland, Germany, and England. Later went to the office. Remained there for two hours. Brought handkerchiefs for my cousins and socks for the husband. Went to Rosslyn, where I had dinner. Remained until 9:30. Had lots of fun. Felt a little disconsolate, however, when I reflected that on other Christmases, Harry and Ernest would have been here with me. Cousins had a delicious dinner. The Christmas tree

was beautifully decorated and held a lot of presents. Some
were mine, also. As usual, they gave me a box of "goodies" to
bring home. I didn't want to take it, but they are so solicitous
for my welfare that I could not refuse. There were fruitcake,
layer cake, candy, nuts, salad, turkey sandwiches, and fresh
rolls. Reminded me of the good old days. They really are
precious.

Suffered no ill effects from Christmas. In fact, felt quite rested.
This morning Dr. [Lorenzo D.] Turner, former head of the
English Department of Howard University, came in to see
me. Was also formerly a teacher of mine at the University. We
are publishing his book, *Anti-Slavery Sentiment in American
Literature*. A fine piece of work, presented as a doctoral dissertation at the University of Chicago. Told me he is collaborat-
ing with Dr. Eva Dykes and a Miss Coleman, of Howard
University, in getting out an *Anthology of Negro Verse*. Also
had some good news for my good friend [Emile] Holley. Fisk
will need a man in English next year. Holley, I told Turner,
will make an excellent teacher and co-author. Ambitious, talented, conscientious. A fine scholar. Turner likes Fisk. Can
save money there. Only handicap—lack of library facilities.
This will be lessened by the proposal to give the teachers three
months off during the summer for research. I would rather
teach at Fisk than at any other Negro school. The University
has a wide-awake, sympathetic, and liberal president in
Thomas Elsa Jones. He is a Columbia University Ph.D. Only
a slip prevented my going there in 1928.

Thursday
December
26
1929

    Called upon Emile to see his mother, who has been here
since Tuesday. I was unspeakably glad to see her. It was mutual. We embraced each other, so glad were we to be together
again. Joked with Miss C[?], who told me that I must have
loved much, to write such poetry as I compose. Told Emile of
Turner's proposition. Emile feels that it is a little far removed
from here. This attitude is colored, no doubt, by the expectancy of his entering the new City College in the fall. Will
consider Fisk, however.
    Went to a party at my friend Jones'. Party dull. Did not

enjoy myself except for a flirtation with a girl whose name I do not even remember.

Friday
December
27
1929

Dr. Thomas I. Brown of Morgan College came in this afternoon. Spent about two hours with me. Consequently, I was unable to do the work I had allotted myself. Told me he will soon leave Morgan to become the Head of the Baltimore Urban League. Brown is an ardent enthusiast in the work of our Association, and, in the mail this week, sent us a contribution collected from his students. We entered into a discussion of the death of Mr. E. C. Williams, former librarian of Howard University, whose passing, due to cancer of the stomach, we thought may have been induced by improper diet. This brought us into a mutual outpouring of confidences concerning the struggles of Negro youth in their attempts to secure an education. Told him of my spending my last eight cents in New York City for rice and apples, and subsisting for two days upon a concoction of them cooked together.

After dinner, returned to the office at 8:30. Remained until 10:30. Met Miss Bowser (now Mrs. Adkins), also Laura, who lives with Mrs. Mahoney. Asked them to help me put up curtains. They did, until the manager called to inform me that the tenants beneath me were complaining about the noise caused by hammering nails and dragging chairs around. Must admit that 11 o'clock at night is no time to be putting up curtains, but then there have been other noises here until the wee hours of the morning, about which I have never expressed my dissatisfaction. But then, no two mortals are alike.

Saturday
December
28
1929

Miss Meyers types so slowly that I took her off the manuscript and substituted Mrs. Harris, placing the former on the letters which are to be sent out January 3. The change was soon evident by the number of pages turned out by Mrs. Harris, who has had more experience in such work than Miss Meyers.

Mrs. Mickey called me this morning to tell me that the check which she cashed for the bags was returned from the bank. Asked if I desired her to send personal check in its stead. Of course not, for I had purposely deposited money last Monday to cover such an emergency. Felt mortified, however, for she and her husband had been so kind to me, and it appeared as if I were presuming upon their goodness. Told her I would straighten the matter out at the bank during the noon break.

Deposited money for the Associated Publishers at the Metropolitan Bank. Did not have time to go to the Liberty Bank. Bought an aluminum double boiler and another smaller saucepan. Needed them, for others have been burned up. Also bought four wine glasses, for Harry [Hipp] and Florence [Bacote] are coming tomorrow. Telegram here at noon from Harry, stating neither Helen [Notis] nor Marguerite [Skeeter] could come.

Sterling Brown, the poet, came in this afternoon. Bought a copy of the *Journal of Negro History* for April, 1927. A very brilliant chap. Phi Beta Kappa from Williams College. (Father was formerly head of Correspondence Study in the School of Religion of Howard University.) Has a deep interest in history. Wanted to read Woodson's reply to one Eaton, who had, in a magazine article, made some remarks upon the Negro which he could not substantiate. Woodson subsequently had torn his argument to shreds.

Went to dinner. Arrived home at 8:30. Ruth [Beverly] came in about 9 o'clock. Had lots of fun until two.

The phone rang about 5:30 a.m. I was so sleepy, however, that I could only answer "yes, yes," and had no idea who was speaking until after I had returned to bed. Then it dawned upon me that it was Harry. I quickly rose, washed, and made myself presentable by the time he and Florence arrived. It was certainly good to see my old pal, Harry. Is dearer than a brother to me. And Florence, despite her youth, feels that she is a member of the "gang." Also Brown, her sweetheart! As I looked at them (Brown and Harry), I felt that, after all, it is a strange world.

After our enjoyable reunion, Harry and Florence left at 3:30. I went to the office, where I remained until 7:00. While writing, Mr. Mickey came in. Chatted about history. Showed him my diary kept while selling magazines last summer (1927).

Sunday
December
29
1929

Became so interested that he overstayed his time. He and his wife are attending a dawn dance at 12:30 a.m.

Monday
December
30
1929

Dr. Woodson was here when I arrived at 8:30 this morning. Gave him my report. Only jarring note was the loss of 200 stamps. Miss Dunlap either lost them or did not receive them or someone mailed Christmas cards with them. Hope they didn't. Dr. Woodson looked very refreshed and rested. I worked quite diligently today. Stopped at bank. Asked Mr. Greene [bank teller], to call Kahn's department store and tell them to return the check. It would be honored.

Dr. Woodson received a fruitcake from his sister in West Virginia. Gave it to me. Said it was too rich for him. Also too rich for me, but I thought of friends who would come in during the remainder of the holiday season. It would come in handy. Very kind of him.

Helen [Massey] was supposed to come help me put up curtains. Did not expect her. Neither did I particularly desire her to come. She did not disappoint me, for, true to her unreliability, she came not. Called, and although I believe she was at home, [her landlady] told me that she would not be in from work until late. If I depended upon her, my curtains would not get up before June.

Mr. Samuels came in to talk about insurance. Advised me to take $5,000 worth in February. Later he brought in Mr. Stevenson, Manager of the Washington Branch of the Supreme Liberty Life Insurance Company, a Negro Company. Told me of interesting experiences in France. Also stated I ought to take the $10,000 policy to which I had partly agreed. I promised with the stipulation that Woodson know nothing of it, for since Mr. [S. W.] Rutherford, President of the National Benefit Insurance Company, is Secretary-Treasurer of the Association for the Study of Negro Life and History, it would logically follow that I would take my insurance from him. Stevenson gave me his word to keep the transaction confidential.

Lovett came in. He had heard that I was getting Chicago on

my radio without an antenna. He stayed for a while. Left after listening to news from St. Louis.

<table>
<tr><td></td><td>Tuesday
December
31
1929</td></tr>
</table>

Last day of the old year. Am making no resolutions, therefore, will have none to break. Put in a hard day's work. Started to have a few friends come in to welcome the advent of the New Year, but decided not to. Mrs. Harris had asked me during the day to have a little party.

Met Samuels. Asked me to come down and play cards, which I did. Told Mr. and Mrs. Mickey to come in after returning from the movies. They came before I returned from Samuels. Left a note. I went up after them. They came down, and between us we prepared a salad with other refreshments and ginger ale. Mr. Mickey went upstairs and brought down some wine. Mrs. Mickey drank a small glassful and it apparently rendered her *hors de combat*. They left about 1:30. I went to the Mahoneys' for a while, returned, and went to bed. I was lonesome. By the way, I received a letter today from Helen [Notis] in Newark. Explained that although she received the bag I sent, it was a little too large. Asked me if I would be kind enough to change it for a smaller one. Mr. Mickey felt that she was ungrateful; Mrs. Mickey was astounded. I realize just how Helen felt. I would take the same attitude about a necktie I did not like. Regardless of how much it cost, I would not wear it. Mrs. Mickey agreed to change it. Helen Grinage was tickled over hers. By the way, Helen Notis sent me a beautiful formal dress set [studs and cuff links] as a Christmas gift. Told me she had also sent a birthday gift, but it was returned.

The dying year has been marked by many epoch-making events.

[18] Preparing for Negro History Week

Wednesday
January 1
1930 The beginning of a new year. Hope springs anew in every heart that this year will be even better than the last. My main desire is the fulfillment of my ambition—completion of the study and then?

Rose late. Went to dinner at 1:30. From there called upon Miss [Ophelia] Davidson to extend New Year's greetings, then to the office.

When I arrived, Woodson was filing and sorting letters obtained from a Mr. Whitefield McKinlay.[1] Woodson has hundreds of them from President [Theodore] Roosevelt, Booker T. Washington, and many other prominent men. Letters from Booker T. to McKinlay show that for every measure or speech of any importance that Roosevelt made concerning Negroes, he first consulted Booker T. Washington. [The letters are] a great storehouse of information. Will immortalize McKinlay, says Dr. Woodson. Letters desiring patronage, asking McKinlay's intercession for some favor, letters concerning impending failures of Negro banks, etc. from 1890 to the present (1929), all were included. Left the office at 6:30. Went to

1. McKinlay, a real estate broker, was Booker T. Washington's closest friend in the nation's capital. President Theodore Roosevelt appointed him to a commission to investigate housing conditions among the poor in Washington, D.C., and President William Howard Taft appointed him Collector of the Port of Georgetown.

Rosslyn. Bertha was to have come. Did not appear before I
left. Returned to town. Went to the movies.

A fire here last night in the Capitol Building destroyed an
architect's office and some duplicate papers, causing damage
estimated at $3,000. About 7:30 Mrs. Harris called me. Sur-
prised me by saying that after I had gone Woodson told her in a
very sarcastic manner he was sorry that she had to be detained,
so that she "could not go home with her boyfriend." I asked
her to whom he was alluding. She answered to me; not only
that, but he taunted her, "You are always talking with him;
you go to see him, and I suppose when he is sick you go there
and nurse him." I was shocked, for although I am civil
towards Mrs. Harris, in no manner has my conversation with
her been other than the merest conventionalism, and most of
the time on some phase of the work. To think that she comes
here habitually is preposterous. He owes not only her, but me,
an apology. True, she did come here once, brought her baby
along one Sunday, and stayed about ten minutes. It was such a
surprise that she caught me looking like a wild man, with
unkempt hair, etc. She made her crowning mistake, however,
by telling him of the visit. And he has not been liberal enough
to interpret it in the proper light. Had there been anything to
hide, common sense might have told him that she would not
have divulged her coming here.

She feels that Woodson is jealous, for he has, in her own
words, made several advances to her. I will not say improper,
for I have never tried to draw her out on this point. But to
intimate that there is any vestige of unconventionality in the
relationship between Mrs. Harris and me is at once to cast a
foul calumny on both of us. And to make matters appear all
the more damnable, Mrs. Harris was so surprised that she
could not respond to his accusation. According to her, she just
remained silent. I would that he approached me. I can assure
him he will find me no Mrs. Harris. *Job* or no *job*; *manhood* first!

Spent two hours at the office, from 8:30 to 10:30. Interested
in perusing book by Ella Lonn, *Desertion During the Civil War.*

She finds that 100,000 men, roughly speaking, deserted from the Confederate Army, and more than twice that number from the Union Armies. For the Negroes, desertion was much lower—only 26,000 Negroes being labeled as deserters. Why? Military service for Negroes meant freedom.

[No entries were made for January 3 and January 4.]

Sunday
January 5
1930

Remained in until 4:45, when I went to Anacostia. Was too beautiful to stay indoors. Can't tell when I have been out to visit on a Sunday. Called upon Leona Turner and her husband. They are cousins of Ruth [Beverly], whom I used to date when we both were students at Howard University. Leona has a beautiful home, with every modern convenience; shower bath, electric range, Frigidaire, sun parlor, study, etc. The kitchen also has a breakfast set built into the wall. The walls and woodwork are decorated in white and blue. I waxed quite flowery over their home; and just young people! Made me feel I, too, should have a home.

Leona asked me about Ruth. Why we were no longer sweethearts, etc. I evaded the question by replying that Ruth was teaching out of town, and when she returned, rushed pell-mell back to school. "Lee"—even as I—sensed my insincerity and tactfully altered the conversation. It was easy to discern, nevertheless, that they half-way looked upon me as a prospective husband for Ruth.

Monday
January 6
1930

Woodson has said nothing to me concerning Saturday's little flare-up in which he virtually accused Mrs. Harris of being intimate with me. Naturally, I did not allude to it. Mrs. Harris, however, continued to work on Dr. Woodson's papers, while Miss Meyers took up the burden of typing my manuscript.

Just before departure, two bits of information came to me. One I mentioned only because of its human side. Mrs. Harris, when Dr. Woodson had gone downstairs, came into my office to inform me that she had acted so mean, and her facial expression had been so forbidding, that Dr. Woodson asked her whether she was ill. I was forced to smile, for I realized that despite her light skin, she has that much Negro indelibly inter-mixed in her that her anger shows through her eyes.

Later Dr. Woodson told me he had called a meeting to draw up plans for a "monster" celebration for Negro History Week in February. In a gala meeting he will bring together the three living [Negro] ex-Congressmen—John R. Lynch (Missis-sippi), Henry P. Cheatham (North Carolina), and Thomas E. Miller (South Carolina), together with the recently-elected one, Oscar DePriest of Illinois. What could be more inspiring for me as the beginning of Negro History Week? It fired my imagination. We are to meet at 7:30 tonight.

By 7:20 I was back at the office. Dr. Woodson had already cleared his desk and made preparation, insofar as chairs, etc. were concerned. I brought up several more chairs from the downstairs office. Dr. Harris, a large, imposing-looking med-ical practitioner, was the first to enter. Dr. John R. Hawkins, financial secretary of the African Methodist Episcopal Church, and a prominent politician, followed. Dr. [W. H.] Jernagin, Pastor of Mt. Carmel Baptist Church, an ardent supporter of the Association, was next.

Beginning promptly at 7:30, as is his custom, Dr. Woodson outlined his plans as follows: (1) to present the current Negro Congressman, Oscar DePriest, together with the three living Negro ex-Congressmen of the Reconstruction Period, in a "monster" program in February as a climax to Negro History Week; (2) to arrange a banquet for about 400 persons; and (3) following the banquet, to hold a mass meeting for approxi-mately 1,200 persons at the Washington auditorium. Senator Otis F. Glenn of Illinois would be the chief speaker.

Mr. Hawkins asked Dr. Woodson how he proposed to fi-nance this program. The latter outlined his plan in the follow-ing manner: a banquet at $1.50 per plate for 400 persons would gross $600, $200 of which ought to be clear. This would leave about $350 to be raised in order to pay expenses for rental of the Auditorium and to defray additional costs of bringing the ex-Congressmen here. To do this, Woodson proposed charg-ing a fee of 50 cents. Hawkins opposed such a small fee, arguing that this would belittle the speakers and have a tendency to keep the crowd away. "Washington Negroes," continued Hawkins, "will patronize dances, but not such an event as this." Reverend Jernagin proposed a reduction of the fee to 25 cents. I felt that would be more unacceptable, if an admission fee *had* to be charged. It was finally decided to charge no admission, but to take up a silver offering. But to do so in the presence of the speakers would be out of place. Woodson proposed it be taken at the door, and the entrant be denied admittance if he refused to contribute, but this idea was voted down as impractical. Finally, we decided to let the matter of raising the remainder of the money be dropped until Friday.

Mr. [Morris] Lewis, DePriest's secretary, now entered. He said he had been under the impression that the meeting was to begin at 8 o'clock. I smiled, for I did not wish to accuse him of having come on "C.P." [colored people's] time. When apprised of the proposed method of collecting sufficient money to cover expenses, Mr. Lewis remarked that he had included that item in the cost, per plate, of the banquet. His figure of $2.50 for 400 persons would gross $1,000, of which $575 could easily be used to defray all extra costs. The Committee thought that price prohibitive, however. "Washington is not New York," said one. We also agreed to settle that question on Friday.

Some complications arose. Mr. Lewis stated that Mr. De-Priest would not be available for February 13, the proposed night of the program. We therefore decided on the night of February 10. I thought it a strategic date, for it would enable Negro History Week to start off with a "bang." Dr. Harris then submitted the name of a printer who, he stated, will publish the programs of the meeting free, in return for advertising. Woodson was skeptical. According to him, he has found from experience that Negro printers cannot get out such material as well or as cheaply as white ones. In addition, he stated that only a certain type of advertisement should be placed on such a program.

Lewis then presented his idea of a format for the program: the cover with an eagle, wings outspread, hovering over the

Capitol Building and the portraits of the Congressmen grouped in the center, with a short biographical sketch of each one under it. I felt that such a program would be too unwieldy. My idea was to place the portrait of each Congressman at the top of the page, with the sketch under it, giving each man a page. We finally decided to postpone anything definite concerning the program until Friday.

Dr. Woodson then drew up a list of people in strategic parts of the East who should be notified concerning the proposed celebration. These people will be notified by letter tomorrow. Mr. Lewis promised to see whether February 10 is satisfactory to Congressman DePriest and Senator Glenn. He will also find out whether the auditorium may be secured for that date. He promised to report to the office tomorrow. The meeting adjourned. I was thrilled over the prospects of a successful observance.

Mr. Lewis called this morning. Has secured the auditorium and Congressman DePriest's consent to be present on the 10th. Lewis will also draw up a list of names during the afternoon.

Secretary of State [Henry] Stimson left today for the Naval Conference at London. Hoover implores the American public to be patient, as well he may, for we all can recall quite clearly the debacle of 1922. Hoover declares that the peace of nations hinges on the arms parley. Senator [Cole] Blease, the demagogue from South Carolina, shocked the gathering yesterday by quoting salacious passages from interdicted books, which the good Senator contends are polluting our American populace. He gives the average American little discretion in the choice of books. Very few persons in South Carolina, I fear, will have their precious morals impaired, for they do not read that much. Fiorello La Guardia, Representative from New York, attacked Senator [William E.] Borah of Idaho, because of the latter's verbal assault on Prohibition last week. Says latter ought to begin to criticize things at home. Just a lot of blah! blah!

Went to the movies after dinner. Came home about 8:30.

Carol [Horne] arrived about ten minutes until nine. Had not seen her in more than a month. She had scarcely been here more than ten minutes before the house phone rang. I knew it was Irene, and straightaway I regretted Carol's presence here. Had to go down, however. No one was there. About half an hour later, the phone again rang. I went downstairs, and there was Irene. Looked so relieved to see me. Got on elevator and asked me to take her to the 4th floor. How disappointed she seemed when I told her I could not see her now. She looked so charming. Told me she would see me tomorrow. Carol left at 11:00.

Wednesday
January 8
1930

Saw Irene. Said she was disappointed last night. Also worrying over her husband and brother. Wanted to talk with me.

Crown Prince Humbert of Italy and the Crown Princess Marie of Belgium were married today. The Chicago *Tribune* (according to its announcer, as I write) had the only representative at the wedding, he having received special invitation from the Italian King. Mr. Julius Rosenwald, famous philanthropist and friend of the Negro, was married today to a St. Paul lady. Mr. Rosenwald's wife recently died. No doubt his hasty marriage was the desire for companionship.

Coast guardsmen confessed today to stealing, smuggling wine, and accepting graft. This happened at Atlantic City last week. And still we try to enforce Prohibition, which has brought in its wake killings by the wholesale, gangs, rackets, hypocrisy, smuggling, and various other evils which are filling our jails.

Saw Bertha tonight. Had to go after check left there last week. How she did scold me for failing to visit, or even call her, all during the holidays! Told her I was busy. Knew she did not believe it. But, nevertheless, it was true. . . . Cousins Susie [Robinson] and Winnie, religious fanatics, tried to frighten me into embracing their faith. I can still think for myself, however. To do as one would be done by is religion enough for me. Let the future take care of itself. Dr. Davis had been here to examine me for an insurance policy.

My friend, Lovett, awakened me at 1:00 a.m. to affix my radio to his aerial, which he had put up this evening. Kept me up until 2:30. Persuaded me at that hour to come to his apartment. Believing his wife had retired, I slipped on a bathrobe over my pajamas. Was shocked to find her reading. It was too late, however, to turn back. She served us ice cream and cake.

The Progressives won their fight in the Senate today. The Old Guard had tried to keep young Senator [Robert] La Follette off the Finance Committee. After the dust of battle had settled, not only was La Follette safely ensconced on the Committee, but also Senator [John] Thomas of Idaho, as well as Senator [John James] Blaine of Wisconsin, on the overwhelmingly conservative Committee on Banking and Currency.

Thursday
January 9
1930

A little scandal in Congressional circles. The secretary of Representative [Harold] Knutson of Minnesota, Joseph Cassel Ridgeway, was arrested yesterday, charged with having embezzled $750 out of the funds of the First National Bank of Block, North Dakota, while acting as receiver in August, 1926. He was released on bond of $2,500 to stand trial in Fargo, North Dakota.

Major floods are threatening the South. Warm weather and rains are the cause. The American delegation to the London Naval Conference sailed from Hoboken today. Ninety-six men and women all told. Mr. Hoover gave a breakfast for the delegates yesterday. The Conference begins on January 20.

Went to Dr. [Rhett] Stewart tonight to be examined before the insurance doctor does so. Just to check. Lungs, heart, kidneys okay. Did not take blood test. Will do so tomorrow. Asked me to join the Continental Insurance Company. Weigh eleven pounds more than when I was there in September. Was gratified.

Mr. [William M.] Brewer came in about lunchtime. Had just read the proof of Dr. Woodson's *Rural Negro*. Extolled it. His words may be taken relatively, however. He worships Woodson's genius. It is *good*, because it is *Woodson's*. Brewer checked

Friday
January 10
1930

a couple of omissions. Told Woodson the work was marvelous. Woodson laughingly remarked he was sorry, for then no one else would attempt to write upon the subject.

Tonight another meeting apropos The Negro History Week Banquet and Mass Meeting. Main question was how to finance the proceedings. Mr. [Garnet C.] Wilkinson, Assistant Superintendent of Washington Schools, proposed that we secure a sufficient number of men and women in town to underwrite the expenses of the Auditorium and cost of bringing the ex-Congressmen here. I suggested that we find 200 persons to subscribe $5 each, said $5 entitling person to two tickets for the banquet. Auditorium admission, programs, etc. would be free.

Woodson objected, at first, to the price of $2.50. [James Lesesne?] Wells agreed with me. Wilkinson, although at first objecting, finally saw the light, after I explained that such persons would be more willing to part with $5 if they saw some tangible return, rather than to subscribe that amount without such a possibility. Wilkinson is *so* deliberate, yet a good thinker. Did not want the necessity of lifting an offering to mar the dignity of the program. No one did, and since no one could devise an unobtrusive, yet efficient, method of taking up such a collection at the Auditorium, the proposal jointly made by Wilkinson and me (or should I say Wilkinson's suggestions, plus my idea that we make the banquet defray all expenses) stood.

Woodson then wanted to know what price should be charged out-of-town persons and other Washingtonians, not listed as patrons? Wells and I were insistent that they pay $2.50, the same as the others. The members finally agreed. Doubt if I acted prudently in pushing my ideas. Ought to have listened. Dr. Woodson, with whom I am affiliated, is sponsoring this affair. If it fails, Woodson will be the loser. He has already given his personal check for $100 as a down payment on the Auditorium. I have to marvel at the man. The secret of his success is that he has the courage to plan, and the confidence that, although the money is not presently available, his project will succeed.

Asked by Wilkinson where the money will ultimately come from, should the subscription fail, Woodson answered, "I am not worried about failure. It will go over. I just start things and never worry where the money will come from. I started the *Journal of Negro History* that way. A white woman, who was a member of the Board of Directors, became indignant, . . . asked me in a letter how dare I plunge the Association some $350 in debt, and sent in her resignation." Woodson laughed. I gazed at him in admiration as he told of it. "That was the first copy," he added, "published in 1916. It has not missed an issue since."

Before adjourning we decided to write all Negro Assemblymen. We will introduce them at the meeting. It will be inspirational. Tickets for the banquet we decided to make *gratis* for the Assemblymen. They will be our guests. Tuesday, we will meet to get a larger committee to raise the $1,000. Letters will go out tomorrow. I believe this affair will be a huge success. It ought to be a tremendous fount of inspiration to all, particularly to me.

Woodson left a note on my desk at noon telling me to return all books to the Library of Congress. He had received another notice about them. Inconveniences me seriously, but I suppose he knows what he is about. Before going home, Woodson asked me to leave the manuscript on his desk, that he might begin reading it tomorrow. I did not wish to do so, for there are certain revisions yet to be made in several chapters. Will comply with his request, however.

Saturday January 11 1930

Very tired. Returned from dinner at 7:30. Took books to library. Placed manuscript on Dr. Woodson's desk. Left two notes attached to each set. One on the unrevised manuscript informed him that it could not be read in that form, that I had not had opportunity to make revisions. On the other, I informed him it could be read. The latter group consisted of almost 325 pages; the first group some 125 pages. The capacity for work on the part of Dr. Woodson is certainly astounding. So tired, I was glad to come home, take a hot bath, and retire.

Sunday
January 12
1930

Rose at 10:30. Did so purposely in order to secure a little much-needed rest. Called Helen [Massey]. Supposed to be ill abed. Called upon her this afternoon. Lo! Instead of finding a sick person, I beheld her sitting at cards—whist to be exact. Putting my religion in my pocket, I played also. Had amazingly good luck. Did not lose a game. Played six. Bohanan, a friend, came in. Looks almost ghostly. I can't realize why. Helen now was not to be seen. Still another, a Mr. Cook, called later. Seems to be the real object of Helen's affections. Left about 5:30. Was eating dinner when Ruth [Beverly] called. Wanted me to come out. Did so. Saw Vashti, her sister, for the first time in more than a year and a half. Has grown quite plump. Ruth said she called me last night. I was out. Just as well, for tired as I was, I desired to see no one. Ruth is coming to town next Sunday. Will see me then.

Monday
January 13
1930

Felt that Dr. Woodson and I would have it hot and heavy today. Did not materialize, fortunately. Woodson said he wanted to have me finish the study this week. (If so, it would certainly lift a load off my mind.) He wants me to reduce the first two chapters on "Antebellum Occupations" to a mere statement. I felt more detail should be included. Spent the day on tables at the library.

Tuesday
January 14
1930

Spent most of the day at the library verifying the tables for the newly-made first chapter, resulting from Dr. Woodson's suggestion to combine chapters one and two.

Went to meeting about 7:30. Only about twenty present. Mr. [S. W.] Rutherford, of the National Benefit Insurance Company, entered. Brought with him two distinguished guests in the persons of Dr. John B. Watson, President of Arkansas A & I College, and a minister from Englewood, New Jersey. Each had a word to say in regard to observance of Negro History Week. Each subscribed to the banquet. Rutherford made himself responsible for five tickets.

Not much business accomplished at the meeting. Members did appoint a banquet committee consisting of Miss [Susie] Quander, a school teacher; Mrs. [G. Dorothy?] Pelham; and

Mr. [Sylvester] McLaurin, a lawyer. Committee is to report as soon as possible. Group feels that we cannot secure the Howard University dining hall because of a conflict with students' dinner hour. Dunbar High School and/or Armstrong High School auditoriums were suggested as alternative places. Mr. Lewis submitted an invitation form. To me it read more like a broadside. Would make a good handbill. Too much in it. A letter, I believe, should go with it under separate cover, or else precede it. Wrote out additional list of names for large committee we were to work with. The meetings have been disappointing so far. Have not had enough persons to work with. By the way, Dr. John W. Davis, President of West Virginia [Collegiate] Institute, came in. Was glad to see me. Asked me to send him a French and Spanish teacher *post haste*.

[No entries were made for January 15 and January 16.]

At the meeting tonight a larger number present. Mr. McLaurin was made chairman of the Executive Committee. Morris Lewis was named secretary. I believe Lewis and Dr. Harris had prearranged that the former should be elected chairman and the latter secretary. As Woodson commented, "Might just as well have elected DePriest."

Friday
January 17
1930

[No entries were made for January 18 through January 25.]

Found my "Lynchburg" (1927) diary today. Was so happy I knew not what to do. Stayed at the office until 4:30. Had engagement with Mr. Lewis at 5 o'clock. Told him that under no consideration should this meeting develop into a political affair. He assured me it would not. Lewis promised to send me the *Congressional Record*. Went to Bertha's. Weinberg [Boyd] was there. Had not left, as she supposed. I could not get away until 10 o'clock.

Sunday
January 26
1930

Terrible day. Raining and snowing. Worked on the second chapter. Had to cut it up yesterday, for the way Woodson had struck out certain parts caused quite a bit of repetition and lack of coherence. Had Miss Meyers type it.

Monday
January 27
1930

Went to the Census Bureau at 3:30. Saw Mr. [William Lane] Austin. Asked him whether there had been a 1927 agricultural census. Told me "No." I felt much relieved. Asked him for a copy of the census monographs on *Farm Population* and *Farm Tenancy*. He gave them to me. Also sent me to the chief clerk for others. Called upon Dr. [Joseph Adna] Hill. He gave me a copy of his *Women in Gainful Occupations*. I returned to the office at 4:30. Left at 6:25. Remained to give Miss Lavertee information about schools. She is a girl from the South who wants to avail herself of opportunites for education here. Very commendable. Only trouble is she belongs to that darned "House of Prayer" and is more or less fanatically religious.

Tuesday
January 28
1930

Dr. Woodson read the chapter on "Manufacturing After the World War." Only correction seemed to be his inability to read part of the manuscript where the typist had either left out words she could not understand or else had interpreted them as best she could, thereby making no sense at all. Was especially evident concerning textile mills. All in all, we got along well. I was quite excited, however, due to the strain, with nerves on edge. Miss Meyers felt it once or twice, but, womanlike, was sympathetic.

Now to pick up subscriptions for the banquet. Left office at 5:20 for this purpose. Went to Emile's [Holley]. Received $7.50 ($2.50 for [Emmett] Dorsey) from him. Stopped by Dr. [William James] Pinkhard's. Induced him and his wife to subscribe. Secured [Edward P.] Lovett's $5.00. Gave my own check, and with $5.00 from Mr. Arnold, went to the meeting armed with $32.50. Woodson reported $30.00. [Roscoe Conklin] Bruce said he had $50.00 but not at hand. We must certainly work faster, insofar as subscriptions are concerned, in order to raise the necessary amount.

A petty discussion then ensued over whether the banquet should be formal or informal. In my mind there should be no question. Banquet begins at 5 o'clock. Lasts until 7 p.m. Therefore, since we will be there after 6 o'clock, a dinner jacket seems to be in order. Mrs. Hilyer supported that view. Ought to make a good appearance, she said, because of the distinguished people who will be there. Mrs. Pelham, more practical, however, replied that it should be left to the individual. If it is made formal, she said, many will stay away because of lack of formal attire. The talk flew back and forth; words upon words, but no one dared to put the question to a vote. I started to interpose my view. Woodson whispered I had better let the dress question drop. I did so. McLaurin, the Chairman, then summed it up by saying, "It is hoped that the banquet will be formal; it is desirable that the banquet be formal, but it is feared that the banquet will be informal." A hearty laugh greeted this play upon words. Dr. Woodson asked McLaurin to repeat it, which the latter did.

Now to the banquet. Bids for catering have run around $600. Would leave $400 net. Dr. Woodson favors Armajean, whose bid was $600. Mrs. Carruthers, a school teacher, favors Greenlease. McLaurin brought up the name of Georges. Said he could not read the latter's writing or translate the French dishes (a hearty laugh) on the menu. Woodson looked at me knowingly, his face wrinkled with laughter. Group could not reach agreement on the caterer. Georges would furnish decorations also. Woodson said under no consideration would he give Georges the banquet. Thought him unreliable. Unfortunately, Woodson does not know of Georges' experience. I could not counter, lest the impression be given that I was personally interested. Was Georges' fault. I had told him on Sunday to submit references. A reverend gentleman finally suggested we write out a menu and submit it to caterers for estimates. Approved.

Mr. Lewis talks about the banquet but brings in no subscriptions. So do most of the others. I shall make a plea at the next meeting for more action.

The Naval Conference is merely making gestures. Only thing members have done is to permit newspapermen to attend plenary sessions. Other meetings of committees will be closed. The poor public! They tell us to be patient!

Georges was waiting for me after the meeting. Persuaded him to go to Mr. McLaurin's home and talk with him. Georges is a good caterer, but diffident about giving references. Doesn't want people to know he is a cook. Foolish, I think. Georges came home with me. Had a little supper. Left about 12 o'clock. Said he had to study.

Received a letter from Helen [Notis] today. She had received the bag. Has promised to cook dinner for Ernest [Bacote]. I wondered whether she realized what she is doing.

Wednesday Today was spent correcting and inserting notes into combined
January 29 chapters. I am happy as the end of this study draws near. So
1930   much more I desire to do.

Dr. Woodson told me tonight we had not yet received $200. Fears that the affair will fail for lack of funds. Says Lewis talks but has collected no money. I went back to the office after dinner. Worked until 9:30. On the way home, it seemed as if it would snow.

Thursday   Snowed all day. Washington's biggest snow storm since 1922,
January 30 when roof of ill-fated Knickerbocker Theater collapsed, kill-
1930   ing and injuring several hundred persons.

Bertha called at noon. Wanted to know if I would return to office. Told her yes, by all means. Spent the remainder of the day putting in footnotes.

Distributed 50 posters for Negro History Week celebration from 9th to 14th Streets N.W. And, of course, all along U Street. Even put some in white business establishments. Met Professor [Lorenzo] Johnson en route home. Asked me if I would call for his subscription. I assured him I would. Returned home about 9 o'clock. Tired, went to bed immediately.

Friday   Collected $12.50 today. Secured $5.00 from Clarence Baker.
January 31 Also, the same amount from Professor Lorenzo Johnson, my
1930   former English teacher at Howard University. Mrs. Morse
            promised me $5.00, but could only spare $2.50. I also have a
            promise of tickets from Mrs. Victoria Bacote, the wife of my
            dear friend, Dr. Ernest Bacote of Newark, New Jersey. I shall
            pick that up later.

The meeting tonight was devoid of great interest. In fact,

Mr. McLaurin stated this was just a sort of "catch up" affair. The committee first discussed the program. Mrs. Carruthers, a teacher, suggested that the cuts of the Congressmen be placed on the inside of the program cover. In my opinion, a fine idea.

Quite a bit of discussion as to the selection of a caterer. Woodson would give it to Armajean's because, I believe, he takes his meals there and likes their food. I believe he is half-way pledged to them. Also, he is a friend of the family.

Georges' name again was suggested. Everyone laughed. Again Woodson took the ground that Georges was just a student—unreliable, unknown, and irresponsible—just trying to make a little money. I felt that, in justice to Georges, his true position should be given to the committee. Therefore, I took the floor, daring to oppose the "master." I told of Georges' experience as a caterer. His services have been employed by white groups alone, which understandably accounted for his being virtually unknown by this group. Told of his opening up the large chain of Maddux Hotels here, the many large banquets which he had served at churches, YMCA's, and the National Press Club. Told them he had enjoyed 15 years' experience in such work. Whether his cause was helped or not, it at least dispelled the suspicion that a totally incompetent and unreliable person had been recommended as caterer to the committee. The committee finally decided to make out a menu, secure its adoption by the committee, and obtain estimates. Latter will be presented at next meeting.

By the way, Dr. Woodson told me confidentially today that the reason the banquet committee failed to secure the Howard University dining hall was that McLaurin had given the impression it was to be used for a political meeting. President [Mordecai] Johnson then called Woodson and told him nothing was said by McLaurin concerning the connection of the Association with the banquet. He, President Johnson, had been informed that a citizen's committee was sponsoring it. McLaurin placed both Johnson and Howard University in an awkward postion. How were they to explain their refusal to accommodate a meeting, the purpose of which was for racial uplift? Conversely, a political meeting might do injury to the chances of the University's securing favorable legislation in Congress. In either case, Howard University stood to lose.

Saturday
February 1
1930

Had to go to Library of Congress today to look up "Jacksonville Agreement," mentioned in [Abram L.] Harris' "Negro Coal Miners" in *Opportunity*, magazine of the National Urban League, for October, 1925. Woodson asked me to define it. I could not. Searched at library until I finally found it. Was just a restatement of the "Cleveland Agreement" of 1920, which fixed the wage scale in the Central Competitive Coal Fields, embracing Ohio, Indiana, Illinois, and western Pennsylvania. Its purpose was to reduce the "cut-throat" competition engendered by cheap coal from the West Virginia coal mines, dug by non-union labor. The Mellon Company of Pennsylvania broke their contract in 1925 and imported 3,000 Negroes into the western Pennsylvania mines.

Just remembered I am to speak at the Vermont Avenue Baptist Church tomorrow. Dorothy Dean called. Informed me she had arranged for Mr. Lewis, DePriest's secretary, and me to speak at several Arlington, Virginia, churches on the same day.

Sunday
February 2
1930

Pretty full day. Went to Vermont Avenue Baptist Church at 11:20. Wanted to make an announcement about the meeting at the Auditorium for Negro History Week. Could not do so before 12 o'clock, I was told, because the pastor began his sermon at 12:40. Although I had previously sent up my card, requesting three minutes to present my information, I had to leave at 12:08, for I had an engagement with Mr. Morris Lewis at 12:15.

Arrived at latter's home, 1744 K Street, N.W., at that hour. We were to leave for Arlington, Virginia, to speak at three churches there, thanks to the arrangements made by Miss Dean. Left about 12:20. Delayed, waiting for a Miss Todd, friend of Mr. Lewis' brother. Went through Rosslyn. Got lost in Fort Meyer. To make matters worse, twice the car got stuck in snow and ice which covered the dirt road. Fortunately, we extricated ourselves by placing dry grass under the back wheels. Finally reached Arlington about 1 o'clock. Then, about a half mile from the church, the car became mired down again. Oh, these country roads!

This time we were the recipients of one of the finest exhibitions of service that I have ever experienced. We were unable to move the car. Seeing a house about 200 feet away, Mr. Lewis suggested we solicit aid there. Arriving, we found that a white family lived there. The door was answered by a woman who communicated our predicament to her husband. He and another man immediately joined us with shovels, bags, pieces of wood, etc. While assisting us, one of the men apologized for their delay, stating that his mother had died just last evening.

We were overcome with their fine show of sportsmanship, their willingness to help us, despite their bereavement, which would have been excellent grounds for refusal. To our amazement, moreover, they refused to accept anything for their services, and we knew only too well that to press the offer would be tantamount to insulting these fine-spirited men. I shall never forget them. Mr. Lewis and I both regretted that we did not think to ask either their names or addresses that we might have sent them, at least, a floral offering of thanks.

Finally reached one church, St. John's Baptist. People were just leaving. I asked the pastor to call them back. He did so. Both Lewis and I spoke, telling them about the program and exhorting them to attend. They seemed interested and vowed they would come to the auditorium. Went next to Mount Zion Baptist Church. Caught Reverend Greene and some of his flock. He also called those of his congregation who had not departed. We got over our message to them.

Now an unexpected occurrence took place. The church where we were booked to speak, Mt. Olive Baptist, threatened to refuse us permission to do so. The deacon there said that they let nothing interfere with Sunday services. One man, in particular, was especially obdurate. Although Mr. Holmes and Mr. James Ball were friends of my family, playmates of my mother, they refused to be swerved. I finally asked to see the pastor, Reverend Lee. He decided that we could speak after communion service about 5:30 p.m. Poor Dorothy Dean, who had arranged for us, was quite outdone. It was too late to speak now, for the congregation had left.

Back to town. Took dinner. Called on Ophelia Davidson. Then back to Arlington. We were given five minutes. I spoke first. Had to counteract the idea that meeting was to be a political confab. (Miss Dean had confided to me that it was mainly on those grounds that our speaking at the church had been refused.) Told congregation about work done by Booker T. Washington. Then compared Woodson's efforts to his. Left Lewis to fill in the gaps.

Back to the office for a meeting of the executive committee. Two important questions had to be settled. How small is the nature of man! McLaurin, the Chairman, refused to allow John R. Hawkins to be master of ceremonies at the Auditorium. Stated it appeared as if he were being shelved. Woodson replied that he was still Chairman, but John Hawkins was President of the Association; hence, had to have some place on the program, and master of ceremonies was the logical position for him. Then, too, Hawkins has more poise, refinement, and dignity than McLaurin. The latter still demurred. Finally, I made him see that he was actually conferring the power upon Hawkins. When assured that he would be the toastmaster at the banquet, and also have a speech to make at the Auditorium, McLaurin finally yielded.

A sharp debate now arose regarding what to do about the National Anthem. Should it be "The Star Spangled Banner," "America," or the so-called Negro National Anthem? Most of them—Lewis, Mrs. Scott, and Miss Quander, a school teacher—stated that we should sing the Negro National Anthem, "Lift Every Voice and Sing." Woodson objected. It was being put to a vote when I called unreadiness. Taking the floor, I spoke at some length, and perhaps a little heatedly, to the point that we are first and foremost American citizens; that to sing "Lift Every Voice and Sing," giving it the same construction as "America" or "The Star Spangled Banner," would not only be tantamount to renunciation of our citizenship, but a voluntary yielding up of those rights and privileges for which we have been so long and bitterly contending. Further, it would also be diametrically opposed to the sum and substance of the purpose of Negro History Week and its program, which is to inspire our youth to become better citizens by acquainting them with their past history. Moreover, it is also meant to teach them to love this country, which they and their forefathers have done so much to develop into the greatest nation in the world. Finally, I added, it would be tantamount to both an insult and an embarrassment to these Congressmen, our guests, who have taken an oath to support the Constitution of the United States. Seems I won my point, for the Committee voted to delete the so-called race anthem at the beginning and at the end of the ceremony. Naturally, I was gratified.

Left the meeting. Went to Bertha's. Ate dinner there. She "berated" me for not taking time to eat regularly.

Nothing of great importance today. Continued to work on manuscript.

Monday February 3 1930

Things brightened up considerably tonight insofar as the banquet was concerned. Prior to the meeting tonight, only some $300 had been subscribed. Mr. Bruce, Superintendent of Washington Schools, however, started things rolling by bringing in $95. Mrs. J. U. King turned in $35. The flow was on. When the final count was announced, more than $275 had been collected, which made things appear much more roseate. Finally, when Dr. Woodson announced that he had $65 here at the office, the subscription of $1,000 seemed assured, with other ticket sellers still to be heard from. Woodson appeared very tired. Seemed encouraged tonight, however.

Tuesday February 4 1930

Spurred by the receipts of last evening, I secured $5.00 from Mrs. McAdoo at the YWCA; $5.00 from Clarence Baker; and $2.50 from Joseph Greene. The latter two are cashier and teller respectively of the Prudential Bank here.

Wednesday February 5 1930

Dr. Woodson is going to New York tomorrow. Asked me to come back tonight in order that he might show me necessary corrections to be made in the program. Among them were placing in order, as to age, the pictures of the Congressmen; deletion of the Tibbs Quartet, and the substitution of Mrs. Ethel E. Gibbs therefor; the rearrangement of the speaking program at the banquet and the like. He not only pointed out the desired corrections to me, but also typed them out in a letter to the printer. I am to take the proof to the printer in the morning, designate the desired revisions, read the corrected proof, and, if "okay," tell the printer to "run" the programs.

A touching incident occurred while I waited for Dr. Woodson to dress in preparation for his train. It showed the sacrifices which this man is making in order to lift up his race. He called downstairs to me that having washed his face, he could not find a clean towel upon which to dry himself, adding: "I do not believe any man in Washington, D.C., neglects himself as much as I." I knew only too well that he was telling the truth. I felt like going out and buying him a dozen towels, but, of course, at twelve midnight, that was out of the question.

But neglect himself he does. I have seen him go until 2 o'clock in the afternoon without eating, have seen him with his shirt tattered and torn about the neck, cuffs soiled, and his shoes sadly in need or repair. Greater things claim his attention; hence, his personal appearance suffers.

He asked me to buy some towels for him tomorrow, also some soap. He advised me, further, that he could be reached tomorrow night at the office, should anyone desire to see him. Instructed me to place no more names on the program, but to accept all subscriptions, telling the subscribers that their names would be taken care of accordingly. He also asked me to try to match envelopes for invitations which were to be sent out.

Waited downstairs until he was ready to leave for the train. Went to the train station with him. From there stopped by a drugstore; took dose of castor oil, for I felt badly. Arrived home about 12:45.

Had to hire a taxi in order to reach the office by 8 o'clock.
Once there, I was kept constantly on the go. Lewis, Mc-
Laurin, Bruce, and others called concerning either the placing
of names on the program or about additional tickets. I replied
evasively to all of them.

The program gave me trouble. I could not find the letter
that Dr. Woodson had typed last night, which was to go to the
printer. Searched his office in vain. Finally, decided to go
without it, since I knew all corrections to be made. Explained
everything to the printer. Told him to call when proof was
ready. Failed to find envelopes to match invitations. Bought
towels and soap for Woodson, also pajamas and table cover for
myself.

Back to the office. Found everyone agog. Thomas I. Brown
had called from Baltimore. Finally called again after I came in.
Ordered three reservations. Mrs. Henry Lincoln Johnson, the
poetess, also called. Wanted one reservation.

Now for trouble! Morris Lewis called. Wanted to know
whether certain names were on the list and the latest hour for
placing them thereon. Told him to refuse no subscriptions and
refer all queries concerning names to me. McLaurin called.
Had two subscriptions from a sergeant and captain from Fort
Myer. Asked if I could get their names on the list. Told him
they would be "taken care of." When I returned to the printer
in the afternoon, I found Mr. McLaurin had telephoned names
there and ordered the printer to publish them. Latter had not
yet done so. I told him to omit them.

Read proof. Certain corrections still not made. Waited for
final draft. Approved it, and told printer to go ahead with
printing them.

Mr. Bruce sent for eighteen sets of tickets. Could not give
them to him. He feared the teachers in outlying districts would
not receive them in time. I assured him they would.

Returned to the office later in the afternoon. McLaurin
called to ask about the names he submitted. I told him they
were in the hands of the printer.

Worked on manuscript. Left office about 7 o'clock. Glad to
get home.

Friday
February 7
1930

Dr. Woodson was in the office when I arrived at 8:15. I spent the day on the manuscript. In the afternoon Woodson received a copy of the program. Read it over. Called me in and told me I had ruined it by neglecting to change *Mrs.* Gibbs to *Miss* on the program. Said I "had ruined *her* by giving her a husband." Told him his correction was to change *Miss* to *Mrs.* Woodson wanted to see the letter he had typed. Told him I could not find it yesterday morning. He was quite angry. Said I was a poor man to attend to business. I swallowed my wrath and walked away.

At the meeting I fortunately met "Mrs." Gibbs. She was introduced to me by her pastor, Rev. Jernagin. I apologized to her, telling her I had made her a *Mrs.* before the world, when she was not married. The lady, however, assured me that she is *very much married.* I chuckled to myself. Told them what Woodson had said. Asked both to say nothing to him about the matter.

Now for the fun. This meeting first assured us of the banquet's success. Woodson feared, however, that the affair at the Auditorium would be a farce, because of meager attendance. It was agreed that several volunteers should speak at the various churches on Sunday. Several quickly offered their services.

Now for the *pièce de résistance.* Mrs. Pelham had been given 100 posters by me to distribute to the schools. Yet several teachers declared they knew nothing about the details of the affair. Woodson wondered what had become of the posters. Suggested I call Mrs. Pelham. I did, but failed to get her. Her daughter Sarah told me, however, that the posters were at her father's printing office. Woodson asked me to get them. When I arrived there the boy gave them to me. As I started down the stairs, he called me back. Told me they were not to be removed from the office. I became a trifle ruffled. Called the Pelhams again. This time Sarah Speaks, the daughter, and a former classmate of mine at Howard, declared, in no uncertain tones, that *nothing* was to leave the office. I reminded her, in tones equally as determined, that I proposed to carry the property of the Association out of that office. She fumed; I raged. I finally hung up. Called Woodson. Was almost too angry to tell him of the situation. He called the Pelhams. Result: I brought the posters and a sorely-rankled disposition away with me.

A whirlwind publicity campaign was then inaugurated. Posters were distributed among the committee members. Each person promised to place them in conspicuous places, either in businesses or in churches. Dr. Harris suggested that the celebration be announced in theaters and schools, either by slides or Speakaphone records. Naturally, Dr. Harris was selected as chairman of this committee. I was appointed to assist him. Dr. Harris pleaded illness and I straightaway realized that the chief burden would fall upon me. Still, I welcomed it. Anything to make this affair a success.

On to the office now. Lewis, McLaurin, Harris, Turner, and a few others came over. Lewis was indignant because certain names which he submitted were not included on the program. He had just picked up one, much to the chagrin of Woodson, who had wanted them to remain unseen until delivered to Major Atwood. Woodson told Lewis frankly that he did not mean to put his names on the list, but had to tell him something to keep him from bothering him. McLaurin looked for his names, but said nothing. Harris picked up another program to offer a similar adverse comment, but Woodson curtly asked him for it, adding: "Don't touch things on my desk." Result: Harris became incensed and quit the meeting.

There were still about 200 tickets to be sent out. Lewis asked if he might help. Woodson politely told him to go home. Lewis did so in a huff. Two Committee members alienated!

Turner, Woodson, and I then set ourselves to the task of getting out invitations. I stamped them with the seal of the Association, until I had blisters on the palm of my hand. We finally had them sealed and stamped by 1:45 a.m. Woodson then took them to the Post Office. I, utterly fatigued, crept home to bed.

Spent the morning trying to secure permission to have the celebration announced in all the Negro theaters. Was successful with the exception of two. These were the Republic and

Saturday
February 8
1930

Dunbar. The owner of the Republic Theater shifted the responsibility to his son, who was conveniently out whenever I called. Finally had a record made over the Speakaphone recording system for announcement of the meeting at the Howard Theater. Mrs. Georges informed me that my voice recorded well. I persuaded her to give the record to the Association for further advertising the observance. Knew Alexander, the owner, would sanction it. If not, we would buy the record.

Dr. Turner came in this morning. Wanted to know what arrangements had been made for checking wraps. I told him McLaurin was to attend to that. Turner replied that the latter had done nothing in that respect. That responsibility was now placed upon me. Called Mrs. [Lucille] Lovett in order to get the address and telephone number of Joe Busch, a "frat" brother and law student at Howard University, to help me. Unfortunately, she could not get the information for me. She did tell me, however, my radio had been going all day. Asked if she would turn it off. She kindly secured the key from the manager, went in, and did so.

People are frantically calling the office. Some want tickets; others are complaining that they have not received their tickets; still others that they have received two sets. I took two sets to persons on my way to dinner. Was also given two extra sets received by two different ladies. Very fine of them! After dinner I assisted girls in getting out 6,000 letters.

Lewis and his daughter came in. He asked me to reserve his group seats to and including "Q," beginning with section "A." Later Dr. Woodson gave me 25 sets of tickets. He then asked me to come down at 9:00 in the morning. He wanted me to assume the following responsibilities: (1) to get out tickets; (2) to reply to queries of newcomers to town, for a place to stay; and (3) to see that publicity is put over. He also gave me a letter of introduction to his cousin, who is a trustee of Shiloh Baptist Church. Further, asked me to get in touch with Messrs. G. Smith Wormley, Lewis, Brewer, and McLaurin to help me with the publicity. Woodson fears the mass meeting will not be a success. He leaves for Pittsburgh at 12:30. Both of

us were utterly fatigued. I felt as if I would collapse. Assured
him, however, I would get out the publicity tomorrow.

Reached home at 1:00 a.m. House upset, dishes unwashed,
and Helen [Notis] coming on the 6 o'clock train in the morning. Cleaned up. Went to bed at 3 o'clock. Nothing to eat in
the house.

Helen called from the station at 6 o'clock. So tired, I could
hardly stagger to the telephone. In fifteen minutes she was
here. Glad to see her, but wish she had not come at a time
when I felt absolutely exhausted.

Sunday
February 9
1930

Rested a while. Left for the office at 9 o'clock. Ordered
groceries from Stein's.

Did not take time to eat breakfast. Started to eat an orange
and while attempting to drink some milk, McLaurin entered.
Told me he proposed going to churches in order to announce
the meeting. I gave him placards and some of the throwaways.
I should state that my efforts to secure the services of Mrs. J. U.
King failed. She was going to Maryland with her husband,
Dr. King. Disappointed, I called Mr. Brewer, only to be disappointed again. He was at church, but Mrs. Brewer told me
she would communicate with me as soon as her husband returned. I then called Mr. G. S. Wormley. Fortunately, he
promised to cooperate with me this evening.

At 1:30, I spoke at Shiloh Baptist Church. The audience was
very attentive. I then rushed back to the office, called a taxi,
and took placards and several thousand throwaways to
Georgetown churches. Stopping at Gethsemane Baptist
Church, Union Wesley Church, Mt. Calvary Church, and
First Baptist Church, I gave ushers at each church placards and
several hundred throwaways, one of which requested the pas-
tor to kindly announce the mass meeting tomorrow. From
Georgetown, I rushed to the Vermont Avenue Baptist
Church. It is the largest Negro Baptist Church in Washington.
Its Pastor is the Reverend Mr. Wills.

I entered just as Reverend Wills was completing his sermon.
That vast audience of some 3,000 persons, crowding the aisles
and balconies and overflowing the spacious church, offered

the most inviting spectacle and opportunity yet to announce this meeting, which has almost become a part of me. I first drew the people to me by joining the church. Then I spoke to that multitude as I perhaps have never spoken before. When I finished, after five or six minutes, the pastor exclaimed, "Let the whole church go to the Auditorium." I was thrilled with the response.

Returning to the office in a glow of exhilaration, I informed Woodson of the response by the churches. He seemed pleased, but expressed some doubt that the ministers could actually get their congregations to attend. He was still busy with Brewer, preparing last minute details for the banquet and mass meeting tomorrow. I believe Woodson still doubts whether a representative audience will attend the program at the auditorium. Admission is free. I busied myself helping Woodson, Brewer, and the girls, answering phone calls, meeting out-of-town people, and getting out flyers.

Rushed home about 5 p.m., changed clothes, and taxied to Helen's cousin's for dinner. Then back to the office. Out again to speak at Shiloh Baptist Church, at 9th and W Streets. I rejoiced when the minister urged the congregation to help fill the auditorium tomorrow night.

I returned home exhausted, and retired about 12:30.

Monday
February
10
1930

This has been an unforgettable day. I reached the office at 8:30, and spent the morning at the Library working on the Negro Labor study.

Later, when I stopped by the office, I found Woodson was busy with people coming from different parts of the country for the Negro History Week celebration. New York, Chicago, Detroit, Pittsburgh, Charleston, St. Louis, Boston, Philadelphia, Newark, Memphis, and Kansas City were some of the cities represented. Woodson introduced me to many of the visitors, including Mrs. Lena Trent Gordon and Judge Edward Wilson and his wife from Philadelphia.

The Banquet in Armstrong High School cafeteria was a tremendous success. The food was delicious. A copy of the menu follows:

MENU
Fruit Cocktail
Consommé
Roast Turkey - Dressing - Gravy
Cream Potatoes—Candied Sweets
Buttered green peas
Hearts of Lettuce salad with French Dressing
Hot Rolls - - - - - - - - Coffee
Nuts - - - - Pickles - - - Olives
Ice Cream - - - - - - Fancy Cakes
1. Custard and Pistachio
2. Chocolate and Macaroon
3. Strawberry and Vanilla

Between 350 and 400 persons attended. The women were superbly gowned. Most of the men wore tuxedos. Woodson was pleased. So was I.

I left the banquet at 7:15 and rushed with Woodson to the Auditorium. The Congressmen traveled in the car with De-Priest. Long lines of people were entering the auditorium when we arrived. The crowd finally numbered between 5,000 and 6,000. Dr. John R. Hawkins presided. He made an excellent Chairman. What a thrill to see three Negro Congressmen in the flesh! Unfortunately, Congressman Henry P. Cheatham could not come. He had been injured in an automobile accident.

Speeches followed speeches. Dr. Woodson, as usual, set the stage by a short historical introduction. Hawkins then introduced the Congressmen: Thomas E. Miller of South Carolina, John R. Lynch of Mississippi, and Oscar DePriest of Illinois. All of them spoke briefly except Lynch. His remarks were particularly impressive, especially to me. By the way, Lynch still practices law in Chicago. He looks sturdy and is an eloquent speaker. Reflecting on the role of black Congressmen during the Reconstruction and post-Reconstruction periods, Lynch stated that their records were no better or worse than those of their white colleagues. He deplored the disfranchisement of the Negroes in the South, charging that the Republicans betrayed them. Continuing, he declared that the practical nullification of the Fifteenth Amendment began with the Taft Administration in 1908. Negroes, he went on, must not only continue to fight for the ballot, they must demand all their rights under the Constitution. To do this intelligently, he strongly advised, Negroes must study the Constitution. For this purpose, he has distributed thousands of copies of the Constitution among Chicago Negroes. In closing, he ardently prayed that his efforts would bear fruit.

At the conclusion, the immense audience of approximately 5,000 gave Lynch and his conferees a prolonged standing ovation. Woodson, Wesley, Hawkins, and others considered the meeting a great success. I was ecstatic; so too was Helen, who had travelled all the way from Newark, New Jersey, for the occasion.

Tonight's involvement makes me a confirmed and dedicated associate of Dr. Woodson. Negro History henceforth shall be my life's work. The Association is indelibly stamped upon me. It is my cause and shall transcend everything else, even my allegiance to Woodson.

I reached home, tired but elated. When I finally retired, I knew I had found my life's vocation and that Dr. Woodson was my historical idol.

[Appendix I] Publications Mentioned in the Diary

Abel, Annie Heloise, and Frank J. Klingberg, eds. *A Side-Light on Anglo-American Relations, 1839–1858, Furnished by the Correspondence of Lewis Tappan and Others with the British and Foreign Anti-Slavery Society.* Washington, D.C., 1927.

Adventures in Vinland. Probably contained in Joseph Fischer. *Discoveries of the Norsemen in America.* St. Louis, 1903; or Arthur Middleton Reeves, ed. and trans. *The Norse Discovery of America: A Compilation in Extensio of All the Sagas, Manuscripts and Inscriptive Memorials Relating to the Finding and Settlement of the New World.* New York, 1911.

Baltimore Afro-American, 1928.

Barry, John Stetson. *A Historical Sketch of the Town of Hanover, Mass., with Family Genealogies.* Boston, 1953.

Bentwich, Norman DeMattos. *Hellenism.* New York, 1920.

Bowers, Claude. *The Tragic Era: The Revolution After Lincoln.* Cambridge, Mass., 1929.

Bragg, George F. *History of the Afro-American Group of the Episcopal Church.* Baltimore, 1922.

Brunner, Edmund de Schweinitz, ed. *Churches of Distinction in Town and Country.* New York, 1923.

Channing, Edward. *Students' History of the United States.* New York, 1924.

Columbus, Christopher. *The Journal of Christopher Columbus (during his first voyage, 1492–1493) and Document Relating the Voyages of John Cabot and Gaspar Corte Real.* Translated, with notes and an introduction, by Clements R. Markham. London, 1893. Reprinted as "Journal of the First Voyage of Columbus," in *The Northmen, Columbus and Cabot.* Translated by Clements R. Markham, with some slight revisions by Edward G. Bourne. New York, 1906. Reprinted as *Christopher Columbus, the Journal of His First Voyage to America* (an abstract of the original journal, made by the Admiral's companion Las Casas). New York, 1924.

Current History, 1910–1920.

Davis, Edwin Griffith. *Text Book of Constitutional Law: Act of March 3, 1875*. Kansas City, Mo., 1906.

Davis, George B. *Elements of International Law, with an Account of Its Origin, Sources, and Historical Development*. New York, 1900.

Douglass, Harlan Paul. *How to Study the City Church*. New York, 1928.

———. *1000 City Churches: Phases of Adaptation to Urban Environment*. New York, 1924.

Dubnow, Semen Markovich. *History of the Jews in Russia and Poland from the Earliest Times to the Present Day*. New York, 1916.

Dubois, Félix. *Timbuctoo, the Mysterious*. New York, 1896.

Du Bois, W. E. B. *The Negro*. New York, 1915.

Dumas, Alexandre. *Adventures of D'Artagnan*. Probably refers to Alexander Dumas. *Twenty Years After*. New York, 1895.

———. *The Three Musketeers*. New York, 1926.

Esenwein, Joseph Bay. *The Art of Public Speaking*. Springfield, Mass., 1915.

Essadi, Abderrahman. *Tarik es Sudan*. Paris, 1898.

Estabrook, Arthur H., and I. E. McDougle. *Mongrel Virginians: The Winn Tribe*. Baltimore, 1926.

Freedom's Journal, 1817.

Frobenius, Leo. *Voice of Africa*. Translated by Rudolf Blind. London, 1913.

Grant, Ulysses S. *Personal Memoirs*. New York, 1909.

Harris, Abram L. "The Plight of the Negro Miners." *Opportunity*, III (October, 1925), 303, 312.

Helper, Hinton Rowan. *The Impending Crisis of the South: How to Meet It*. New York, 1857.

———. *Nojoque: A Question for a Continent*. New York, 1867.

Hill, Joseph Adna. *Women in Gainful Occupations, 1870–1920: A Study of the Trend of Recent Changes in the Numbers, Occupational Distribution, and Family Relationship of Women Reported in the Census*. Washington, D.C., 1929.

Historical Status and New Haven Society. Probably refers to William Chaunery Fowler. *The Historical Status of the Negro in Connecticut: A Paper Read Before the New Haven Colony Historical Society*. New Haven, 1875.

Jernegan, Marcus W. "Slavery and Conversion in the American Colonies." *American Historical Review*, XXI (1916), 504–27.

Johnson, Charles Spurgeon. *Ebony and Topaz: A Collectanea*. New York, 1927.

Locke, Mary S. *Anti-Slavery in America, from the Introduction of African Slaves to the Prohibition of the Slave Trade, 1619–1807*. Boston, 1901.

Logan, H. Raymond. "The Operation of the Mandate System in Africa." *Journal of Negro History*, XIII (October, 1928), 423–77.

Lonn, Ella. *Desertion During the Civil War*. New York, 1928.

Lugard, Lady Flora Louisa Shaw. *A Tropical Dependency*. London, 1906.

Maran, René. *Batualo or Batouala*. Translated by A. S. Seltzer. New York, 1922.

Mather, Cotton. *Diary*. Probably Murdock, Kenneth B., ed. *Selections from Cotton Mather*. New York, 1926.

Moon, Parker Thomas. *Imperialism and World Politics*. New York, 1926.

Moore, George Henry. *Historical Notes on the Employment of Negroes in the American Army of the Revolution*. New York, 1862.

_____. *Notes on the History of Slavery in Massachusetts*. New York, 1866.

Nell, William Cooper. *The Colored Patriots of the Revolution*. Boston, 1855.

Phillips, Ulrich B. *American Negro Slavery*. London, 1918.

Pittsburgh Courier, 1928.

Rhodes, James Ford. *History of the United States from Hayes to McKinley*. New York, 1918.

_____. *The McKinley and Roosevelt Administrations, 1897–1909*. New York, 1922.

Saga of Eric the Red. Probably contained in Joseph Fischer. *Discoveries of Norsemen in America*. St. Louis, 1903; or Arthur Middleton Reeves, ed. and trans. *The Norse Discovery of America: A Compilation in Extension of All the Sagas, Manuscripts and Inscriptive Memorials Relating to the Finding and Settlement of the New World*. New York, 1911.

Schlesinger, Arthur Meier. *Political and Social History of the United States, 1829–1925*. New York, 1925.

Seligman, Edwin R. A. *Principles of Economics, with Special References to American Conditions*. New York, 1926.

Small, Albion W., and George E. Vincent. *An Introduction to the Study of Society*. New York, 1922.

Story of 100 Operas. Possibly E. Markham Lee. *Story of Opera*. New York, 1909.

Taylor, Alrutheus Ambush. *The Negro in the Reconstruction of Virginia*. Washington, D.C., 1926.

_____. *The Negro in South Carolina During the Reconstruction*. Washington, D.C., 1924.

Turner, E. Raymond. *The Negro in Pennyslvania, Slavery—Servitude—Freedom, 1639–1861*. Washington, D.C., 1911.

Turner, Lorenzo D. *Anti-Slavery Sentiment in American Literature Prior to 1865*. Washington, D.C., 1929.

U.S. War Department. *The War of the Rebellion: A Compilation of the Official Records of the Union and Confederate Armies*. Washington, D.C., 1880–1901.

Washington, D.C., Sun, 1928.

Weishampel, J. F. *History of Baptist Churches in Maryland Connected with the Maryland Baptist Union Association*. Baltimore, 1885.

Wesley, Charles Harris. *Negro Labor in the United States, 1850–1925*. New York, 1927.

Wiener, Leo. *Africa and the Discovery of America*. Philadelphia, 1920–1922.
Woodson, Carter G. *African Myths, Together with Proverbs*. Washington, D.C., 1928.
_____. *A Century of Negro Migration*. Washington, D.C., 1918.
_____. *Free Negro Heads of Families in the United States in 1830*. Washington, D.C., 1925.
_____. *The Negro as Businessman*. Washington, D.C., 1929.
_____. *Negro in Our History*. Washington, D.C., 1927.
_____. *Negro Makers of History*. Washington, D.C., 1922–1928.
_____. *Rural Negro*. Washington, D.C., 1930.
_____, ed. *Journal of Negro History*. Washington, D.C.
Work, Monroe Nathan, comp. *Negro Year Book and Annual Encyclopedia of the Negro*. Tuskegee, Alabama, 1912–1938.
Young, Donald, ed. *The American Negro*. Philadelphia, 1928.

[Appendix II] Two Poems by Lorenzo J. Greene

To the Unknown Soldier

What means this sad, yet gorgeous sight?
    What mean these flowers so rare?
Is all this splendor, all this pomp,
    For one dead soldier there?

Who is this warrior bold deceased?
    What glories does he claim?
What honor to his country brought
    That merits him this fame?

What valiant deeds did he perform
    On Flanders' reeking strand?
Was he like mighty Ajax, chief,
    Of some heroic band?

Did he into the battle's din
    Rush in midst shot and shell,
And slay until he lifeless sank
    Amidst that raging Hell?

What matter what of honor, fame,
    He has his country brought?
What matter whether in the strife,
    Great deeds of arms he wrought?

Think not of glory— but a breath!
    But think of what he gave:
Ambition, loved ones, even life,
    His native land to save.

In him a grateful nation shrines
    Her nameless heroes lost;
Reveres her sons who, with their lives,
    Paid war's supremest cost.

This tribute breathes a nation's prayer,
    That war forever may cease;
That over this bleeding earth may dawn
    A day of lasting peace.

                November 11, 1921

The New Negro

Ah used to heah de ole folks say,
"Dis worl' ain't gwine to las'
Dat eberything down heah below
Will fall wif Gabriel's blas'."

I'se often heard dem in de church
A'shoutin' "Lawd t'will please us,
To let de white folks hab de worl',
But gib us Massa Jesus."

An' den ah laffs an' snickers so,
Cause folks like me an' you,
Knows dat de white folks got de worl',
And Massa Jesus too.

Ah don' know what de futah holds,
But sence I'se heah below,
I'se gwine ter git some ob dis worl',
An' let Massa Jesus go.

                  April, 1927

Editor's Bibliography

A. *Government Publications*

U.S. Bureau of the Census. *Negro Population, 1790–1915.* 1918.
_____. *Negroes in the United States, 1920–1932.* 1935.
_____. *Tenth Census of the United States, 1880,* Virginia, Vol. I.

B. *Newspapers*

Chicago *Defender,* 1928.
Kansas City (Mo.) *Call,* 1928.
New York *Times,* 1913–1930.
Pittsburgh *Courier,* 1928.
St. Louis *Argus,* 1928.
Savannah *Tribune,* 1928.

C. *Books and Periodicals*

Allen, Frederick Lewis. *Only Yesterday: An Informal History of the 1920's.* 1931; rpr. New York, 1964.
Bergman, Peter M. *The Chronological History of the Negro in America.* New York, 1969.
Berry, Mary Frances, and John W. Blassingame. *Long Memory: The Black Experience in America.* New York, 1982.
Bragg, George F., Jr. *History of the Afro-American Group of the Episcopal Church.* Baltimore, 1922.
Brawley, Benjamin. *A Social History of the American Negro.* 1921; rpr. London, 1970.
Brawley, James P. *Two Centuries of Methodist Concern: Bondage, Freedom and Education of Black People.* New York, 1974.
Current Biography: Who's News and Why, 1944. New York, 1944.
Daniel, W. A. *The Education of Negro Ministers.* 1925; rpr. New York, 1969.

Fauset, Arthur Huff. *Black Gods of the Metropolis: Negro Religious Cults of the Urban North.* Philadelphia, 1944.

Franklin, John Hope. *From Slavery to Freedom: A History of Negro Americans.* 5th ed. New York, 1980.

Frazier, E. Franklin. *The Negro Church in America.* New York, 1966.

Garvey, Amy Jacques. *Garvey and Garveyism.* Introduction by John Hendrik Clarke. 1963; rpr. New York, 1970.

———, ed. *Philosophy and Opinions of Marcus Garvey.* New preface by Hollis R. Lynch. 1925; rpr. New York, 1970.

Gosnell, Harold F. *Negro Politicians: The Rise of Negro Politics in Chicago.* Chicago, 1935.

Handlin, Oscar, *et al. Harvard Guide to American History.* New York, 1954.

Hill, Roy L. *Booker T's Child: The Life and Times of Portia Marshall Washington Pittman.* Newark, 1974.

Journal of Negro History, XIII–XV (1928–1930).

Locher, Frances C., ed. *Contemporary Authors: A Bio-bibliographical Guide to Current Writers in Fiction, General Nonfiction, Poetry, Journalism, Drama, Motion Pictures, Television, and Other Fields.* Vol. CI. Detroit, 1981.

Meier, August. *Negro Thought in America, 1880–1915: Racial Ideologies in the Age of Booker T. Washington.* Ann Arbor, Mich., 1963.

Meier, August, and Elliott Rudwick. *Black History and the Historical Profession, 1915–1980.* Urbana and Chicago, 1986.

Melton, J. Gordon. *Encyclopedia of American Religions.* Vol. II of 2 vols. Wilmington, N.C., 1978.

Richard B. Morris, ed. *Encyclopedia of American History.* Updated and revised. New York, 1965.

Mosley, Leonard. *Lindbergh: A Biography.* Garden City, N.Y., 1976.

Mowry, George E. *The Era of Theodore Roosevelt, 1900–1912.* New York, 1958.

Negro History Bulletin, XVIII (February, 1965).

Polk's Baltimore City Directory, 1928–1930.

Shulman, Albert M. *The Religious Heritage of America.* La Jolla, Calif., 1981.

Stewart, Ruth Ann. *Portia: The Life of Portia Washington Pittman, the Daughter of Booker T. Washington.* Garden City, N.Y., 1977.

Suffolk, Virginia, City Directory, 1927–1928. Asheville, N.C., 1927.

Thorpe, Earl E. *Black Historians: A Critique.* New York, 1971.

Toppin, Edgar A. *A Biographical History of Blacks in America Since 1528.* New York, 1971.

Who's Who in Colored America: A Biographical Dictionary of Notable Living Persons of African Descent in America. 5th ed. Brooklyn, N.Y., 1940.

Who's Who in Colored America: A Biographical Dictionary of Notable Living Persons of African Descent in America. 6th ed. Brooklyn, N.Y., 1944.

Who's Who in Colored America: A Biographical Dictionary of Notable Living Persons of Negro Descent in America. New York, 1927.

Wilkinson, Frederick D., ed. *Directory of Graduates: Howard University, 1870–1963.* Washington, D.C., 1965.

Woodson, Carter G. *The History of the Negro Church.* 3rd ed. 1921; rpr. Washington, D.C., 1985.

_____. "Negro History Week." *Journal of Negro History,* XI (April, 1926), 238–42.

Index